Advance Praise f

" jQuery makes doing amazing things with JavaScript so easy it feels like cheating. This ___ demonstrates how to solve real-world problems quickly. As a bonus, you'll learn key asp___ how to set up a web development environment, and some PHP/MySQL. This is a soli___

— **Jim Doran, software engineer at Johns Hopkins University**

"Unlike those abstruse programming books filled with technical jargon, *Head First jQuery* guides beginners through the steps to create their first jQuery pages in a fun and understandable way."

— **Lindsey Skouras, attorney and self-taught programmer**

"Ryan Benedetti and Ronan Cranley have taken a potentially intimidating stew of technologies (jQuery, DOM, Ajax, HTML5, CSS) and broken them down into approachable concepts that actually make learning the material fun."

— **Bill Mietelski, software engineer**

"JavaScript has reemerged as a programming language of some merit due in no small part to a collection of best-of-breed add-on libraries, of which jQuery is a key player. *Head First jQuery* provides the modern web developer with a focused heads-up and hands-on treatment to this key JavaScript technology."

— **Paul Barry, author and lecturer on computing at the Institute of Technology, Carlow**

"Another nice thing about *Head First Java, Second Edition,* is that it whets the appetite for more. With later coverage of more advanced topics such as Swing and RMI, you just can't wait to dive into those APIs and code that flawless, 100,000-line program on Java.net that will bring you fame and venture-capital fortune. There's also a great deal of material, and even some best practices, on networking and threads— my own weak spot. In this case, I couldn't help but crack up a little when the authors use a 1950s telephone operator—yeah, you got it, that lady with a beehive hairdo that manually hooks in patch lines—as an analogy for TCP/IP ports…you really should go to the bookstore and thumb through *Head First Java, Second Edition.* Even if you already know Java, you may pick up a thing or two. And if not, just thumbing through the pages is a great deal of fun."

> — **Robert Eckstein, Java.sun.com**

"Of course it's not the range of material that makes *Head First Java* stand out, it's the style and approach. This book is about as far removed from a computer science textbook or technical manual as you can get [with its] use of cartoons, quizzes, fridge magnets (yep, fridge magnets…). And, in place of the usual kind of reader exercises, you are asked to pretend to be the compiler and compile the code, or perhaps to piece some code together by filling in the blanks or…you get the picture.… The first edition of this book was one of our recommended titles for those new to Java and objects. This new edition doesn't disappoint and rightfully steps into the shoes of its predecessor. If you are one of those people who falls asleep with a traditional computer book, then this one is likely to keep you awake and learning."

> — **TechBookReport.com**

"*Head First Web Design* is your ticket to mastering all of these complex topics, and understanding what's really going on in the world of web design.… If you have not been baptized by fire in using something as involved as Dreamweaver, then this book will be a great way to learn good web design. "

> — **Robert Pritchett, MacCompanion**

"Is it possible to learn real web design from a book format? *Head First Web Design* is the key to designing user-friendly sites, from customer requirements to hand-drawn storyboards to online sites that work well. What sets this apart from other 'how to build a website' books is that it uses the latest research in cognitive science and learning to provide a visual learning experience rich in images and designed for how the brain works and learns best. The result is a powerful tribute to web design basics that any general-interest computer library will find an important key to success."

> — **Diane C. Donovan, California Bookwatch: The Computer Shelf**

"I definitely recommend *Head First Web Design* to all of my fellow programmers who want to get a grip on the more artistic side of the business. "

> — **Claron Twitchell, Utah Java User Group**

Other related books from O'Reilly

jQuery Cookbook

jQuery Pocket Reference

jQuery Mobile

JavaScript and jQuery: The Missing Manual

Other books in O'Reilly's Head First series

Head First C#

Head First Java

Head First Object-Oriented Analysis and Design (OOA&D)

Head First HTML with CSS and XHTML

Head First Design Patterns

Head First Servlets and JSP

Head First EJB

Head First SQL

Head First Software Development

Head First JavaScript

Head First Physics

Head First Statistics

Head First Ajax

Head First Rails

Head First Algebra

Head First PHP & MySQL

Head First PMP

Head First Web Design

Head First Networking

Head First iPhone and iPad Development

Head First jQuery

Wouldn't it be dreamy if there were a book to help me learn how to use jQuery that was more fun than going to the dentist? It's probably nothing but a fantasy...

Ryan Benedetti
Ronan Cranley

O'REILLY®

Beijing • Cambridge • Farnham • Köln • Sebastopol • Tokyo

Head First jQuery

by Ryan Benedetti and Ronan Cranley

Copyright © 2011 Ryan Benedetti and Ronan Cranley. All rights reserved.

Printed in the United States of America.

Published by O'Reilly Media, Inc., 1005 Gravenstein Highway North, Sebastopol, CA 95472.

O'Reilly Media books may be purchased for educational, business, or sales promotional use. Online editions are also available for most titles (*http://my.safaribooksonline.com*). For more information, contact our corporate/institutional sales department: (800) 998-9938 or *corporate@oreilly.com*.

Series Creators:	Kathy Sierra, Bert Bates
Editor:	Courtney Nash
Design Editor:	Louise Barr
Cover Designer:	Karen Montgomery
Production Editor:	Teresa Elsey
Production Services:	Rachel Monaghan
Indexing:	Potomac Indexing, LLC
Page Viewers:	Ronan: Caitlin and Bono; Ryan: Shonna, Josie, Vin, Rocky, and Munch

Printing History:

September 2011: First Edition.

Ronan

Ryan, Rocky, Shonna

Vin, Josie, and Munch

Caitlin

Bono

ISBN: 978-1-449-39321-2

We dedicate this book to the JavaScript Jedi Masters: John Resig (creator and lead developer of the jQuery library), Douglas Crockford, David Flanagan, and Brandon Eich.

To my three miracles: Josie, Vin, and Shonna.

—Ryan

To Caitlin and Bono: Thank you for everything!

—Ronan

Ryan

Ronan

Ryan Benedetti holds a Master of Fine Arts degree in creative writing from the University of Montana and works as a web developer/multimedia specialist for the University of Portland. He works with jQuery, Flash, ActionScript, Adobe's Creative Suite, Liferay Portal, Apache's Jakarta Velocity Templating language, and Drupal.

For seven years, Ryan served as department head for Information Technology and Computer Engineering at Salish Kooteni College. Prior to that, he worked as editor and information systems specialist for a river, stream, and wetland research program in the School of Forestry at the University of Montana.

Ryan's poems have been published in *Cut Bank* and Andrei Codrescu's *Exquisite Corpse*. He spends his free hours painting, cartooning, playing blues harmonica, and practicing zazen. He spends his best moments with his daughter, his son, and his sweetheart, Shonna, in Portland, Oregon. He also digs hanging out with his animal compadres: Rocky, Munch, Fester, and Taz.

Ronan Cranley has worked for the University of Portland—going from web developer to senior web developer/systems manager to assistant director of web and admin systems—since moving from Dublin, Ireland, to Portland, Oregon, in 2006.

He earned his bachelor's degree in computer science from Dublin Institute of Technology, graduating with honors in 2003. In his college career, and in both his previous position in ESB International in Dublin and his current one for the University of Portland, Ronan has worked on an array of different projects in PHP, VB.NET, C#, and Java. These include, but are not limited to, a client-side GIS system, a homegrown content management system, a calendaring/scheduling system, and a jQuery/Google Maps mashup.

When he's not designing and building front-end web applications, he also serves as the SQL Server DBA for the university. In his spare time, Ronan spends many hours on the soccer field, on the golf course, hanging out with his wife, Caitlin, and their English bulldog, Bono, and sampling as much of the Pacific Northwest as he can.

Table of Contents (Summary)

Table of Contents (the real thing)

Intro

Your brain on jQuery. Here *you* are trying to *learn* something, while here your *brain* is doing you a favor by making sure the learning doesn't *stick*. Your brain's thinking, "Better leave room for more important things, like which wild animals to avoid and whether naked snowboarding is a bad idea." So how *do* you trick your brain into thinking that your life depends on knowing jQuery?

getting started with jQuery

Web page action

You want more for your web pages.

You've got HTML and CSS under your belt and want to add scripting to your skill set, but you don't want to spend your life writing lines and lines of script. You need a scripting library that allows you to change web pages on the fly. And since we're wishing, can it play well with AJAX and PHP, too? Can it do in 3 lines of code what most client-side languages do in 15? Wishful thinking? No way! You need to meet jQuery.

1

```
jQuery ( )
     ⇓
   $ ( )
```

JavaScript interpreter

selectors and methods

2 Grab and go

jQuery helps you grab web page elements and do all kinds

of things with them. In this chapter, we'll dig into jQuery selectors and methods. With jQuery selectors, we can grab elements on our page, and with methods we can do stuff to those elements. Like a massive book of magic spells, the jQuery library lets us change tons of things on the fly. We can make images disappear and reappear out of thin air. We can select a certain piece of text and animate the change to its font size. So, on with the show—let's grab some web page elements and go!

jQuery events and functions

Making things happen on your page

3

jQuery makes it easy to add action and interactivity to any web page. In this chapter, we'll look at making your page react when people interact with it. Making your code run in response to user actions takes your website to a whole new level. We'll also look at building reusable functions so you can write the code once and use it multiple times.

The Event Listener hears the event and passes it on to...

...the JavaScript interpreter that works out what needs to happen for each event...

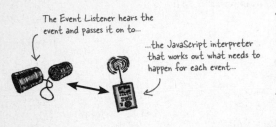

var pts = 250;

=250

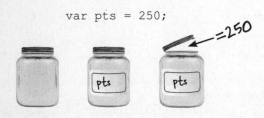

jQuery web page manipulation

Mod the DOM

4

Just because the page is finished loading doesn't mean it has to keep the same structure. Back in Chapter 1, we saw how the DOM gets built as the page loads to set up the page's structure. In this chapter, we'll look at how to move up and down through the DOM structure and work with element hierarchy and parent/ child relationships to change the page structure on the fly using jQuery.

jQuery effects and animation

5 A little glide in your stride

Making things happen on you page is all well and good,

but if you can't make it look cool, people won't want to use your site. That's where jQuery effects and animation come in. In this chapter, you'll learn how to make elements transition on your page over time, show or hide specific pieces of elements that are relevant, and shrink or grow an element on the page, all before your users' eyes. You'll also see how to schedule these animations so they happen at various intervals to give your page a very dynamic appearance.

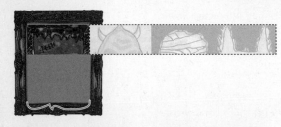

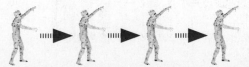

jQuery and JavaScript

~~Luke~~ jQuery, I am your father!

6

jQuery can't do it all alone. Although it is a
JavaScript library, unfortunately it can't do everything its parent
language can do. In this chapter, we'll look at some of the
features of JavaScript that you'll need to create really compelling
sites, and how jQuery can use them to create custom lists and
objects as well as loop through those lists and objects to make
your life much easier.

custom functions for custom effects

What have you done for me lately?

When you combine jQuery's custom effects with

JavaScript functions you can make your code—and your web app—more efficient, more effective, and more *powerful*. In this chapter, you'll dig deeper into improving your jQuery effects by handling **browser events**, working with **timed functions**, and improving the **organization and reusability** of your custom JavaScript functions.

My teeth *are* my best feature, but I could still use the rest of my face for crying out loud!

setTimeout()   **setInterval()**   **delay()**

jQuery and Ajax

Please pass the data

Using jQuery to do some cool CSS and DOM tricks is fun,

but soon you'll need to read information (or data) from a server and display it. You may even have to update small pieces of the page with the information from the server, without having to reload the page. Enter Ajax. Combined with jQuery and JavaScript, it can do just that. In this chapter, we'll learn how jQuery deals with making Ajax calls to the server and what it can do with the information returned.

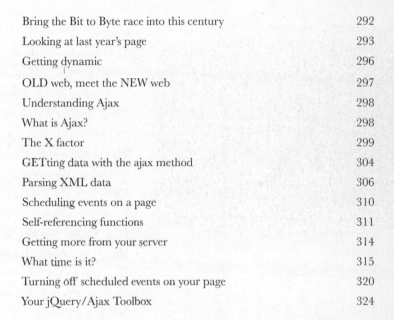

handling JSON data

Client, meet server

9

As useful as reading data from an XML file was, that won't always cut the mustard. A more efficient data interchange format (JavaScript Object Notation, aka JSON) will make it easier to get data from the server side. JSON is easier to generate and read than XML, too. Using jQuery, PHP, and SQL, you'll learn how to create a database to store information so you can retrieve it later, using JSON, and display it on the screen using jQuery. A true web application superpower!

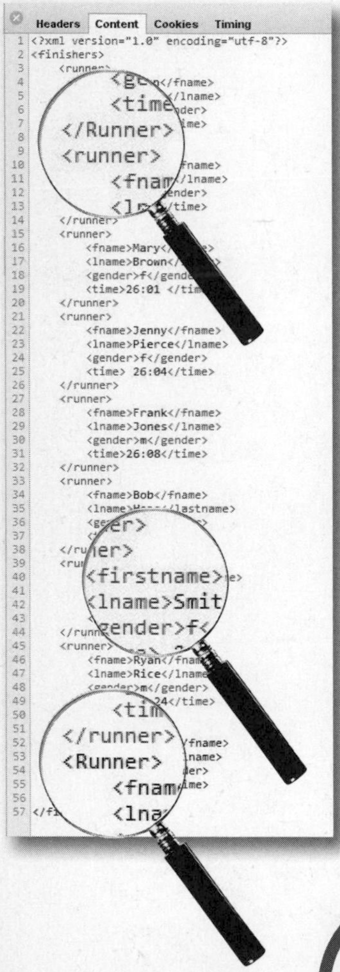

jQuery UI

Extreme form makeover

10

The Web lives and dies by users and their data.

Collecting data from users is a big business and can be a time-consuming challenge for a web developer. You've seen how jQuery can help make Ajax, PHP, and MySQL web apps work more effectively. Now let's look at how jQuery can help us build the user interface for the forms that collect data from users. Along the way, you'll get a healthy dose of jQuery UI, the official user interface library for jQuery.

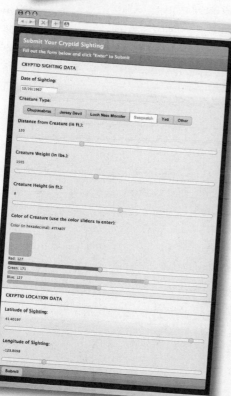

I wish I could get the paparazzi off my back!

jQuery and APIs

Objects, objects everywhere

11

As talented a developer as you are, you can't do it all alone... We've seen how we can include jQuery plug-ins, like jQuery UI or the tabs navigation to help boost our jQuery app, without much effort. To take our applications to the next level, apply some of the really cool tools out there on the Internet, and use information provided by the big hitters—like Google, Twitter, or Yahoo!—we need something...more. Those companies, and many others, provide APIs (application programming interfaces) to their services so you can include them in your site. In this chapter, we'll look at some API basics and use a very common one: the Google Maps API.

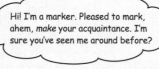

Hi! I'm a marker. Pleased to mark, ahem, *make* your acquaintance. I'm sure you've seen me around before?

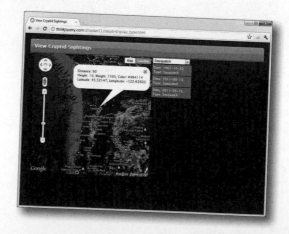

leftovers

The top ten things (we didn't cover)

Even after all that, there's still plenty we didn't get around to. There are lots of other jQuery and JavaScript goodies we didn't manage to squeeze into the book. It would be unfair not to tell you about them, so you can be more prepared for any other facet of jQuery you might encounter on your travels.

set up a development environment

Get ready for the big times

You need a place to practice your newfound PHP skills without making your data vulnerable on the Web.
It's always a good idea to have a safe place to develop your PHP application before unleashing it on the world (wide web). This appendix contains instructions for installing a web server, MySQL, and PHP to give you a safe place to work and practice.

how to use this book

Intro

In this section, we answer the burning question:
"So why <u>DID</u> they put that in a jQuery book?"

Who is this book for?

If you can answer "yes" to all of these:

1. Do you have previous web design or development experience?

    It definitely helps if you've already got some scripting chops, too. Experience with JavaScript is helpful, but definitely not required.

2. Do you want to **learn**, **understand**, **remember**, and **apply** important jQuery and JavaScript concepts so that you can make your web pages more interactive and exciting?

3. Do you prefer **stimulating dinner-party conversation** to **dry**, **dull**, **academic lectures**?

this book is for you.

Who should probably back away from this book?

If you can answer "yes" to any of these:

1. Are you **completely new** to web development?

    Check out Head First HTML with CSS & XHTML for an excellent introduction to web development, and then come back and join us in jQueryville.

2. Are you already developing web apps and looking for a **reference** book on jQuery?

3. Are you **afraid to try something different**? Would you rather have a root canal than mix stripes with plaid? Do you believe that a technical book can't be serious if Bigfoot is in it?

this book is not for you.

[Note from Marketing: This book is for anyone with a credit card. Or cash. Cash is nice, too. —Ed]

We know what you're thinking.

"How can *this* be a serious jQuery development book?"

"What's with all the graphics?"

"Can I actually *learn* it this way?"

And we know what your *brain* is thinking.

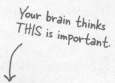

Your brain thinks THIS is important.

Your brain craves novelty. It's always searching, scanning, *waiting* for something unusual. It was built that way, and it helps you stay alive.

So what does your brain do with all the routine, ordinary, normal things you encounter? Everything it *can* to stop them from interfering with the brain's *real* job—recording things that *matter*. It doesn't bother saving the boring things; they never make it past the "this is obviously not important" filter.

How does your brain *know* what's important? Suppose you're out for a day hike and a tiger jumps in front of you. What happens inside your head and body?

Neurons fire. Emotions crank up. *Chemicals surge.*

And that's how your brain knows...

This must be important! Don't forget it!

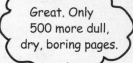

Great. Only 500 more dull, dry, boring pages.

But imagine you're at home or in a library. It's a safe, warm, tiger-free zone. You're studying. Getting ready for an exam. Or trying to learn some tough technical topic your boss thinks will take a week, 10 days at the most.

Just one problem. Your brain's trying to do you a big favor. It's trying to make sure that this *obviously* unimportant content doesn't clutter up scarce resources. Resources that are better spent storing the really *big* things. Like tigers. Like the danger of fire. Like how you should never again snowboard in shorts.

Your brain thinks THIS isn't worth saving.

And there's no simple way to tell your brain, "Hey, brain, thank you very much, but no matter how dull this book is, and how little I'm registering on the emotional Richter scale right now, I really *do* want you to keep this stuff around."

We think of a "Head First" reader as a <u>learner</u>.

So what does it take to *learn* something? First, you have to *get* it, and then make sure you don't *forget* it. It's not about pushing facts into your head. Based on the latest research in cognitive science, neurobiology, and educational psychology, *learning* takes a lot more than text on a page. We know what turns your brain on.

Some of the Head First learning principles:

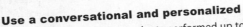

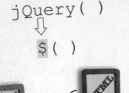

Make it visual. Images are far more memorable than words alone, and make learning much more effective (up to 89% improvement in recall and transfer studies). It also makes things more understandable.

Put the words within or near the graphics they relate to, rather than on the bottom or on another page, and learners will be up to *twice* as likely to solve problems related to the content.

Also, the furry friend picture just pops up. Can you make it slide slower and sort of fade in as it does?

Use a conversational and personalized style. In recent studies, students performed up to 40% better on post-learning tests if the content spoke directly to the reader, using a first-person, conversational style rather than taking a formal tone. Tell stories instead of lecturing. Use casual language. Don't take yourself too seriously. Which would *you* pay more attention to: a stimulating dinner-party companion, or a lecture?

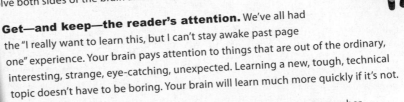

Get the learner to think more deeply. In other words, unless you actively flex your neurons, nothing much happens in your head. A reader has to be motivated, engaged, curious, and inspired to solve problems, draw conclusions, and generate new knowledge. And for that, you need challenges, exercises, thought-provoking questions, and activities that involve both sides of the brain and multiple senses.

Get—and keep—the reader's attention. We've all had the "I really want to learn this, but I can't stay awake past page one" experience. Your brain pays attention to things that are out of the ordinary, interesting, strange, eye-catching, unexpected. Learning a new, tough, technical topic doesn't have to be boring. Your brain will learn much more quickly if it's not.

Touch their emotions. We now know that your ability to remember something is largely dependent on its emotional content. You remember what you care about. You remember when you *feel* something. No, we're not talking heart-wrenching stories about a boy and his dog. We're talking emotions like surprise, curiosity, fun, "what the...?", and the feeling of "I rule!" that comes when you solve a puzzle, learn something everybody else thinks is hard, or realize you know something that "I'm more technical than thou" Bob from Engineering *doesn't*.

Metacognition: thinking about thinking

If you really want to learn, and you want to learn more quickly and more deeply, pay attention to how you pay attention. Think about how you think. Learn how you learn.

Most of us did not take courses on metacognition or learning theory when we were growing up. We were *expected* to learn, but rarely *taught* to learn.

I wonder how I can trick my brain into remembering this stuff...

But we assume that if you're holding this book, you really want to learn about jQuery. And you probably don't want to spend a lot of time. And since you're going to work with it more in the future, you need to *remember* what you read. And for that, you've got to *understand* it. To get the most from this book, or *any* book or learning experience, take responsibility for your brain. Your brain on *this* content.

The trick is to get your brain to see the new material you're learning as Really Important. Crucial to your well-being. As important as a tiger. Otherwise, you're in for a constant battle, with your brain doing its best to keep the new content from sticking.

So just how *DO* you get your brain to think that jQuery development is a hungry tiger?

There's the slow, tedious way, or the faster, more effective way. The slow way is about sheer repetition. You obviously know that you *are* able to learn and remember even the dullest of topics if you keep pounding the same thing into your brain. With enough repetition, your brain says, "This doesn't *feel* important to him, but he keeps looking at the same thing *over* and *over* and *over*, so I suppose it must be."

The faster way is to do *anything that increases brain activity,* especially different *types* of brain activity. The things on the previous page are a big part of the solution, and they're all things that have been proven to help your brain work in your favor. For example, studies show that putting words *within* the pictures they describe (as opposed to somewhere else in the page, like a caption or in the body text) causes your brain to try to makes sense of how the words and picture relate, and this causes more neurons to fire. More neurons firing = more chances for your brain to *get* that this is something worth paying attention to, and possibly recording.

A conversational style helps because people tend to pay more attention when they perceive that they're in a conversation, since they're expected to follow along and hold up their end. The amazing thing is, your brain doesn't necessarily *care* that the "conversation" is between you and a book! On the other hand, if the writing style is formal and dry, your brain perceives it the same way you experience being lectured to while sitting in a roomful of passive attendees. No need to stay awake.

But pictures and conversational style are just the beginning.

Here's what WE did:

We used **pictures**, because your brain is tuned for visuals, not text. As far as your brain's concerned, a picture really *is* worth a thousand words. And when text and pictures work together, we embedded the text *in* the pictures because your brain works more effectively when the text is *within* the thing the text refers to, as opposed to in a caption or buried in the text somewhere.

We used **redundancy**, saying the same thing in *different* ways and with different media types, and *multiple senses*, to increase the chance that the content gets coded into more than one area of your brain.

We used concepts and pictures in **unexpected** ways because your brain is tuned for novelty, and we used pictures and ideas with at least *some* **emotional** *content*, because your brain is tuned to pay attention to the biochemistry of emotions. That which causes you to *feel* something is more likely to be remembered, even if that feeling is nothing more than a little **humor**, **surprise**, or **interest.**

We used a personalized, **conversational style**, because your brain is tuned to pay more attention when it believes you're in a conversation than if it thinks you're passively listening to a presentation. Your brain does this even when you're *reading*.

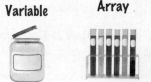

We included loads of **activities**, because your brain is tuned to learn and remember more when you **do** things than when you *read* about things. And we made the exercises challenging-yet-doable, because that's what most people prefer.

We used **multiple learning styles**, because *you* might prefer step-by-step procedures, while someone else wants to understand the big picture first, and someone else just wants to see an example. But regardless of your own learning preference, *everyone* benefits from seeing the same content represented in multiple ways.

We include content for **both sides of your brain**, because the more of your brain you engage, the more likely you are to learn and remember, and the longer you can stay focused. Since working one side of the brain often means giving the other side a chance to rest, you can be more productive at learning for a longer period of time.

And we included **stories** and exercises that present **more than one point of view,** because your brain is tuned to learn more deeply when it's forced to make evaluations and judgments.

We included **challenges**, with exercises, and by asking **questions** that don't always have a straight answer, because your brain is tuned to learn and remember when it has to *work* at something. Think about it—you can't get your *body* in shape just by *watching* people at the gym. But we did our best to make sure that when you're working hard, it's on the *right* things. That **you're not spending one extra dendrite** processing a hard-to-understand example, or parsing difficult, jargon-laden, or overly terse text.

We used **people**. In stories, examples, pictures, etc., because, well, because *you're* a person. And your brain pays more attention to *people* than it does to *things*.

Here's what YOU can do to bend your brain into submission

So, we did our part. The rest is up to you. These tips are a starting point; listen to your brain and figure out what works for you and what doesn't. Try new things.

Cut this out and stick it on your refrigerator.

- -

① Slow down. The more you understand, the less you have to memorize.

Don't just *read*. Stop and think. When the book asks you a question, don't just skip to the answer. Imagine that someone really *is* asking the question. The more deeply you force your brain to think, the better chance you have of learning and remembering.

② Do the exercises. Write your own notes.

We put them in, but if we did them for you, that would be like having someone else do your workouts for you. And don't just *look* at the exercises. **Use a pencil.** There's plenty of evidence that physical activity *while* learning can increase the learning.

③ Read the "There are No Dumb Questions."

That means all of them. They're not optional sidebars—*they're part of the core content!* Don't skip them.

④ Make this the last thing you read before bed. Or at least the last challenging thing.

Part of the learning (especially the transfer to long-term memory) happens *after* you put the book down. Your brain needs time on its own, to do more processing. If you put in something new during that processing time, some of what you just learned will be lost.

⑤ Drink water. Lots of it.

Your brain works best in a nice bath of fluid. Dehydration (which can happen before you ever feel thirsty) decreases cognitive function.

⑥ Talk about it. Out loud.

Speaking activates a different part of the brain. If you're trying to understand something, or increase your chance of remembering it later, say it out loud. Better still, try to explain it out loud to someone else. You'll learn more quickly, and you might uncover ideas you hadn't known were there when you were reading about it.

⑦ Listen to your brain.

Pay attention to whether your brain is getting overloaded. If you find yourself starting to skim the surface or forget what you just read, it's time for a break. Once you go past a certain point, you won't learn faster by trying to shove more in, and you might even hurt the process.

⑧ Feel something!

Your brain needs to know that this *matters*. Get involved with the stories. Make up your own captions for the photos. Groaning over a bad joke is *still* better than feeling nothing at all.

⑨ Create something!

Apply this to your daily work; use what you are learning to make decisions on your projects. Just do something to get some experience beyond the exercises and activities in this book. All you need is a pencil and a problem to solve…a problem that might benefit from using the tools and techniques you're studying for the exam.

Read me

This is a learning experience, not a reference book. We deliberately stripped out everything that might get in the way of learning whatever it is we're working on at that point in the book. And the first time through, you need to begin at the beginning, because the book makes assumptions about what you've already seen and learned.

We expect you to know HTML and CSS.

If you don't know HTML and CSS, pick up a copy of *Head First HTML with CSS & XHTML* before starting this book. We will do some refreshers on CSS selectors, but don't expect to learn all of what you need to know about CSS here.

We don't expect you to know JavaScript.

We know, we know…this is a controversial opinion, but we feel that you can learn jQuery without knowing JavaScript first. You need to know some JavaScript to write jQuery, and we teach you all those important JavaScript concepts side-by-side with the jQuery code. We truly and deeply believe in the jQuery motto: Write Less. Do More.

We encourage you to use more than one browser with this book.

We encourage you to test your pages using at least three up-to-date browsers. This will give you experience in seeing the differences among browsers and in creating pages that work well in a variety of browsers.

This is not Head First Browser Dev Tools...

…but we expect you to know how to use them. We highly recommend Google Chrome, which you can download here: *http://www.google.com/chrome*. You can visit the following sites for more information on the following browsers and their dev tools:

Google Chrome	*http://code.google.com/chrome/devtools/docs/overview.html*
Firefox's Firebug	*http://getfirebug.com/wiki/index.php/FAQ*
Safari	*http://www.apple.com/safari/features.html#developer*
Internet Explorer 8	*http://msdn.microsoft.com/en-us/library/dd565628(v=vs.85).aspx*
Internet Explorer 9	*http://msdn.microsoft.com/en-us/ie/aa740478*
Opera's Dragonfly	*http://www.opera.com/dragonfly/*

We expect you to go beyond this book

The best thing you can do when you're learning something new is to join a learning community. We feel that the jQuery community is one of the best and most active communities in the world of technology. You can find out more here: *http://www.jquery.com*.

The activities are NOT optional.

The exercises and activities are not add-ons; they're part of the core content of the book. Some of them are to help with memory, some are for understanding, and some will help you apply what you've learned. ***Don't skip the exercises.*** Even crossword puzzles are important—they'll help get concepts into your brain. But more importantly, they're good for giving your brain a chance to think about the words and terms you've been learning in a different context.

The redundancy is intentional and important.

One distinct difference in a Head First book is that we want you to *really* get it. And we want you to finish the book remembering what you've learned. Most reference books don't have retention and recall as a goal, but this book is about *learning*, so you'll see some of the same concepts come up more than once.

The Brain Power exercises don't have answers.

For some of them, there is no right answer, and for others, part of the learning experience of the Brain Power activities is for you to decide if and when your answers are right. In some of the Brain Power exercises, you will find hints to point you in the right direction.

Software requirements

To write jQuery code, you need a text editor, a browser, a web server (it can be locally hosted on your personal desktop), and the jQuery library.

The text editors we recommend for Windows are PSPad, TextPad, or EditPlus (but you can use Notepad if you have to). The text editor we recommend for Mac is TextWrangler. If you're on a Linux system, you've got plenty of text editors built in, and we trust you don't need us to tell you about them.

If you are going to do web development, you need a web server. For the later chapters (9, 10, and 11), you need to go to the appendix on installing PHP, MySQL, and a web server (Apache or IIS) and follow the instructions. We recommend doing that now. No, seriously, head there now, follow the instructions, and come back to this page when you're done.

You'll also need a browser, and you'll need to use the Browser Developer tools. Please read the previous page. Learning how to use the JavaScript console in Google's Chrome Dev Tools is well worth the time. This is homework you need to do on your own.

Last of all, you need the jQuery library; turn the page and we'll show you where to get it.

Download jQuery

It's time to dive in. Head over to the jQuery website and download a copy to use throughout this book.

Step One:

Open your favorite browser and point it to this address: *http://www.jquery.com*.

Step Two:

Find the section labeled "Grab the Latest Version!" Then, select the checkbox next to "Production."

Step Three:

Click the "Download jQuery" button.

Step Four:

The next page you'll see will look something like this.

Save the page into a folder called *scripts* on your drive.

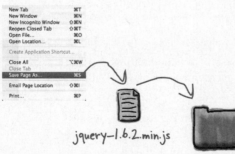

What's the difference between the Production and Development versions?

The **Production** version of jQuery is a minified version, intended for speed of execution on a web server. The **Development** version is intended for developers interested in exploring and extending the inner workings of the jQuery library. Get a copy of both if you're the type who likes to have a look inside the engine.

Folder setup

After downloading and unzipping the code for the book from Head First labs (*http://www.headfirstlabs.com/books/hfjquery*), you'll find that it's structured in folders organized by each chapter. Let's look at *ch03*, for example:

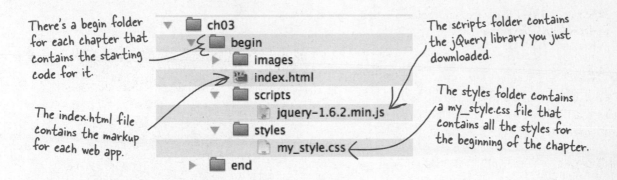

There's a begin folder for each chapter that contains the starting code for it.

The index.html file contains the markup for each web app.

The scripts folder contains the jQuery library you just downloaded.

The styles folder contains a my_style.css file that contains all the styles for the beginning of the chapter.

The *end* folder of every chapter contains the final code for that chapter. We encourage you to use the *end* folder only when you need it for reference.

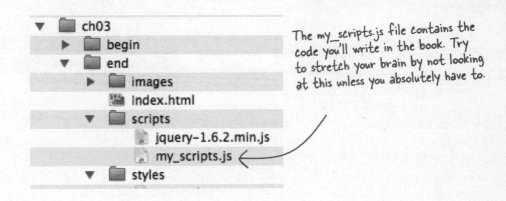

The my_scripts.js file contains the code you'll write in the book. Try to stretch your brain by not looking at this unless you absolutely have to.

You can use the jQuery library in any of your own projects. For your convenience, we include the jQuery library in the code folder for the book, but you need to know where to get it for use in future projects and for when the jQuery library is updated. The jQuery folks update the library regularly.

The technical review team

Lindsey Skouras

Paul Barry

Bill Mietelski

Jim Doran

Jim Doran works as a software engineer at Johns Hopkins University in Baltimore, Maryland. He teaches JavaScript at the Community College of Baltimore County and speaks about jQuery at web conferences. When not doing these things, Jim blogs his art at *http://jimdoran.net* and skates in a coed roller derby league.

Bill Mietelski has been a technical reviewer of several Head First titles. He's currently a software engineer at a leading national academic medical center in the Chicagoland area, working on biostatistical research. When he's not collecting or shepherding data, you'll find him at a local golf course chasing a little white ball.

Lindsey Skouras is an attorney in the Washington, DC, area. She has been teaching herself how to code in her spare time by working her way through the Head First series. Her other interests include reading, crafting, visiting museums, and spending time with her husband and dogs.

Paul Barry lectures in computing at the Institute of Technology, Carlow, in Ireland. Paul is a contributing editor to *Linux Journal* magazine as well as a published technical author. He is also the author of *Head First Python* and coauthor of *Head First Programming*. When he gets time, Paul consults with SMEs and startups on software development projects.

Acknowledgments

Our editor:

Thanks (and congratulations!) to **Courtney Nash**, who pushed us to create the best book we possibly could. She has endured a huge portion of emails, questions, ramblings, and occasional crankiness. She stuck with us throughout this book and trusted us to trust our guts.

Courtney Nash

The O'Reilly team:

Thanks to **Lou Barr** for the speedy, excellent, and magical work she did to shape this book up and make it look beautiful.

Thanks to **Laurie Petrycki** for giving us the green light. Ryan has fond memories of HF training in Boston and will never forget the cool, family-like atmosphere Laurie created there.

Thanks to **Karen Shaner**. Thanks to everyone on the tech review team.

Ryan will never forget the day he discovered the Head First series at the bookstore. Thanks to Kathy Sierra and Bert Bates for lighting up the neurons of geeks everywhere. Thanks to Bert for listening to us ramble, pulling us out of the closure quagmire, and keeping our object-ives clear. ;)

Thanks to Tim O'Reilly for his vision in creating the best geek press ever!

Lou Barr

Ronan's friends and family:

A special thanks to my wife, Caitlin, who helped make this book a reality through her fantastic design abilities and knowledge of all things Adobe. And for her patience—I couldn't have done this without you! A big thank you to everyone who supported both of us in this effort—my great neighbors, our fellow basement-dwelling colleagues at the University of Portland, my understanding soccer teams and golfing buddies. Thanks to my family back in Ireland for their support and encouragement. Most of all, thanks to Ryan Benedetti, my awesome coauthor, colleague, and friend. Thank you for taking me on this journey and giving me this opportunity. It's been quite the experience!

Ryan's friends and family:

Thank you to my daughter, Josie; my son, Vinny; and my fiancée, Shonna, who believed in me and supported me in so many ways on a daily basis throughout this book. *Ti amo, i miei tre miracoli.* I love each of you so much, my three miracles!

Thanks also to my Mom and Pops; my brother, Jeff; and my nieces, Claire and Quinn. Thanks to my fellow basement dwellers and the WAS team at University of Portland—namely, Jenny Walsh, Jacob Caniparoli, and the Tuesday morning tech team (you know who you are). Thanks to Caitlin Pierce-Cranley for her awesome design skills. Thanks to my pal, the Irish Ninja (aka Ronan Cranley), for bringing his excellent jQuery, JavaScript, and PHP coding skills; his sense of humor; and incredible work ethic to this book.

Safari® Books Online

 Safari® Books Online is an on-demand digital library that lets you easily search over 7,500 technology and creative reference books and videos to find the answers you need quickly.

With a subscription, you can read any page and watch any video from our library online. Read books on your cell phone and mobile devices. Access new titles before they are available for print, and get exclusive access to manuscripts in development and post feedback for the authors. Copy and paste code samples, organize your favorites, download chapters, bookmark key sections, create notes, print out pages, and benefit from tons of other time-saving features.

O'Reilly Media has uploaded this book to the Safari Books Online service. To have full digital access to this book and others on similar topics from O'Reilly and other publishers, sign up for free at *http://my.safaribooksonline.com*.

1 getting started with jQuery

Web page action

Maybe there's something in here that will make my web pages more interactive.

You want more for your web pages. You've got HTML and CSS

under your belt and want to add scripting to your skill set, but you don't want to spend your

life writing lines and lines of script. You need a scripting library that allows you to change web

pages on the fly. And since we're wishing, can it play well with AJAX and PHP, too?

Can it do in 3 lines of code what most client-side languages do in 15? Wishful thinking?

No way! You need to meet jQuery.

You want web page power

You already know how to build great-looking web pages with clean, valid HTML and CSS. But static web pages just don't cut it anymore—people want a responsive web page. They want action, animation, interaction, and lots of cool effects.

My clients love my web page designs, but they want more interactivity.

Our company website is so boring. We refuse to use it until someone makes it more responsive.

✏️ Sharpen your pencil

Do you want to take control of your web pages and make them more useful for your visitors? Check all the options that apply from the list below:

- [ ] Dynamically add elements to the web page without reloading every time.
- [ ] Change menu items when users mouse over them.
- [ ] Alert your user when a form field is missing.
- [ ] Add motion and transitions to text and pictures.
- [ ] Load data from a server just when a user needs it.

HTML and CSS are fine, but...

Plain old HTML and CSS are good for giving your page structure and style. Once you have a rendered HTML page, it's there, but it's *static*.

What if you want to change how the page looks, or add or remove something from it? You either have to do some really crazy CSS gymnastics, or you simply have to load a new page. And that can get ugly fast. Why? Because all you're really doing with HTML and CSS is controlling how a page is displayed.

1 The browser requests a web page from a server when someone types a web address into the browser's URL bar.

2 The server finds the requested file(s) and sends them to the browser.

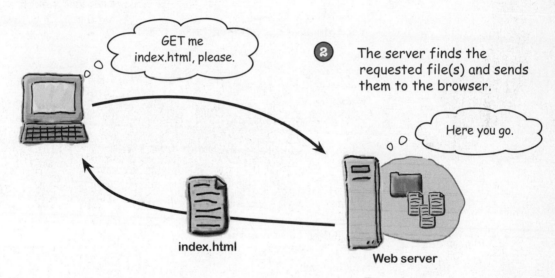

index.html

Web server

3 The browser displays a rendered HTML page based on the file sent from the server.

index.html

The browser loads the page and displays it to the user.

...you need the power of script

To change your web pages **on the fly**, without reloading, you need to talk to your browser. How do you pull that off? With an HTML tag known as `<script>`.

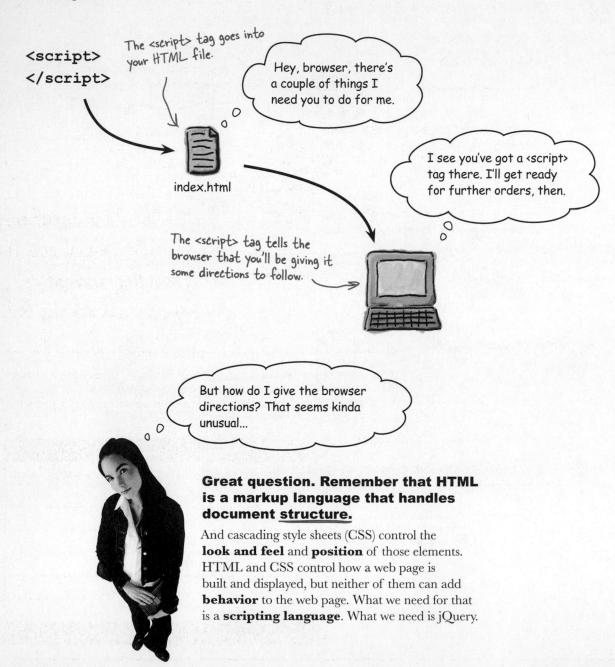

```
<script>
</script>
```

The `<script>` tag goes into your HTML file.

index.html

Hey, browser, there's a couple of things I need you to do for me.

I see you've got a `<script>` tag there. I'll get ready for further orders, then.

The `<script>` tag tells the browser that you'll be giving it some directions to follow.

But how do I give the browser directions? That seems kinda unusual...

Great question. Remember that HTML is a markup language that handles document <u>structure</u>.

And cascading style sheets (CSS) control the **look and feel** and **position** of those elements. HTML and CSS control how a web page is built and displayed, but neither of them can add **behavior** to the web page. What we need for that is a **scripting language**. What we need is jQuery.

Enter jQuery (and JavaScript)!

The language we use to give the browser directions is JavaScript. Every browser comes with a built-in JavaScript interpreter that takes the directions you write in between the `<script>` tags and translates those directions into different kinds of action on the web page.

The user just clicked!

Hey, browser, update that img element for me, will ya?

The JavaScript interpreter "listens" for events that happen on the page, like a mouse-click.

The JavaScript interpreter can give the browser commands too.

To give the interpreter directions, you ultimately need to speak JavaScript. But don't worry! This is where jQuery comes in. jQuery is a JavaScript **library** specialized for changing web page documents on the fly. Let's check some jQuery out.

jQuery is a JavaScript library specialized for changing web page documents on the fly.

Sharpen your pencil

The script below dynamically changes a web page. Read each line and think about what it might do based on what you already know about HTML and CSS. Then, write down what you think the code does. If you're not sure what a line does, it's perfectly OK to guess. We did one for you.

```
<script>
$(document).ready(function(){
    $("button").click(function(){
        $("h1").hide("slow");
        $("h2").show("fast");
        $("img").slideUp();
    });
});
</script>
```

When the web page document is ready, do what's below.

Sharpen your pencil
Solution

The script below dynamically changes a web page. Read each line and think about what it might do based on what you already know about HTML and CSS. Then, write down what you think the code does. If you're not sure what a line does, it's perfectly OK to guess. Here's our solution.

```
<script>
$(document).ready(function(){
  $("button").click(function(){
    $("h1").hide("slow");
    $("h2").show("fast");
    $("img").slideUp();
  });
});
</script>
```

When the web page document is ready, do what's below.
When any button element is clicked, do this stuff:
Make all h1 elements disappear slowly from the page.
Make all h2 elements show quickly on the page.
Make all img elements slide upward and disappear.
End the click function.
End the document ready function.

But if I don't refresh the browser, how does the browser know to hide an element or slide it up?

That's a great question. It does seem a bit like magic, right?

Let's look at a web page from the perspective of the browser—specifically, how jQuery can change the web page from *within* the browser.

Look into the browser

It's time to pull back the curtain to see what's really going on behind a web page as a browser displays it. Your browser uses the HTML Document Object Model (DOM) to build a page from simple HTML markup and CSS code into a clickable page complete with text, images, videos, and all the other great content we love to browse.

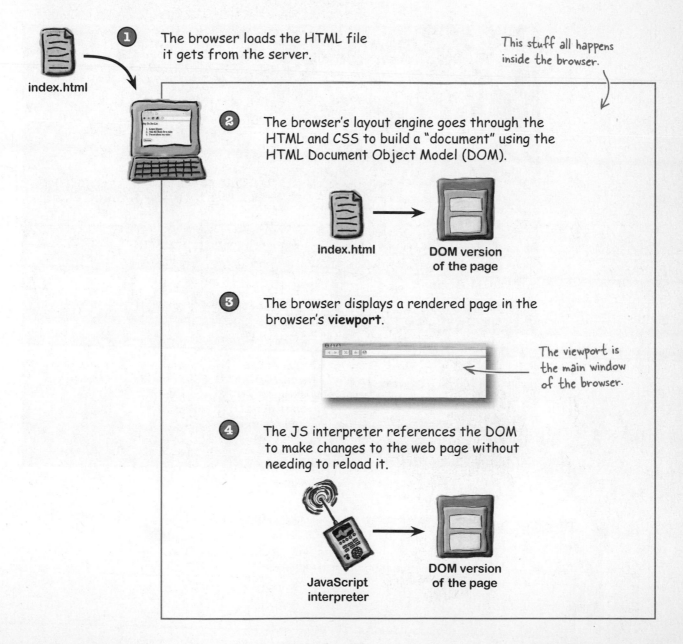

index.html

1 The browser loads the HTML file it gets from the server.

This stuff all happens inside the browser.

2 The browser's layout engine goes through the HTML and CSS to build a "document" using the HTML Document Object Model (DOM).

index.html → DOM version of the page

3 The browser displays a rendered page in the browser's **viewport**.

The viewport is the main window of the browser.

4 The JS interpreter references the DOM to make changes to the web page without needing to reload it.

JavaScript interpreter → DOM version of the page

The hidden structure of a web page

Over the years, the DOM has helped HTML, CSS, and JavaScript work together more effectively. It provides a standardized skeleton that all modern browsers use to make browsing the Web more effective. Many people think of the DOM as being built like a tree: it has a *root* and *branches* with *nodes* at the end. Alternatively, you can think of it as an x-ray for how the page is built.

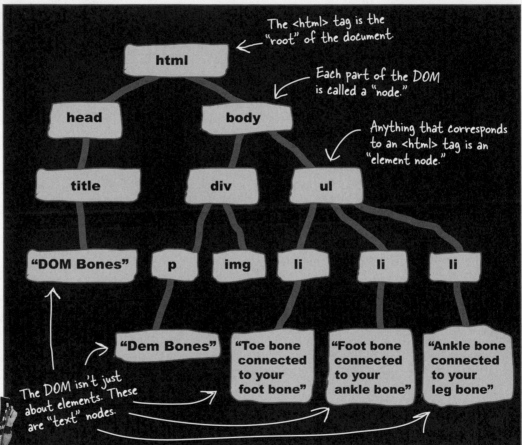

The <html> tag is the "root" of the document.

html

Each part of the DOM is called a "node."

head　　**body**

Anything that corresponds to an <html> tag is an "element node."

title　　**div**　　**ul**

"DOM Bones"　　**p**　　**img**　　**li**　　**li**　　**li**

The DOM isn't just about elements. These are "text" nodes.

"Dem Bones"　　**"Toe bone connected to your foot bone"**　　**"Foot bone connected to your ankle bone"**　　**"Ankle bone connected to your leg bone"**

An x-ray tells a doctor what's going on with the body's hidden structure. Like an x-ray, the DOM shows us the hidden structure behind the page. But unlike an x-ray, JavaScript and jQuery use the DOM to *change the structure* on the page.

jQuery makes the DOM less scary

The DOM can seem complex and intimidating, but luckily for us, jQuery keeps it simple. Don't forget: jQuery *is* JavaScript, but a much more approachable version. When you want to control the DOM, jQuery makes it much easier. For instance, let's say we want to change the HTML inside of the *only* paragraph element on our page.

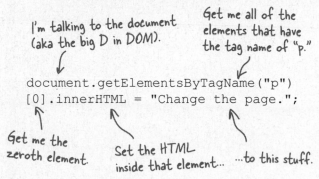

The raw JavaScript way

I'm talking to the document (aka the big D in DOM).

Get me all of the elements that have the tag name of "p."

```
document.getElementsByTagName("p")
[0].innerHTML = "Change the page.";
```

Get me the zeroth element.

Set the HTML inside that element...

...to this stuff.

The jQuery way

Grab me a paragraph element.

Change the HTML of that element to what's in these parentheses.

```
$("p").html("Change the page.");
```

jQuery uses a "selector engine," which means you can get at stuff with selectors just like CSS does.

Or let's say we want to change the HTML inside of *five* paragraph elements on our page:

Loop through the number of elements I want to change.

```
for (i = 0; i <= 4; i++)
{
    document.getElementsByTagName("p")
[i].innerHTML="Change the page";
}
```

Get me the element we're looping over.

Because jQuery uses CSS selectors, we can say it the same way as above.

```
$("p").html("Change the page.");
```

One of jQuery's main strengths is that it allows you to work with the DOM without having to know every little thing about it. Underneath it all, JavaScript is doing the heavy lifting. Throughout this book, you'll learn to use JavaScript and jQuery together. In Chapter 6, we'll learn more about jQuery's relationship to JavaScript, and we'll beef up our JavaScript skills along the way. For now, when you need to work with the DOM, you'll use jQuery.

Let's take jQuery for a spin around DOM-ville, shall we?

 Ready Bake Code

Enter the following code into a text editor. Then save it, open it in your browser, and try out each of the buttons. (It won't hurt to take a look at the code and try to figure out what it's doing while you're at it...)

```html
<!DOCTYPE html>
<html><head> <title>jQuery goes to DOM-ville</title>
<style>
        #change_me {
        position: absolute;
        top: 100px;
        left: 400px;
        font: 24px arial;}

        #move_up #move_down #color #disappear {
        padding: 5px;}
</style>
<script src="scripts/jquery-1.6.2.min.js"></script>
</head>
<body>
        <button id="move_up">Move Up</button>
        <button id="move_down">Move Down</button>
        <button id="color">Change Color</button>
        <button id="disappear">Disappear/Re-appear</button>

        <div id="change_me">Make Me Do Stuff!</div>
        <script>
            $(document).ready(function() {
                $("#move_up").click( function() {
                    $("#change_me").animate({top:30},200);
                });//end move_up
                $("#move_down").click( function() {
                    $("#change_me").animate({top:500},2000);
                });//end move_down
                $("#color").click( function() {
                    $("#change_me").css("color", "purple");
                });//end color
                $("#disappear").click( function() {
                    $("#change_me").toggle("slow");
                });//end disappear
            });//end doc ready
        </script>
</body>
</html>
```

index.html

How does *that* work?

Pretty nifty how jQuery can manipulate the page, isn't it? The important part to keep in mind is that **none of the original HTML and CSS changed** when you pressed each button. So how did jQuery do it? Check it out:

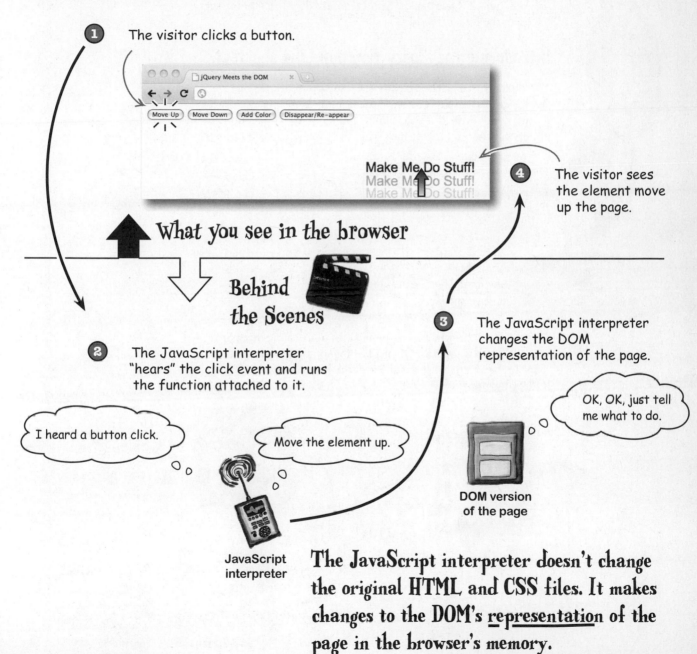

1 The visitor clicks a button.

What you see in the browser

Behind the Scenes

2 The JavaScript interpreter "hears" the click event and runs the function attached to it.

I heard a button click.

Move the element up.

JavaScript interpreter

4 The visitor sees the element move up the page.

3 The JavaScript interpreter changes the DOM representation of the page.

OK, OK, just tell me what to do.

DOM version of the page

The JavaScript interpreter doesn't change the original HTML and CSS files. It makes changes to the DOM's <u>representation</u> of the page in the browser's memory.

What's with all of those dollar signs in the code?

The dollar sign represents all of the cash you'll rake in with your newly acquired jQuery skills. Kidding, but it does bring home the bacon in the jQuery world.

Introducing the jQuery function (and shortcut)

The dollar sign with the parentheses is the shorter name of the jQuery **function**. This shortcut saves us from writing "jQuery()" every time we want to call the jQuery function. The jQuery function is also often referred to as the jQuery **wrapper**.

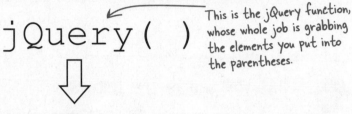

This is the jQuery function, whose whole job is grabbing the elements you put into the parentheses.

This is the jQuery shortcut. Instead of typing the six characters that make up "jQuery," you just type one.

The short name and the long name point to the same thing: the big code block known as jQuery. Throughout this book, we'll use the shortcut. Here are three different things you can put into the jQuery function.

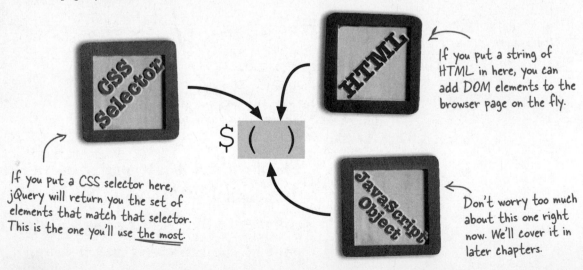

If you put a string of HTML in here, you can add DOM elements to the browser page on the fly.

If you put a CSS selector here, jQuery will return you the set of elements that match that selector. This is the one you'll use <u>the most</u>.

Don't worry too much about this one right now. We'll cover it in later chapters.

jQuery selects elements the same way CSS does

You already know more about jQuery than you realize. The main way you get at stuff with jQuery is to use **selectors**—the same selectors you've used with CSS. If you're a little fuzzy on CSS selectors, it's OK. Let's have a quick refresher.

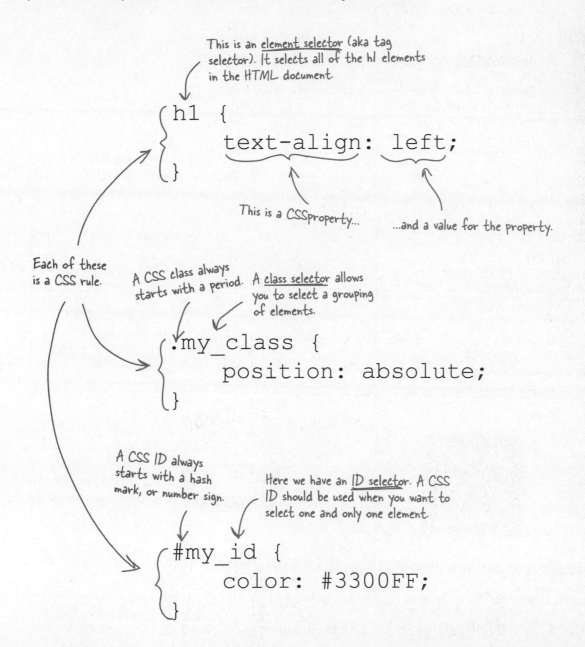

This is an element selector (aka tag selector). It selects all of the h1 elements in the HTML document.

```
h1 {
    text-align: left;
}
```

This is a CSSproperty...

...and a value for the property.

Each of these is a CSS rule.

A CSS class always starts with a period.

A class selector allows you to select a grouping of elements.

```
.my_class {
    position: absolute;
}
```

A CSS ID always starts with a hash mark, or number sign.

Here we have an ID selector. A CSS ID should be used when you want to select one and only one element.

```
#my_id {
    color: #3300FF;
}
```

Style, meet script

The great thing about jQuery is that it uses those same CSS selectors we use to style our page to *manipulate elements* on the page.

CSS selector

Element selector

```
h1 {
      text-align: left;
}
```

Class selector

```
.my_class{
      position: absolute;
}
```

ID selector

```
#my_id {
      color: #3300FF;
};
```

jQuery selector

jQuery element selector

Method

```
$("h1").hide();
```

This hides all of the h1 elements on the page.

jQuery class selector

Method

```
$(".my_class").slideUp();
```

Slides up all of the elements that are members of the CSS class my_class

jQuery ID selector

Method

```
$("#my_id").fadeOut();
```

And this jQuery statement fades out an element that has a CSS ID of my_id until it's invisible.

CSS selectors select elements to add <u>style</u> to those elements; jQuery selectors select elements to add <u>behavior</u> to those elements.

You'll do more with combining selectors and methods in Chapter 2 and the rest of this book.

jQuery selectors at your service

As its name suggests, jQuery is all about *querying*. You ask for something with a selector, and the JavaScript interpreter asks the DOM to get it for you. If you ask for an element with nested elements, jQuery will give you the nested elements too. Let's take apart a jQuery selector a bit more to make sure we know how it works.

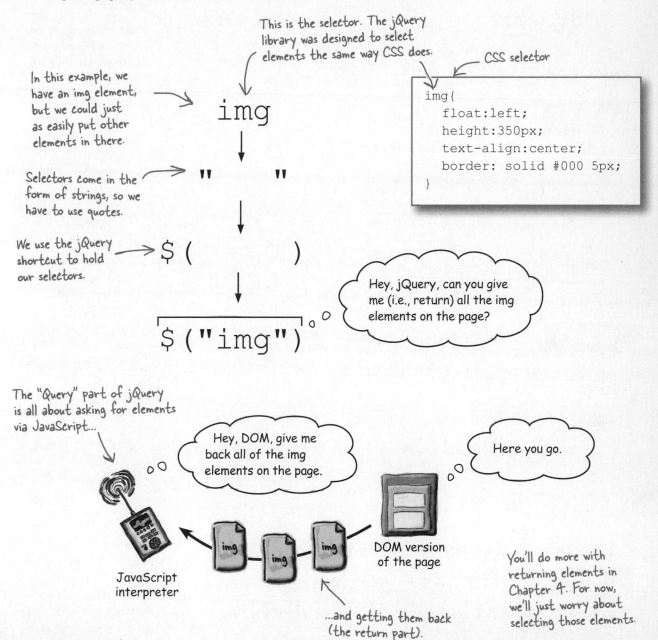

This is the selector. The jQuery library was designed to select elements the same way CSS does.

CSS selector

```
img{
    float:left;
    height:350px;
    text-align:center;
    border: solid #000 5px;
}
```

In this example, we have an img element, but we could just as easily put other elements in there.

img

Selectors come in the form of strings, so we have to use quotes.

" "

We use the jQuery shortcut to hold our selectors.

$ (   )

$ ("img")

Hey, jQuery, can you give me (i.e., return) all the img elements on the page?

The "Query" part of jQuery is all about asking for elements via JavaScript...

Hey, DOM, give me back all of the img elements on the page.

Here you go.

JavaScript interpreter

DOM version of the page

...and getting them back (the return part).

You'll do more with returning elements in Chapter 4. For now, we'll just worry about selecting those elements.

jQuery in translation

To show you just how easy it is to learn jQuery, here's a little breakdown of a few jQuery phrases to use when travelling in DOM country.

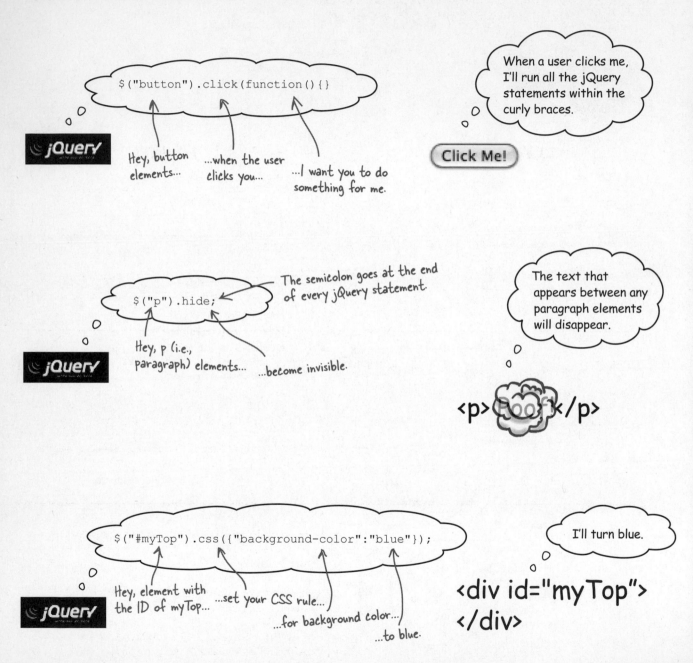

BE the browser

Your job is to play the browser and circle the HTML elements (on the right) that the jQuery statement (on the left) will affect.

jQuery statement	HTML elements
	`<p>One morning, when Gregor Samsa woke from troubled dreams . . .</p>`
`$("p").hide();`	`<p>he found himself transformed in his bed into a horrible vermin.</p>`
	`<p>He lay on his armour-like back, and if he lifted his head a little . . . </p>`

	`<span class="Italian">Nel Mezzo del cammin di nostra vita</span>`
`$("span.Italian").toggle();`	`<span class="English">In the middle of this road called "our life"</span>`
	`<span class="Italian">mi ritrovai per una selva oscura</span>`

	`<p id="mytext">One morning, when Gregor Samsa woke from troubled dreams . . . </p>`
`$("p#mytext").show();`	`<p id="mytext">he found himself transformed in his bed into a horrible vermin.</p>`
	`<p>He lay on his armour-like back, and if he lifted his head a little . . . </p>`

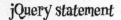

BE the browser Solution

Your job is to play the browser and circle the HTML elements (on the right) that the jQuery statement (on the left) will affect. Here's our solution.

jQuery statement	HTML elements

jQuery statement

HTML elements

`$("p").hide();`

> `<p>One morning, when Gregor Samsa woke from troubled dreams . . .</p>`

> `<p>he found himself transformed in his bed into a horrible vermin.</p>`

> `<p>He lay on his armour-like back, and if he lifted his head a little . . . </p>`

`$("span.Italian").toggle();`

> `<span class="Italian">Nel Mezzo del cammin di nostra vita</span>`

> `<span class="English">In the middle of this road called "our life"</span>`

> `<span class="Italian">mi ritrovai per una selva oscura</span>`

`$("p#mytext").show();`

> `<p id="mytext">One morning, when Gregor Samsa woke from troubled dreams . . . </p>`

> `<p id="mytext">he found himself transformed in his bed into a horrible vermin.</p>`

`<p>He lay on his armour-like back, and if he lifted his head a little . . . </p>`

there are no
Dumb Questions

Q: So why create jQuery if all it does is use JavaScript? Isn't JavaScript enough on its own?

A: JavaScript is great for a lot of things—especially manipulating the DOM—but it's pretty complex stuff. DOM manipulation is by no means straightforward at the base level, and that's where jQuery comes in. It abstracts away a lot of the complexity involved in dealing wlth the DOM, and makes creating effects super easy. (It was created by John Resig; you can find out more about him here; *http://ejohn. org/about.*)

Q: What's this business with the dollar sign all about?

A: It's just a shortcut so you don't have to write "jQuery" over and over! But when you're working with other client-side languages, using `jQuery()` helps avoid naming conflicts.

Q: You've mentioned "client-side scripting" before, too. What's that again, exactly?

A: Web developers often refer to the web browser as a *client* because it consumes data from a (web) server. A client-side scripting language is one that can give directions to the browser behind the scenes, while a server-side language gives directions to the server. We'll cover this more in Chapters 8 and 9.

Q: Where did this whole DOM thing come from?

A: Good question. Web developers and designers were tired of inconsistencies across browsers and decided they needed a standard they could use to add behavior to and interact with web pages on any browser. The World Wide Web Consortium (aka W3C) worked to define the standard collaboratively with these various groups. You can find out more about that here: *http://w3.org/dom.*

Q: When I go to download jQuery, there's a production version and a developer version. What's the difference between the two?

A: The production version is *minified*, which means that a bunch of unnecessary characters and whitespace have been removed. It is optimized to run faster in a production environment, but it's kind of harder to see what's going on. The developer version is nicely spaced and much more readable. It's intended for anyone who wants to dig around in the jQuery code to change or even extend it (it is open source, after all!).

Your first jQuery gig

You just landed a job as the new web developer for the Webville Pet Rescue Foundation. The marketing team wants to kick off their annual fundraising campaign with a revamp of last year's "Help Our Furry Friends" web page. They gave you a screen shot from last year with details on what they want the page to do.

Well, no one wants to let Marketing down on the first day—you don't want to be on their bad side! So let's see what we're working with here…

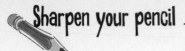

Sharpen your pencil

Before you figure out how to add jQuery functionality to the page, let's look at how the HTML and CSS are set up. We've given you the files for last year's campaign below. Next to the elements that you think you'll need, write what you'll have to do to provide the functionality that Marketing is looking for. We've filled in the first one for you.

```
<!DOCTYPE html><html> <head>
<title>Furry Friends Campaign: jQuery
Proof-of-Concept</title>
<link rel="stylesheet" type="text/
css" href="styles/my_style.css">
</head>

<body>

<div id="showfriend">

<a href="#">Our Furry Friends Need
Your Help
<img src="images/furry_friend.jpg">
</a>

</div>
```

This anchor tag has "hover" and "active" states set in the CSS. The user hovers over the link, and the image appears.
....
....
....
....
....

index.html

```
a:link img, a:visited img {
display:none;
}


a:hover img, a:active img {
display:block;
}
a{
text-decoration:none;
color: #000;
}
```
....
....
....
....
....
....
....

my_style.css

Sharpen your pencil
Solution

Before you figure out how to add jQuery functionality to the page, let's look at how the HTML and CSS are set up. We've given you the files for last year's campaign below. Next to the elements that you think you'll need, write what you'll have to do to provide the functionality that Marketing is looking for. Here are our answers, but don't worry if yours aren't exactly the same as what we came up with.

```
<!DOCTYPE html><html> <head>
<title>Furry Friends Campaign: jQuery
Proof-of-Concept</title>
<link rel="stylesheet" type="text/
css" href="styles/my_style.css">
</head>

<body>

<div id="showfriend">

<a href="#">Our Furry Friends Need
Your Help
<img src="images/furry_friend.jpg">
</a>

</div>
```

index.html

This anchor tag has "hover" and "active" states set in the CSS. The user hovers over the link, and the image appears.

The furry friend image of the dog is nested inside the anchor tag. This image shouldn't show up until the user clicks the link in the anchor tag.

```
a:link img, a:visited img {
display:none;
}

a:hover img, a:active img {
display:block;
}
a{
text-decoration:none;
color: #000;
}
```

my_style.css

This CSS selector changes the display property of the nested image to "none" so it's not visible when the page first loads.

When the user hovers her mouse over or clicks on the anchor tag, the img element's display property will change to "block." The image will then suddenly appear.

OK, so now we can just dive in and start writing jQuery for all the functionality we want, right?

You could, but things might get messy.

Before we can use jQuery to make the cool effects that Marketing wants, we need to make sure that jQuery has everything in place to work its magic. As you already know now, one of jQuery's main jobs is to manipulate HTML elements, so we need to have good *structure*. To get at elements, jQuery uses the same selectors that CSS uses, so we also need to have well-defined *styles*.

Revisit your requirements

When you're thinking about your structure, it's always good to go back to what you're trying to build. Marketing wants an image to slide down and fade in when people click on the "Show Me the Furry Friend of the Day" section of the page. What changes to the HTML and CSS might you need to make?

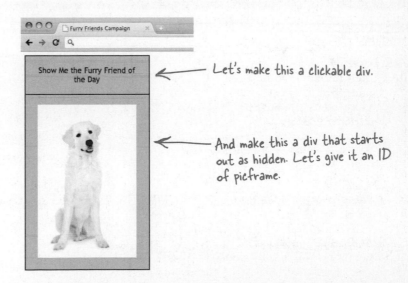

Let's make this a clickable div.

And make this a div that starts out as hidden. Let's give it an ID of picframe.

Set up your HTML and CSS files

Let's think about what we'll have to set up in our HTML and CSS files before you write any jQuery statements. Open up the jQuery files for Chapter 1 (if you haven't done that yet, be sure to go back to the opening section "How to use this book" for details). Find the *Begin* folder in Chapter 1. Then, add the code in bold below to the files, as shown here.

Do this!

```
<!DOCTYPE html>
<html><head>
    <title>Furry Friends Campaign</title>
    <link rel="stylesheet" type="text/css" href="styles/my_style.css">
</head>
<body>
    <div id="clickMe">Show Me the Furry Friend of the Day</div>
    <div id="picframe">
      <img src="images/furry_friend.jpg">
    </div>
    <script src="scripts/jquery-1.6.2.min.js"></script>
    <script>
      $(document).ready(function(){
        $("#clickMe").click(function() {

        });
      });
    </script>
</body>
</html>
```

This makes a clickable div, and we'll style it in the CSS file below so it has the same look and feel as the picframe div.

Here's the picframe div that will slide open to show the furry friend picture.

Nest the furry_friend.jpg image inside the picframe.

index.html

```
#clickMe {
    background: #D8B36E;
    padding: 20px;
    text-align: center;
    width: 205px;
    display: block;
    border: 2px solid #000;
}
#picframe {
    background: #D8B36E;
    padding: 20px;
    width: 205px;
    display: none;
    border: 2px solid #000;
}
```

This styles the clickMe div so that so it has the same look and feel as the picframe div.

Set the picframe selector to "display: none" so that it won't show when the page loads.

my_style.css

jQuery Up Close

Now that you have your HTML and CSS files set up, let's break down the code that's sitting between the `<script>` tags.

As soon as I possibly can, I'll start executing code within the curly braces!

The DOM

Hey, DOM...

...whenever you're ready and loaded...

...I want you to do something for me.

```
$(document).ready(function(){
```

Here's our ID selector for the clickMe div.

```
$("#clickMe").click(function()
{
```

The dot separates the selector part from the method part.

Connecting the button with an ID of clickMe to the click event, this code makes the button clickable.

The code for what will happen when the button is pressed will go between these curly braces (aka the "code block").

The semicolon is a <u>terminator</u>. It ends our jQuery click statement.

```
});
```

```
});
```

This semicolon ends our jQuery ready function.

 **Relax**

There are a lot of potentially new terms here.

We'll get into events, methods, and functions in a lot more detail soon.

But our page still doesn't **do** anything new yet!

You're right. Our HTML and CSS are ready; now we need some jQuery.

We want the `picframe div` to slide and to fade. Fortunately, the jQuery folks have built *effects* that let us control both of these rich visual actions: *slides* and *fades*. We've devoted a whole chapter later in the book to jQuery effects (Chapter 5), so don't worry about getting every little thing down now. Let's just start sliding and fading first.

Slide on in...

The first effect we'll implement is having the image slide into view, which is one of the things the marketing team manager wants to have happen. There are three ways to deal with sliding:

```
$("div").slideUp();          $("div").slideDown();          $("div").slideToggle();
```

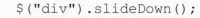

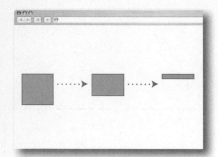
The slideUp method changes the height property of the element until it's 0, and then hides the element.

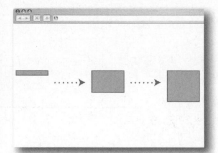
The slideDown method changes the height property of the element from 0 to whatever it's set to in the CSS style.

The slideToggle action says, "If it's up, slide it down; if it's down, slide it up."

May the fade be with you

We also want the image to gradually appear, going from invisible to fully visible. Again, jQuery has a method for that, and that method is called a *fade*. The fade methods are pretty similar to what you just saw for sliding: you have `FadeIn`, `FadeOut`, `FadeTo`, and `FadeToggle`. For now, let's just use `FadeIn`, which gives us control over the opacity and transparency properties of HTML elements.

Here's what we want to fade in; in this case, it is an image.

You can specify how fast it fades in by putting a value inside the parentheses, typically represented in milliseconds (ms).

```
$("img").fadeIn();
```

When an element fades in, it goes from being invisible (transparent) to being visible (opaque).

BRAIN POWER

How many jQuery statements do you think it will take us to accomplish the effect we want?

Take a shot at writing those statements on a piece of scratch paper. If you're not sure, try to write it out first in plain English; then you'll start getting your brain to think in jQuery.

That's it?

Amazingly, you only need to write **two lines** of jQuery code to get these effects to work. Now you're probably beginning to get a sense of why so many people like jQuery. Add the bolded lines below to your *index.html* file, and you're good to go.

Do this!

```
<!DOCTYPE html>
<html>
  <head>
    <title>Furry Friends Campaign</title>
    <link rel="stylesheet" type="text/css" href="styles/my_style.
css">
  </head>
  <body>
    <div id="clickMe">Show me the Furry Friend of the Day</div>
    <div id="picframe">
    <img src="images/furry_friend.jpg">
    </div>
    <script src="scripts/jquery-1.6.2.min.js"></script>
    <script>
      $(document).ready(function(){
        $("#clickMe").click(function() {

          $("img").fadeIn(1000);
          $("#picframe").slideToggle("slow");

        });
      });
    </script>
  </body>
</html>
```

In jQuery, it's important to sequence our effects in such a way that they don't run over one another. We'll deal with this issue throughout the book.

We run the fade effect on our image first.

We added some extra stuff in the parentheses to juice up the effects. We'll look at these in more depth in Chapter 5.

index.html

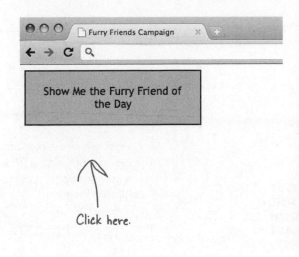

Test Drive

Open the page up in your favorite browser to make sure everything's working.

Click here.

Your image should fade in and slide down.

Watch it!

Check it across multiple browsers.

Just because jQuery will work the same across all browsers doesn't mean the styles you define in your CSS file, or any dynamic styles you apply to elements in your page, will react the same in all browsers!

You rescued the Furry Friends campaign

You got the job done with some HTML and CSS fine-tuning, and just two lines of jQuery. Just think of all the puppies you've saved…

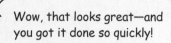

jQuerycross

It's time to sit back and give your left brain
something to do. It's your standard crossword;
all of the solution words are from this chapter.

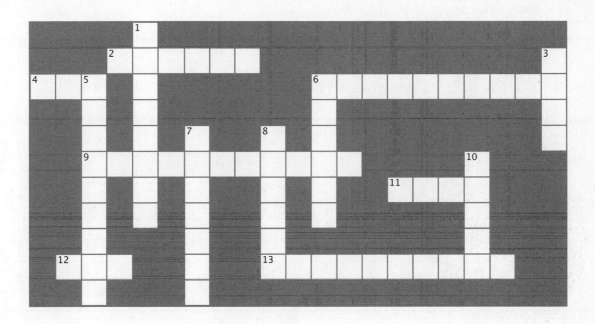

Across

2. After your browser receives a web page from a web server, it loads that web page into its _____.
4. Adds style to a web page.
6. The language jQuery is written in.
9. The JavaScript _____ translates directions you give it into different actions on the page.
11. A CSS setting that makes sure an element won't show when the page loads, `display: _____` .
12. Name of the character used to separate a jQuery selector from a jQuery method.
13. The name of the symbol we use for the jQuery shortcut.

Down

1. A _____ is used by jQuery to locate and return an element from the web page.
3. This kind of file builds the structure of the web page.
5. The name of the symbol that ends a jQuery statement.
6. JavaScript library specialized for complex interactivity and rich visual effects.
7. Use a _____ to test that your jQuery scripts are working.
8. You know you're dealing with a _____ when you see a set of parentheses after a keyword.
10. Creator of the jQuery library, John _____.

 jQuerycross Solution

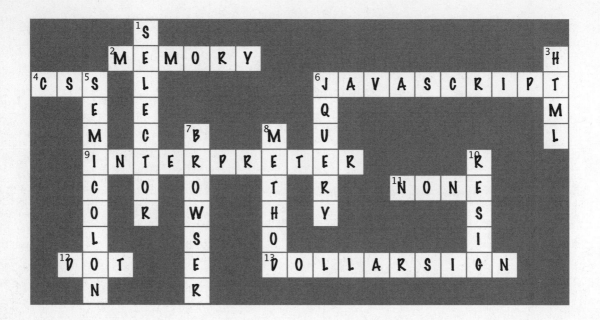

Your jQuery Toolbox

You've got Chapter 1 under your belt and now you've added the basic jQuery function, selectors, click events, and the fade effect to your toolbox.

jQuery function

You use this to select elements from an HTML page to manipulate.

The $ shortcut means you don't have to type "jQuery" over and over.

The jQuery function can handle selectors, straight HTML, and even JavaScript objects.

Selectors

jQuery selects elements the same way CSS does: with selectors.

Just about any kind of HTML element is fair game for a jQuery selector.

Fade effect

Once you've selected an element, you can fade it in a variety of ways, using FadeIn, FadeOut, FadeTo, and FadeToggle.

You can fade in all kinds of elements, from text to images and more.

Control the speed of your fade effect by putting a time (in milliseconds) value inside the parentheses at the end of the statement.

2 selectors and methods

Grab and go

Oh baby, could my selectors and methods make magic with *your* web page elements...

jQuery helps you grab web page elements and do all kinds of things with them. In this chapter, we'll dig into jQuery selectors and methods. With jQuery selectors, we can grab elements on our page, and with methods we can do stuff to those elements. Like a massive book of magic spells, the jQuery library lets us change tons of things on the fly. We can make images disappear and reappear out of thin air. We can select a certain piece of text and animate the change to its font size. So, on with the show—let's grab some web page elements and go!

Jump for Joy needs your help

You receive an email from your friend, who is a professional portrait photographer. She wants to roll out a "Jump for Joy" promotion that allows users to win deals on a package of prints. She needs your help making the promotion work.

From: **Emily**
Subject: **Jump for Joy Promotion!**

Hey,

I saw your tweet that you're doing more interactive web work these days, so I was hoping you could help me with making some interactive stuff for the "Jump for Joy" promotion on my website. I'd like to give my visitors a chance to receive a discount off their purchase before they check out, to encourage them to click around the site some more (and hopefully buy more as a result!).

The page should have four sections with one of four images per section. I need a message that says "Your Discount is" that displays a random discount amount (between 5 and 10 percent). When a user clicks on one of the sections, the message should appear below the image in that section. If a user clicks again, I'd like to get rid of the last message and display a new one.

I've attached a mockup of how I want it to look.

Think you can help??

--

Emily

What are the project requirements?

Emily is a great photographer, but her request is kind of all over the place. Let's take a closer look at that email and figure out what she is really asking for. Before you can even start writing any jQuery, you want to be super clear on what the project (or user) requirements are.

Sharpen your pencil

Take the requests in the email and break them down into a list of things our web app needs to do. This list will be our guide for ensuring that our web app meets the client's needs.

To-Do List:

1.

2.

3.

4.

5.

Converting user *requests* into actual *project requirements* is an important skill that gets better with practice and time.

Make it Stick

Sharpen your pencil
Solution

Take the requests in the email and break them down into a list of things our web app needs to do. This list will be our guide for ensuring that our web app meets the client's needs. Here's our solution.

To-Do List:

1. The page should have four sections with one of four "jump for joy" images per section.

2. The sections should be clickable.

3. We need a message that says "Your Discount is" along with a random discount amount (between 5 and 10 percent).

4. When a user clicks on one of the sections, the message should appear below the image in that section.

5. If a user clicks again, get rid of the last message and make a new one.

Great, now that we've worked out the project requirements, let's jump in and get started with the jQuery already!

Whoa! Hold your horses there, hoss!

Working out project requirements first is a good habit to get into for every jQuery project you'll work on. But before we jump right into writing jQuery code, we need to do a little work setting up the structure and styles first. We did a bit of this in Chapter 1, and now we've got even more to set up before we get any jQuery goodness going.

Dig in with divs

We need four clickable areas on the page, so let's make those first. The most useful and flexible HTML element for our purposes is the `<div>` tag. The `<div>` tag serves very well in the structure role, since it's a block-level element. We can also easily style `div` elements to act exactly as we want them to.

Exercise

Open your favorite text editor to create the HTML and CSS files you'll need. Below is the starter code with some key elements missing. Add the following items to the page and check them off as you're done:

☐ A tag to include the jQuery library, version 1.6.2.

☐ A `<div>` tag with the ID of `header`.

☐ A `<div>` tag with the ID of `main`.

☐ Inside each of the four `div` elements inside of the `main` div, put a different image (get the images here: *www.thinkjquery.com/chapter02/images.zip*).

```
<html>
  <head>
    <title>Jump for Joy</title>
    <link href="styles/my_style.css" rel="stylesheet">
  </head>
  <body>
.................................................
      <h2>Jump for Joy Sale</h2>
  </div>
.................................................
      <div><img src="images/jump1.jpg"/></div>
      <div> .......................................... </div>
      <div> .......................................... </div>
      <div> .......................................... </div>
  </div>
.................................................
<script > </script>   </body>
</html>
```

index.html

```
div{
  float:left;
  height:245px;
  text-align:left;
  border: solid #000 3px;
}
#header{
  width:100%;
  border: 0px;
  height:50px;
}
#main{
  background-color: grey;
  height: 500px;
}
```

my_style.css

EXERCISE SOLUTION

Open your favorite text editor and create the HTML and CSS files to solve this exercise. Below is the starter code with some key elements missing. Once you've added the following items, your page should look like our solution.

☑ A tag to include the jQuery library, version 1.6.2.

☑ A `<div>` tag with the ID of `header`.

☑ A `<div>` tag with the ID of `main`.

☑ Inside each of the four `div` elements inside of the `main` div, put a different image.

Your HTML and CSS files should look like this.

```
<html>
  <head>
    <title>Jump for Joy</title>
    <link href="styles/my_style.css" rel="stylesheet">
  </head>
  <body>
  <div id="header">

      <h2>Jump for Joy Sale</h2>
  </div>
  <div id="main">

      <div><img src="images/jump1.jpg"/></div>
      <div> <img src="images/jump2.jpg"> </div>
      <div> <img src="images/jump3.jpg"> </div>
      <div> <img src="images/jump4.jpg"> </div>
  </div>
<script src="scripts/jquery-1.6.2.min.js"></script>
<script > </script>  </body>
</html>
```

A div element with the ID of header

A div element with the ID of main

The div elements for the images

Include the jQuery library.

index.html

```
div{
      float:left;
      height:245px;
      text-align:left;
      border: solid #000 3px;
}
#header{
      width:100%;
      border: 0px;
      height:50px;
}
#main{
      background-color: grey;
      height: 500px;
}
```

my_style.css

Test Drive

Open the page up in your favorite browser to make sure everything's working.
This will give us an opportunity to note how we want the page to function.

A div
element
with the ID
of header

A div element with
the ID of main,
containing...

...the four div elements
for the images.

We now have four areas on our page with images.
How do we make them clickable?

A click event up close

As we've seen, making an element clickable with jQuery is easy.

Clicking on a page element causes an *event* to trigger on the page, and can also run *functions*. We'll get more in depth into events and functions later on, but for now, let's just review how the **click** event works on a paragraph (or <div>) tag.

Here, we tell the JS interpreter that we want to make paragraph elements do something when we click on them.

This is the element we want to attach the click event to.

A function is a way to collect together a bunch of things we want to do.

```
$("p").click( function() {
```

Because it's inside the parentheses that belong to the click action, the function will run when the click is triggered by the user.

We use opening curly braces to start a "block" of code. A block is a lot like a paragraph: it contains related statements.

```
alert("You rang?");
```

We use the alert statement when we want to test that our function was called properly.

Whatever we put into the quotes will pop up in a new window.

```
});
```

We use closing curly braces to end a "block" of code.

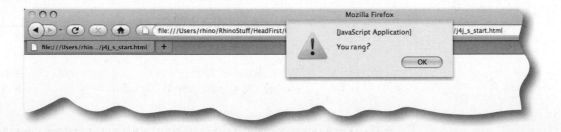

jQuery Code Magnets

Move the magnets to write the code that will make all the `div` elements clickable. When a `div` is clicked, use a JavaScript alert function to display the text "You clicked me." We've put a few in place for you already.

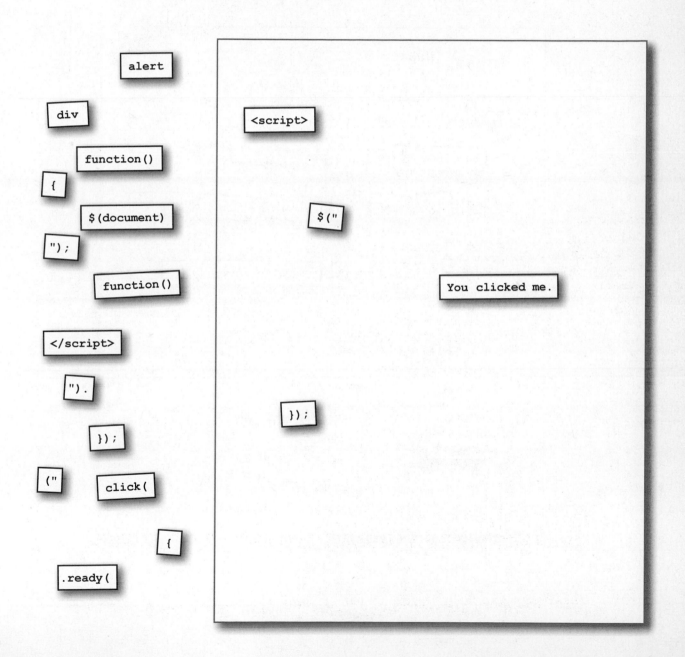

alert

div

function()

{

$(document)

");

function()

</script>

").

});

("

click(

{

.ready(

<script>

$("

You clicked me.

});

jQuery Code Magnets Solution

Move the magnets to write the code that will make all the `div` elements clickable. When a `div` is clicked, use a JavaScript alert function to display the text "You clicked me."

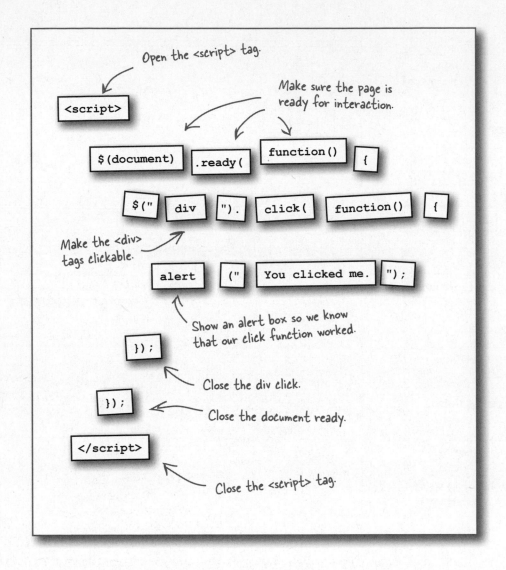

Open the `<script>` tag.

`<script>`

Make sure the page is ready for interaction.

`$(document)` `.ready(` `function()` `{`

`$("` `div` `").` `click(` `function()` `{`

Make the `<div>` tags clickable.

`alert` `("` `You clicked me.` `");`

Show an alert box so we know that our click function worked.

`});`

Close the div click.

`});`

Close the document ready.

`</script>`

Close the `<script>` tag.

Add the click method to your page

Using the code you put together in the magnets solution on the previous page, update your HTML file to include this script. Don't forget to put it inside a `<script>` tag!

Do this!

```html
<html>
  <head>
    <title>Jump for Joy</title>
    <link href="styles/my_style.css" rel="stylesheet">
  </head>
  <body>
    <div id="header">
      <h2>Jump for Joy Sale</h2>
    </div>
    <div id="main">
      <div><img src="images/jump1.jpg"/></div>
      <div><img src="images/jump2.jpg"/></div>
      <div><img src="images/jump3.jpg"/></div>
      <div><img src="images/jump4.jpg"/></div>
    </div>
    <script src="scripts/jquery-1.6.2.min.js"></script>
    <script >
      $(document).ready(function() {
          $("div").click(function() {
              alert("You clicked me.");
          });//end click function
      });//end doc ready
    </script>
  </body>
</html>
```

The alert function calls up a window in your browser with a message inside it. We'll use it whenever we want to see the results of things we've added to code like variables and functions.

Add these lines between your `<script>` tags to make the divs clickable.

Some programmers add comments to help identify parentheses and curly braces. It's a matter of coding style that's entirely up to you.

index.html

TEST DRIVE

Open the page up in your favorite browser to make sure everything's working. You should see the alert message now as you click around the images on the page.

Here's the alert box you added. You can see that the click function worked.

> Yes, but no matter *where* I click, I get the alert message. Why is that?

Hmmm, that is a problem.

It looks like we've gotten a bit click-happy. Let's take a look at that click event again.

The JS interpreter did exactly what we asked it to do. It selected all the divs...

...and added a click method to each of them.

```
$("div").click( );
```

In fact, you don't even have to click on the images to get that message. Our page structure has `div` elements nested in another `div`, so when you click on those, the browser thinks you've clicked on both, and you might get two alerts in that case. Clearly, we need to narrow down what we're asking jQuery to do here...

Get more specific

The issue is that we haven't been specific enough in our selection. So how can we get at the four sub-divs and leave out the larger container div? Remember from Chapter 1 that jQuery selectors use CSS classes and IDs. We can get even more specific about which elements we want jQuery to grab by adding classes and IDs to those elements.

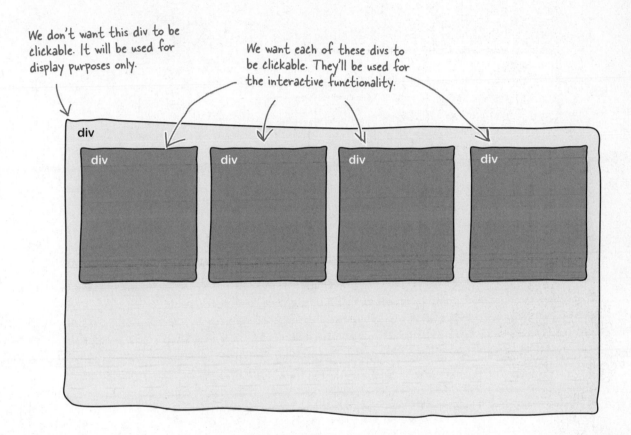

We don't want this div to be clickable. It will be used for display purposes only.

We want each of these divs to be clickable. They'll be used for the interactive functionality.

div

div   div   div   div

Would you use just CSS classes or IDs separately, or a combination of both, to specify the div elements above? Which would work best, and why?

Classing up your elements

In CSS, classes are used to group elements together and give them common style attributes. You can have one or more elements on the page that have the same class. For jQuery, we can use the same class selector, and affect the same group of elements with jQuery methods. Both CSS and jQuery use the "." to signify a class, which makes it super easy to start classing up your code.

The DOM tree structure of the web page

```
html
```

```
body
```

```
div
```

```
div class="nav"
```
```
div class="nav"
```
```
p id="my_blurb"
```

The DOM tree

Class selectors match any elements that are members of the class.

```css
.nav {
    display: block;
    border: solid #00f 1px;
    width: 100%;
}
```

CSS code

```javascript
$(".nav").click( function(){
    alert("You clicked me!");
});
```

jQuery code

ID-entifying elements

An ID selector is used to identify a single, unique element on a page. In jQuery, as in CSS, the # symbol is used to identify an ID selector. IDs are great when you want to get specific with an element, or when there is only going to be one of that kind of element on the page, like a page header or footer.

ID selectors match one unique element.

```css
#my_blurb {
    display: block;
    border: 0px;
    height: 50%;
}
```

CSS code

```
$("#my_blurb").slideToggle("slow");
```

jQuery code

WHO DOES WHAT?

Check the boxes in the appropriate columns to indicate what you can use classes for and what you can use IDs for. Remember, sometimes a class and an ID can do the same job!

	Class	ID
Uniquely identify a single element on the page	☐	☐
Can identify one or more elements on the page	☐	☐
Can be used by a single JavaScript method, cross-browser, to identify an element	☐	☐
Can be used by CSS to apply style to elements	☐	☐
More than one of these can be applied to an element at the same time	☐	☐

WHO DOES WHAT? SOLUTION

Check the boxes in the appropriate columns to indicate what you can use classes for and what you can use IDs for. Remember, sometimes a class and an ID can do the same job!

	Class	ID
Uniquely identify a single element on the page	☐	☑
Can identify one or more elements on the page	☑	☐
Can be used by a single JavaScript method, cross-browser, to identify an element	☐	☑
Can be used by CSS to apply style to elements	☑	☑
More than one of these can be applied to an element at the same time	☑	☐

there are no Dumb Questions

Q: What is a *block-level* element?

A: Block-level elements appear within their parent elements as rectangular objects that do not break across lines. They also appear with block margins, width and height properties that can be set independently of the surrounding elements.

Q: Why is the `<script>` tag at the bottom of the page before the `</body>` tag? I thought it was always supposed to be inside the `<head> </head>` tags?

A: Yes, that used to be (and for some people, still is) the suggested best practice. However, the problem caused by scripts is that they block parallel downloads in the browser. Images from different servers can be downloaded more than two at a time, but once your browser encounters a `<script>` tag, it can no longer download multiple items in parallel. Having them at the bottom means it will help speed up your page load time.

Q: What's up with that whole JavaScript alert thing?

A: The ones we used didn't look that pretty, but alerts are useful for a variety of reasons. Really, a JavaScript alert is a simple window containing a message. The text inside the parentheses is what is shown in the alert message. If you want to show a string of text, enclose the text in quotes. To display variable values, enter the variable name without quotes. You can also combine variable values and text strings by using the + sign. You probably see these all the time and don't think about it, like when you don't fill in a required field in a form. In our case, we're using them more for testing and debugging purposes. There are certainly more robust ways to do that, and we'll get into those in later chapters in the book.

Fireside Chats

Tonight's talk: **CSS and jQuery Selectors discuss their differences.**

CSS Selector:	**jQuery Selector:**
Howdy, jQuery Selector. I'm relieved that you're here to let everyone know that you owe your entire existence to me.	
	Uh, thanks, I guess. I certainly get a lot of my power from your approach to picking out elements. However, I'm more about behavior than style. You just sit around and make things look nice, while I actually get some serious action going.
Well, I've definitely got style, but I've got quite a bit of power. I can change the look and feel of things in the blink of an eye.	
	I won't argue about your usefulness on a page. You've got your job, which is changing how elements look, and I've got mine, which is very different.
And what is it you can do that I can't do?	
	My job is to find elements and return them so that a method can do something to the returned set.
Hello, fancy jargon! What do you mean, you "return" elements?	
	Say someone uses me to select all the paragraph elements on the page. I grab that set of paragraphs and hold them so that a jQuery method can do whatever it wants to them.
But I can affect all the elements I select, too. I can change all of their background colors to fuchsia if I want. And don't forget that my engine gives you all the power you have.	
	Your selector engine gives me a good chunk of power, but another chunk of my power comes from JavaScript. Don't forget the "Query" part of my name. I can actually ask the browser for an element, hold on to that element, and pass it off to a jQuery method to make it fly across the page or even disappear.
I've got to admit, that does sound pretty cool.	
	Yeah, and you're right that I couldn't do it without you.

Wire up your web page

Classes and IDs are common ground for the three layers of a web page that we looked at in Chapter 1: structure, style, and script. Selectors are where those layers get *wired* together so they can all work in concert. HTML provides the building blocks (i.e., elements and their attributes), or **structure** of the web page. CSS provides the **style**, or the presentation and position of those elements. JavaScript and jQuery provide the **script** that controls the behavior or function of those elements.

Imagine that we have a class called `slideshow` for an image we want to run the `slideUp` method on:

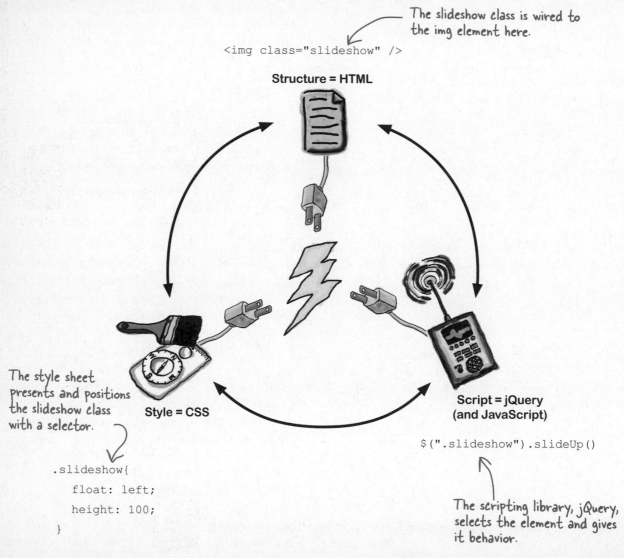

The slideshow class is wired to the img element here.

`<img class="slideshow" />`

Structure = HTML

The style sheet presents and positions the slideshow class with a selector.

Style = CSS

```
.slideshow{
    float: left;
    height: 100;
}
```

Script = jQuery (and JavaScript)

`$(".slideshow").slideUp()`

The scripting library, jQuery, selects the element and gives it behavior.

Sharpen your pencil

Update the structure, style, and script in your page to make only the four image `div` sections clickable. In the CSS file, create a CSS class (called `guess_box`) and apply it to the `html` and the `script`. It looks like one of our `div` elements lost its ID attribute too. Can you figure out which one and put it back?

```css
div{
    float:left;
    height:245px;
    text-align:left;
    border: solid #000 3px;
}
#header{
    width:100%;
    border: 0px;
    height:50px;
}
#main{
    background-color: grey;
    height: 500px;
}

.........................................................
......height. 245px;.....................................
.........................................................
```

my_style.css

```html
<html>
  <head>
    <title>Jump for Joy</title>
    <link href="styles/my_style.css" rel="stylesheet">
  </head>
  <body>
    <div id="header">
      <h2>Jump for Joy Sale</h2>
    </div>
    <div ...........................>
     <div ...........................><img src="images/jump1.jpg"/></div>
     <div ...........................><img src="images/jump2.jpg"/></div>
     <div ...........................><img src="images/jump3.jpg"/></div>
     <div ...........................><img src="images/jump4.jpg"/></div>
    </div>
    <script src="scripts/jquery-1.6.2.min.js"></script>
    <script>
      $(document).ready(function() {
        $(" ...........................").click(function() {
          alert("You clicked me.");
        });
      });
    </script>
  </body>
</html>
```

index.html

Sharpen your pencil Solution

Add the `guess_box` class to all the `div` elements that will be used to hide the discount code. Also, update our selector to use this class, and add it into our CSS file. And it was the `main` `div` element that needed to get its ID attribute back.

```css
div{
    float:left;
    height:245px;
    text-align:left;
    border: solid #000 3px;
}
#header{
    width:100%;
    border: 0px;
    height:50px;
}
#main{
    background-color: grey;
    height: 500px;
}
.guess_box{
    height 245px;
}
```

my_style.css

Here's where you add a class for the guess boxes. The height matches the height of the images in the boxes, so everything lines up nicely.

```html
<html>
  <head>
    <title>Jump for Joy</title>
    <link href="styles/my_style.css" rel="stylesheet">
  </head>
  <body>
    <div id="header">
      <h2>Jump for Joy Sale</h2>
    </div>
    <div      id="main"           >
      <div   class="guess_box"       ><img src="images/jump1.jpg"/></div>
      <div   class="guess_box"       ><img src="images/jump2.jpg"/></div>
      <div   class="guess_box"       ><img src="images/jump3.jpg"/></div>
      <div   class="guess_box"       ><img src="images/jump4.jpg"/></div>
    </div>
    <script src="scripts/jquery-1.6.2.min.js"></script>
    <script>
      $(document).ready(function() {
        $("     .guess_box          ").click(function() {
          alert("You clicked me.");
        });
      });
    </script>
  </body>
</html>
```

Attach the click method to the guess_box class only and not all div elements.

index.html

Meanwhile, back to our list

Let's have a look at our requirements to-do list to see where we are on
building everything that Emily asked for:

- ☑ The page should have four sections with one of four "jump for joy" images per section.

- ☑ The sections should be clickable.

- ☐ We need a message that says "Your Discount is" along with a random discount amount (between 5 and 10 percent).

- ☐ When a user clicks on one of the sections, the message should appear below the image in that section.

- ☐ If a user clicks again, get rid of the last message and make a new one.

Wow, that was easy. We're almost halfway
through our list already. The next few things don't
look too bad either. We have to create some text
and a number. How hard can that be?

Actually, not very hard.

There are several things involved in displaying a
message to the user. Don't forget, it could be a different
message for each user who visits the site.

BRAIN POWER

You're going to have to create a message
and store it somewhere to display it to your
visitors. How do you think you can do that?

Creating some storage space

The next requirement on our list is to show some text that will stay the same as our script runs: "Your Discount is". But beside that, we need to hold a number that will change or **vary** depending on the random amount. We need a way to carry that information throughout the script—our page needs a way to store that information. Storing information (or data) that varies is a perfect job for **variables**. When we want variables in jQuery, we use JavaScript variables.

After the var keyword, you name your variable.

The var keyword lets you declare a variable.

This is how we set the value of the variable in code.

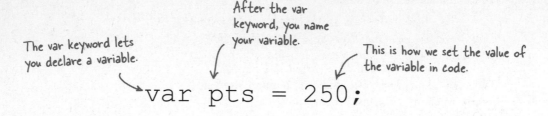

```
var pts = 250;
```

When we declare a variable, the JavaScript interpreter gives us some browser memory in which we can store your data.

We name a variable so that we can reference it later in our script.

We place a value into our variable using an equals sign.

=250

pts

pts

Now, whenever we want to get the data we stored, we just ask for it by its variable name.

If you want to know more about JavaScript variables and the math functions, pick up a copy of Head First JavaScript!

Mix things up with concatenation

For many of our jQuery scripts, we'll be storing different kinds of data: numbers, text, or true or false values. In many cases, especially when we need to display different messages to our visitors, we'll be mixing HTML with these other kinds of data, which gives our web pages even more power. So, how do we go about combining our variables with other values? We use *concatenation*. Imagine you have a video game where you have a variable called `pts` that stores the highest score, and you need to display it to the winner:

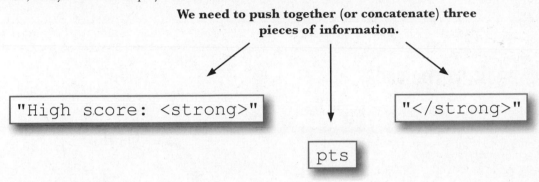

We need to push together (or concatenate) three pieces of information.

```
"High score: <strong>"
```

```
pts
```

```
"</strong>"
```

Which give us:

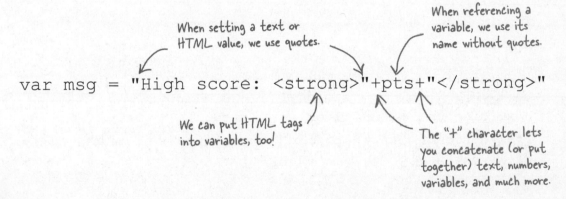

When setting a text or HTML value, we use quotes.

When referencing a variable, we use its name without quotes.

```
var msg = "High score: <strong>"+pts+"</strong>"
```

We can put HTML tags into variables, too!

The "+" character lets you concatenate (or put together) text, numbers, variables, and much more.

Exercise

We'll give you the JavaScript code to make a variable called `discount` that holds a random number from 5 to 10. Write the code for a `discount_msg` variable that shows the message and the random variable. Make sure the discount message appears inside a paragraph element.

```
var discount = Math.floor((Math.random()*5) + 5);
```

....

Exercise Solution

We'll give you the JavaScript code to make a variable called `discount` that holds a random number from 5 to 10. Write the code for a `discount_msg` variable that shows the message and the random variable. Make sure the discount message appears inside a paragraph element.

Don't worry, we'll explain the math and random function in Chapter 3.

```
var discount = Math.floor((Math.random()*5) + 5);
```

var discount_msg = "<p>Your Discount is "+ discount +"%</p>";

Meanwhile, back in the code...

Now that you've got a variable set up to store your concatenated discount message, you just need to update what's in between your <script> tags, so let's focus there.

Do this!

```
<script>
  $(document).ready(function() {

    $(".guess_box").click( function() {

      var discount = Math.floor((Math.random()*5) + 5);
      var discount_msg = "<p>Your Discount is "+ discount +"%</p>";
      alert(discount);

    });
  });
</script>
```

Create new JavaScript variables.

We put the discount variable in our alert to make sure it's doing what we want it to.

index.html

Insert your message with append

You've got your message ready to go, but how do you display it on the page below the image that's been clicked? If you think of adding a new message as *inserting* it into the page, jQuery provides several ways to insert content into an existing element. We'll cover some more useful ones in more depth in Chapter 4, but for now, let's just look quickly at the append action.

```
<p>jQuery lets me add stuff onto my web page
without having to reload it.</p>
```

This jQuery statement is telling the JS interpreter to append the content in quotes to all paragraph elements.

```
$("p").append(" <strong>Like me, for instance.</strong>");
```

If you run this in your script, the text in bold appears on your page.

jQuery lets me add stuff onto my web page
without having to reload it.
Like me, for instance.

The resulting HTML as seen in the DOM

```
<p>jQuery lets me add stuff onto my web page
without having to reload it.</p> <strong>Like me,
for instance.</strong>
```

Exercise

With what you know about selectors already and your new `append` powers, write the code to append the `discount` variable to your `guess_box` element.

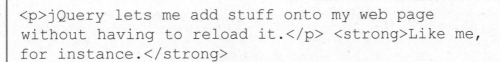

EXERCISE SOLUTION

Adding a new message to a web page is really just this simple!

```
$(".guess_box").append(discount_msg);
```

append is a jQuery method. You use methods to do stuff in jQuery.

there are no
Dumb Questions

Q: Are there any restrictions on what I can use for class names?

A: A class name must begin with an underscore (_), a dash (-), or a letter (a–z), followed by any number of dashes, underscores, letters, or numbers. There is a catch: if the first character is a dash, the second character must be a letter or underscore, and the name must be at least two characters long.

Q: Are there any restrictions on what I can call variables?

A: Yes! Variables cannot begin with numbers. Also, they cannot contain any mathematical operators (+ * - ^ / ! \), spaces, or punctuation marks. They can, however, contain underscores. They cannot be named after any JavaScript keywords (like `window`, `open`, `array`, `string`, `location`), and are case sensitive.

Q: How many classes can I give to elements?

A: There is no defined maximum, according to the standards, but the number in real-world usage is around 2,000 classes per element.

Q: Is there a way to select every element on the page?

A: Yes! Simply pass in a "*" into the jQuery wrapper to get all the elements.

Q: If I give my elements a class or ID, without any style, will that have any effect on how they look in a browser?

A: No, there are no browser defaults for classes or IDs. Some browsers do treat elements differently, but a class or ID without any CSS applied to it will not have any effect.

TEST DRIVE

Open the page up in your favorite browser to make sure everything's working. Pay special attention to the alert to make sure that the discount variable is set up properly.

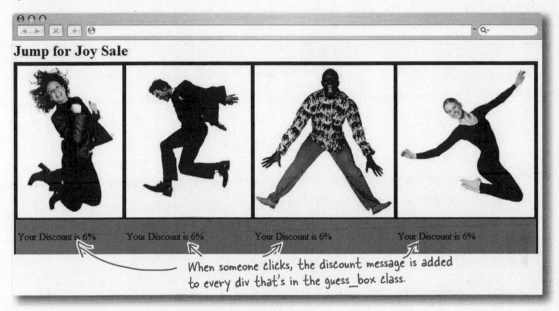

Jump for Joy Sale

Your Discount is 6%   Your Discount is 6%   Your Discount is 6%   Your Discount is 6%

When someone clicks, the discount message is added to every div that's in the guess_box class.

Everything works great, but...

The discount variable is generating a random number and appends the message to our page the way we expected, but it has an unexpected side effect: the discount shows up over and over again in every div.

That's not what we wanted to happen. So what went wrong?

```
<script>
  $(document).ready(function() {
    $(".guess_box").click( function() {
      var discount = Math.floor((Math.random()*5) + 5);
      var discount_msg = "<p>Your Discount is "+discount+"%</p>";
      alert(discount_msg);
      $(".guess_box").append(discount_msg);
    });
  });
</script>
```

This applied the click method so that each member of the guess_box class is clickable.

This is just to test the variable.

Our selector is specific enough to grab a class, but we end up affecting all the divs in the class

We need to append the discount variable **only** to the individual div that's clicked. So, how do we select only the one that was clicked and append the discount variable to that one?

Give me $(this) one

Throughout this chapter, we've been looking at jQuery selectors and how they return elements that jQuery methods use. And very often, we want to be really specific about which element we're selecting. When it comes to specificity, the simplest selector to write is `$(this)`. (All you have to remember is the pronoun "this," after all.) The `$(this)` selector gives us an easy way to point to the *current* element.

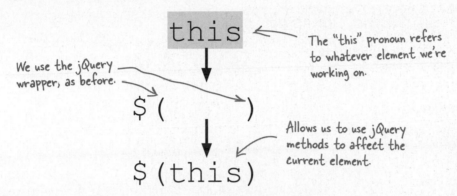

We use the jQuery wrapper, as before.

The "this" pronoun refers to whatever element we're working on.

Allows us to use jQuery methods to affect the current element.

It's important to think about `$(this)` as **context-dependent**. In other words, `$(this)` means different things depending on where or when you use it. One of the **best** places to use it is within a function that runs when a jQuery method is called:

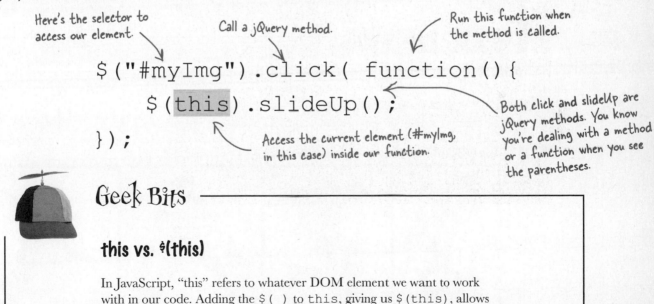

Here's the selector to access our element.

Call a jQuery method.

Run this function when the method is called.

```
$("#myImg").click( function(){
    $(this).slideUp();
});
```

Access the current element (#myImg, in this case) inside our function.

Both click and slideUp are jQuery methods. You know you're dealing with a method or a function when you see the parentheses.

Geek Bits

this vs. $(this)

In JavaScript, "this" refers to whatever DOM element we want to work with in our code. Adding the `$( )` to `this`, giving us `$(this)`, allows us to interact with our DOM element using jQuery methods.

Put $(this) to work

Let's see if $ (this) can help us solve our problem. Update your
code to use $ (this), as shown in bold below.

Do this!

```
<script type="text/javascript">
  $(document).ready(function() {

    $(".guess_box").click( function() {

      var discount = Math.floor((Math.random()*5) + 5);
      var discount_msg = "<p>Your Discount is "+ discount +"%</p>";
      alert(discount_msg);
      $(this).append(discount_msg);

    });
  });//end doc ready
</script>
```

Now we're telling our guess
boxes to append the discount
code only to the one clicked.

index.html

Test Drive

Open the page up in your favorite browser to make sure everything's working. Pay special attention to the
alert to make sure that we got the discount variable right. Make sure to click several times to check that
the random number concatenated into the discount variable works too.

Jump for Joy Sale

Your Discount is 6%

$(this) worked great! But now every time I click, I keep getting discount codes. How can I stop that happening?

Great question!

That leads us right to the last step on our to-do list:

- ☑ The page should have four sections with one of four "jump for joy" images per section.
- ☑ The sections should be clickable.
- ☑ We need a message that says "Your Discount is" along with a random discount amount (between 5 and 10 percent).
- ☑ When a user clicks on one of the sections, the message should appear below the image in that section.
- ☐ If a user clicks again, get rid of the last message and make a new one.

BRAIN POWER

How do you think you can remove the last message?

Good riddance with remove

So how do we get rid of the last message and make a new one? Use the `remove` method. The `remove` method allows us to take an element, or a group of elements, off of the page. Let's have a look at a really simple page with a list and a button.

1 Here's what it looks like in the browser, and the HTML that creates it.

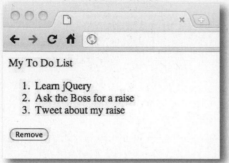

Browser view

HTML view

```
<div>My To Do List</div>
<ol>
    <li>Learn jQuery</li>
    <li>Ask the Boss for a raise</li>
    <li>Tweet about my raise</li>
</ol>
<button id="btnRemove">
```

2 And here's the code for the button, which will remove all the list items from your list:

```
$("#btnRemove").click(function(){
    $("li").remove();
});
```

remove is another jQuery method. Think of a jQuery method as a verb—it's all about web page action.

3 Looking again at the page in the browser and the HTML—after jQuery is finished—we can see that all our list items are gone, even in the HTML!

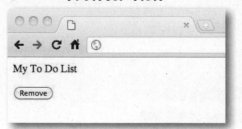

Browser view

HTML view

```
<div>My To Do List</div>
<ol>
</ol>
<button id="btnRemove">
```

BRAIN POWER

Which selector do you need to use to remove just the discount message from the page?

Dig down with descendant selectors

Descendant selectors are yet another selector we can use with jQuery, and they happen to fit our situation perfectly. With descendant selectors, we can specify *relationships between elements*. We can select children, parents, or siblings.

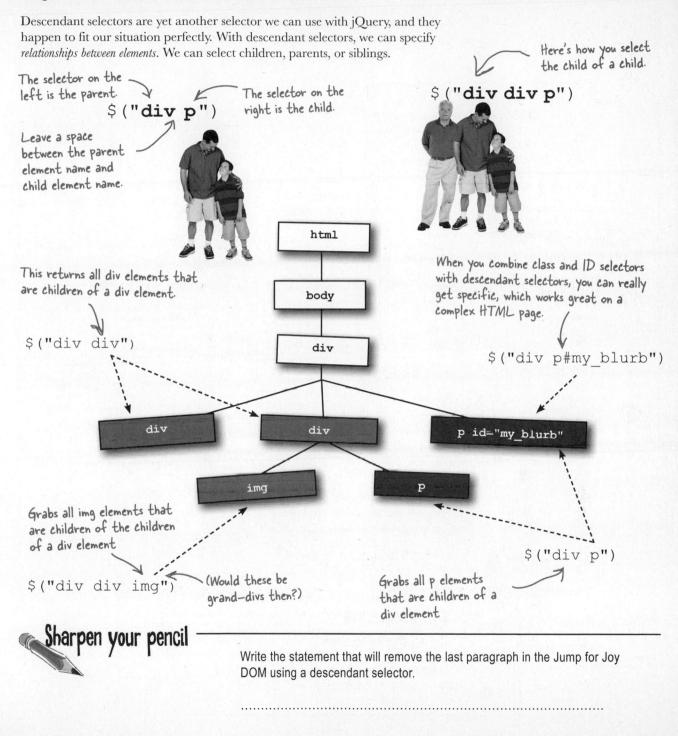

The selector on the left is the parent.

$("div p")

The selector on the right is the child.

Leave a space between the parent element name and child element name.

Here's how you select the child of a child.

$("div div p")

This returns all div elements that are children of a div element.

$("div div")

When you combine class and ID selectors with descendant selectors, you can really get specific, which works great on a complex HTML page.

$("div p#my_blurb")

```
html
```

```
body
```

```
div
```

```
div
```

```
div
```

```
p id="my_blurb"
```

```
img
```

```
p
```

Grabs all img elements that are children of the children of a div element

$("div div img")

(Would these be grand-divs then?)

Grabs all p elements that are children of a div element

$("div p")

Sharpen your pencil

Write the statement that will remove the last paragraph in the Jump for Joy DOM using a descendant selector.

....

Sharpen your pencil
Solution

Start by using the `.guess_box` class selector, followed by a descendant p selector to access the paragraph you added. Then, use the `remove` method to take all the p elements in any element with the class of `guess_box` off the page.

$("`.guess_box p`").remove();

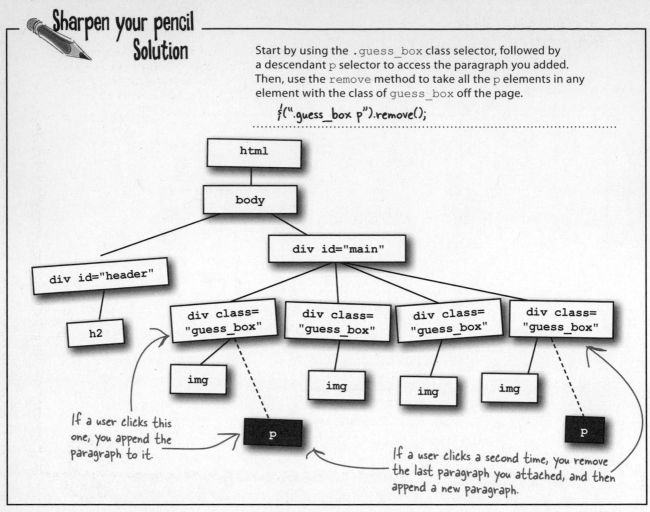

If a user clicks this one, you append the paragraph to it.

If a user clicks a second time, you remove the last paragraph you attached, and then append a new paragraph.

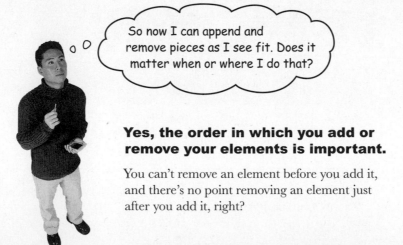

So now I can append and remove pieces as I see fit. Does it matter when or where I do that?

Yes, the order in which you add or remove your elements is important.

You can't remove an element before you add it, and there's no point removing an element just after you add it, right?

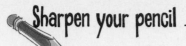

Sharpen your pencil

Your job is to decide where the remove statement should go. Write the statement on the line numbered 1, 2, or 3 below. Then explain why you put it there. Think about *when* you need to remove the paragraph, and use the process of elimination to pick the correct place to do that.

```
<script>
  $(document).ready(function() {

  1. ................................................................

     $(".guess_box").click( function() {

  2. ................................................................

       var discount = Math.floor((Math.random()*5) + 5);
       var discount_msg = "<p>Your Discount is "+ discount +"%</p>";
       alert(discount_msg);
       $(this).append(discount_msg);

  3. ................................................................

     });
  });
</script>
```

index.html

Why I think the statement goes there:

....

....

....

....

....

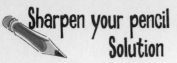

Sharpen your pencil
Solution

Your job is to decide where the `remove` statement should go. Write the statement on the line numbered 1, 2, or 3 below. Then explain why you put it there. Think about *when* you need to remove the paragraph, and use the process of elimination to pick the correct place to do that.

```
<script>
    $(document).ready(function() {

    1. ........................................................
       $(".guess_box").click( function() {
            $(".guess_box p").remove();
    2. ........................................................
          var discount = Math.floor((Math.random()*5) + 5);
          var discount_msg = "<p>Your Discount is "+ discount +"%</p>";
          alert(discount_msg);
          $(this).append(discount_msg);

    3. ........................................................
       });
    });
</script>
```

index.html

Why I think the statement goes there:

The remove statement can't go on line 1 because it would be outside of the click function for the guess box. The statement can't go on line 3 because that would remove what I just appended. I want to remove the last discount message before generating a new one, so I'll put it as the first line of the code block (inside the curly braces) for the guess_box click.

The order and timing of when you make your jQuery calls is important.

Watch it! *This is true especially when you are giving important information to your visitors and removing it again. We'll look more into the timing and order of on-screen effects in Chapter 5.*

<h1>there are no
Dumb Questions</h1>

Q: Sometimes, after calling the `remove` method, I still see the elements I removed in the source of the page. Why is that?

A: Oftentimes, browsers actually make a fresh call to the server to get the source of the page when you use the View Source option. Using DOM inspectors, like Chrome Developer tools or Firebug for Firefox, should show you the DOM as it is displayed on the page.

Q: What do the `Math.floor` and `Math.random` methods mean?

A: The `floor` method rounds a number down to the nearest integer and returns the result. The `random` method returns a random number between 0 and 1. When we multiply it by a number, we guarantee getting a number between 0 and whatever number we multiply by.

Q: Where did `this` come from?

A: In many object-oriented programming languages, `this` (or `self`) is a keyword that can be used in instance methods to refer to the object on which the currently executing method has been invoked.

Q: So I can display a random discount only when someone clicks one of the images, and remove it when he clicks another one. But really, that's not all we need to do to make this work for real, right?

A: You're right, you've got us there. This is only the first piece of the puzzle, really. People are going to need to have that code carry over when they check out to buy their photos. To pass the discount code to a shopping cart, you'll need to send the code back to the server for processing. We'll work on that kind of functionality in more detail in Chapters 8–10.

Test Drive

Add the line of code you just wrote to your *index.html* file. Then, open the page up in your favorite browser to make sure everything's working. Click several times to check that the random number concatenated into the `discount` variable works too, and that the old discount values are removed properly, before appending the new code.

Your turn to jump for joy

Congratulations! You nailed the requirements and made the campaign work.

☑ The page should have four sections with one of four "jump for joy" images per section.

☑ The sections should be clickable.

☑ We need a message that says "Your Discount is" along with a random discount amount (between 5 and 10 percent).

☑ When a user clicks on one of the sections, the message should appear below the image in that section.

☑ If a user clicks again, get rid of the last message and make a new one.

From: **Emily**
Subject: **Re: Jump for Joy Promotion!**

Thank you so much for doing this for me. My site is so much better.

I hope people enjoy my photos as much as I enjoy my new page!

--
Emily

> PS. I've attached a self-portrait of me with my photo gear when I saw the new web page... No prizes for guessing what I'm doing!

Your jQuery Toolbox

You've got Chapter 2 under your belt and now you've added the basics of jQuery selectors and jQuery methods to your toolbox.

$(this)

Selects the "current" element.

The meaning of $(this) will change throughout your code, depending on where it is being referenced.

jQuery methods

method — A jQuery method is reusable code defined in the jQuery library. You use methods to do stuff in jQuery and in JavaScript. Think of a method as a verb—it's all about web page action.

.append — Inserts the specified content into the DOM. It gets added to the end of whatever element calls it.

.remove — Takes elements out of the DOM.

Selectors

$(this) — Selects the current element.

$("div") — Selects all the div elements on the page.

$("div p") — Selects all the p elements that are directly inside div elements.

$(".my_class") — Selects all the elements with the my_class class.

$("div.my_class") — Selects only the divs that have the my_class class. (Different types of elements can share a class.)

$("#my_id") — Selects the element that has the ID of my_id.

3 jQuery events and functions

Making things happen on your page

How many times do I have to dig this out?!

jQuery makes it easy to add action and interactivity to any web page. In this chapter, we'll look at making your page react when people interact with it. Making your code run in response to user actions takes your website to a whole new level. We'll also look at building reusable functions so you can write the code once and use it multiple times.

Your jQuery skillz are in demand again

Emily was pleased with the work you did for her Jump for Joy promotion, but she's met with her accountant and now has a few changes she'd like you to make.

From: **Jump for Joy**
Subject: **RE: Jump for Joy Promotion**

Hey,

You did a great job of making the web promotion work! I met with my accountant and crunched some numbers on the success of the promotion.

My accountant suggested some changes to the app that should bring in more sales.

Visitors should still get four options to pick from for the chance to receive a discount. However, now let's make it the same discount amount each time. My accountant recommends offering 20% off visitors' purchases before they check out. That should be more enticing for them.

Visitors should only get one chance to find the discount code, which should be in a random square for each visit. If a visitor finds the discount code when she clicks, show it to her on the screen before she proceeds. Otherwise, show her the box where the code was hiding.

Think you can do this as well as you did the first part?

--
Emily Saunders
jumpforjoyphotos.hg

Emily's taken some photos of her accountant for his profile, but she couldn't get him to jump for joy. Can your changes to the site help?

The money man has a point...

Making the promotion limited to only one square keeps Emily from having to hand out so many discount codes, and it keeps people clicking around the site. Seems like these new features are *all* about clicking...

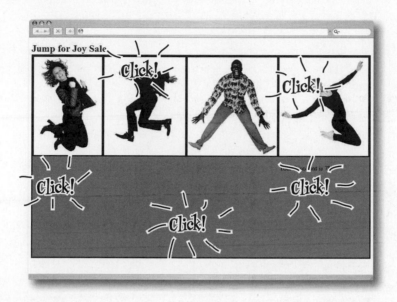

Sharpen your pencil

It's time for another list of requirements. You know what to do: look at Emily's email again and pick out all the new features she's asking for. Write out in plain English what you think each feature is.

Requirements:

Sharpen your pencil
Solution

It's time for another list of requirements. You know what to do: look at Emily's email again and pick out all the new features she's asking for. Write out in plain English what you think each feature is. Here's our solution.

Requirements:

- The discount should only be in one of the four image boxes, and the images should be in a different (random) box each time the page loads.

- Visitors should only get one chance to find the discount when they load the page. So we'll need to stop them from clicking more than once in order to find a better discount.

- After the visitor has made his guess and clicked on a box, the answer should be revealed as to whether or not he got it right. If he chose correctly, show him the discount so he can apply it to his order.

- There will be a standard 20% discount, instead of a variable one. So instead of a percentage, give visitors a discount code.

What our solution currently does

Geesh! This guy really is click-happy.

What we need our solution to do

You only get one chance with me!

BRAIN POWER

You know how to add a click to your page. But how do you make sure a user can only do it once?

You also learned in the previous chapters how to run code when a click gets called. Can you think of a way we could use that to help us complete our solution?

Making your page eventful

The Jump for Joy application is all about the clicks. In jQuery and
JavaScript, a click is referred to as an *event* (there are plenty of other
events, but for our purposes, we'll just focus on clicks for now). An event
is a mechanism that allows you to run a piece of code when something
happens on the page (like a user clicking a button). The code that gets
run is a *function*, and functions allow you to make your jQuery more
efficient and reusable. We'll look more closely at functions in a minute,
but for now, let's look at how a click event really works.

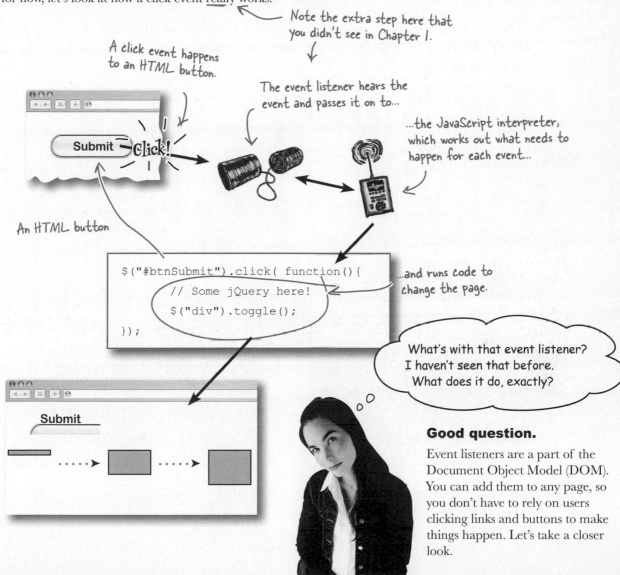

Note the extra step here that
you didn't see in Chapter 1.

A click event happens
to an HTML button.

The event listener hears the
event and passes it on to...

...the JavaScript interpreter,
which works out what needs to
happen for each event...

An HTML button

```
$("#btnSubmit").click( function(){
    // Some jQuery here!
    $("div").toggle();
});
```

...and runs code to
change the page.

What's with that event listener?
I haven't seen that before.
What does it do, exactly?

Good question.

Event listeners are a part of the
Document Object Model (DOM).
You can add them to any page, so
you don't have to rely on users
clicking links and buttons to make
things happen. Let's take a closer
look.

Behind the scenes of an event listener

Event listeners are the browser's way of paying attention to what a person does on a page, and then telling the JavaScript interpreter if it needs to do something or not.

jQuery gives us very easy ways to add event listeners to *any element* on the page, so users are no longer just clicking on links and buttons!

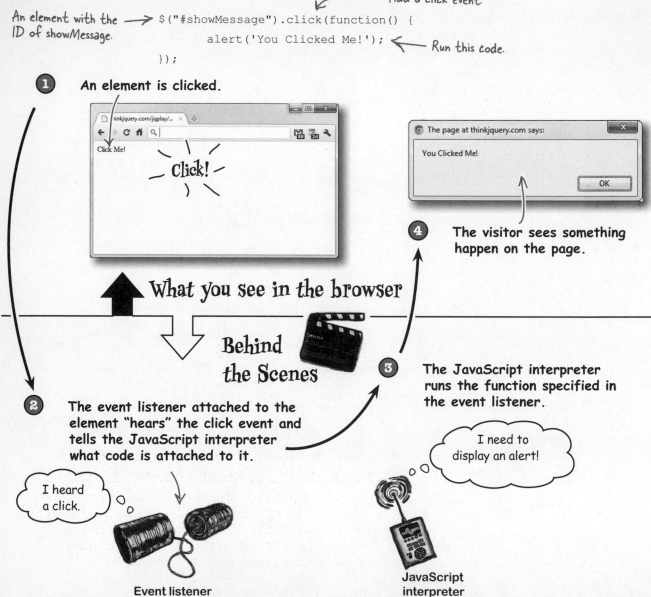

Add a click event.

An element with the ID of showMessage.

```
$("#showMessage").click(function() {
    alert('You Clicked Me!');
});
```

Run this code.

1 An element is clicked.

Click Me!

Click!

4 The visitor sees something happen on the page.

The page at thinkjquery.com says:

You Clicked Me!

OK

What you see in the browser

Behind the Scenes

2 The event listener attached to the element "hears" the click event and tells the JavaScript interpreter what code is attached to it.

I heard a click.

Event listener

3 The JavaScript interpreter runs the function specified in the event listener.

I need to display an alert!

JavaScript interpreter

Binding an event

When we add an event to an element, we call this *binding* an event to that element. When we do this, the event listener knows to tell the JavaScript interpreter what function to call.

There are two ways of binding events to elements.

Method 1

We use this method to add events to elements as the page is getting loaded.

This is often known as the *convenience* method.

```
$("#myElement").click( function() {
        alert($(this).text());
});
```

Method 2

We use this method just like Method 1, but we can also use it to add events to elements that get added to the page after it is loaded, like when we create new DOM elements.

Both methods add a click event listener for our element with the ID of myElement.

```
$("#myElement").bind('click', function() {
        alert($(this).text());
});
```

Watch it!

Method 1—the convenience method—is simply a shortcut for Method 2, but only when the <u>DOM elements exist already</u>.

jQuery offers many shortcuts like this to help you keep your code cleaner. They are known as convenience methods because they are included solely for ease of use—but they do have limits. You'll want to use Method 2 to add events to new DOM elements that you create within your code, like if you added a new clickable image, or a new item to a list that you want the user to interact with.

Triggering events

Events can be triggered by a wide variety of things on any given page. In fact, your entire browser is eventful, and pretty much any part of it can trigger events!

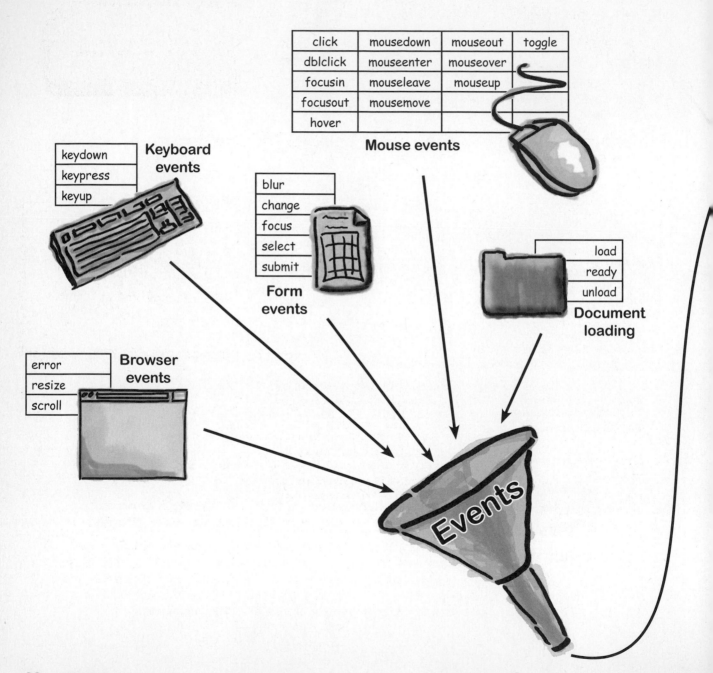

click	mousedown	mouseout	toggle
dblclick	mouseenter	mouseover	
focusin	mouseleave	mouseup	
focusout	mousemove		
hover			

Mouse events

keydown
keypress
keyup

Keyboard events

blur
change
focus
select
submit

Form events

load
ready
unload

Document loading

error
resize
scroll

Browser events

Events

Event is triggered

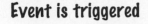

Event listener

Run a function

JavaScript interpreter

```
function () {
    [this is the code
    block. do stuff here]
}
```

Selector + Event + Function = Complex interaction

there are no Dumb Questions

Q: What about those functions inside the events?

A: They are called *handler functions*. A handler function is a block of code that runs when the event is triggered. We'll see more on functions later in this chapter.

Q: Where can I find all the different types of events?

A: On the jquery.com website, under Documentation → Events.

Q: How many different categories of events are there?

A: jQuery groups events into five different categories: browser events, document loading events, form events, keyboard events, and mouse events.

Q: How many different events are there?

A: There are nearly 30 different types, between all the different event categories.

Q: What can trigger an event (i.e., make an event happen) on the page?

A: It's mostly input devices (keyboard and mouse) that trigger the different event types. However, your browser, the page document, your jQuery code, and even an HTML form on your page can trigger events, too.

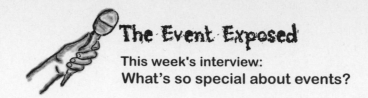

The Event Exposed

This week's interview:
What's so special about events?

HeadFirst: Hi, Event, it's nice to be able to talk to you.

Event: It's great to be here.

HeadFirst: So, who are you? Who's the real Event?

Event: These days, I've really come into my own, but before jQuery came along, I was a little scattered. I'm an object that helps people interact with a web page.

HeadFirst: That sounds cool. I'll come back to that in a bit, but why were you scattered? Where did you come from?

Event: It's a long story. Back in the mid 1990s, Netscape released Navigator 2.0. It was great. I was a really simple model. The DOM, JavaScript, and I were the new kids on the block. There was a W3C standard on how we were supposed to be implemented in browsers and everything!

HeadFirst: That was a long time ago. You've come a long way.

Event: Yes, we all have. Along the way, we got caught up on the browser wars between Microsoft Internet Explorer and Netscape. Eventually, Microsoft won out, after both companies tried to one-up each other with cool tricks that were not in the standard, but only supported in each company's browser.

HeadFirst: That sounds like a tough time.

Event: It was, but good things came out of it. In 1997, both Netscape and Microsoft released version 4.0 of their respective browsers. There were many new events, and we could do so much more with the page. It was a great time to be an event.

HeadFirst: So what happened?

Event: Things got out of control. Netscape went open source, and later became Mozilla Firefox. But there was still a Netscape too, for a while. Both it and Internet Explorer had different event models. Many things would only work on one browser, leaving people frustrated when they got to a website with the wrong browser. Netscape eventually went away, but several other browsers came on the scene.

HeadFirst: So why are things so great now?

Event: Browser by browser, things are still not ideal. Internet Explorer supports different events than Firefox, Google Chrome, Apple's Safari, and Opera. But that is changing with each release. They are starting to get more in line with the standards. But the really great news is that jQuery handles these issues for the web developer.

HeadFirst: Really? That's great! How? What's this object you said you were?

Event: jQuery knows which browser is being used, so it decides how to deal with events, depending on what browsers your website viewer is using. As for an object, it's nothing fancy. In practical terms, an object is really just variables and functions combined into a single structure.

HeadFirst: Where can we go to read more about these variables and functions?

Event: You can find out more about me in jQuery's official documentation here: *http://api.jquery.com/category/events/event-object/*.

HeadFirst: Thanks! I'll be sure to check that out. How do we go about using you on our pages?

Event: Well, first, I have to be bound to something, so the event listener knows to listen out for me. Then, something has to trigger me, so I can run whatever code I'm supposed to when an event happens.

HeadFirst: OK, but how do you know what code to run?

Event: That happens when I get bound to an element. Pretty much any code can get called when I get bound to an element. That's what makes me so useful. I can also be unbound from an element. If that happens, the event listener will no longer listen out for events on that element, so whatever code was supposed to run when I was triggered won't run.

HeadFirst: That sounds pretty slick, but we're running out of time. Where can I find out more about you and the types of events that happen on the page?

Event: The link I gave you already will explain what makes me an object. There's more information about me and all the types of events on the jQuery website, in the Documentation section. Thanks for having me.

HeadFirst: Thanks for being here. We're looking forward to using you in our code.

We'll dive into functions and variables later in this chapter.

Plus, we'll look more at JavaScript in coming chapters.

Removing an event

Just like binding events to elements, you often need to *remove* events from elements—for example, when you don't want people to click a submit button twice on a form, or you only want to allow them to do something once on a page. That's just what you need for these new Jump for Joy requirements.

After an element has an event bound to it, we can remove that event from the element so it doesn't get triggered.

To remove one event:

The unbind command tells the web browser to no longer listen for this particular event for this element.

Add a click event listener to the element with an ID of myElement.

Run this code when myElement gets clicked.

```
$("#myElement").bind ('click', function() {
    alert($(this).text());
});
```

Remove the click event from myElement.

```
$("#myElement").unbind('click');
```

To remove all events:

Add a focus event listener to the element with an ID of myElement.

```
$("#myElement").bind ('focus', function() {
    alert("I've got focus");
});
```

Add a click event listener to the element with an ID of myElement.

```
$("#myElement").click(function(){
    alert('You clicked me.');
});
```

Tell the browser to no longer listen for events from myElement.

```
$("#myElement").unbind();
```

So, an event listener sits inside the browser, attached to elements, waiting for events to happen, and tells the JavaScript interpreter to do something when they do happen, right?

Yes! That's exactly right.

Let's see how events can help us tackle the first requirement.

• Visitors should only get one chance to find the discount when they load the page. So we'll need to stop them from clicking more than once in order to find a better discount.

Don't let users have another try at finding the discount.

Sharpen your pencil

Using what you know about `$(this)` and what you learned about events, update the code from the last chapter and add in the code to remove the click event from the `div` sections.

```
$(".guess_box").click( function() {
    $(".guess_box p").remove();
    var my_num = Math.floor((Math.random()*5) + 5);
    var discount = "<p>Your Discount is "+my_num+"%</p>";
    $(this).append(discount);

    ...................................................................................................

    ...................................................................................................

    ...........................................................................................

});
```

index.html

Sharpen your pencil
Solution

Using what you know about $(this) and what you learned about events, update the code from the last chapter and add in the code to remove the click event from the div sections.

```
$(".guess_box").click( function() {
    $(".guess_box p").remove();
    var my_num = Math.floor((Math.random()*5) + 5);
    var discount = "<p>Your Discount is "+my_num+"%</p>";
    $(this).append(discount);

    $(this).unbind("click");



});
```

Tell the browser to no longer listen for events from the current element.

index.html

TEST DRIVE

Update your *index.html* file with this new code, save it, and click around to make sure everything is working as it should.

Jump for Joy Sale

Your Discount is 9%

Did you try clicking around the page when you test drove it? What happened?

I'm guessing your page is acting a lot like mine. And it's not doing what you said it would at all...

You're right, it's not removing the click from all the events yet.

This only removes the click from whatever box you click on. You could still click on the other boxes. If only you could stop the click happening on each of the other elements...

BRAIN POWER

How would you remove the click event **from every box** after the visitor **clicks one box**? Do you have to go through the elements one by one?

Going through the ~~motions~~ elements

Oftentimes, we need to interact with a group of elements *one by one*.

Thankfully jQuery gives us the ability to *loop* through groups of elements, based on whatever selector we choose. Looping, also known as *iteration*, is simply going through a group of elements one at a time, and doing something to each element along the way.

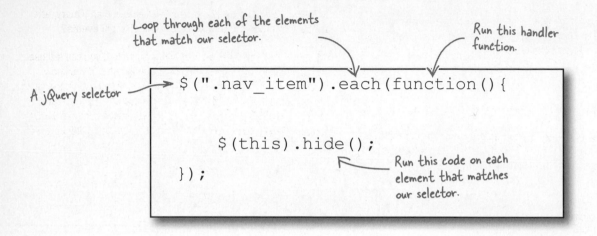

Loop through each of the elements that match our selector.

Run this handler function.

A jQuery selector

```
$(".nav_item").each(function(){

    $(this).hide();
});
```

Run this code on each element that matches our selector.

You'll see more of me from here on out, especially in the next chapter...

The .each iterator takes a group of elements and does something to every element in the group in turn.

We'll look at iteration in more depth later in the book.

there are no
Dumb Questions

Q: Can I trigger events in my code?

A: Yes! This is relatively common. Good examples of this are submitting forms for validation or hiding modal pop-up boxes, to name a couple.

Q: So, how do I trigger an event then?

A: Just like most things in jQuery, its creators tried to make things memorable. You can just use the `.trigger` method, combined with a selector; for example, `$("button:first").trigger('click');` or `$("form").trigger('submit');`.

Q: Can I use events in a web page without jQuery?

A: Yes, you can. jQuery just makes it much easier to bind events to any element because it's cross-browser compatible and uses easy-to-use functions to help bind the events to elements.

Q: How does `.each` work?

A: `.each` uses the selector that calls it and creates an array of elements identified by that selector. It then loops through each element in the array sequentially. Don't worry, though, we'll explain arrays and loops a little later on!

Q: So, I've seen that I can create elements with jQuery, after the page is loaded. Can these elements also get events?

A: Yes, they can. After an element gets created, you can still use the `.bind` method to give it an event listener. Also, if you know ahead of time that your element will behave like some other elements already created, you can use the `.live` method. This will attach a handler to the event for all elements that match the current selector, now and in the future. This will work even for elements that have not yet been added to the DOM.

Sharpen your pencil

Write the code to use iteration to remove the **click** event from every clickable box on your Jump for Joy page. Also, read your code carefully to see if there are any pieces you don't need anymore.

```
$(".guess_box").click( function() {
    $(".guess_box p").remove();
    var my_num = Math.floor((Math.random()*5) + 5);
    var discount = "<p>Your Discount is "+my_num+"%</p>";
    $(this).append(discount);



    $(this).unbind('click');

});
```

index.html

Sharpen your pencil
Solution

Since you're only allowing people to click once, you don't need to remove the old one!

Calling the `.each` method on the `.guess_box` class loops through all of the elements with that class. You can then unbind the click method from each one of them in turn. You also no longer need our `.remove` code; since visitors can only click once, there won't be anything to remove anymore.

```
$(".guess_box").click( function(){
    $(".guess_box p").remove();
    var my_num = Math.floor((Math.random()*5) + 5);
    var discount = "<p>Your Discount is "+my_num+"%</p>"
    $(this).append(discount);

    $(".guess_box").each( function(){
        $(this).unbind('click');
    });
});
```

Loop through each .guess_box element and remove the click event from it.

index.html

Hold on!
Is your HTML file getting a little heavy on the script side there? Before you go on, we really should try to find a way to slim things down a little...

Can we just set up a separate script file from our HTML? We already do it with our CSS...

Good thinking. In fact, there are several reasons to create a separate file for your jQuery code:

1 You can include it in more than one page (code reuse).

2 Your page will load faster.

3 The HTML code you write will be cleaner and easier to read.

Exercise

You already know how to include CSS files, and you've seen how to include the jQuery library. Including your own JavaScript/jQuery file is no different!

You should already have a folder called *scripts* in your root web directory (where you put the jQuery library).

1 Using your favorite text editor, create a file called *my_scripts.js* and save it in the *scripts* folder.

2 Take all the JavaScript and jQuery code from our *index.html* file and move it into this new file. There is no need to put the `<script>` and `</script>` tags in the new file.

3 Create the link to this file in your HTML page by putting the following code just before the closing `</body>` tag:

```
<script src="scripts/my_scripts.js"></script>
```

Exercise Solution

You already know how to include CSS files, and you've seen how to include the jQuery library. Including your own JavaScript/jQuery file is no different!

1 Using your favorite text editor, create a file called *my_scripts.js* and save it in the *scripts* folder.

2 Take all the JavaScript and jQuery code from our *index.html* file and move it into this new file. There is no need to put the `<script>` and `</script>` tags in the new file.

```
$(document).ready(function() {
  $(".guess_box").click( function() {
    var my_num = Math.floor((Math.random()*5) + 5);
    var discount = "<p>Your Discount is "+my_num+"%</p>";
    $(this).append(discount);

    $(".guess_box").each( function(){
      $(this).unbind('click');
    });
  });
});
```

my_scripts.js

Now, if you include this file in every HTML file you have for this project, you can access the same jQuery code. You don't have to repeat it in every file.

Create the link to this file in your HTML page by putting the following code just before the closing </body> tag.

```html
<!DOCTYPE html>
<html>
  <head>
    <title>Jump for Joy</title>
    <link href="styles/styles.css" rel="stylesheet">
  </head>
<body>
  <div id="header">
    <h2>Jump for Joy Sale</h2>
  </div>
  <div id="main ">
    <div class="guess_box"><img src="images/jump1.jpg"/></div>
    <div class="guess_box"><img src="images/jump2.jpg"/></div>
    <div class="guess_box"><img src="images/jump3.jpg"/></div>
    <div class="guess_box"><img src="images/jump4.jpg"/></div>
  </div>
  <script src="scripts/jquery.1.6.2.min.js"></script>
  <script src="scripts/my_scripts.js"></script>
</body>
<html>
```

index.html

All right, that's more like it. Nice and organized. Move along...

Your project structure

You just made some important changes to
how your files are structured. Let's look at
how these all fit together. We've added several
things since the last time we looked at it.

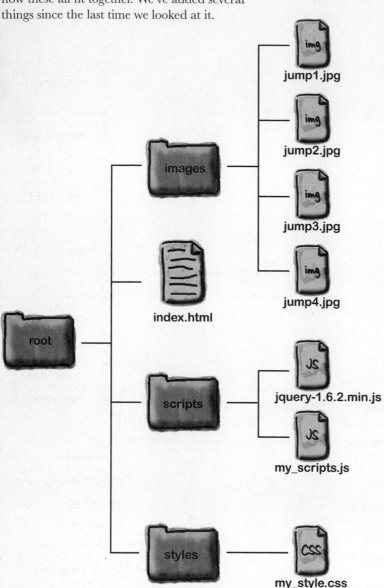

Q: Why does this file have a
.js extension?

A: Because jQuery is a
JavaScript library, any code we write
needs to be included as if it were
JavaScript.

Q: How does this help speed
things up on our page?

A: If your *.js* file is included in
several HTML files, your browser
only asks for it once. It stores it in
the browser cache so it doesn't have
to ask the server for the file every
time we go to another HTML page
that references your script file.

Q: Why don't we need the
`<script>` and `</script>` tags
in our *my_scripts.js* file?

A: They are HTML tags. Since
this is already being included in
our page as a JavaScript file, the
browser already knows what to
expect in the file.

jQuery Magnets

Use the magnets below to organize your project files so you
know how to separate out your HTML, CSS, and jQuery code.
Let's make sure you can get this right every time.

```
<!DOCTYPE html>
<html>

 ...................................
   <title>Jump for Joy</title>
     <link href="styles/styles.css" rel="stylesheet">
   </head>

 ...................................
   <div id="header">
     <h2>Jump for Joy Sale</h2>

 ...................................
   <div   id="main">
     <div ...................><img src="images/jump1.jpg"/></div>
     <div class="guess_box"><img src="images/jump2.jpg"/></div>
     <div class="guess_box"><img src="images/jump3.jpg"/></div>
     <div ...................><img src="images/jump4.jpg"/></div>
   </div>
   <script src="scripts/...................."></script>
   <........ src="scripts/my_scripts.js"></script>
</body>
<html>
```

index.html

```
my_num
```

```
this
```

```
});
```

```
<head>
```

```
".guess_box"
```

```
</div>
```

```
$(document).ready(function() {
  $(.................).click( function() {
    var.............= Math.floor((Math.random()*5) + 5);
    var discount = "<p>Your Discount is "+my_num+"%</p>";
    $(.......).append(discount);

    $(".guess_box").each( function(){
      $(this).unbind('click');
    });

..........................................
});
```

my_scripts.js

```
jquery-1.6.2.min.js
```

```
<body>
```

```
class="guess_box"
```

```
script
```

```
class="guess_box"
```

jQuery Magnets Solution

Use the magnets below to organize your project files so you
know how to separate out your HTML, CSS, and jQuery code.
Let's make sure you can get this right every time.

```html
<!DOCTYPE html>
<html>
    <head>
    <title>Jump for Joy</title>
        <link href="styles/styles.css" rel="stylesheet">
    </head>
    <body>
    <div id="header">
        <h2>Jump for Joy Sale</h2>
        </div>
    <div  id="main">
        <div class="guess_box"><img src="images/jump1.jpg"/></div>
        <div class="guess_box"><img src="images/jump2.jpg"/></div>
        <div class="guess_box"><img src="images/jump3.jpg"/></div>
        <div class="guess_box"><img src="images/jump4.jpg"/></div>
    </div>
    <script src="scripts/jquery-1.6.2.min.js"></script>
    <script src="scripts/my_scripts.js"></script>
</body>
<html>
```

index.html

```javascript
$(document).ready(function() {
  $(".guess_box").click( function() {
    var my_num = Math.floor((Math.random()*5) + 5);
    var discount = "<p>Your Discount is "+my_num+"%</p>";
    $(this).append(discount);

    $(".guess_box").each( function(){
      $(this).unbind('click');
    });
  });
});
```

my_scripts.js

Wouldn't it be dreamy if we could write our jQuery code *once*, but use it again whenever we need? But I know it's just a fantasy...

Making things function-al

Now that we've seen how to add and remove events on our page, let's look at another important feature that will help us master our websites with jQuery: *functions*.

A function is a block of code, separate from the rest of your code, that you can execute wherever you want in your script.

Believe it or not, we've been using functions all throughout the book. Remember these?

These are all things we have already called in our code throughout the book so far.

```js
$(document).ready(function(){

  $("#clickMe").click(function(){

  //Do stuff in here!

  });

  $(".guess_box").click(function(){

  //Do stuff in here!

  });

});
```

Look at all those functions!

jQuery provides a lot of functions for you, but you can also write your own custom functions to provide features not supplied by jQuery. By creating a custom function, you can use your own code again and again without repeating it in your script. Instead, you just call the function by name when you want to run its code.

Custom functions allow you to organize a chunk of jQuery code by name so that it can be easily reused.

The nuts and bolts of a function

To create a function, you need to use a consistent syntax that ties the name of the function with the code that it runs. This is the syntax for the most basic JavaScript function:

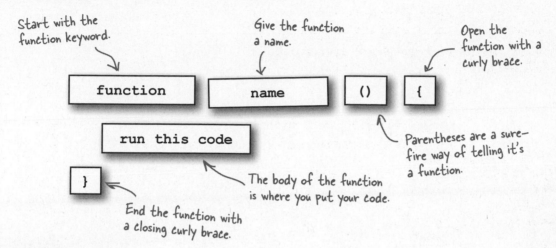

Start with the function keyword.

Give the function a name.

Open the function with a curly brace.

`function` `name` `()` `{`

Parentheses are a sure-fire way of telling it's a function.

`run this code`

The body of the function is where you put your code.

`}`

End the function with a closing curly brace.

Giving functions names

There are two ways to give names to functions.

Function declaration

The first method is a *function declaration*, which defines a named function variable without requiring variable assignment. This one starts with `function`, like so:

```
function myFunc1(){        The function name
    $("div").hide();
}
```

Function expression

A named *function expression* defines a function as part of a larger expression syntax (typically, a variable assignment):

```
var myFunc2 = function() {
    $("div").show();
}
```

This assigns a variable while you're at it.

Function names? But all the functions we've used so far didn't have names. Why start giving them names now?

Good point.

Naming your functions allows you to call them from more than one place in your code. Unnamed functions—also known as *anonymous* functions—are pretty limited in how you can use them. Let's look at anonymous functions in more detail so you can see how limiting it is not to have a name.

The anonymous function

Anonymous, or *self-executing*, functions don't have a name, and they get called immediately when they're encountered in the code. Also, any variables declared inside these functions are available only *when the function is running*.

We can't call this function from anywhere else in our code.

```javascript
$(document).ready(function() {
    $(".guess_box").click( function() {

        var my_num = Math.floor((Math.random()*5) + 5);
        var discount = "<p>Your Discount is "+my_num+"%</p>";
        $(this).append(discount);                    variables

        $(".guess_box").each( function(){
            $(this).unbind('click');
        });
    });
});
```

If we want to use this code elsewhere, we'll have to duplicate it.

variables

my_scripts.js

BANG!

Since we didn't give this function a name, we can't call it from anywhere else in our code.

Watch it!

there are no
Dumb Questions

Q: What is the difference between the function declaration and the named function expression?

A: The main difference is one of timing. While they do the same thing, a function declared as a *named function expression* cannot be used in code until after it is encountered and defined. On the other hand, the function defined using the *function declaration* method can be called whenever you want to on the page, even as an onload handler.

Q: Are there any restrictions on what names we give to our functions?

A: Yes. Function names should never start with a number and must not use any mathematical operators or punctuation marks of any kind other than an underscore (_). Also, spaces are not allowed in any part of the name, and both function names and variable names are case sensitive.

Named functions as event handlers

Earlier, we saw how anonymous functions can be used as handler functions for events. We can also use our own custom, named functions as these handlers, and call them directly from our code. Let's look closer at the two functions we named two pages ago.

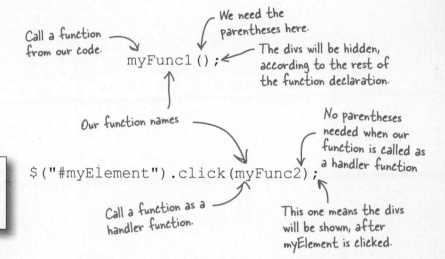

Function declaration

```
function myFunc1(){
        $("div").hide();
}
```

Call a function from our code.

We need the parentheses here.

myFunc1();

The divs will be hidden, according to the rest of the function declaration.

Function expression

```
var myFunc2 = function() {
        $("div").show();
}
```

Our function names

No parentheses needed when our function is called as a handler function

$("#myElement").click(myFunc2);

Call a function as a handler function.

This one means the divs will be shown, after myElement is clicked.

jQuery Magnets

See if you can arrange the magnets to move the code that checks for the discount code into its own named function called `checkForCode`, and use it as the handler for the click event on the boxes.

```
$(document).ready(function() {
  $(".guess_box").click( checkForCode );

...........................................................

    var my_num = Math.floor((Math.random()*5) + 5);
        discount = "<p>Your Discount is "+my_num+"%</p>";
.............
    $(this).append(            );
                   .................

    $(".guess_box").each( function(){
      $(this).unbind('          ');
                      ...................
    });

});
```

Magnets:
```
"+my_num+"
function
}
()
discount
(
{
click
checkForCode
append
)
var
```

my_scripts.js

jQuery Magnets Solution

See if you can arrange the magnets to move the code that checks for the discount code into its own named function called `checkForCode`, and use it as the handler for the click event on the boxes.

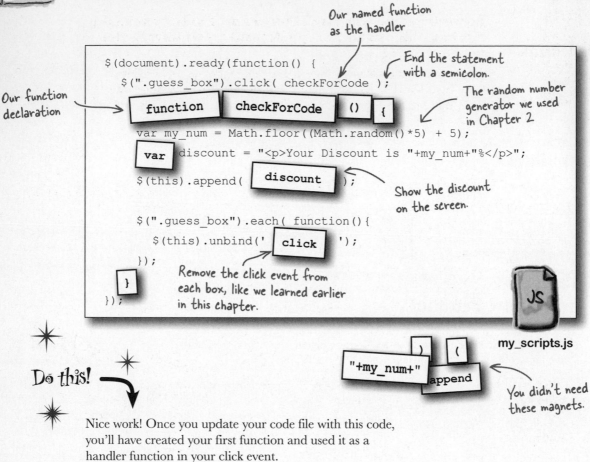

Our named function as the handler

End the statement with a semicolon.

The random number generator we used in Chapter 2

```
$(document).ready(function() {
    $(".guess_box").click( checkForCode );

    function   checkForCode   ()   {
    var my_num = Math.floor((Math.random()*5) + 5);
    var   discount = "<p>Your Discount is "+my_num+"%</p>";
    $(this).append(   discount   );

    $(".guess_box").each( function(){
        $(this).unbind('   click   ');
    });
    }
});
```

Our function declaration

Show the discount on the screen.

Remove the click event from each box, like we learned earlier in this chapter.

JS

my_scripts.js

`"+my_num+"` `(` `)` `append`

You didn't need these magnets.

Do this!

Nice work! Once you update your code file with this code, you'll have created your first function and used it as a handler function in your click event.

BRAIN POWER

How would you create a function to hide the discount code in a random box, and another to generate a random number for the discount code itself?

Hint: Now that it's part of a function declaration, you can use the random number generator in both our existing checkForCode function AND your soon-to-be-made function to put the discount code in a random box.

So, really, we need to have our function do something different based on which box is clicked...how can we do that?

Sometimes we want functions to do a task repeatedly, but have the result change depending on information we give it.

Our functions can accept *variables* passed into them—as you recall from Chapter 2, a variable is used to store information that can change over time. We've already looked at variables. Let's remind ourselves how they work.

After the var keyword, you name your variable.

The var keyword lets you declare a variable.

This is how we set the value of the variable in code.

$$\text{var pts = 250;}$$

When we declare a variable, the JavaScript interpreter gives us some browser memory in which we can store stuff.

We name a variable so that we can reference it later in our script.

We place a value into our variable using an equals sign.

=250

pts

pts

We're already using some variables in our code, remember?

```
var my_num = Math.floor((Math.random()*5) + 5);

var discount = "Your Discount is "+my_num+"%";
```

Passing a variable to a function

When variables are added (or passed) into functions, they are known as *arguments*. (Sometimes you may see them referred to as *parameters* too.) Let's take a closer look at how to pass an argument to a function.

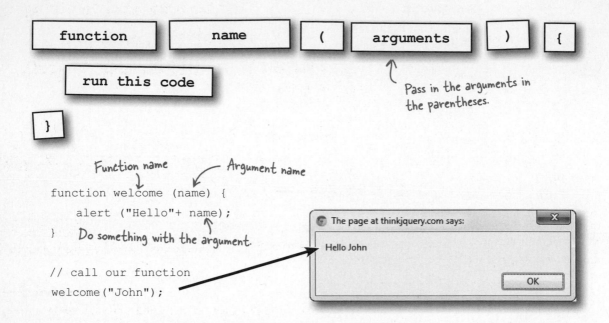

Pass in the arguments in the parentheses.

Function name

Argument name

```
function welcome (name) {
    alert ("Hello"+ name);
}
```

Do something with the argument.

```
// call our function
welcome("John");
```

The page at thinkjquery.com says:

Hello John

OK

The function doesn't need to know what's contained in the variable; it just displays whatever is currently stored. That way, you can change what the function displays simply by changing the variable, instead of having to change your function (which wouldn't make it a very reusable function!).

Relax

Combining variables and functions might seem a bit hairy.

But really, you can think of your function as a *recipe*—in this case, let's say it's for making a drink. You have the basic, repeatable steps for assembling a drink—a shot of this, a splash of that, swirl together, etc.—that compose your function, and the ingredients are your variables that you pass in. Gin and tonic, anyone?

Functions can return a value, too

Returning information from a function involves using the `return` keyword, followed by what should be returned. The result is then returned to the code that called the function, so we can use it in the rest of our code.

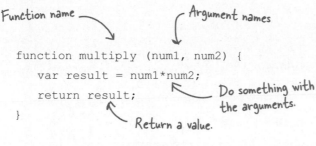

Function name

Argument names

```
function multiply (num1, num2) {
    var result = num1*num2;
    return result;
}
```

Do something with the arguments.

Return a value.

```
// Call our function
var total = multiply (6, 7);

alert (total);
```

The return type can be a number, a string of text, or even a DOM element (object).

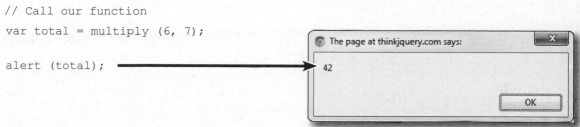

The page at thinkjquery.com says:

42

OK

Sharpen your pencil

Now that you can create your own functions, add a new function to your *my_scripts.js* file that accepts a single argument (called `num`), and then returns a random number based on the argument you give it. Call the function `getRandom`.

Hint: Remember the code that you have already used to generate a random number. Think where you'd place it to call the function.

JS

my_scripts.js

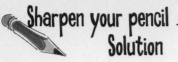

Sharpen your pencil Solution

Now that you can create your own functions, add a new function to your *my_scripts.js* file that accepts a single argument (called num) and then returns a random number based on the argument you give it. Call the function getRandom.

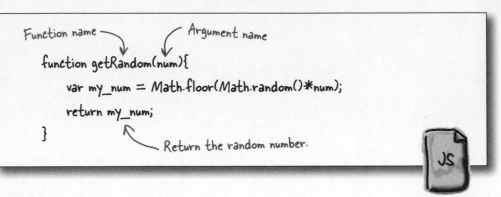

Function name ⟶   Argument name ⟵

```
function getRandom(num){
    var my_num = Math.floor(Math.random()*num);
    return my_num;
}
```

← Return the random number.

my_scripts.js

Looking good! But there's still plenty more to do—let's see what your team has to say about checking for the "right" box...

> OK, all that function and argument stuff is great, but how much nearer are we to finishing off the code for the Jump for Joy page?

Jim: Well, along with our new getRandom function, we still need another one...

Frank: ...Right, one to put the discount code in a random box that can use the getRandom function.

Joe: That makes sense. Then, after a click happens, we can check to see if the user clicked the right box.

Jim: Wait, what? How can we tell if someone clicked on the right box?

Frank: Conditional logic!

Jim: What?

Frank: Conditionals allow us to check for a particular situation and run the code accordingly.

Joe: So we could say, check if a variable has a certain value, or if two values are equal?

Frank: Exactly! We can even check if there is an element inside another element, which I think will help us here.

Jim: Wow, I can't wait to see this!

Frank   Jim   Joe

Use conditional logic to make decisions

jQuery uses JavaScript's *conditional logic* features. Using conditional logic, you can run different code based on decisions you want your code to make, using information it already has. The code below is just one example of conditional logic with JavaScript. We'll look at some others in Chapter 6.

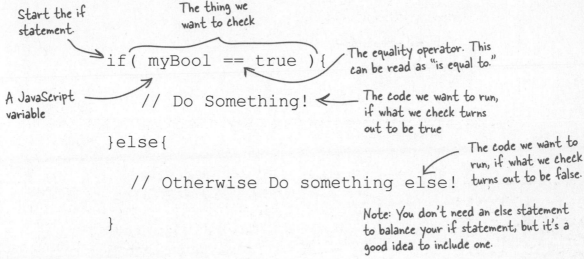

Start the if statement.

The thing we want to check

```
if( myBool == true ){
```

The equality operator. This can be read as "is equal to."

A JavaScript variable

```
    // Do Something!
```

The code we want to run, if what we check turns out to be true

```
}else{
```

```
    // Otherwise Do something else!
```

The code we want to run, if what we check turns out to be false.

```
}
```

Note: You don't need an else statement to balance your if statement, but it's a good idea to include one.

jQuery Magnets

See if you can arrange the magnets to create a new named function called `hideCode` that uses conditional logic to hide a new `span` element, with the ID of `has_discount`, in one of the existing clickable `.guess_box` div elements randomly each time.

```
var ............. = function (){
    var numRand = ........................(4);
    $(....................).each(function(index, value) {
        if(numRand == index){
            $(this).append("<span id='.................'></.............>");
            return false;
        }
    ..........
    }
```

my_scripts.js

Magnets:
```
".guess_box"
span
()
hideCode
{
});
)
getRandom
has_discount
(
}
```

jQuery Magnets Solution

See if you can arrange the magnets to create a new named function called `hideCode` that uses conditional logic to hide a new `span` element, with the ID of `has_discount`, in one of the existing clickable `.guess_box div` elements randomly each time. Here's our solution.

Our named function

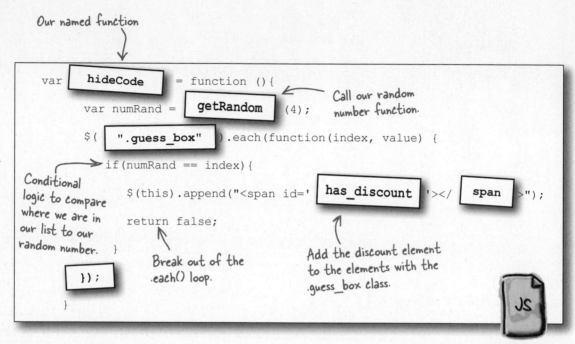

```
var   hideCode    = function (){
    var numRand =    getRandom    (4);
    $(   ".guess_box"   ).each(function(index, value) {
        if(numRand == index){
            $(this).append("<span id='   has_discount   '></   span   >");
            return false;
        }
    });
}
```

Call our random number function.

Conditional logic to compare where we are in our list to our random number.

Break out of the .each() loop.

Add the discount element to the elements with the .guess_box class.

my_scripts.js

Watch it!

The *index* of an element in a list refers to where it appears on the list.

Indexes always start at 0.

So, the first element in the list has an index of 0, the second has an index of 1, and so on. We'll see more about using the index when we look at arrays and loops in Chapter 6.

Awesome! The discount will hide itself in a different box each time. These functions are getting to be really useful.

Frank: Yes, they are. But now that you've hidden the code, can you find it again?

Jim: Oh, uh, good question. I don't know.

Joe: I'm guessing we'll need some of this conditional magic again?

Frank: Exactly. Now, rather than picking a random index in our list of .guess_box elements, we'll have to loop through them again to see if they contain our has_discount element.

Joe: "Contain?" Hey, Frank, you might be on to something there.

Frank: Yep. Let's take a look at what jQuery has along these lines.

Do this!

Update your checkForCode function to include some new code based on Jim, Frank, and Joe's discovery.

Declare the discount variable.

Conditional logic to see if the user has found the discount code

The current element—i.e., the one that called the function

Look for a DOM element with the ID of has_discount.

A jQuery method that checks if whatever is in the first parameter contains whatever is in the second parameter. The clue's in the name.

Set the message so that it will be different depending on whether users find the discount code or not.

```js
function checkForCode(){

    var discount;
    if($.contains(this, document.getElementById("has_discount") ) )
    {
        var my_num = getRandom(5);
        discount = "<p>Your Discount is "+my_num+"%</p>";
    }else{
        discount = "<p>Sorry, no discount this time!</p>" ;
    }
    $(this).append(discount);

    $(".guess_box").each( function(){
        $(this).unbind('click');
    });

}
```

my_scripts.js

Do this, too!

Time to add some custom functions: one for generating a random number, one for hiding the code, and one for checking for the discount code.

```javascript
$(document).ready(function() {
    $(".guess_box").click( checkForCode );
    function getRandom(num){
        var my_num = Math.floor(Math.random()*num);
        return my_num;
    }
    var hideCode = function(){
        var numRand = getRandom(4);
        $(".guess_box").each(function(index, value) {
            if(numRand == index){
                $(this).append("<span id='has_discount'></span>");
                return false;
            }
        });
    }
    hideCode();
    function checkForCode(){
        var discount;
        if($.contains(this, document.getElementById("has_discount") ) )
        {
            var my_num = getRandom(5);
            discount =  "<p>Your Discount is "+my_num+"%</p>" ;
        }else{
            discount = "<p>Sorry, no discount this time!</p>" ;
        }
        $(this).append(discount);
        $(".guess_box").each( function(){
            $(this).unbind('click');
        });
    }
}); //End document.ready()
```

Call the function when an element with the .guess_box class is clicked.

Our random number generator function

The named function that hides the discount variable

Call the named function...

...that tells you what the discount code is.

JS

my_scripts.js

Jump for Joy needs even more help

Just when you thought you were done with the Jump for Joy campaign,
it looks like Emily has a few more requirements...

From: **Jump for Joy**
Subject: **RE: Jump for Joy Promotion**

Hey,

Thanks so much for all your work on this.

I was wondering, is there a way you could highlight the box before people click
on it? That way, they'll know which box they're on, and it will lessen any confusion
before they click.

Also, instead of popping up the code, can you put it into its own easy-to-read area
below the boxes on the screen? Can the discount code be some text together with
a number? I was thinking that might be nice... Oh, and can the number be bigger
than just between 1 and 10? How about up to 100?

Let me know if you think we can make these little changes!

--
Emily Saunders
jumpforjoyphotos.hg

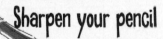 Sharpen your pencil

You know what to do. Pick out all the new requirements from Emily's email.

Requirements:

Sharpen your pencil
Solution

You know what to do. Pick out all the new requirements from Emily's email.

Requirements:

● Highlight whatever box visitors are on before they click it, so they know for sure what option they are choosing.

● Put the discount code into its own area on the screen. The discount code should be text and a number between 1 and 100.

there are no
Dumb Questions

Q: Do we need to specify a return value for all our functions?

A: Technically, no. All functions return a value whether you specify one or not. If you don't tell a function what value to return, it will return a value of `undefined`. If your code is not able to handle an `undefined` value, it will cause an error. So, it is a good idea to specify a return value, even if it is something like `return false;`.

Q: Are there any restrictions on arguments or parameters that I can pass into a function?

A: No, you can pass any object, element, variable, or value into a function. You can also pass in more parameters than your function is expecting. These will be ignored. If you pass in too few, the remaining parameters will automatically be set to `undefined`.

Q: What does the `$.contains` method do?

A: This is a static method of the jQuery library that takes two parameters. It checks all the child elements of the first parameter, seeing whether it contains the second parameter, and returns a `true` or `false`. In our case, `$.contains(document. body, document. getElementById("header"))` is `true`; on the other hand, `$.contains(document. getElementById("header"), document.body)` would be `false`.

Q: What is a static method in jQuery?

A: That means it is a function that is associated with the jQuery library, as opposed to any specific object. We do not need a selector to call this method, only the jQuery name or its shortcut (`$`).

Q: What was that `index` and `value` about in our `.each` handler function?

A: The `index` refers to where in the loop we are, starting at 0 for the first item in the array returned by the selector. The `value` refers to the current object. It is the same as `$(this)` inside the `.each` loop.

Q: Why does our `.each` loop in the `hideCode` function return `false`?

A: Returning `false` in an `.each` loop tells it to stop executing and move on. If any non-`false` return value is returned, it will move on to the next item in the list. For our purposes, we know we have already hidden the code, so we can stop going through the rest of the elements.

BRAIN POWER

Can you think of a way to tell the user what square she's about to choose *before* she clicks?

Methods can change the CSS

To complete our solution, we'll need to highlight whatever box the user is hovering over before she clicks. The easiest way we can change how an element looks is with CSS and CSS classes.

Thankfully, jQuery provides an easy way to give elements CSS classes and remove them again, with a few easy-to-use <u>methods</u>. Let's have a look at how we can put them to use in our solution.

Remember those from Chapters 1 and 2?

Ready Bake Code

Create these new files, separate from your Jump for Joy files, so you can observe these methods in action. That should help you figure out how you can highlight the box before a user clicks on it.

```css
.hover{
  border: solid #f00 3px;
}
.no_hover{
  border: solid #000 3px;
}
```
test_style.css

```html
<html>
  <head>
    <link href="styles/test_style.css" rel="stylesheet">
  </head>
  <body>
    <div id="header" class="no_hover"><h1>Header</h1></div>
    <button type="button" id="btn1">Click to Add</button>
    <button type="button" id="btn2">Click to Remove</button>
    <script src="scripts/jquery.1.6.2.js"></script>
    <script src="scripts/my_test_scripts.js"></script>
  </body>
</html>
```

class_test.html

```javascript
$(document).ready(function() {
  $("#btn1").click( function(){
    $("#header").addClass("hover");
    $("#header").removeClass("no_hover");
  });
  $("#btn2").click( function(){
    $("#header").removeClass("hover");
    $("#header").addClass("no_hover");
  });
});
```

my_test_scripts.js

TEST DRIVE

Open your newly created *class_test.html* file in your browser. After clicking on the Add button, your class gets applied to the `div`, with the ID of `header`. Clicking the Remove button removes the class again!

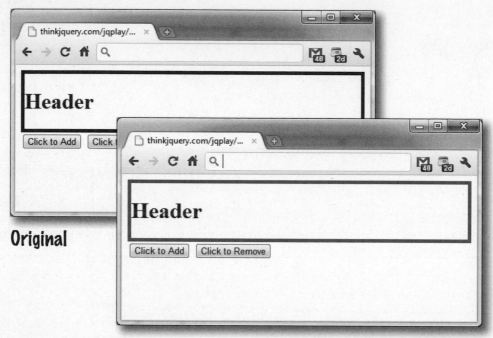

Original

After click

Sweet! If only everything were this easy. Does this CSS change work on anything other than a click event?

Yes, it does. And it's just as easy...

You can switch up the CSS for any event type. But for this solution, you'll need another event to help you out. Take a look at the list back on page 82 and see if you can figure out which event you'll need to use.

Add a hover event

The `hover` event can take two handler functions as parameters: one
for the `mouseenter` event and another for the `mouseleave` event.
These handler functions can be named or anonymous functions. Take
a closer look at the test script you just used to see how we can use the
`hover` event to apply behavior to an element during the time the
mouse is over the element.

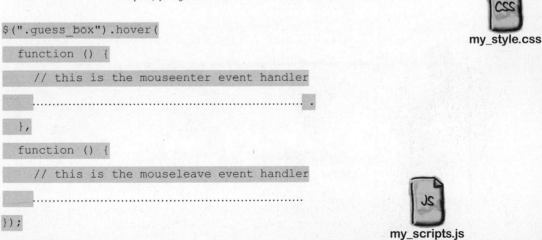

my_test_scripts.js

```
$(document).ready(function() {
  $("#btn1").click( function(){
    $("#header").addClass("hover");
    $("#header").removeClass("no_hover");
  });
  $("#btn2").click( function(){
    $("#header").removeClass("hover");
    $("#header").addClass("no_hover");
  });
});
```

The removeClass jQuery method
allows us to remove a CSS class
from an element.

The addClass jQuery method allows us
to add a CSS class to an element. It
does not affect any CSS classes the
element already has.

Exercise

Update your *my_style.css* and *my_scripts.js* files so that the image boxes are highlighted
when the user places the cursor over them. You'll need a new CSS class to apply the
hover to, and two handler functions in your script file (after your `checkForCode`
function) that use the `addClass` and `removeClass` methods to set the CSS class.
We've started those for you; you just need to write in the functions below.

my_style.css

```
$(".guess_box").hover(
  function () {
    // this is the mouseenter event handler
    ....................................................... .
  },
  function () {
    // this is the mouseleave event handler
    .......................................................
});
```

my_scripts.js

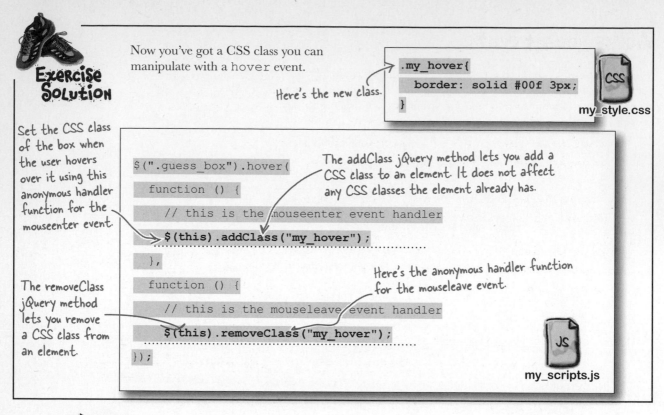

Exercise Solution

Now you've got a CSS class you can manipulate with a hover event.

Here's the new class.

```css
.my_hover{
    border: solid #00f 3px;
}
```

my_style.css

Set the CSS class of the box when the user hovers over it using this anonymous handler function for the mouseenter event.

```javascript
$(".guess_box").hover(
  function () {
    // this is the mouseenter event handler
    $(this).addClass("my_hover");
  },
  function () {
    // this is the mouseleave event handler
    $(this).removeClass("my_hover");
});
```

The addClass jQuery method lets you add a CSS class to an element. It does not affect any CSS classes the element already has.

Here's the anonymous handler function for the mouseleave event.

The removeClass jQuery method lets you remove a CSS class from an element.

my_scripts.js

Test Drive

Open your *index.html* file in your browser, which should include your new *my_scripts.js* file. Move your mouse over the images and see if the border changes.

Jump for Joy Sale

Sorry, no discount this time!

Hmm. The image border color changes now, but there's still more to do...

You're almost there...

That's definitely good progress, but the message still appears in the wrong place, and it doesn't look the way you were asked to make it look. Plus, there's still one requirement from the first email we didn't cover yet. Here's the requirements list as it stands right now:

- ~~Highlight whatever box visitors are on before they click it, so they know for sure what option they are choosing.~~

- Put the discount code into its own area on the screen. The discount code should be text and a number between 1 and 100.

- After the visitor has made his guess and clicked on a box, the answer should be revealed as to whether or not he got it right. If he chose correctly, show him the discount so he can apply it to his order.

} This one's from the first email!

Exercise

Update your `checkForCode` function to complete these last three things:

1. Put the discount code in its own area on the screen.

2. Make the code a combination of letters and a number between 1 and 100.

3. Show the visitor where the code was hiding, if she guessed wrong.

To help you out, we've created these CSS classes that you can add to your *my_styles.css* file to indicate if the code was found or not.

While you're at it, add a `span` element with the ID of `result` below the four boxes to display the discount code.

```css
.discount{
    border: solid #0f0 3px;
}
.no_discount{
    border: solid #f00 3px;
}
```

my_style.css

Exercise Solution

Now you've updated your `checkForCode` function with all the pieces you were asked for: a separate place on the screen for a discount code, a discount code consisting of text and a number up to 100, and indications of where the discount code was, after the visitor clicks.

```js
function checkForCode(){

  var discount;

  if($.contains(this, document.getElementById("has_discount") ) )
  {

    var my_num = getRandom(100);

    discount = "<p>Your Code: CODE"+my_num+"</p>" ;
  }else{

    discount = "<p>Sorry, no discount this time!</p>" ;
  }

  $(".guess_box").each(function() {

    if($.contains(this, document.getElementById("has_discount")))

    {

      $(this).addClass("discount");

    }else{

      $(this).addClass("no_discount");

    }

    $(this).unbind();

  });

  $("#result").append(discount);

} // End checkForCode function
```

Check to see if this box has the discount code, using the jQuery contains function.

Use the getRandom function to increase the discount code to a value up to 100.

Set the output message, indicating whether the code is found or not.

If it does, visually change the box to tell people where the code was...

...if it does not, show that to the user.

Write the output message onto the page into its own area.

my_scripts.js

Test Drive

Now that you've updated your `checkForCode` function, test out all the new features on the Jump for Joy website. (For comparison, your code should look like what is in this file: *http://thinkjquery.com/chapter03/end/scripts/my_scripts.js.*)

Loaded page

Jump for Joy Sale

Sorry, no discount this time!

No discount code

Jump for Joy Sale

Your Code: CODE48

Discount code

Nice work! That's more like it. This should really help the site, and will save Emily some dough!

Your jQuery Toolbox

You've got Chapter 3 under your belt and now you've added events, reusable functions, and conditionals to your toolbox.

Conditionals

Test for logical conditions (if XYZ = true) before doing something.

Often come with an else statement if the conditional result is false, but it's not required.

Functions

Reusable chunks of code that you can use elsewhere in your code...

...but only if they are named.

Unnamed functions only run right where they are called in the code and can't be used anywhere else.

You can pass variables (or arguments or parameters) to functions, and functions can return results, too.

Events

Objects that help users interact with a web page.

There are around 30 of them, and just about anything that can happen on a browser can trigger an event.

CHAPTER 3

Mod the DOM

Just because we've got the same parents doesn't make us the same elements!

Just because the page is finished loading doesn't mean it has to keep the same structure. Back in Chapter 1, we saw how the DOM gets built as the page loads to set up the page's structure. In this chapter, we'll look at how to move up and down through the DOM structure and work with element hierarchy and parent/child relationships to change the page structure on the fly using jQuery.

The Webville Eatery wants an interactive menu

Alexandra, the head chef of the Webville Eatery, has a job for you. She's been maintaining separate web pages for different versions of her menu: the regular menu and the menu with vegetarian substitutions. She wants you to make one page that will adjust the menu for the restaurant's vegetarian customers.

We put our menu on the Web a few years ago, and our customers love it! We'd like you to add some buttons that let our customers change and highlight the web menu on the fly.

Go vegetarian

Here's what Alexandra would like you to do.

We want a "Go Vegetarian" button that automatically substitutes the vegetarian options on our web page menu.

Here's how our substitutions work:

— We offer no substitutes for our fish entrées, so we need those removed.

— We offer giant portobello mushrooms as a vegetarian substitute for our hamburgers.

— We offer tofu as a vegetarian substitute for all of our meat and egg dishes except hamburgers.

— We'll need a button that restores the menu to its original state.

P.S. If you can pull it off, we'd also like a leaf icon to show up next to the substituted vegetarian entrees.

I had the web designer email you the files for the current menu so you can get started.

The Webville Eatery ©

There's no exercise for it this time around—because you're probably already thinking it—but be sure to write down what the requirements are in your own words so you know what you're building here.

Before we write any jQuery, let's look at the HTML and CSS files the web designer sent us, and see if their style and structure are up to snuff.

DOM Tree Magnets

Dig into the current structure of the web menu by diagramming how the DOM sees it. Below, you'll find all the element magnets you need to complete the tree. Using the HTML fragment for the menu on the right, complete the tree. Each magnet will fit where you see a hollow circle. We've done a few for you already.

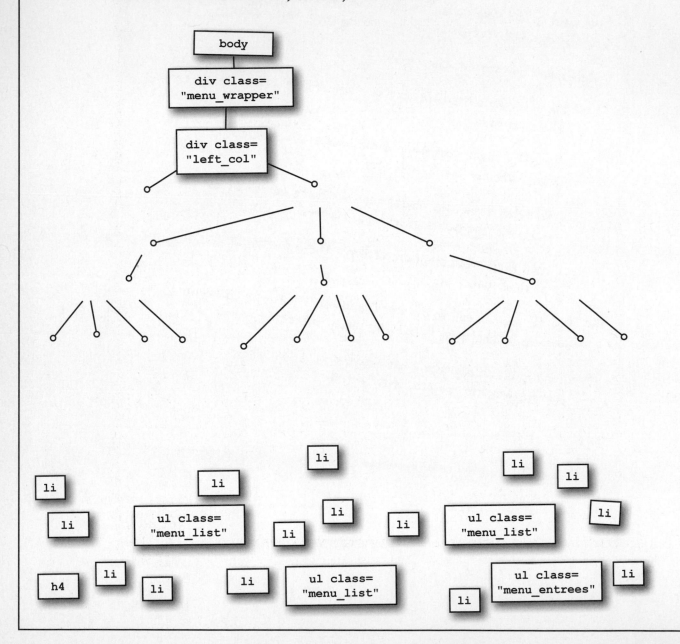

This is just a fragment of the actual HTML page.

```html
<body>
 <div id="menu_wrapper">
  <div class="left_col">
   <h4>Dinner Entrees</h4>
   <ul class="menu_entrees">
      <li>Thai-style Halibut
            <ul class="menu_list">
                  <li>coconut milk</li>
                  <li>pan-fried halibut</li>
                  <li>early autumn vegetables</li>
                  <li>Thai spices </li>
            </ul>
      </li>
      <li>House Grilled Panini
            <ul class="menu_list">
                  <li>prosciutto</li>
                  <li>provolone</li>
                  <li>avocado</li>
                  <li>sourdough roll</li>
            </ul>
      </li>
      <li>Southwest Slider
            <ul class="menu_list">
                  <li>whole chiles</li>
                  <li>hamburger</li>
                  <li>pepperjack cheese</li>
                  <li>multigrain roll</li>
            </ul>
      </li>
   </ul>
  </div>
 </div>
</body>
```

index.html

DOM Tree Magnets Solution

It looks like all the ingredients are set up as child list items of the parent entrée list items. They aren't really labeled very clearly or uniquely, now are they?

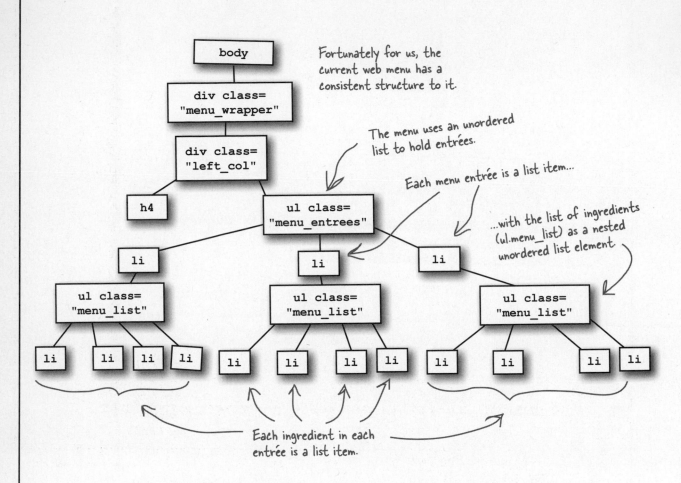

Fortunately for us, the current web menu has a consistent structure to it.

The menu uses an unordered list to hold entrées.

Each menu entrée is a list item...

...with the list of ingredients (ul.menu_list) as a nested unordered list element.

Each ingredient in each entrée is a list item.

We need to write selectors that will find the ingredients we need to change. At this level, they're all list elements...

...so how can we distinguish the ingredients we want to substitute from the rest?

```
<body>
 <div id="menu_wrapper">
  <div class="left_col">
   <h4>Dinner Entrees</h4>
   <ul class="menu_entrees">
     <li>Thai-style Halibut
         <ul class="menu_list">
             <li>coconut milk</li>
             <li>pan-fried halibut</li>
             <li>early autumn vegetables</li>
             <li>Thai spices </li>
         </ul>
     </li>
     <li>House Grilled Panini
         <ul class="menu_list">
             <li>prosciutto</li>
             <li>provolone</li>
             <li>avocado</li>
             <li>sourdough roll</li>
         </ul>
     </li>
     <li>Southwest Slider
         <ul class="menu_list">
             <li>whole chiles</li>
             <li>hamburger</li>
             <li>pepperjack cheese</li>
             <li>multigrain roll</li>
         </ul>
     </li>
   </ul>
  </div>
 </div>
</body>
```

This is just a fragment of the actual HTML page.

index.html

BRAIN POWER

Regular web page structure (HTML) makes writing jQuery code much easier, but the ingredient elements we want to find aren't labeled in a way that will make our jQuery code easier to write. How can we make our elements easier to select?

Class up your elements

As we've seen in each chapter so far, we can help jQuery find elements on web pages more effectively by setting up our HTML and CSS properly. To really make our structure sing, we should add classes and IDs to our style sheet and set our HTML elements' attributes with the appropriate classes and IDs. This makes selecting elements easier and saves you coding time later on.

For jQuery, selectors aren't just about controlling the look and feel of your page. Selectors allow jQuery to match (or query) elements on the page, too.

You can write a selector for each ingredient you need to match...

`<li>chicken</li>` `<li>eggs</li>` `<li>turkey</li>` `<li>lamb shoulder</li>`

...or you can group them in a class and write one selector to match them all.

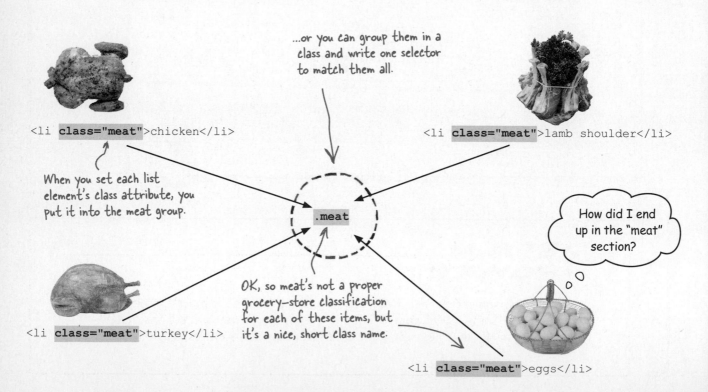

`<li `**`class="meat"`**`>chicken</li>`

When you set each list element's class attribute, you put it into the meat group.

`<li `**`class="meat"`**`>lamb shoulder</li>`

`.meat`

How did I end up in the "meat" section?

`<li `**`class="meat"`**`>turkey</li>`

OK, so meat's not a proper grocery-store classification for each of these items, but it's a nice, short class name.

`<li `**`class="meat"`**`>eggs</li>`

Exercise

Find the menu substitutions the head chef wants and label each one with the appropriate class (fish, meat, or hamburger). If an ingredient doesn't need a class, leave the line blank. The HTML is laid out just like your menu will appear on the page.

```
<li>Thai-style Halibut
   <ul class="menu_list">
      <li.....................>coconut milk</li>
      <li.....................>pan-fried halibut</li>
      <li.....................>lemongrass broth</li>
      <li.....................>vegetables</li>
      <li.....................>Thai spices </li>
   </ul>
</li>


<li>Braised Delight
   <ul class="menu_list">
      <li.....................>lamb shoulder</li>
      <li.....................>cippolini onions</li>
      <li.....................>carrots</li>
      <li.....................>baby turnip</li>
      <li.....................>braising jus</li>
   </ul>
</li>


<li>House Grilled Panini
   <ul class="menu_list">
      <li.....................>prosciutto</li>
      <li.....................>provolone</li>
      <li.....................>avocado</li>
      <li.....................>cherry tomatoes</li>
      <li.....................>sourdough roll</li>
      <li.....................>shoestring fries </li>
   </ul>
</li>

<li>House Slider
   <ul class="menu_list">
      <li.....................>eggplant</li>
      <li.....................>zucchini</li>
      <li.....................>hamburger</li>
      <li.....................>balsamic vinegar</li>
      <li.....................>onion</li>
      <li.....................>carrots</li>
      <li.....................>multigrain roll</li>
      <li.....................>goat cheese</li>
   </ul>
</li>
```

```
<li>Frittata
   <ul class="menu_list">
      <li.....................>eggs</li>
      <li.....................>Asiago cheese</li>
      <li.....................>potatoes </li>
   </ul>
</li>


<li>Coconut Soup
   <ul class="menu_list">
      <li.....................>coconut milk</li>
      <li.....................>chicken</li>
      <li.....................>vegetable broth</li>
   </ul>
</li>


<li>Soup Du Jour
   <ul class="menu_list">
      <li.....................>grilled steak</li>
      <li.....................>mushrooms</li>
      <li.....................>vegetables</li>
      <li.....................>vegetable broth </li>
   </ul>
</li>


<li>Hot and Sour Soup
   <ul class="menu list">
      <li class="meat">roasted pork</li>
      <li.....................>carrots</li>
      <li.....................>Chinese mushrooms</li>
      <li.....................>chili</li>
      <li.....................>vegetable broth </li>
   </ul>
</li>


<li>Avocado Rolls
   <ul class="menu_list">
      <li.....................>avocado</li>
      <li.....................>whole chiles</li>
      <li.....................>sweet red peppers</li>
      <li.....................>ginger sauce</li>
   </ul>
</li>
```

Exercise Solution

Find the menu substitutions the head chef wants and label each one with the appropriate class (fish, meat, or hamburger). If an ingredient doesn't need a class, leave the line blank.

```
<li>Thai-style Halibut
   <ul class="menu_list">
     <li                  >coconut milk</li>
     <li class="fish"     >pan-fried halibut</li>
     <li                  >lemongrass broth</li>
     <li                  >vegetables</li>
     <li                  >Thai spices </li>
   </ul>
</li>


<li>Braised Delight
   <ul class="menu_list">
     <li class="meat"     >lamb shoulder</li>
     <li                  >cippolini onions</li>
     <li                  >carrots</li>
     <li                  >baby turnip</li>
     <li                  >braising jus</li>
   </ul>
</li>


<li>House Grilled Panini
   <ul class="menu_list">
     <li class="meat"     >prosciutto</li>
     <li                  >provolone</li>
     <li                  >avocado</li>
     <li                  >cherry tomatoes</li>
     <li                  >sourdough roll</li>
     <li                  >shoestring fries </li>
   </ul>
</li>


<li>House Slider
   <ul class="menu_list">
     <li                   >eggplant</li>
     <li                   >zucchini</li>
     <li class="hamburger" >hamburger</li>
     <li                   >balsamic vinegar</li>
     <li                   >onion</li>
     <li                   >carrots</li>
     <li                   >multigrain roll</li>
     <li                   >goat cheese</li>
   </ul>
</li>
```

```
<li>Frittata
   <ul class="menu_list">
     <li class="meat"     >eggs</li>
     <li                  >Asiago cheese</li>
     <li                  >potatoes </li>
   </ul>
</li>


<li>Coconut Soup
   <ul class="menu_list">
     <li                  >coconut milk</li>
     <li class="meat"     >chicken</li>
     <li                  >vegetable broth</li>
   </ul>
</li>


<li>Soup Du Jour
   <ul class="menu_list">
     <li class="meat"     >grilled steak</li>
     <li                  >mushrooms</li>
     <li                  >vegetables</li>
     <li                  >vegetable broth </li>
   </ul>
</li>


<li>Hot and Sour Soup
   <ul class="menu_list">
     <li class="meat"     >roasted pork</li>
     <li                  >carrots</li>
     <li                  >Chinese mushrooms</li>
     <li                  >chili</li>
     <li                  >vegetable broth </li>
   </ul>
</li>


<li>Avocado Rolls
   <ul class="menu_list">
     <li                  >avocado</li>
     <li                  >whole chiles</li>
     <li                  >sweet red peppers</li>
     <li                  >ginger sauce</li>
   </ul>
</li>
```

Button things up

Now that you've got things mostly set up, let's go back to the napkin with
the head chef's requirements. Next up, you need to build two buttons.

— We want a "Go Vegetarian" button that automatically
substitutes the right vegetarian option on our web page menu.

— We'll need a second button that restores the menu to its
original state.

Sharpen your pencil

Update the structure and script to make the two buttons from the napkin. Give the "Go Vegetarian" button an ID of `vegOn` and the "Restore Menu" button an ID of `restoreMe`.

```
<div class="topper">
  <h2>Our Menu</h2>
    <ul>
      <li class="nav">.............................................</li>
      <li class="nav">.............................................</li>
    </ul>
</div>
```

index.html

```
$(document).ready(function() {
    var v = false;

    ....................................................................

        if (v == false){

          v = true}
    });//end button

    ....................................................................

        if (v == true){

          v = false;}
    });//end button
});//end document ready
```

my_scripts.js

Sharpen your pencil
Solution

Update the structure and script to make the two buttons from the napkin. Give the "Go Vegetarian" button an ID of vegOn and the "Restore Menu" button an ID of restoreMe.

```
<div class="topper">
  <h2>Our Menu</h2>
    <ul>
      <li class="nav">  <button id="vegOn">Go Vegetarian</button>    </li>
      <li class="nav">  <button id="restoreMe">Restore Menu</button>  </li>
    </ul>
</div>
```

Build button elements with IDs of vegOn and restoreMe.

index.html

```
$(document).ready(function() {
    var v = f;
    $("button#vegOn").click(function(){

        if (v == false){

            v = true;}
    });//end button
    $("button#restoreMe").click(function(){

        if (v == true){

            v = false;}
    });//end button
});//end document ready
```

A more specific selector, using the element type and ID

Attach the click method to the buttons.

my_scripts.js

What's next?

That was quick! You've got the two buttons set up. Let's check those items off of the napkin and move on to the stuff that the "Go Vegetarian" button needs to do.

~~We want a "Go Vegetarian" button that automatically substitutes the right vegetarian option on our web page menu.~~

~~We'll need a second button that restores the menu to its original state.~~

Here's how our substitutions work:

— We offer no substitutes for our fish entrées, so we need those removed.

— We offer giant portobello mushrooms as a vegetarian substitute for our hamburgers.

— We offer tofu as a vegetarian substitute for all of our meat and egg dishes except hamburgers.

Exercise

In your own words, write the three things that the "Go Vegetarian" button needs to do.

1. ....
   ....

2. ....
   ....

3. ....
   ....

In your own words, write the three things that the "Go Vegetarian" button needs to do.

1. Match li elements of the fish class and remove those entrées from the menu.

2. Match li elements in the hamburger class and replace them with portobello mushrooms.

3. Match li elements in the meat class and replace them with tofu.

Don't worry if your answers were a bit different. Translating requirements into stuff that your web app needs to do takes practice.

Our next task is to tackle item 1 above: match li elements of the fish class and remove them from the menu. We matched elements with class selectors and used remove to take elements out of the DOM in Chapter 2.

jQuery also offers us the detach method. detach and remove both take elements out of the DOM. So what's the difference between the two methods, and which one should we use?

remove

You need something torn out of the DOM for good?

div id="top"

div class="pic_box"

img id="thumbnail"

The remove method drops the element out of the DOM.

```
$("img#thumbnail").remove();
```

detach

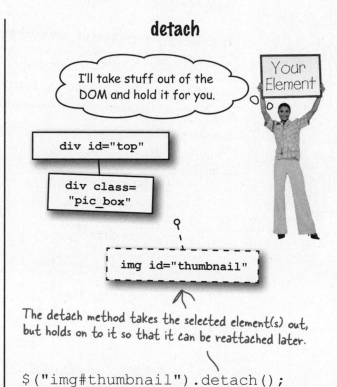

I'll take stuff out of the DOM and hold it for you.

Your Element

div id="top"

div class="pic_box"

img id="thumbnail"

The detach method takes the selected element(s) out, but holds on to it so that it can be reattached later.

```
$("img#thumbnail").detach();
```

Sharpen your pencil

In the space provided, write the selector and `remove` or `detach` code that will create the result shown on the right.

DOM result   jQuery statement

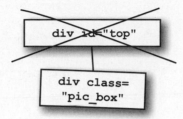

....

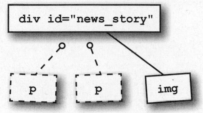

....

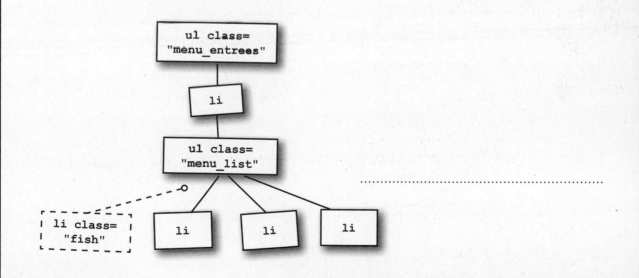

....

Sharpen your pencil
Solution

In the space provided, write the selector and remove or detach code that will create the result shown on the right.

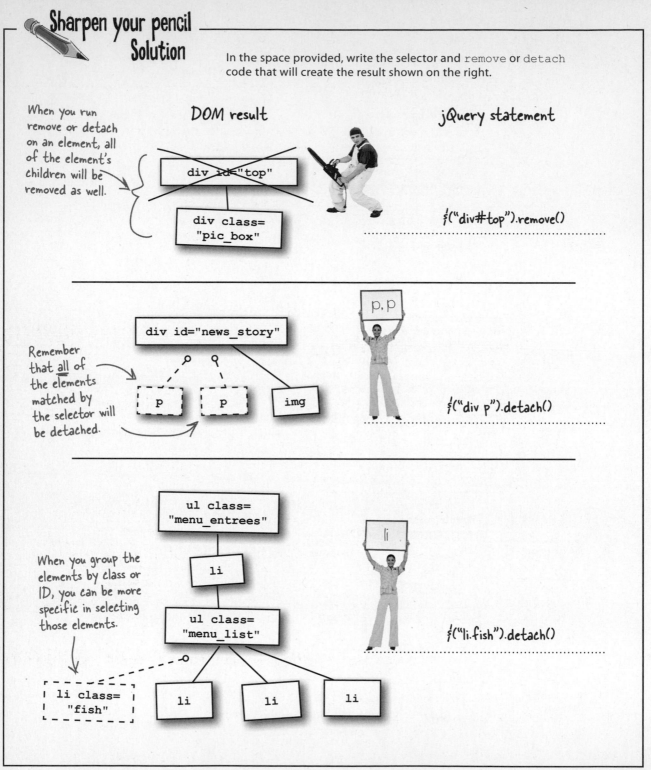

When you run remove or detach on an element, all of the element's children will be removed as well.

DOM result

div id="top"

div class="pic_box"

jQuery statement

$("div#top").remove()

Remember that all of the elements matched by the selector will be detached.

div id="news_story"

p   p   img

p, p

$("div p").detach()

When you group the elements by class or ID, you can be more specific in selecting those elements.

ul class="menu_entrees"

li

ul class="menu_list"

li class="fish"   li   li   li

li

$("li.fish").detach()

TEST DRIVE

Add the line of code for the third Sharpen Your Pencil solution inside the `vegOn` button click function in your *my_scripts.js* file. Then, open the page up in your favorite browser to make sure everything's working.

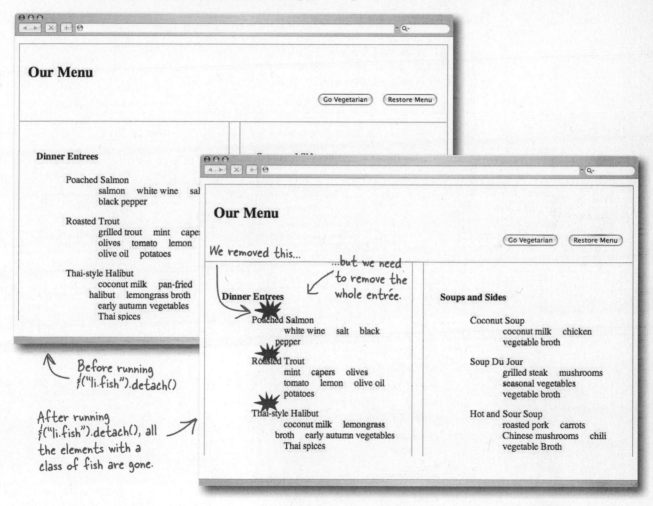

Before running ƒ("li.fish").detach()

After running ƒ("li.fish").detach(), all the elements with a class of fish are gone.

We removed this...

...but we need to remove the whole entrée.

The `detach` method definitely got rid of stuff, just not everything we wanted to remove. We removed the list element of the entrée. What we need to do is to remove the entire entrée inside which the `.fish` list element is nested.

How do we tell the DOM to detach the entire entrée?

Swinging through the DOM tree

In Chapter 1, we learned that the DOM is built like a tree. It has a root, branches, and nodes. The JavaScript interpreter in a browser can *traverse* (and then manipulate) the DOM, and jQuery is especially good at it. DOM traversal simply means climbing up and down and across the DOM.

We've been manipulating the DOM since Chapter 1. The detach method we just looked at is an example of DOM manipulation (i.e., we dynamically take elements out of the DOM).

But what is traversal really all about? Let's take one section of the menu and visualize it as a DOM tree to see how traversal works.

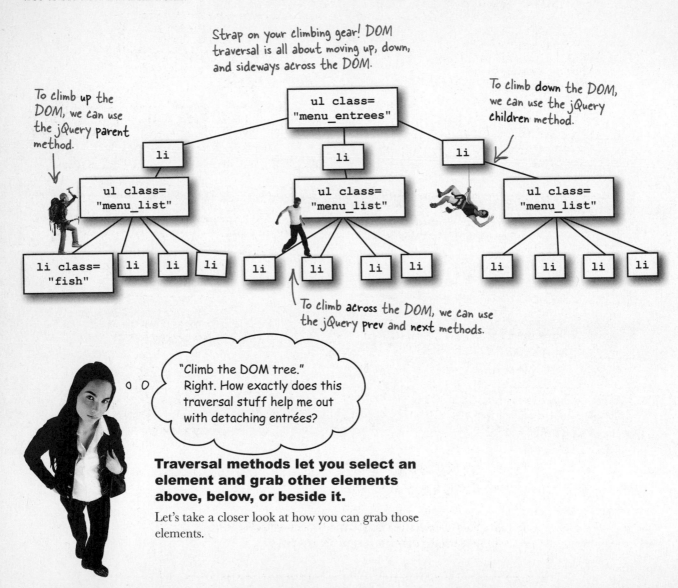

Strap on your climbing gear! DOM traversal is all about moving up, down, and sideways across the DOM.

To climb up the DOM, we can use the jQuery **parent** method.

To climb **down** the DOM, we can use the jQuery **children** method.

To climb **across** the DOM, we can use the jQuery **prev** and **next** methods.

"Climb the DOM tree." Right. How exactly does this traversal stuff help me out with detaching entrées?

Traversal methods let you select an element and grab other elements above, below, or beside it.

Let's take a closer look at how you can grab those elements.

Traversal methods climb the DOM

To tell the DOM that we want to detach entrées whose menu lists contain fish, we have to reference elements by their relationship. jQuery's traversal methods allow us to get at those element relationships.

Select all the elements in the fish class.

Then get the element <u>above</u> those elements.

```
$(".fish").parent()
```

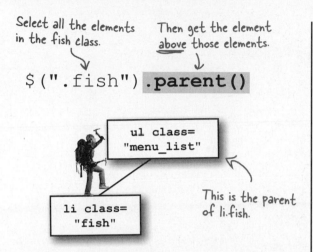

ul class="menu_list"

li class="fish"

This is the parent of li.fish.

Select all the elements in the menu_list class.

Then get the element below those elements.

```
$(".menu_list").children()
```

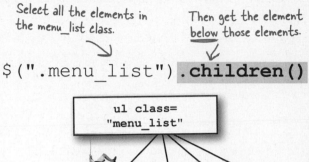
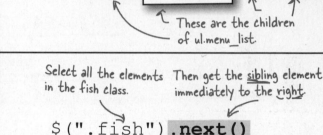

ul class="menu_list"

li | li class="fish" | li | li

These are the children of ul.menu_list.

Select all the elements in the fish class.

Then get the <u>sibling</u> element immediately to the <u>left</u>.

```
$(".fish").prev()
```

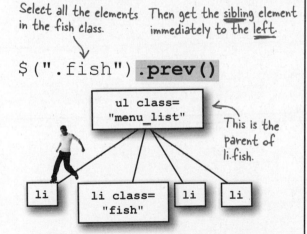

ul class="menu_list"

This is the parent of li.fish.

li | li class="fish" | li | li

Select all the elements in the fish class.

Then get the <u>sibling</u> element immediately to the <u>right</u>.

```
$(".fish").next()
```

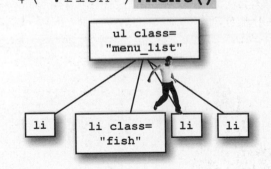

ul class="menu_list"

li | li class="fish" | li | li

BRAIN POWER

Which of these methods can help us detach menu entrées with elements in the `fish` class?

Chain methods to climb farther

What if we want to climb higher, lower, or deeper? Strap on the chains, man! jQuery offers us method *chaining*. Method chaining lets us manipulate and traverse our pages in a more effective way. Here's how it works:

To go one parent higher, just add another method to the method chain.

$(".fish").parent().**.parent()**

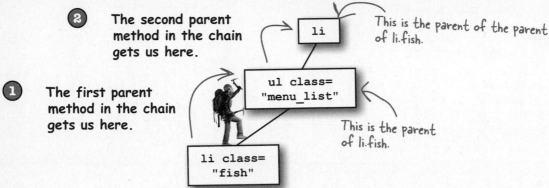

2 The second parent method in the chain gets us here.

li

This is the parent of the parent of li.fish.

1 The first parent method in the chain gets us here.

ul class= "menu_list"

This is the parent of li.fish.

li class= "fish"

You can mix and match methods too.

$(".menu_list")**.parent().next().remove()**

2 The next method climbs to the sibling to the right.

ul class= "menu_entrees"

1 The parent method climbs up to the element that encloses the selected element(s).

li

3 The remove method takes the element we traversed to out of the DOM.

li

ul class= "menu_list"

Exercise

Go to *http://www.thinkjquery.com/chapter04/traversal/* and open the JavaScript console in your favorite browser's developer tools. The "Read Me" section at the front of the book covers browser developer tools. Run each of the four traversal methods along with the chained `detach` method as shown below. Then, write why or why not this will help us with the problem at hand.

Important: Make sure to *refresh the browser* after running each statement.

```
$(".menu_entrees").children().detach()
```

....

....

....

```
$(".menu_list").children().detach()
```

....

....

....

```
$(".fish").parent().detach()
```

....

....

....

```
$(".fish").parent().parent().detach()
```

....

....

....

Go to *http://www.thinkjquery.com/chapter04/traversal/* and open the JavaScript console in your favorite browser's developer tools. Don't remember how to use browser dev tools? Head back to the "Read Me" section of the book to refresh yourself. Run each of the four traversal methods along with the chained `detach` method as shown below. Then, write why or why not this will help us with the problem at hand.

Important: Make sure to *refresh the browser* after running each statement.

```
$(".menu_entrees").children().detach()
```

This traversal method detaches the children element of menu_entrees. It won't work for removing entrées that contain fish because it removes ALL of the entrée lists. Crud! Not what we needed.

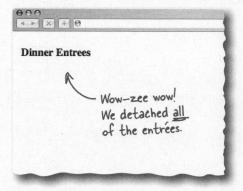

Wow-zee wow! We detached all of the entrées.

```
$(".menu_list").children().detach()
```

This traversal method detaches the children element of .menu_list. It won't work for removing entrées that contain fish because it removes the list of ingredients from every ul.menu_list. Oops! Not what we wanted at all.

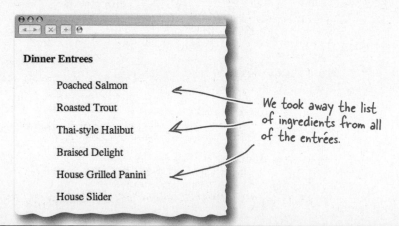

We took away the list of ingredients from all of the entrées.

```
$(".fish").parent().detach()
```

This traversal method detaches the parent element of .fish. It won't work for removing entrées that contain fish because it doesn't go far enough up the DOM tree. Instead, it removes the ul.menu_list (and everything below it).

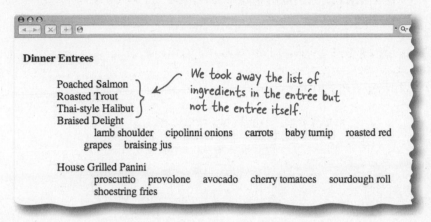

```
$(".fish").parent().parent().detach()
```

This traversal method detaches the parent of the parent element of .fish. It does just what we need it to do.

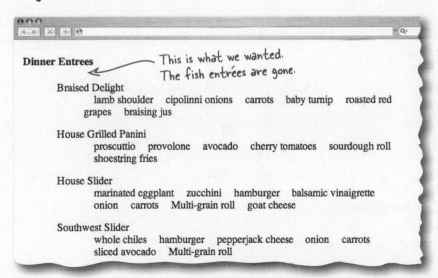

Wait a second—don't we need to restore the fish entrées when we program the "Restore Menu" button?

Right. We can't just detach the fish entrées and forget about them.

We'll have to rethink our code a bit to make this work.

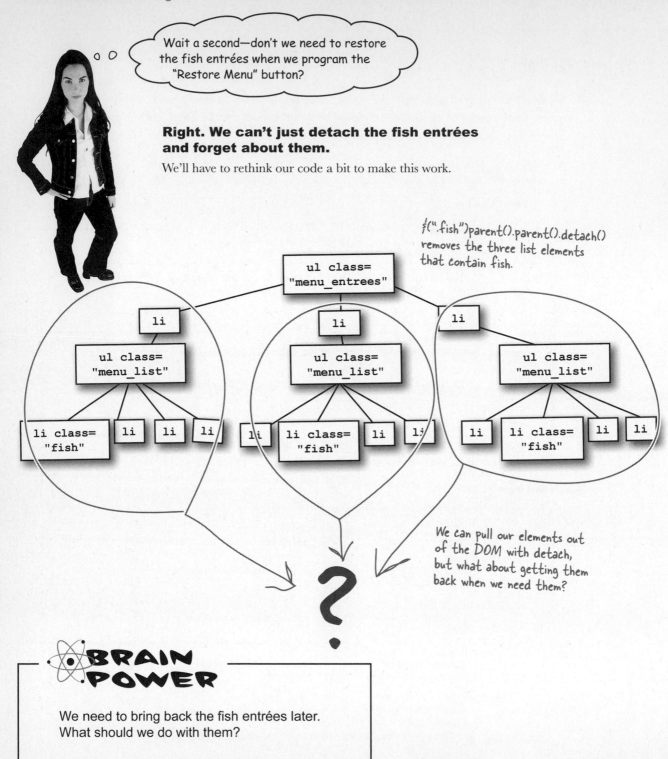

$("fish").parent().parent().detach() removes the three list elements that contain fish.

We can pull our elements out of the DOM with detach, but what about getting them back when we need them?

BRAIN POWER

We need to bring back the fish entrées later. What should we do with them?

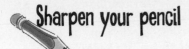
Sharpen your pencil

We've seen quite a few jQuery and JavaScript constructs so far. Which ones do we need so that we don't forget the `.fish` class elements? Write a "Yes" or "No" in the "Should we use it?" column for each, and explain why you chose or didn't choose it. We did one for you, so now you're down to three.

	Should we use it?	Why?
Terminator	No	A terminator simply ends a statement. It won't solve the problem of remembering the detached elements.
Variable		
Function		
Selector		

Sharpen your pencil
Solution

We've seen quite a few jQuery and JavaScript constructs so far. Which one do we need so that we don't forget the `.fish` class elements? Write a "Yes" or "No" in the "Should we use it?" column for each, and explain why you chose or didn't choose it. Here's our solution.

	Should we use it?	Why?
Terminator	No	A terminator simply ends a statement. It won't solve the problem of remembering the detached elements.
Variable	Yes	A variable stores stuff for us. If we store the detached elements, we can bring them back later by simply referencing the variable.
Function	No	A function lets us perform manipulations on data. The problem with the detached elements is a problem of storing data, not manipulating it.
Selector	No	A selector selects elements based on what's in the DOM. We've already selected our elements. What we need is a way to store those elements.

there are no
Dumb Questions

Q: I get `remove` and `detach`, but what if I just want to get rid of something inside an element and not the element itself?

A: To get rid of the content in an element, you can use the `empty` method. Let's say you want to delete all of the stuff inside the paragraphs on a page; just do this: `$("p").empty();`.

Q: Is there a way to traverse all of an element's parent elements?

A: Yes. In addition to the `parent` method, jQuery also offers the `parents` method, which lets you traverse all of the selected element's parent elements. You'll see this method in action later in this chapter.

Q: What if I want to get the parent element nearest to the selected element?

A: You can use the `closest` method. Like the `parents` method, the `closest` method will climb through an element's parent elements, but it stops when it finds a match. For example, if you want to find the closest `ul` above a list item, use this: `$("li").closest("ul")`.

Q: I know about `next` and `previous`, but what if I want to traverse all of the elements on the same level of the DOM tree?

A: Fortunately, the jQuery team has thought of that one, too. The `siblings` method will traverse all of the elements at the same level as the selected element.

Q: Does Google Chrome have jQuery built in?

A: No. The reason we can run jQuery in Chrome's browser dev tools is that we've included jQuery in the HTML page. If you visit a web page that doesn't use jQuery, don't expect the Chrome JavaScript console to run jQuery statements.

Variables can store elements, too

Variables must be pretty useful because we find ourselves needing them again. We've seen variables throughout the first three chapters, but we've only used them to store numbers and text strings. Wouldn't it be convenient if JavaScript variables could store our elements too? As it turns out, they can.

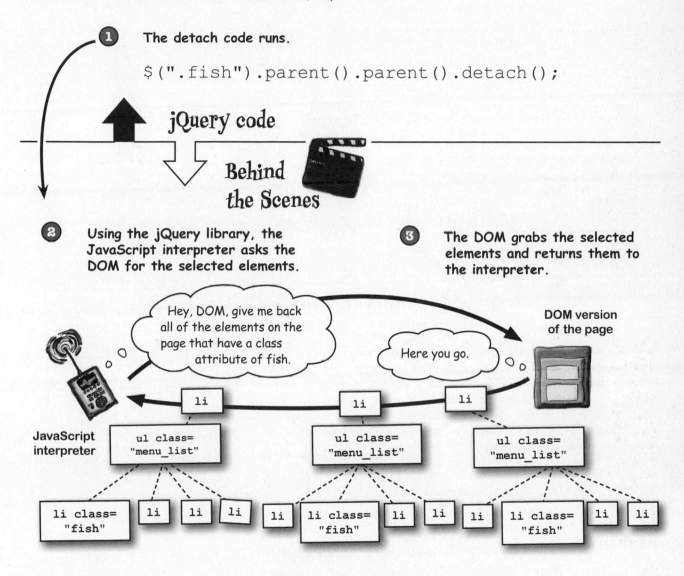

1 The detach code runs.

```
$(".fish").parent().parent().detach();
```

jQuery code

Behind the Scenes

2 Using the jQuery library, the JavaScript interpreter asks the DOM for the selected elements.

3 The DOM grabs the selected elements and returns them to the interpreter.

Hey, DOM, give me back all of the elements on the page that have a class attribute of fish.

Here you go.

DOM version of the page

JavaScript interpreter

The browser will hold those elements in memory temporarily. If we want to keep them to use in our program later, it's a good idea to put them into a variable. But how do we do that?

There's that dollar sign again...

Storing our elements is simple. We create a variable, just as we have for numbers and text strings, and set the variable (using the equals sign) to the statement that returns elements. But wouldn't it be good to know when the variable is storing *special* stuff like elements (versus just numbers or text strings)? It's common practice among jQuery coders to place a dollar sign in front of a variable that will be used to store elements returned from jQuery. That way, anyone else who looks at our code knows that we are using the variable to store stuff that we got from jQuery.

```
$f = $(".fish").parent().parent().detach();
```

Putting a dollar sign in front of the variable indicates that it's storing elements returned from jQuery.

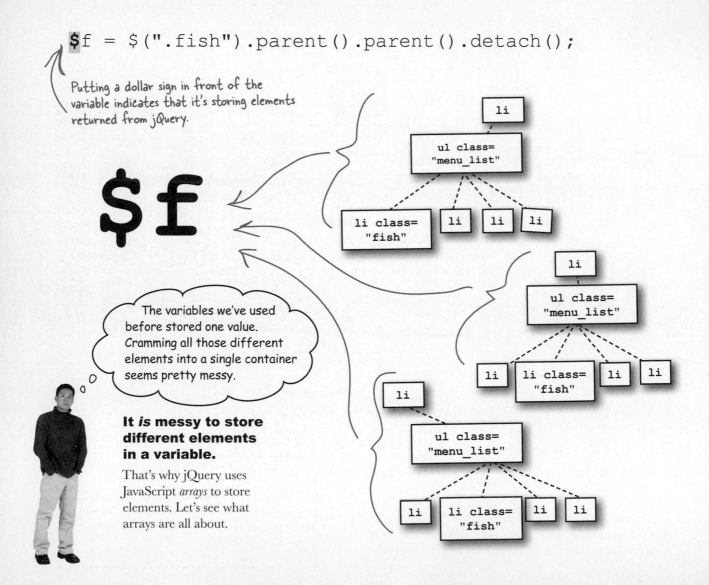

The variables we've used before stored one value. Cramming all those different elements into a single container seems pretty messy.

It *is* messy to store different elements in a variable.

That's why jQuery uses JavaScript *arrays* to store elements. Let's see what arrays are all about.

Expand your storage options with arrays

Any time we select elements from the DOM and store them in a variable, jQuery returns the data as an *array*. An array is simply a variable with greater storage options.

A basic <u>variable</u> stores <u>one</u> value.

An <u>array</u> stores <u>many</u> values.

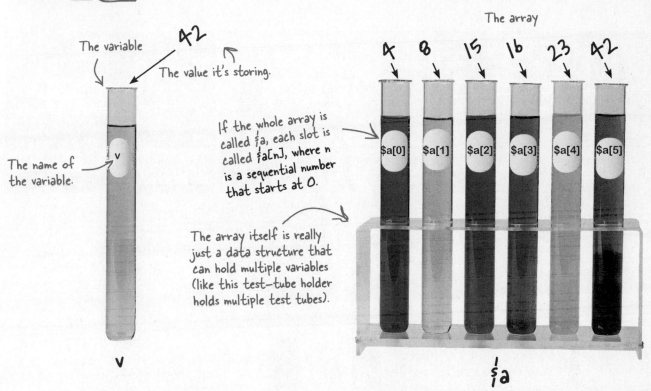

The variable

42

The value it's storing.

The name of the variable.

v

v

The array

4   8   15   16   23   42

If the whole array is called $a, each slot is called $a[n], where n is a sequential number that starts at 0.

$a[0] $a[1] $a[2] $a[3] $a[4] $a[5]

The array itself is really just a data structure that can hold multiple variables (like this test–tube holder holds multiple test tubes).

$a

We can put stuff in and take things out of each storage slot. To put the value "15" into the third slot, we would write this:

```
$a[2] = 15;
```

The third slot is numbered 2 because we started at 0.

Geek Bits

Arrays don't **have** to start with a dollar sign ($). The practice of indicating a jQuery array with a dollar sign is a coding convention of jQuery developers.

Store elements in an array

When we select and detach the `li` elements and set a variable (`$f`) to the result, jQuery takes the elements the DOM returns and stores them neatly for us in a JavaScript array. When we want to put those elements back with the restore button, our job will be way less messy.

$$\texttt{\$f = \$(".fish").parent().parent().detach();}$$

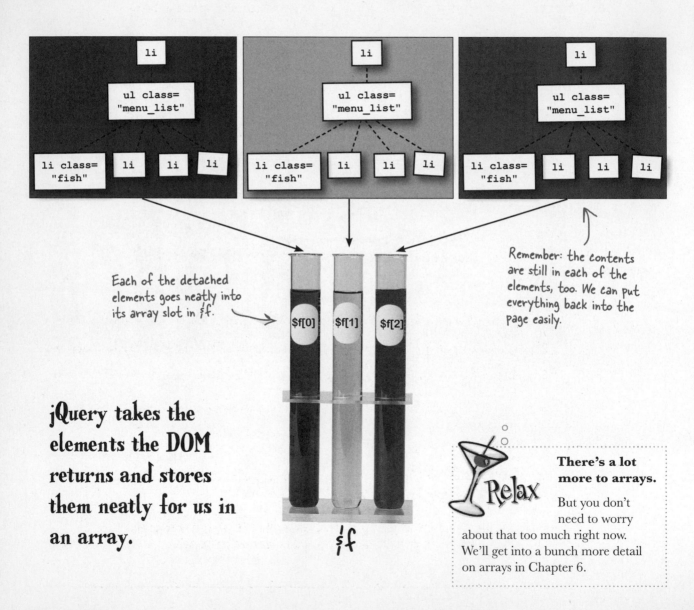

Each of the detached elements goes neatly into its array slot in $f.

Remember: the contents are still in each of the elements, too. We can put everything back into the page easily.

jQuery takes the elements the DOM returns and stores them neatly for us in an array.

There's a lot more to arrays.

Relax

But you don't need to worry about that too much right now. We'll get into a bunch more detail on arrays in Chapter 6.

TEST DRIVE

Add the line of code on the previous page, which will detach the parents of the parents of the `#fish` elements, inside the `vegOn` button click function in your *my_scripts.js* file. Then, open the page up in your favorite browser to make sure everything's working.

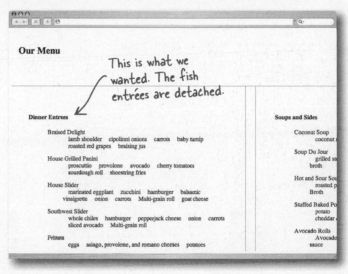

You did it. Now let's update the checklist.

☑ 1. Match li elements of the fish class and remove those entrées from the menu.

☐ 2. Match li elements in the hamburger class and replace them with portobello mushrooms.

☐ 3. Match li elements in the meat class and replace them with tofu.

Next up, you need to find entrées that contain hamburger and replace the hamburger with portobello mushrooms.

BRAIN POWER

We've seen how to take elements out of the DOM, but how do we dynamically replace DOM content with different content?

Change out elements with replaceWith

The replaceWith method allows you to replace selected element(s) with new ones.
Whenever you want modify the DOM by exchanging one thing for another, you can
use this handy jQuery method. Let's say we want to dynamically change the heading
level 2 element that says "Our Menu" to a heading level 1 that says "My Menu."
Here's how you can do it using the replaceWith method:

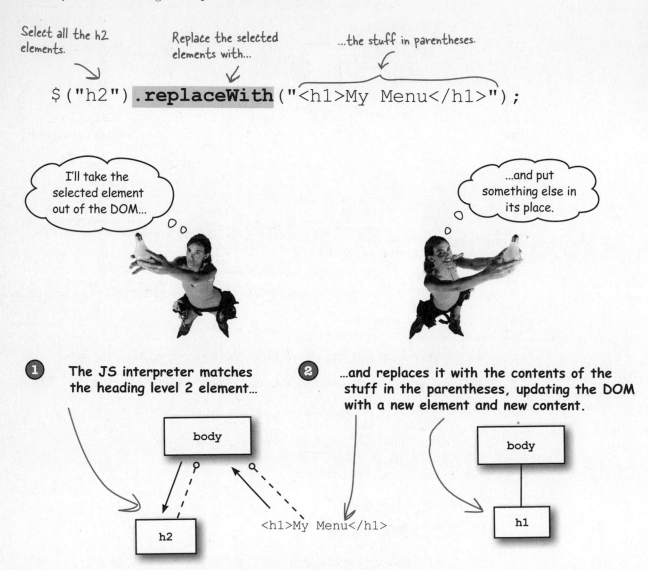

Select all the h2 elements.

Replace the selected elements with...

...the stuff in parentheses.

$("h2").replaceWith("<h1>My Menu</h1>");

I'll take the selected element out of the DOM...

...and put something else in its place.

1 The JS interpreter matches the heading level 2 element...

2 ...and replaces it with the contents of the stuff in the parentheses, updating the DOM with a new element and new content.

body

h2

<h1>My Menu</h1>

body

h1

How can replaceWith help?

You need to match `li` elements in the `hamburger` class and replace them with an `li` element of the `portobello` class. Let's think about that problem before we write our code.

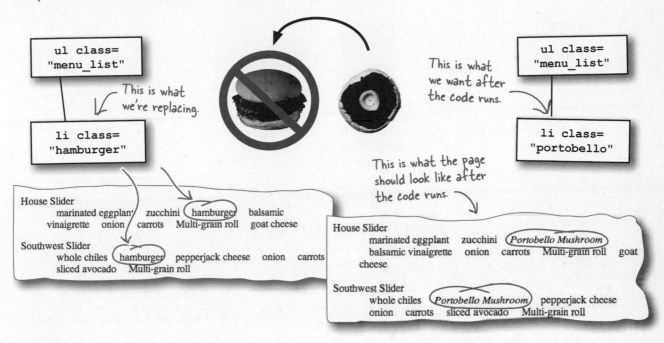

Exercise

Write the code that will find the `li` elements in the `hamburger` class and replace them with `li` elements in the `portobello` class. The diagram below should help you think it out. We wrote part of the answer for you. You do the rest.

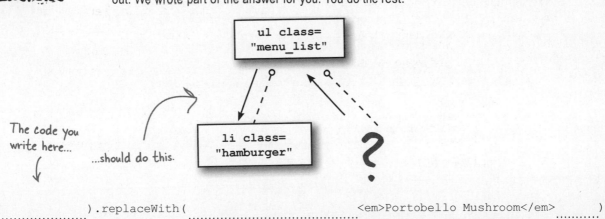

```
$(                ).replaceWith(                                    <em>Portobello Mushroom</em>        );
```

Exercise Solution

Write the code that will find the `li` elements in the `hamburger` class and replace them with `li` elements in the `portobello` class. Here's our solution.

Select all elements in the hamburger class.

The replaceWith method dynamically trades the selected content for the element in the parentheses. The main thing to remember is that you can put HTML in the parentheses.

```
$(".hamburger").replaceWith("<li class='portobello'><em>Portobello Mushroom</em></li>");
```

Test Drive

Add the `replaceWith` code inside the `vegOn` button click function in your *my_scripts.js* file. Then, open the page up in your favorite browser and press the "Go Vegetarian" button to make sure everything's working.

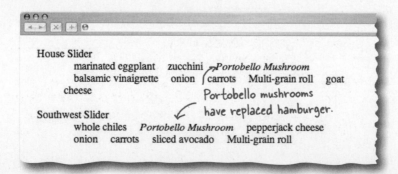

House Slider
  marinated eggplant   zucchini   *Portobello Mushroom*
  balsamic vinaigrette   onion   carrots   Multi-grain roll   goat
  cheese

Southwest Slider
  whole chiles   *Portobello Mushroom*   pepperjack cheese
  onion   carrots   sliced avocado   Multi-grain roll

Portobello mushrooms have replaced hamburger.

Think ahead before using replaceWith

What's next on the checklist?

☑ 1.   Match li elements of the fish class and remove those entrées from the menu.

☑ 2.   Match li elements in the hamburger class and replace them with portobello mushrooms.

☐ 3.   Match li elements in the meat class and replace them with tofu.

You need to find entrées in the meat class and replace them with tofu.

That's easy! We just use replaceWith again, right?

Actually, we can't use `replaceWith` **for this one.**

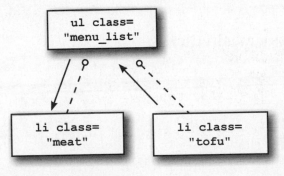

jQuery's `replaceWith` method is straightforward and powerful, but unfortunately, it won't help us solve this one. Why not?

replaceWith doesn't work for every situation

The replaceWith method works well when you have a **one-to-one** replacement like exchanging the hamburger class for portbello class.

One-to-one substitution

One-to-many substitution

But the scenario of trading out elements for the next item on our checklist isn't one for one. We have to replace many *different* kinds of ingredients (i.e., turkey, eggs, steak, lamb chops) with one ingredient (tofu).

One-to-many substitution

We can take items in the meat class and replace them all with tofu.

Many-to-one substitution

But when we want to select tofu and replace it later, we have a problem. When we want to put the different kinds of meat back in, the DOM has forgotten about them.

We could replace tofu with just *one* of the types of meat, but that's not what we wanted at all.

So we'll need to accomplish this menu substitution in two steps:

Many-to-one substitution

Later on, the DOM's forgotten all the different types of meat.

1. Insert li elements of the tofu class into the DOM after the meat elements.

2. Detach the elements of the meat class and hold them in a variable.

Insert HTML content into the DOM

Up to this point, we've either removed or replaced elements in the DOM. Fortunately for us, the creators of the jQuery library gave us many ways to insert stuff into the DOM. The ones we'll look at are `before` and `after`.

`before` inserts content before the selected element.

```
$(".meat").before("<li>Tofu</li>");
```

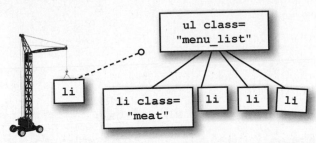

`after` inserts content after the selected element.

```
$(".meat").after("<li>Tofu</li>");
```

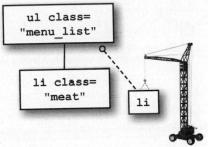

Sharpen your pencil

Write the jQuery code that will accomplish each step to our solution.

① Insert li elements of the tofu class into the DOM after the meat elements.

....

② Detach the elements of the meat class and hold them in a variable.

....

Sharpen your pencil
Solution

Write the jQuery code that will accomplish each step to our solution.

1 Insert li elements of the tofu class into the DOM after the meat elements.

$(".meat").after("<li class='tofu'>Tofu</li>");

2 Detach the elements of the meat class and hold them in a variable.

$m = $(".meat").detach();

You've accomplished each of the steps for the "Go Vegetarian" button:

☑ 1. Match li elements of the fish class and remove those entrées from the menu.

☑ 2. Match li elements in the hamburger class and replace them with portobello mushrooms.

☑ 3. Match li elements in the meat class and replace them with tofu.

Up next, we need to build the "Restore Menu" button. Here's what that button needs to do.

☐ Put the fish entrées back into the menu where we removed them (i.e., before the first menu item in the left column).

☐ Find entrées that contain portobello mushrooms and replace them with hamburger.

☐ Find entrées that contain tofu and replace them with the different kinds of meat (in the right order).

Let's dig right in and look at what we need to do for the first one.

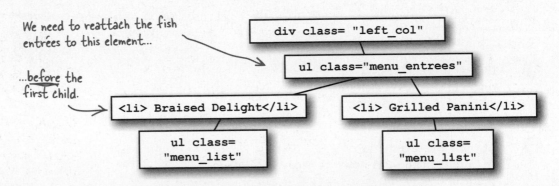

We need to reattach the fish entrées to this element...

...before the first child.

div class= "left_col"

ul class="menu_entrees"

<li> Braised Delight</li>

<li> Grilled Panini</li>

ul class= "menu_list"

ul class= "menu_list"

We know how to use before, **but how do we specify the *first* child?**

Use filter methods to narrow your selections (Part 1)

Fortunately, jQuery provides filtering methods that let us narrow our selection for problems like finding the first child. Let's look at six of them (three on this page, three on the next).

`first`

The `first` method will filter out *everything but the first element* in a selected set of elements.

`eq`

The `eq` method will filter out *everything but the element whose index number is equal* to what you put in the parentheses in a selected set of elements.

`last`

The `last` method will filter out *everything but the last element* in a selected set of elements.

Let's look at one item from our menu to see how these methods work:

The *first* method narrows down the selected elements to just the *first* one.

The *last* method narrows down the selected elements to just the *last* one.

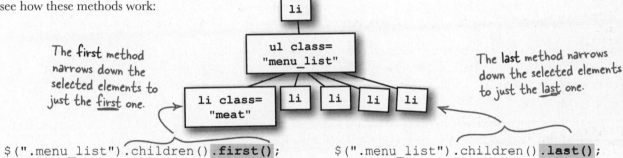

```
$(".menu_list").children().first();
```

```
$(".menu_list").children().last();
```

The *eq* method narrows down the selected elements to just the element whose index number is in the parentheses.

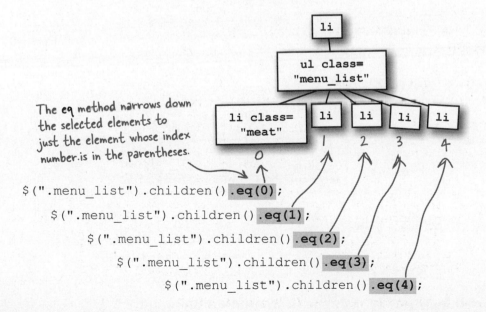

```
$(".menu_list").children().eq(0);
   $(".menu_list").children().eq(1);
      $(".menu_list").children().eq(2);
         $(".menu_list").children().eq(3);
            $(".menu_list").children().eq(4);
```

Remember that jQuery returns our selected elements in an array. The index number we put in the eq method refers to its slot in the array.

Use filter methods to narrow your selections (Part 2)

Now let's check out the `slice`, `filter`, and `not` methods, and how they work.

slice

The `slice` method will filter out everything but elements with an index *between the index numbers* you put in its parentheses.

filter

The `filter` method will filter out everything but elements that *match the selector* you put in its parentheses.

not

The `not` method will filter out everything that *does not match the selector* you place in the parentheses.

The slice method narrows down the selected elements to those between the two index numbers you put in parentheses.

`$(".menu_list").children().slice(1,3);`

In this case, only one element will be returned—the second li element.

The `filter` and `not` methods let us use selectors to create a subset from the matched set using selectors as arguments of their methods.

The filter method narrows down the selected elements to the selector you put in parentheses.

`$(".menu_list").parents().filter(".organic");`

The filter and not methods work great with the **parents** and **children** methods.

The parents method lets us grab all the elements that are parents, grandparents, great-grandparents, etc., of the selected element.

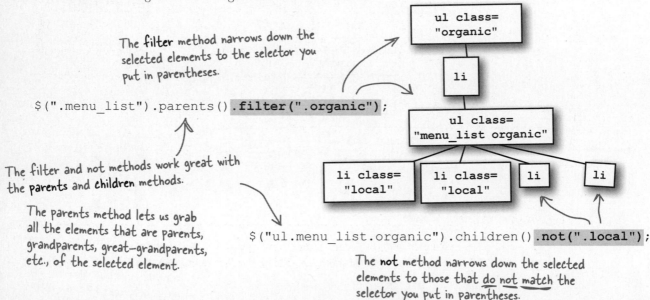

`$("ul.menu_list.organic").children().not(".local");`

The **not** method narrows down the selected elements to those that <u>do not match</u> the selector you put in parentheses.

Which of these methods will help you specify the first child on the menu?

BE the DOM

Your job is to play the DOM. Draw a line from the jQuery statement to the element(s) in the DOM the selector will return. Assume that these are the only elements on the page. We've done the first one for you.

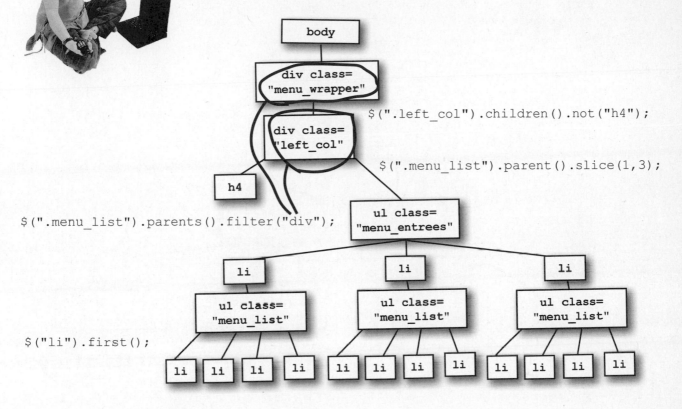

```
$(".left_col").children().not("h4");
```

```
$(".menu_list").parent().slice(1,3);
```

```
$(".menu_list").parents().filter("div");
```

```
$("li").first();
```

```
$(".menu_list li").eq(3);          $(".menu_list").children().last();
```

Sharpen your pencil

Write the line of jQuery code that will put the fish entrées back into the menu where we removed them (i.e., before the first menu item below menu_entrees.

....`.before($f);`

BE the DOM Solution

Your job is to play the DOM. Draw a line from the jQuery statement to the element(s) in the DOM the selector will return. Assume that these are the only elements on the page. We've done the first one for you.

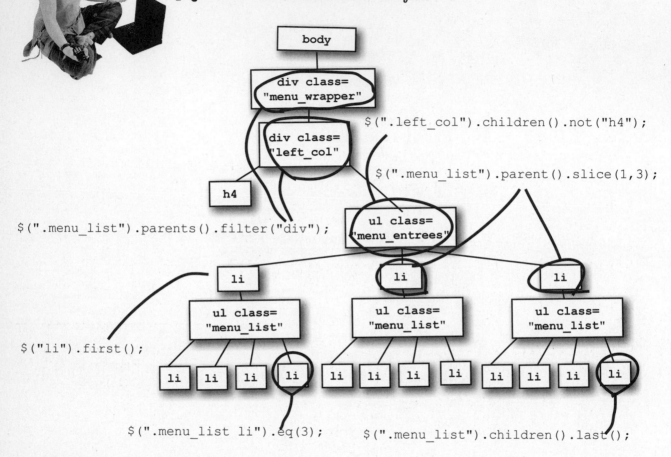

`$(".left_col").children().not("h4");`

`$(".menu_list").parent().slice(1,3);`

`$(".menu_list").parents().filter("div");`

`$("li").first();`

`$(".menu_list li").eq(3);`

`$(".menu_list").children().last();`

Sharpen your pencil Solution

Write the line of jQuery code that will put the fish entrées back into the menu where we removed them (i.e., before the first menu item below `menu_entrees`.

$(".menu_entrees li").first().`before($f);`

Bring the burger back

So far for the "Restore Menu" requirement, we've got one
item down, two to go:

☑ Put the fish entrées back into the menu where we removed
them (i.e., before the first menu item in the left column).

☐ Find entrées that contain portobello mushrooms and
replace them with hamburger.

☐ Find entrées that contain tofu and replace them with the
different kinds of meat (in the right order).

Our next checklist item seems a bit like déjà vu, doesn't it? All we really
need to do is reverse what we did for the original substitution. Why?
Because we're dealing with a one-to-one substitution, and we love
one-to-one substitutions because they're logically simple.

One-to-one substitution

I'm baaa-aaa-aaack.

Exercise

Remember this exercise? We're going to flip it. Write the code that will find the `li` elements in the
`portobello` class and replace them with `li` elements in the `hamburger` class. The diagram
below should help you think it out. We wrote part of the answer for you—you've got the rest.

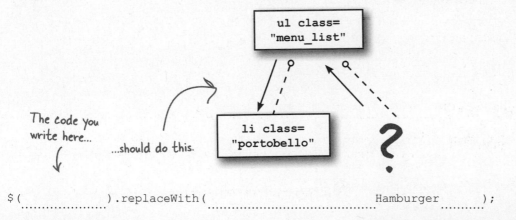

```
ul class=
"menu_list"
```

The code you
write here...

...should do this.

```
li class=
"portobello"
```

?

$(.................).replaceWith(................................. Hamburger ....);

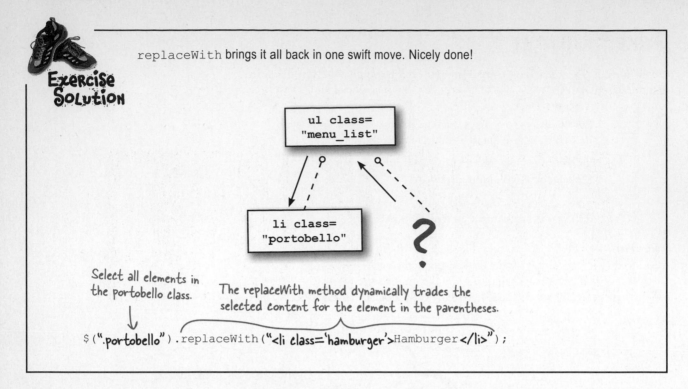

Exercise Solution

replaceWith brings it all back in one swift move. Nicely done!

Select all elements in the portobello class.

The replaceWith method dynamically trades the selected content for the element in the parentheses.

$(".portobello").replaceWith("<li class='hamburger'>Hamburger</li>");

Where's the beef (er...meat)?

We're down to our last item for the "Restore Menu" button:

☑ Put the fish entrées back into the menu where we removed them (i.e., before the first menu item in the left column).

☑ Find entrées that contain portobello mushrooms and replace them with hamburger.

☐ Find entrées that contain tofu and replace them with the different kinds of meat (in the right order).

What did we do with those li.meat elements again? Let's review:

We put li.tofu elements into the DOM after the meat elements.

```
$(".meat").after("<li class='tofu'><em>Tofu</em></li>");
```

Then, we detached the li.meat elements but held on to them by saving them into $m.

```
$m = $(".meat").detach();
```

So where are those elements, and how do we bring them back?

A meaty array

Remember that whenever we store jQuery elements, we give the variable a
dollar sign to signify that the variable we're using has a special kind of storage.
In this case, it's a jQuery array, and here's how the elements in $m are stored:

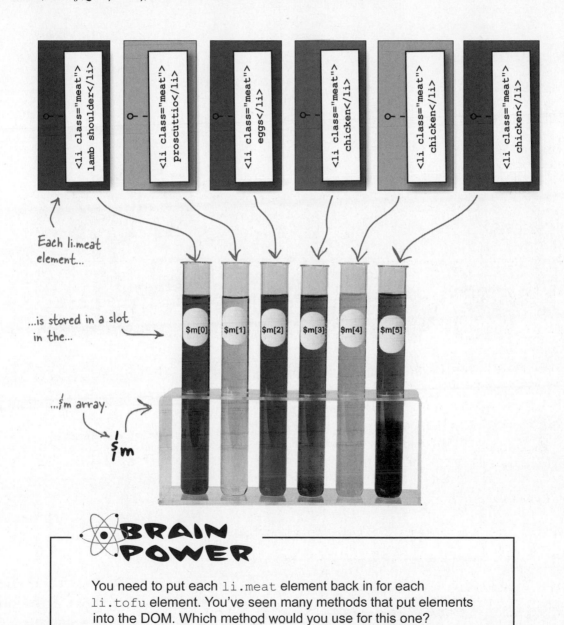

Each li.meat element...

...is stored in a slot in the...

...$m array.

$m

⚛ BRAIN POWER

You need to put each `li.meat` element back in for each
`li.tofu` element. You've seen many methods that put elements
into the DOM. Which method would you use for this one?

The each method loops through arrays

In Chapter 3, you saw how to use the each method to loop through elements. We can use it again here to loop through all the meat elements in the $m array and put them back where they were. But to do that, we'll need to check out a bit more about how the each method works.

The each method is like an assembly-line machine for your elements.

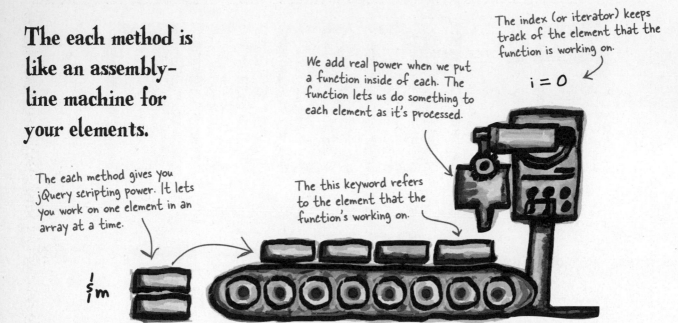

The index (or iterator) keeps track of the element that the function is working on.

We add real power when we put a function inside of each. The function lets us do something to each element as it's processed.

$i = 0$

The this keyword refers to the element that the function's working on.

The each method gives you jQuery scripting power. It lets you work on one element in an array at a time.

$m

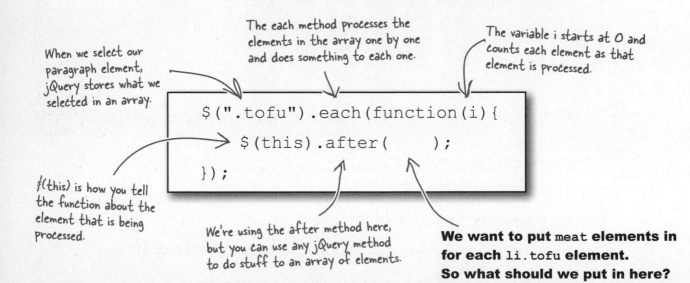

When we select our paragraph element, jQuery stores what we selected in an array.

The each method processes the elements in the array one by one and does something to each one.

The variable i starts at 0 and counts each element as that element is processed.

```
$(".tofu").each(function(i){
    $(this).after(    );
});
```

$(this) is how you tell the function about the element that is being processed.

We're using the after method here, but you can use any jQuery method to do stuff to an array of elements.

We want to put meat elements in for each li.tofu element. So what should we put in here?

jQuery Magnets

Put back the code magnets in the proper order to get the `restoreMenu` button finished and working. We put in a few for you.

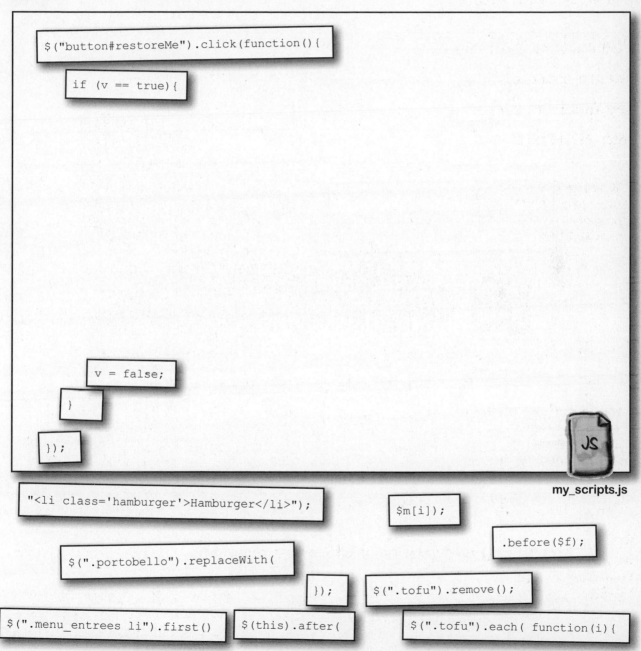

```
$("button#restoreMe").click(function(){

    if (v == true){
```

```
        v = false;
```

```
    }
```

```
});
```

```
"<li class='hamburger'>Hamburger</li>");
```

```
$m[i]);
```

```
.before($f);
```

```
$(".portobello").replaceWith(
```

```
});
```

```
$(".tofu").remove();
```

```
$(".menu_entrees li").first()
```

```
$(this).after(
```

```
$(".tofu").each( function(i){
```

my_scripts.js

jQuery Magnets Solution

Put back the code magnets in the proper order to get the `restoreMenu` button finished and working. We put in a few for you.

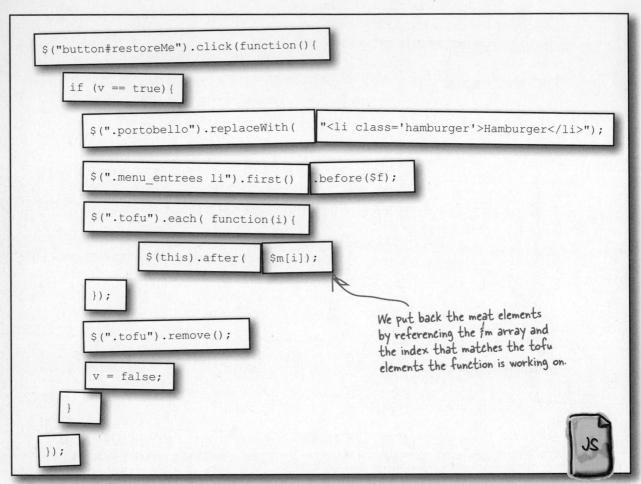

```
$("button#restoreMe").click(function(){

    if (v == true){

        $(".portobello").replaceWith(    "<li class='hamburger'>Hamburger</li>");

        $(".menu_entrees li").first()  .before($f);

        $(".tofu").each( function(i){

            $(this).after(    $m[i]);

        });

        $(".tofu").remove();

        v = false;

    }

});
```

We put back the meat elements by referencing the `$m` array and the index that matches the tofu elements the function is working on.

my_scripts.js

That's it...right?

You did everything required for the "Restore Menu" button.
Let's update our files and call this project done.

- ☑ Put the fish entrées back into the menu where we removed them (i.e., before the first menu item in the left column).
- ☑ Find entrées that contain portobello mushrooms and replace them with hamburger.
- ☑ Find entrées that contain tofu and replace them with the different kinds of meat (in the right order).

> Wait. We forgot about the P.S. on the cocktail napkin.

P.S. If you can pull it off, we'd also like a leaf icon to show up next to the substituted vegetarian entrées.

Oops, you're right.

Luckily, the web designer already put the `veg_leaf` class in the *my_style.css* file. Let's have a look at it.

```
.veg_leaf{
    list-style-image:url('../images/leaf.png');
    }
```

my_style.css

Exercise

Write the statement that will add the `veg_leaf` class to the parent of the parent of the `tofu` classes.

....

Hint: addClass is your friend here.

Exercise Solution

Just a little DOM transversing, plus some `addClass` magic, and you're done!

```
$(".tofu").parent().parent().addClass("veg_leaf");
```

there are no Dumb Questions

Q: I get the other filter methods, but `slice` still confuses the heck out of me. Can you give me a more in-depth explanation of it?

A: The `slice` method can be confusing. The most confusing thing about `slice` are its parameters: `slice(start, end)`.

The first parameter is the `start` parameter, and you have to include it, or `slice` won't work. The `start` parameter tells where to start the selection within an array of elements. Remember that the first element in an array has a "zero index," which means you have to start counting at 0. The `start` parameter will also take a negative number. If you put in a negative number, `slice` will start counting backward from the end of the array rather than forward from the beginning.

Q: OK, so what does the `end` parameter of the `slice` method do?

A: The `slice` method's second parameter, the `end` parameter, is not required. If you don't include it, `slice` will select all elements from whatever the `start` parameter is set to and will select all of the elements in the array that are greater than the `start` parameter. The `end` parameter can be counterintuitive if you don't remind yourself that the array starts counting at 0.

Q: The `each` method seems pretty powerful. How does `each` know what element it's working on?

A: The real power comes from combining `each` with the `this` keyword. The `each` method keeps track of its index automatically and "knows" which element it's working on. You should only use `each` when you've selected multiple elements. To reference the current element, you use `this` but wrap it with the jQuery shortcut: `$(this)`.

Q: Why do I have to put the "i" or "index" inside the `each` function?

A: The `index` variable, often called "i" or "index," is used by the `each` function to keep a count of the element `each` is working on. That way, the `each` function knows when it's done processing. If `each` didn't have an `index` variable, it wouldn't know which function to work on and it wouldn't be able to stop.

Q: How can I find elements within a jQuery array?

A: You can find elements within a jQuery array using the `find` method. Let's say you have an array of `li` elements in a jQuery array:

```
var $my_elements = $("li");
```

Now, you want to find all of the anchor elements in that array. Here's what you do:

```
$my_elements.find("a");
```

Q: Does jQuery give us a way to wrap an element inside of another element?

A: Indeed, it does. Let's say you want to surround an image with an ID of `oreilly` inside of an anchor element. Here's how you do it:

```
$("img#oreilly").wrap("<a
href='http://www.oreilly.
com'></a>");
```

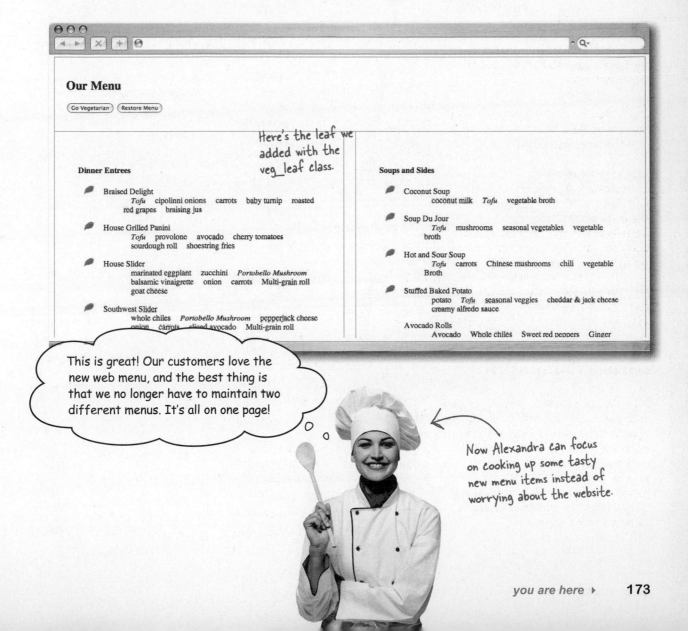

TEST DRIVE

It's been a while since you updated your files. Add the code for the "Restore Menu" button and the code for adding and removing the `veg_leaf` class where you make vegetarian substitutions. You can always download the files for this chapter from *http://www.thinkjquery.com/chapter04/* and compare them to your code.

Our Menu

(Go Vegetarian) (Restore Menu)

Here's the leaf we added with the veg_leaf class.

Dinner Entrees

- Braised Delight
  Tofu   cipolinni onions   carrots   baby turnip   roasted red grapes   braising jus

- House Grilled Panini
  Tofu   provolone   avocado   cherry tomatoes sourdough roll   shoestring fries

- House Slider
  marinated eggplant   zucchini   *Portobello Mushroom* balsamic vinaigrette   onion   carrots   Multi-grain roll goat cheese

- Southwest Slider
  whole chiles   *Portobello Mushroom*   pepperjack cheese onion   carrots   sliced avocado   Multi-grain roll

Soups and Sides

- Coconut Soup
  coconut milk   *Tofu*   vegetable broth

- Soup Du Jour
  Tofu   mushrooms   seasonal vegetables   vegetable broth

- Hot and Sour Soup
  Tofu   carrots   Chinese mushrooms   chili   vegetable Broth

- Stuffed Baked Potato
  potato   *Tofu*   seasonal veggies   cheddar & jack cheese creamy alfredo sauce

Avocado Rolls
  Avocado   Whole chiles   Sweet red peppers   Ginger

This is great! Our customers love the new web menu, and the best thing is that we no longer have to maintain two different menus. It's all on one page!

Now Alexandra can focus on cooking up some tasty new menu items instead of worrying about the website.

Your jQuery Toolbox

You've got Chapter 4 under your belt and now you've added DOM manipulation and traversal, arrays, and filters to your toolbox.

DOM manipulation

You can add to, replace, and remove things from the DOM at will:

detach

remove

replaceWith

before

after

DOM traversal

This is all about climbing around the DOM tree so you can manipulate it.

You use element relationships with associated methods like parent and child to get where you want.

Chaining methods is an efficient way to traverse the DOM quickly.

Arrays

jQuery arrays store all kinds of things, including elements, so you can access them later.

Just like with variables, put a $ in front of your array to signify that it is storing special jQuery goodies.

Filters

Filter methods help you narrow down a set of selected elements:

first

equal

last

slice

filter

not

CHAPTER 4

5 jQuery effects and animation

A little glide in your stride

Look at how well I can move around; I'm so graceful. I bet *you* can't do that!

Making things happen on your page is all well and good,

but if you can't make it look cool, people won't want to use your site. That's
where jQuery effects and animation come in. In this chapter, you'll learn how to
make elements transition on your page over time, show or hide specific pieces
of elements that are relevant, and shrink or grow an element on the page, all
before your users' eyes. You'll also see how to schedule these animations so they
happen at various intervals to give your page a very dynamic appearance.

DoodleStuff needs a web app

DoodleStuff supplies Webville kids with cool art supplies. A few years ago, DoodleStuff started up a popular website that provides interactive art apps for kids. The company's fan base has grown so fast that it has trouble keeping up with requests.

To cater to DoodleStuff's new, wider audience, the web projects director wants to build an app that doesn't use Flash or any other browser plug-ins.

> Our kids' projects are all about making things fun and being hands on. Can you build us an app for our 6- to 10-year age group? We need a lot of visual effects and some interactivity on this one. But no Flash, please!

Do the Monster Mashup

Here's the project blueprint from the web projects director, along with the graphic designer's files for the app.

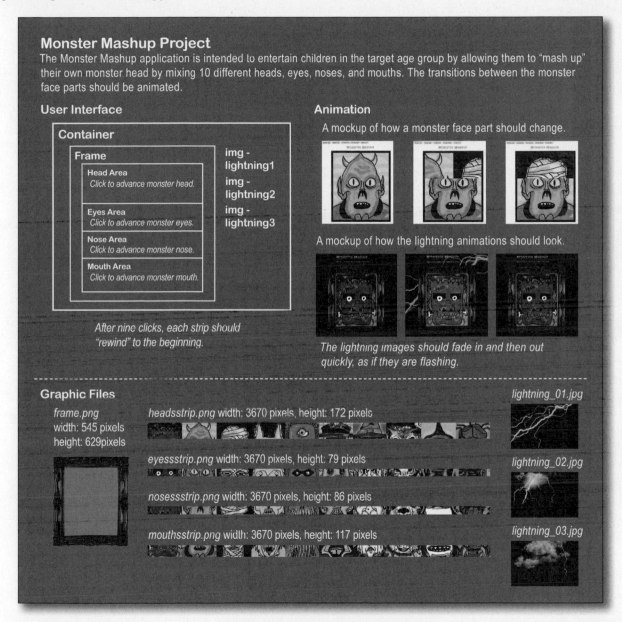

Monster Mashup Project

The Monster Mashup application is intended to entertain children in the target age group by allowing them to "mash up" their own monster head by mixing 10 different heads, eyes, noses, and mouths. The transitions between the monster face parts should be animated.

User Interface

Container

Frame

Head Area
Click to advance monster head.

Eyes Area
Click to advance monster eyes.

Nose Area
Click to advance monster nose.

Mouth Area
Click to advance monster mouth.

img - lightning1

img - lightning2

img - lightning3

After nine clicks, each strip should "rewind" to the beginning.

Animation

A mockup of how a monster face part should change.

A mockup of how the lightning animations should look.

The lightning images should fade in and then out quickly, as if they are flashing.

Graphic Files

frame.png
width: 545 pixels
height: 629pixels

headsstrip.png width: 3670 pixels, height: 172 pixels

eyessstrip.png width: 3670 pixels, height: 79 pixels

nosessstrip.png width: 3670 pixels, height: 86 pixels

mouthsstrip.png width: 3670 pixels, height: 117 pixels

lightning_01.jpg

lightning_02.jpg

lightning_03.jpg

You have a lot of detail on the project requirements and the graphic files you need, but the graphic designer didn't write any HTML or CSS—that's where you'll need to get started. What do you need to do to set that up?

Monster Mashup needs layout and positioning

We've certainly had a lot to say about getting your structure and style right out of the gate before you write any jQuery. And it's even more important now—if you don't get your layout and position right up front, your effects and animations can go wrong, *fast*. There's nothing worse than staring at your jQuery code and wondering why it's not doing what you want it to do in the browser. It's a good idea to sketch up your ideas and think about what's going to happen on screen.

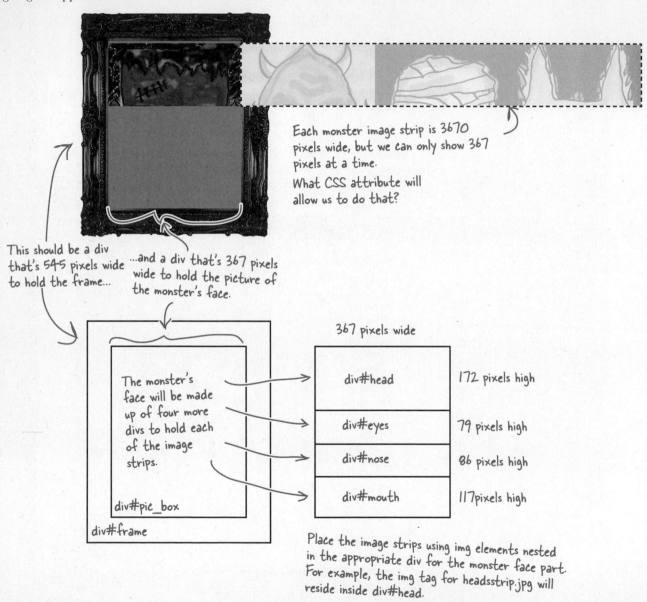

Each monster image strip is 3670 pixels wide, but we can only show 367 pixels at a time.

What CSS attribute will allow us to do that?

This should be a div that's 545 pixels wide to hold the frame...

...and a div that's 367 pixels wide to hold the picture of the monster's face.

367 pixels wide

The monster's face will be made up of four more divs to hold each of the image strips.

div#pic_box

div#frame

div#head	172 pixels high
div#eyes	79 pixels high
div#nose	86 pixels high
div#mouth	117 pixels high

Place the image strips using img elements nested in the appropriate div for the monster face part. For example, the img tag for headsstrip.jpg will reside inside div#head.

Exercise

For each blank line in the HTML and CSS files, write in the CSS ID, property, or setting that will help lay out and position the Monster Mashup app. When in doubt, look at the previous two pages for guidance. We've done a few for you.

```
body>
<header id="top"><img src="images/Monster_Mashup.png" />
<p>Make your own monster face by clicking on the picture.</p></header>

<div id="frame">
    <div id=..."pic_box".>
        <div id=.............class="face"><img src="images/headsstrip.jpg"></div>
        <div id=.............class="face"><img src="images/eyesstrip.jpg"></div>
        <div id=.............class="face"><img src="images/nosesstrip.jpg"></div>
        <div id=.............class="face"><img src="images/mouthsstrip.jpg"></div>
    </div>
</div>
  <script type="text/javascript" src="scripts/jquery-1.6.2.min.js"></script>
  <script type="text/javascript" src="scripts/my_scripts.js"></script>
</body>
```

index.html

```
#frame {                                  .face{
  position:.........................        position:........................
  left:100px;                               left:0px;
  top:100px;                                top:0px;
  width:545px;                              z-index: 0;
  height:629px;                           }
  background-image:url(images/frame.png);
  z-index: 2;                             #head{
  overflow:.........................          height:172px;
}                                         }

#pic_box{                                 #eyes{
  position: relative;                       ........................
  left:91px;                              }
  top:84px;
  .........................               #nose{
  height:460px;                             ........................
  z-index: 1;                             }
  overflow:.........................
}                                         #mouth{
                                            ........................
                                          }
```

my_style.css

For each blank line in the HTML and CSS files, write in the CSS ID, property, or setting that will help lay out and position the Monster Mashup app. When in doubt, look at the previous two pages for guidance. We've done a few for you.

```
body>
<header id="top"><img src="images/Monster_Mashup.png" />
<p>Make your own monster face by clicking on the picture.</p></header>

<div id="frame">
   <div id="pic-box">
       <div id="head" class="face"><img src="images/headsstrip.jpg"></div>
       <div id="eyes" class="face"><img src="images/eyesstrip.jpg"></div>
       <div id="nose" class="face"><img src="images/nosesstrip.jpg"></div>
       <div id="mouth" class="face"><img src="images/mouthsstrip.jpg"></div>
   </div>
</div>
   <script type="text/javascript" src="scripts/jquery-1.6.2.min.js"></script>
   <script type="text/javascript" src="scripts/my_scripts.js"></script>
</body>
```

index.html

```
#frame {
   position: absolute;
   left:100px;
   top:100px;
   width:545px;
   height:629px;
   background-image:url(images/frame.png);
   z-index: 2;
   overflow: hidden;
}

#pic_box{
   position: relative;
   left:91px;
   top:84px;
   width:367px;
   height:460px;
   z-index: 1;
   overflow: hidden;
}
```

When we animate the position of elements, we need to use absolute or relative positioning.

Setting the overflow property to "hidden" allows us to hide the part of the image strip that extends beyond the pic_box area.

You could also use the CSS "clip" property for this.

```
.face{
   position: relative;
   left:0px;
   top:0px;
   z-index: 0;
}

#head{
   height:172px;
}

#eyes{
   height:79px;
}

#nose{
   height:86px;
}

#mouth{
   height:117px;
}
```

my_style.css

A little more structure and style

Next up are the structural changes to the HTML and CSS files. Add the code below to your *index.html* and *my_style.css* files. You can grab the image files from *www.thinkjquery.com/chapter05*.

Add a container and nest the lightning images inside of it.

Do this!

```html
<div id="container">
  <img class="lightning" id="lightning1" src="images/lightning-01.jpg" />
  <img class="lightning" id="lightning2" src="images/lightning-02.jpg" />
  <img class="lightning" id="lightning3" src="images/lightning-03.jpg" />
  <div id="frame">
    <div id="pic_box">
      <div id="head" class="face"><img src="images/headsstrip.jpg"></div>
      <div id="eyes" class="face"><img src="images/eyesstrip.jpg"></div>
      <div id="nose" class="face"><img src="images/nosesstrip.jpg"></div>
      <div id="mouth" class="face"><img src="images/mouthsstrip.jpg"></div>
    </div>
  </div>
</div>
```

index.html

```css
#container{
    position:absolute;
    left:0px;
    top:0px;
    z-index: 0;
}

.lightning{
    display:none;
    position:absolute;
    left:0px;
    top:0px;
    z-index: 0;
}
```

We want the lightning images to start out as invisible.

When we want to animate elements, we need their position property set to absolute, fixed, or relative.

```css
body{
    background-color:#000000;
}
p{
    color:#33FF66;
    font-family: Tahoma, Verdana, Arial,
Helvetica, sans-serif;
    font-size:12px;
}
#text_top {
    position:relative;
    z-index: 4;
}
```

CSS

my_style.css

Make the interface click

Now that we have the Monster Mashup laid out visually, let's set up the rest of the user interface section called for in the blueprint. This part is all about clicking to make stuff happen, and you've done that for four chapters now. Setting this up should be a cake walk.

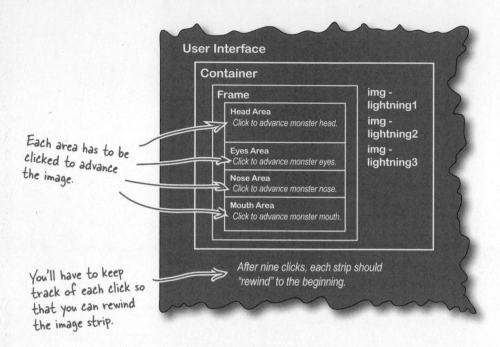

Each area has to be clicked to advance the image.

You'll have to keep track of each click so that you can rewind the image strip.

there are no
Dumb Questions

Q: I'm a little rusty on CSS positioning. Why do we need it for jQuery effects and animation?

A: `position` is a CSS property that controls how and where elements are placed by the browser's layout engine. jQuery accomplishes many of its effects using the CSS `position` property. If you're rusty and need a refresher, check out this excellent explanation at Mozilla's developer's center:

http://developer.mozilla.org/en/CSS/ position#Relative_positioning

Q: Why do we have to set the CSS position property to `absolute`, `fixed`, or `relative` when we want to animate elements ?

A: If we leave the CSS `position` property set to its default setting (i.e., `static`), then we can't apply top,right, left, or bottom positioning. When we get to the `animate` function, we'll need to be able to set those positions, and `static` simply doesn't allow for that. The other position settings—`absolute`, `fixed`, and `relative`—do.

Q: You mentioned a browser layout engine. What the heck is *that*?

A: The browser layout engine is the core part of a browser that interprets the HTML and CSS code and displays it in the browser's *viewport* (the window that displays content to the viewer). Google's Chrome and Apple's Safari use the Webkit browser layout engine. Firefox uses the Gecko layout engine, and Microsoft Internet Explorer use a layout engine called Trident.

jQuery Magnets

Put the code magnets in proper order to make the `div#head` element clickable. Make sure to sequence the variables and conditional statements in the right order so that you can detect the ninth click.

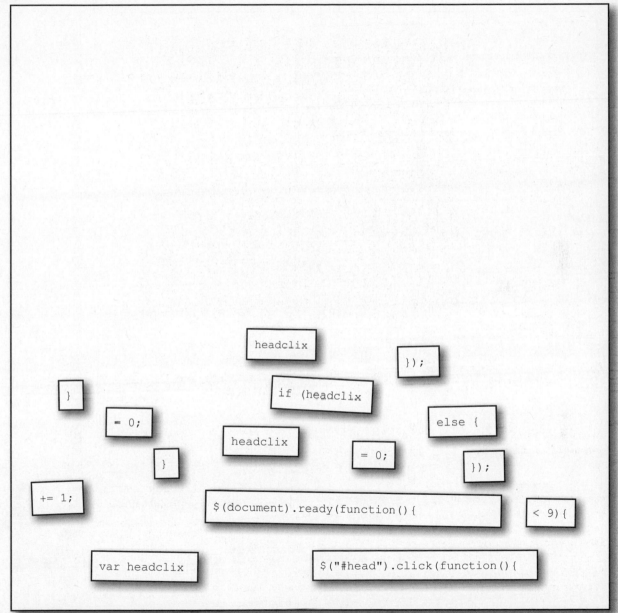

```
headclix

});

}                    if (headclix

= 0;                          else {

headclix
}              = 0;        });

+= 1;    $(document).ready(function(){      < 9){

var headclix      $("#head").click(function(){
```

jQuery Magnets Solution

Put the code magnets in proper order to make the `div#head` element clickable. Make sure to sequence the variables and conditional statements in the right order so that you can detect the ninth click.

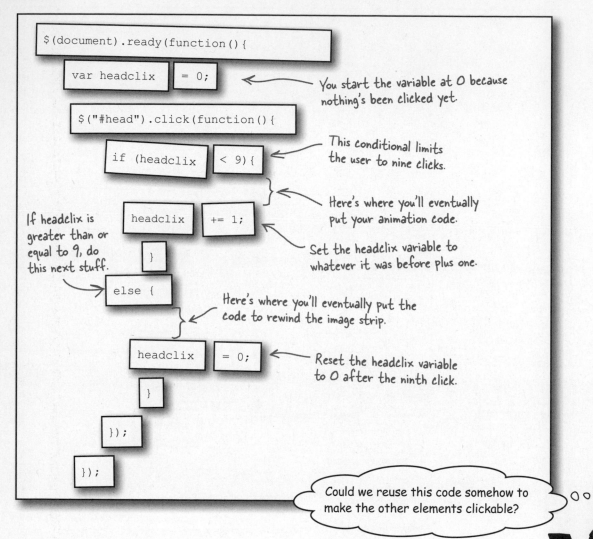

```
$(document).ready(function(){

    var headclix = 0;

    $("#head").click(function(){

        if (headclix < 9){

            headclix += 1;

        }
        else {

            headclix = 0;

        }

    });

});
```

You start the variable at 0 because nothing's been clicked yet.

This conditional limits the user to nine clicks.

Here's where you'll eventually put your animation code.

Set the headclix variable to whatever it was before plus one.

If headclix is greater than or equal to 9, do this next stuff.

Here's where you'll eventually put the code to rewind the image strip.

Reset the headclix variable to 0 after the ninth click.

Could we reuse this code somehow to make the other elements clickable?

Absolutely!

Each of the elements follows a similar pattern to the `div#head` element (with a few variations in things like the variable name).

Sharpen your pencil

Fill in the jQuery script below to make the eyes, nose, and mouth elements clickable. We'll add some functionality to each click in a bit. Make sure to sequence the variables and conditional statements in the right order so that you can detect the ninth click.

```
$(document).ready(function(){

        $("#head").click(function(){
            if (headclix < 9){
                headclix += 1;
                }
                else{
                headclix = 0;
                }
        });











});
```

my_scripts.js

Sharpen your pencil
Solution

You've made the eyes, nose, and mouth elements clickable by sequencing the variables and conditional statements in the right order so that you can detect the ninth click.

```
$(document).ready(function(){
    var headclix = 0, eyeclix=0, noseclix= 0, mouthclix = 0;
        $("#head").click(function(){
            if (headclix < 9){
                    headclix += 1;
            }
            else{
                    headclix = 0;
            }
        });
        $("#eyes").click(function() {
            if (eyeclix < 9){
                    eyeclix += 1;
            }
            else{
                    eyeclix = 0;
            }
        });
        $("#nose").click(function() {
            if (noseclix < 9){
                    noseclix += 1;
            }
            else{
                    noseclix = 0;
            }
        });
        $("#mouth").click(function() {
            if (mouthclix < 9){
                    mouthclix += 1;
            }
            else{
                    mouthclix = 0;
            }
        });
});
```

We can declare and set multiple variables by putting commas between them.

Each part of the monster face is now clickable and is set up to allow only nine clicks before rewinding the image strip

Notice how each function inside the click is structured in a similar way with minor variations? This might be a good case for reuse.

Patience, grasshopper—we'll get to that in Chapter 7.

my_scripts.js

Make the lightning effect

Next up is the lightning effect. Let's review what the blueprint calls for before trying to make the effect work.

The lightning images are nested in the container div...

...and the lightning images need to fade in and out quickly.

A mockup of how the lightning animations should look.

The lightning images should fade in and then out quickly, as if they are flashing.

We did something kinda similar in Chapter 1 with slides and fades. Can't we just use those to make the Monster Mashup work?

Potentially. But there might be a better way.

We looked at jQuery's out-of-the-box effects in Chapter 1, but let's dig in a little more.

How does jQuery animate elements?

When the browser loads a CSS file, it sets the visual properties of the elements on the page. Using jQuery's built-in effects, the JS interpreter changes those CSS properties and animates the change right before your eyes. But it's not magic…it's all about CSS properties. Let's look again at a few you've already seen.

hide, show, and toggle change the CSS display property

hide

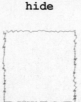

The JS interpreter changes the CSS `display` property of the selected element to `none` and removes it from the layout.

show

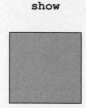

The JS interpreter changes the CSS `display` property of the selected element so that it becomes visible.

toggle

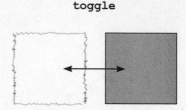

If an element is hidden, the JS interpreter will show it, and vice versa.

jQuery effects change CSS properties on the fly, making the page change right before your users' eyes.

hide, show, and toggle are all about the `display` property. But we need to slide the face parts around and fade the lightning in and out this time around. What CSS properties do you think jQuery changes with fades and slides?

Fade effects animate the CSS opacity property

fadeIn

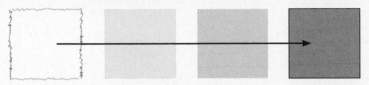

With `fadeIn`, the JavaScript interpreter changes the CSS `opacity` property for the selected element from 0 to 100.

fadeTo

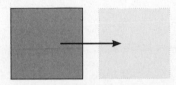

`fadeTo` lets you animate the selected element to a specific opacity percentage.

fadeOut

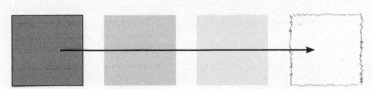

With `fadeOut`, the JavaScript interpreter changes the CSS opacity property for the selected element from 100 to 0, but it keeps space on the page for the element.

Geek Bits

The CSS `opacity` property doesn't work the same across browsers. Fortunately, jQuery takes care of that for us. And, really, that's all you have to know about that!

Sliding is all about height

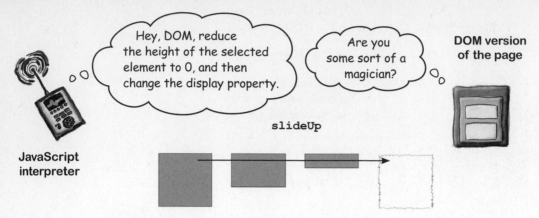

slideUp

The JavaScript interpreter tells the DOM to change the CSS height property for the selected element(s) to 0 and then sets the display property to none. It's essentially a hide with a slide.

slideDown

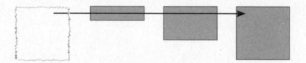

The JavaScript interpreter makes the selected element(s) appear by animating its height from 0 to whatever the height is set to in the CSS style.

slideToggle

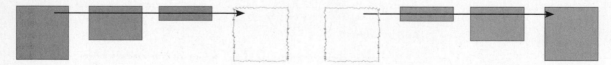

The JavaScript interpreter checks if the image is at full height or 0 height and switches the slide effect depending on what it finds. If the element has a height of 0, the JavaScript interpreter slides it down. If the element is at its full height, the JavaScript interpreter slides the elements up.

So I can only slide stuff up and down? What if I want to slide something to the left or the right?

jQuery only includes out-of-the-box effects for sliding elements up or down.

You won't find a `slideRight` or `slideLeft` method in jQuery (at least at the time of this writing). Don't worry, we'll sort this out a bit later...

You won't find a slideRight or slideLeft method in jQuery.

Sharpen your pencil

Which of jQuery's out-of-the-box effects will work for the Monster Mashup app? For each effect group, answer whether it will help us and explain why you chose or didn't choose each one.

Effect	Can we use it?	Why?
Show/Hide		
Slides		
Fades		

Sharpen your pencil Solution

Which of jQuery's out-of-the-box effects will work for the Monster Mashup app?

Effect	Can we use it?	Why?
Show/Hide	No	Show/hide effects won't help us with Monster Mashup because we don't need to animate the display property of anything.
Slides	No	Close, but no cigar. We need to slide the image strip left. SlideUp, slideDown, and slides only let us change the height property. We need something that changes the left property.
Fades	Yes	We can use the fade to meet the spec on the blueprint that says the lightning images should fade in and then out quickly, as if they are flashing.

Put fade effects to work

The blueprint calls for the lightning images to fade in and out, but we need to do this quickly so it looks like they're flashing. Let's dig into fade effects a bit deeper to see how we can make the lightning work.

Here's the ID for the first img element.

This is where the "duration" parameter goes. It controls how long it takes for the effect to complete.

```
$("#lightning1").fadeIn("fast");
```

You can use one of the string parameters: slow, normal, or fast...

...or you can use a value in milliseconds. For example, you could put in 1000, and the effect would take one second to animate.

Make it Stick

1 second = 1,000 milliseconds

```
$("#lightning1").fadeIn(1000);
```

Combine effects with method chains

The lightning will need to fade in and out, and over and over again. Instead of writing those effects separately, you can use chaining, which you used briefly in Chapter 4 when you needed to climb up the DOM. Method chains are a feature of jQuery that links together methods to run on a returned set of elements. They'll make the lightning effects easier and cleaner to write, so let's take a closer look.

The element's display will change from hidden to visible with full opacity...

...then it will fade back to totally transparent.

If you don't put a duration in the parentheses, the effect will default to normal, which is 400 milliseconds or 0.4 seconds.

```
$("#lightning1").fadeIn().fadeOut();
```

Each method you add is like a link in a chain.

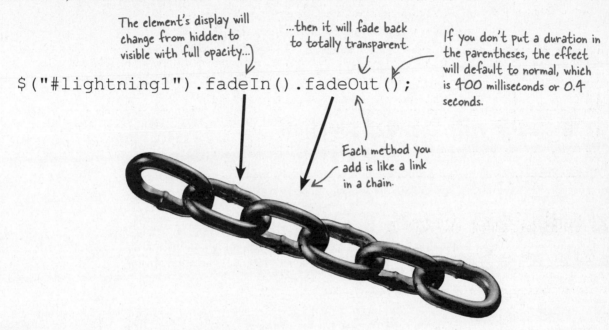

Exercise

Write the line of jQuery code that will accomplish each of the steps shown below.

1 Fade in the `#lightning1` element with a duration of one-quarter of a second.

....

2 Chain another effect that fades out the `#lightning1` element in one-quarter of a second.

....

Write the line of jQuery code that will accomplish each of the steps shown below.

1 Fade in the #lightning1 element with a duration of one-quarter of a second.

$("#lightning1").fadeIn("250");

2 Chain another effect that fades out the #lightning1 element in one-quarter of a second.

$("#lightning1").fadeIn("250").fadeOut("250");

Striking back with a timed function

So now you've got lightning that can fade in and out, but the project requirements are for the lightning to keep striking. Real lightning zaps through the sky and then there's usually an interval of time before another zap crosses the sky. So we need a way to do the fade *repeatedly*.

Think back to earlier chapters where you needed to do a repeated task; what did you use? That's right: functions! They showed up first in Chapter 3 to make a reusable click function and a randomizer, and now you can use functions to run the fades, wait a bit, and then do them again at a given interval. That will provide the slick effect of lots of flashing lighting for the Monster Mashup. Let's take a look at a function that will do this.

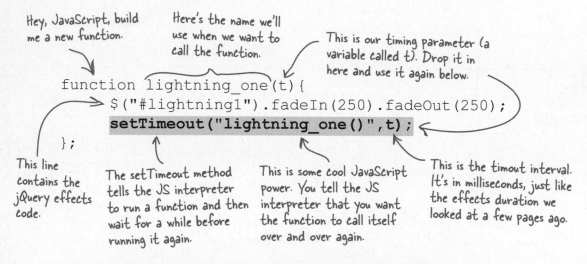

Hey, JavaScript, build me a new function.

Here's the name we'll use when we want to call the function.

This is our timing parameter (a variable called t). Drop it in here and use it again below.

```
function lightning_one(t){
    $("#lightning1").fadeIn(250).fadeOut(250);
    setTimeout("lightning_one()",t);
};
```

This line contains the jQuery effects code.

The setTimeout method tells the JS interpreter to run a function and then wait for a while before running it again.

This is some cool JavaScript power. You tell the JS interpreter that you want the function to call itself over and over again.

This is the timout interval. It's in milliseconds, just like the effects duration we looked at a few pages ago.

In just three lines of code, you have a timed lightning function for the first lightning image. Now, try writing the functions for the other two lightning images.

jQuery Magnets

Put the code magnets in the right order to make the timed lightning functions for the other two lightning elements.

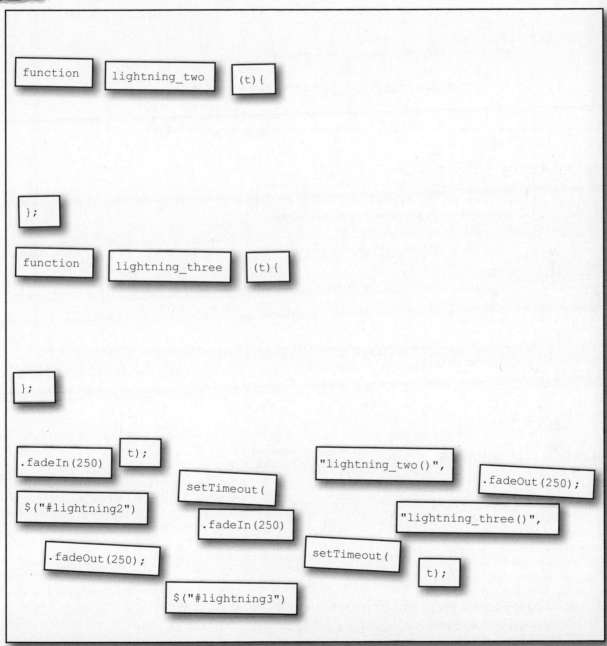

```
function   lightning_two   (t){
```

```
};
```

```
function   lightning_three   (t){
```

```
};
```

```
.fadeIn(250)   t);                    "lightning_two()",
                                                          .fadeOut(250);
          setTimeout(
$("#lightning2")                        "lightning_three()",
           .fadeIn(250)
                              setTimeout(
  .fadeOut(250);                         t);
      $("#lightning3")
```

jQuery Magnets Solution

Put the code magnets in the right order to make the timed lightning functions for the other two lightning elements.

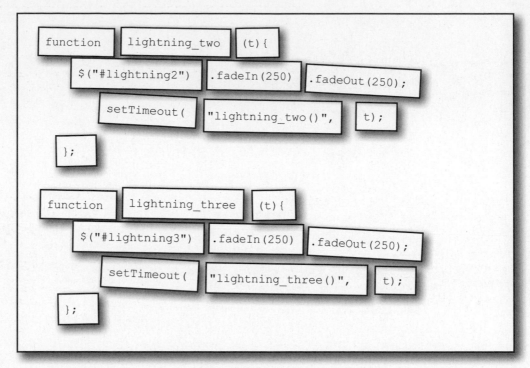

```
function    lightning_two    (t){
    $("#lightning2")    .fadeIn(250)    .fadeOut(250);
        setTimeout(    "lightning_two()",    t);
    };


function    lightning_three    (t){
    $("#lightning3")    .fadeIn(250)    .fadeOut(250);
        setTimeout(    "lightning_three()",    t);
    };
```

---

there are no
Dumb Questions

Q: Is `fadeIn().fadeOut()` not the same as `toggle`?

A: Great question! They are not the same. The `toggle` method is a single method that just switches the selected element from its hidden state to its visible state or vice versa, depending on what the selected element's current state is. Placing `fadeIn` and `fadeOut` in a chain creates a sequential effect that will first make the selected element(s) fade into view and then, when that effect has finished, fade it out of view.

Q: The `setTimeout` method is new. Is that a jQuery thing or a JavaScript thing?

A: The `setTimeout` method is actually a JavaScript method that you can use to control some aspects of jQuery animations. We'll get more into the `setTimeout` function in later chapters, especially Chapter 7.

If you want to read about it now, visit the Mozilla Developer's Center: *https://developer.mozilla.org/en/window.setTimeout*, or, if you really want to dig in, pick up a copy of David Flanagan's excellent and

thorough JavaScript book, *JavaScript: The Definitive Guide* (O'Reilly; *http://oreilly.com/catalog/9780596805531*).

Q: When I use the `hide` effect, the element just disappears. How do I slow that down?

A: To "slow down" the `hide`, `show`, or `toggle` effect, give a `duration` parameter in the parentheses. Here's how we could've done the Chapter 1 hide:

```
$("#picframe").hide(500);
```

Add the lightning functions to your script

Using the code you put together in the exercise on the previous page, update your script file for Monster Mashup.

Do this!

```
$(document).ready(function(){
    var headclix = 0, eyeclix = 0, noseclix = 0, mouthclix = 0;
    lightning_one(4000);
    lightning_two(5000);
    lightning_three(7000);

    $("#head").click(function(){
        if (headclix < 9){headclix+=1;}
        else{headclix = 0;}
    });

    $("#eyes").click(function(){
        if (eyeclix < 9){eyeclix+=1;}
        else{eyeclix = 0;}
    });

    $("#nose").click(function(){
        if (noseclix < 9){noseclix+=1;}
        else{noseclix = 0;}
    });

    $("#mouth").click(function(){
        if (mouthclix < 9){mouthclix+=1;}
        else{mouthclix = 0;}
    });

});//end doc.onready function

function lightning_one(t){
    $("#container #lightning1").fadeIn(250).fadeOut(250);
    setTimeout("lightning_one()",t);
};
function lightning_two(t){
    $("#container #lightning2").fadeIn("fast").fadeOut("fast");
    setTimeout("lightning_two()",t);
};
function lightning_three(t){
    $("#container #lightning3").fadeIn("fast").fadeOut("fast");
    setTimeout("lightning_three()",t);
};
```

These lines call the functions that are defined in bold at the very bottom.

The numbers in parentheses are parameters in milliseconds that will be passed to the setTimeout method. With these, you can alternate the flashes of lightning.

We took out some of the line breaks to save space on this page. Don't worry if your script's line breaks are different.

These are the lightning function definitions.

JS

my_scripts.js

TEST DRIVE

Open the page up in your favorite browser to see if your lightning effect was successful.

You accomplished the lightning fade effect by combining it with JavaScript's setTimeout method.

The lightning fades in and out quickly at different intervals, simulating real lightning.

So far, you've got the click functions working, and you made the three lightning images fade in and out at different intervals. Let's take a look at the blueprint to see what's left to do.

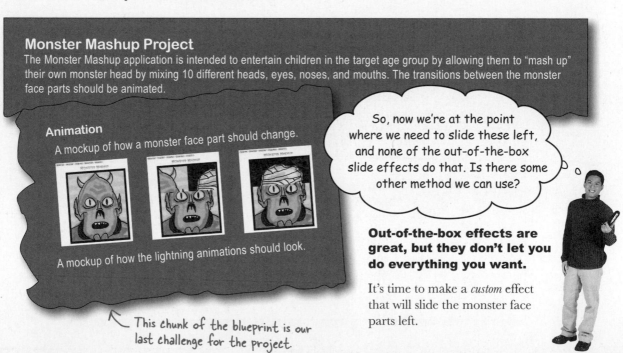

Monster Mashup Project

The Monster Mashup application is intended to entertain children in the target age group by allowing them to "mash up" their own monster head by mixing 10 different heads, eyes, noses, and mouths. The transitions between the monster face parts should be animated.

Animation

A mockup of how a monster face part should change.

A mockup of how the lightning animations should look.

This chunk of the blueprint is our last challenge for the project.

So, now we're at the point where we need to slide these left, and none of the out-of-the-box slide effects do that. Is there some other method we can use?

Out-of-the-box effects are great, but they don't let you do everything you want.

It's time to make a *custom* effect that will slide the monster face parts left.

DIY effects with animate

So jQuery has no `slideRight` or `slideLeft` method, and that's exactly what you need to do at this stage of the project. Does this mean that your Monster Mashup project is dead?

Never fear—jQuery offers the `animate` method for building your own effects. With `animate`, you can create custom animations that do many more things than the out-of-the-box effects do. The `animate` method allows you to animate CSS properties of the selected element(s), and it also allows you to animate multiple properties at the same time.

Let's have a look at some of the things you can do with the `animate` method.

Motion effects

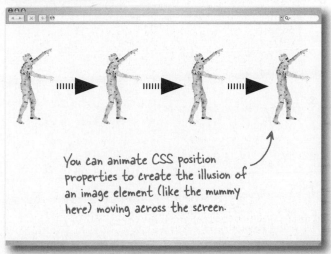

You can animate CSS position properties to create the illusion of an image element (like the mummy here) moving across the screen.

Scale effects

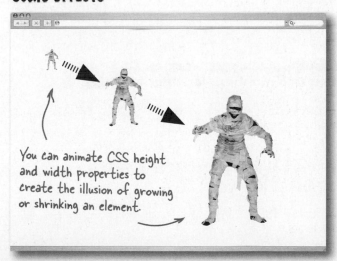

You can animate CSS height and width properties to create the illusion of growing or shrinking an element.

What CSS property will you need to animate to make the monster face parts slide left on each click?

What can and can't be animated

With the `animate` method, you can also dynamically alter font properties to create text effects. You can also animate multiple CSS properties in one animation call, which adds to the palette of cool stuff your web app can do.

As cool as the `animate` method is, it has some limits. Under the hood, animation uses lots of math (which, thankfully, you don't have to worry about), so you are limited to working only with CSS properties that have *numerical* settings. Know your limits, but let your imagination run wild—`animate` offers all kinds of flexibility and fun.

Text effects

I'm shrinking, shrinking!
Oh, what a world, what a world!

I'm shrinking, shrinking!
Oh, what a world, what a world!

I'm shrinking, shrinking!
Oh, what a world, what a world!

I'm shrinking, shrinking!
Oh, what a world, what a world!

I'm shrinking, shrinking!
Oh, what a world, what a world!

You can animate CSS font properties to create the illusion of text flying, growing, or shrinking.

These are just a few examples. We'd need many, many, many more pages to show all of the possibilities.

Watch it!

The `animate` method will only work on CSS properties that use numbers for their settings.

- borders, margin, padding
- element height, min-height, and max-height
- element width, min-width, and max-width
- font size

- bottom, left, right, and top position
- background position
- letter spacing, word spacing
- text indent
- line height

The animate Method Up Close

On the surface, `animate` works a lot like other methods you've already worked with.

Select the element(s) you want to animate.

Call the animate method.

The first parameter of animate allows you to select the CSS property you want to animate.

The second parameter is the duration in milliseconds. This lets you control how long it takes for the animation to complete.

```
$("#my_div").animate({left:"100px"},500);
```

In this example, we're animating the CSS property left...

...and setting it to 100 px.

The first argument is required—you have to put it in there for animate to work. The second parameter is optional.

But one of the most powerful features of `animate` is its ability to change multiple properties of the selected element(s) at the same time.

```
$("#my_div").animate({
    opacity: 0,
    width: "200",
    height: "800"
}, 5000);
```

In this example, we're animating the element's opacity and size simultaneously.

The parameters for CSS properties have to be set using the <u>DOM</u> standard, not the CSS standard.

Watch it!

BRAIN BARBELL

What do you think is happening behind the scenes in the browser that allows the `animate` method to change things in front of the user's eyes?

animate changes style over time

The visual effects and animation you see on a movie or television screen use the illusion of motion. Effects technicians and animators take a sequence of images and play them **one at a time at a specific rate** to accomplish that illusion—you've likely seen the low-tech flip books that accomplish this effect as you fan through the pages.

The same thing happens with a browser screen, except that we don't have a series of images to work with. Instead, the JavaScript interpreter **repeatedly runs a function that changes the style of the animated element**. The browser draws (or *repaints*) these changes to the screen. The user sees an illusion of motion or change to an element as that element's style changes.

1 When animate runs, the JavaScript interpreter sets a timer for the duration of the animation.

Change the CSS left property to 500px over a duration of 400 milliseconds.

JavaScript interpreter

If you don't specify a value for the duration parameter in the animate method, it will default to 400 milliseconds.

2 The JavaScript interpreter tells the browser's layout engine to change the CSS property specified in the parameters of the animate method. The browser's layout engine renders those CSS properties visually onto the screen.

I'd like to schedule a repaint of the screen, please.

Looks like I can fit that in over a few milliseconds.

The browser's layout engine

JavaScript interpreter

3 The JavaScript interpreter repeatedly calls the function that changes the CSS property of the element until the timer set in step 1 runs out. Each time that function runs, the change shows on screen.

4 The visitor sees the illusion of movement as the browser renders the changes to the element.

The browser

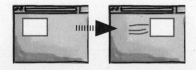

Match each chunk of custom animation code to what it does when it runs.

```
$("#my_div").animate({top: "150px"}, "slow")
```
                            Animates the change to all paragraphs'
                            left and right margins simultaneously.

```
$("p").animate({
    marginLeft:"150px",
    marginRight:"150px"
});
```
        Animates the right position of
        #my_div to 0 in half a second.

```
$("#my_div").animate({width: "30%"}, 250)
```
        Animates the space between letters for
        all paragraphs with default duration
        of 400 seconds.

```
$("#my_div").animate({right: "0"}, 500)
```
        Animates the change to #my_div's
        padding and width simultaneously.

```
$("p").animate({letterSpacing:"15px"});
```
        Animates the change to #my_div's
        top position with a slow duration.

```
$("#my_div").animate({
    padding: "200px",
    width: "30%"
}, "slow")
```
        Animates the height of all images with
        a fast duration.

```
$("img").animate({height: "20px"}, "fast")
```
        Animates the change to #my_div's
        width in a quarter of a second.

Match each chunk of custom animation code to what it does when it runs.

```
$("#my_div").animate({top: "150px"}, "slow")
```

Animates the change to all paragraphs' left and right margins simultaneously.

```
$("p").animate({
      marginLeft:"150px",
      marginRight:"150px"
});
```

Animates the right position of #my_div to 0 in half a second.

```
$("#my_div").animate({width: "30%"}, 250)
```

Animates the space between letters for all paragraphs with default duration of 400 seconds.

```
$("#my_div").animate({right: "0"}, 500)
```

Animates the change to #my_div's padding and width simultaneously.

```
$("p").animate({letterSpacing:"15px"});
```

Animates the change to #my_div's top position with a slow duration.

```
$("#my_div").animate({
      padding: "200px",
      width: "30%"
}, "slow")
```

Animates the height of all images with a fast duration.

```
$("img").animate({height: "20px"}, "fast")
```

Animates the change to #my_div's width in a quarter of a second.

From where to where *exactly?*

An important thing to remember about `animate` is that it changes the *current* CSS property to the CSS property that you set *in the first parameter*. To make your custom animation effective, you need to think hard about what you have currently set in the CSS. In the previous example, we changed the left position of `#my_div` to 100px. What will happen on screen depends entirely on the current CSS `left` property setting of `#my_div`.

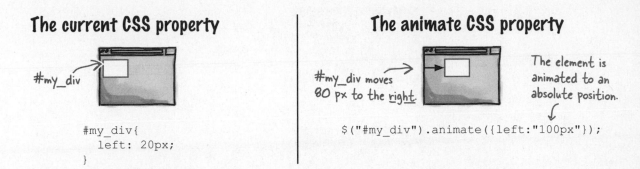

The current CSS property

#my_div

```
#my_div{
    left: 20px;
}
```

The animate CSS property

#my_div moves 80 px to the right.

The element is animated to an absolute position.

```
$("#my_div").animate({left:"100px"});
```

If the current property is a different value, we'll get a different result.

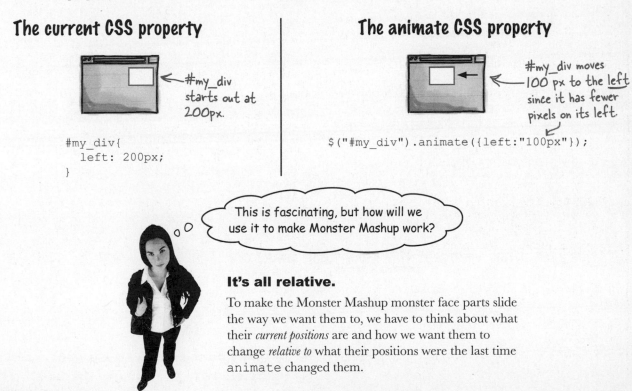

The current CSS property

#my_div starts out at 200px.

```
#my_div{
    left: 200px;
}
```

The animate CSS property

#my_div moves 100 px to the left since it has fewer pixels on its left.

```
$("#my_div").animate({left:"100px"});
```

> This is fascinating, but how will we use it to make Monster Mashup work?

It's all relative.

To make the Monster Mashup monster face parts slide the way we want them to, we have to think about what their *current positions* are and how we want them to change *relative to* what their positions were the last time `animate` changed them.

Absolute vs. relative element movement

Remember that we nested the image strips we want to show inside a `div` with an ID of `#pic_box`. The `left` property of `div#pic_box` is set to 91px in the current CSS. To achieve the left slide effect that we want, let's think about how we want to move the image strips.

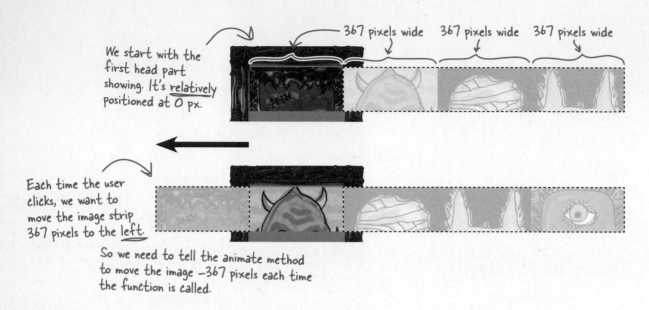

We start with the first head part showing. It's relatively positioned at 0 px.

367 pixels wide   367 pixels wide   367 pixels wide

Each time the user clicks, we want to move the image strip 367 pixels to the left.

So we need to tell the animate method to move the image −367 pixels each time the function is called.

Think about the example of absolute animation on the previous page.

This tells the animate method to set the left position of #my_div to 100 pixels exactly.

But how do we tell it to move an element −367 pixels every time the animate method is called?

```
$("#my_div").animate({left:"100px"});
```

```
$("#head").animate({left:"???"});
```

Relative animation = move it <u>this</u> much each time

With an *absolute* animation, you move an element to an *absolute postion* on the visual grid. With a *relative* animation, you move the element relative to where it was the *last time* any animation moved it.

But how do we make an element move relatively with the `animate` method?

Move stuff relatively with operator combinations

There are some special JavaScript operators that move element(s) the same amount every time the `animate` method is called. These are known as *assignment operators* because they are normally used to assign a value to a variable in such a way that the variable adds the new value to its current value. It sounds a lot more complex than it really is.

The equals sign is an assignment operator.

When you combine arithmetic operators with equals, you end up with some useful shorthand.

$$a = 20$$

$$a \mathrel{+}= 30 \qquad a \mathrel{-}= 10$$

The = operator assigns the value 20 to the variable a.

The plus combined with the equals operator is shorthand for "a = a + 30."

Here, the minus combined with the equals operator is shorthand for "a = a - 10."

These operator combinations help you create a relative animation by allowing you to set a value to what it's currently at *plus or minus* a number of pixels.

This moves the element with an ID of box 20 pixels every time the animate method is called.

```
$("#box").animate({left:"+=20"});
```

Here's what will happen to `#box` every time the `animate` method above is called.

Let's say left starts at 0.

animate runs and sets left to += 20.

animate runs and sets left to += 20.

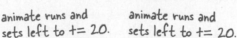

left = 0   left = 20   left = 40

By advancing the element's left position each time, we're actually moving it to the right in the browser window.

BULLET POINTS

Some other assignment operator combinations:

- a `*=` 5 is shorthand for "multiply 5 by the current value of a and assign that value to a.

- a `/=` 2 is shorthand for "dIvide the current value of a by 2 and assign that value to a.

Exercise

Write the line of jQuery code that will accomplish each of the steps shown below.

1 Move the `#head` element 367 pixels to the left every time `animate` is called. Give it a duration of half a second.

....

2 Move the `#head` element back to its original position (`left:0px`). Give it a duration of half a second.

....

Exercise Solution

Write the line of jQuery code that will accomplish each of the steps shown below.

1 Move the `#head` element 367 pixels to the left every time `animate` is called.
Give it a duration of half a second.

$("#head").animate({left:"-=367px"},500);

2 Move the `#head` element back to its original position (`left:0px`).
Give it a duration of half a second.

$("#head").animate({left:"0px"},500); ← *This absolute animation resets the monster head, giving it the appearance of rewinding.*

---

there are no
Dumb Questions

Q: Some people don't want animation to interfere with their web page experience. What do I do if I want to let a user turn off the animation?

A: That's an excellent point. Animation can cause annoyance and accessibility problems. If you want users to turn off your web page animation, you can wire up a click button (you already know how to do that) to this line of code:

```
$.fx.off = true;
```

Another useful method for stopping animation is a jQuery method called `stop`. You can find out more about both of these topics at the jQuery site:

http://api.jquery.com/jQuery.fx.off/
http://api.jquery.com/stop/

Q: You say, "The parameters for CSS properties have to be set using the DOM standard, not the CSS standard." What the heck does that mean?

A: Great question! The `animate` method takes parameters written in the DOM standard (aka DOM notation) instead of CSS notation.

Here's a concrete example that illustrates the difference. To set the width of a border for a `div` in CSS notation, you would do this:

```
div {
border-style:solid;
border-width:5px;
}
```

Now, let's say you want to animate that border's width. In jQuery you set the border width property using DOM notation, like this:

```
$("div").animate({borderWi
dth:30},"slow");
```

Note that in the CSS notation, you write `border-width` for the property, whereas in DOM notation, you write `borderWidth` property.

If you want to read more about the difference between these two notation styles, read this article:

http://www.oxfordu.net/webdesign/dom/straight_text.html

Q: What if I want to animate a color change?

A: To animate color transitions, you need to use jQuery UI, which adds more effects than are included in jQuery. We cover jQuery UI in Chapter 10, but not effects. Once you know how to download, theme, and include jQuery UI in your web app, animating color is pretty easy.

Add the animate functions to your script

Using the code you put together in the exercise on the previous page,
update your script file for Monster Mashup.

Do this!

```
$("#head").click(function(){
    if (headclix < 9){
        $(this).animate({left:"-=367px"},500);
        headclix+=1;
    }
    else{
        $(this).animate({left:"0px"},500);
        headclix = 0;
    }
});
```

We can use the "this" keyword here,
because we're inside the function for
the element we clicked.

```
$("#eyes").click(function(){
    if (eyeclix < 9){
        $(this).animate({left:"-=367px"},500);
        eyeclix+=1;
    }
    else{
        $(this).animate({left:"0px"},500);
        eyeclix = 0;
    }
});

$("#nose").click(function(){
    if (noseclix < 9){
        $(this).animate({left:"-=367px"},500);
        noseclix+=1;
    }
    else{
        $(this).animate({left:"0px"},500);
        noseclix = 0;
    }
});

$("#mouth").click(function(){
    if (mouthclix < 9){
        $(this).animate({left:"-=367px"},500);
        mouthclix+=1;
    }
    else{
        $(this).animate({left:"0px"},500);
        mouthclix = 0;
    }
```

my_scripts.js

TEST DRIVE

Open the page up in your favorite browser to make sure everything's working.

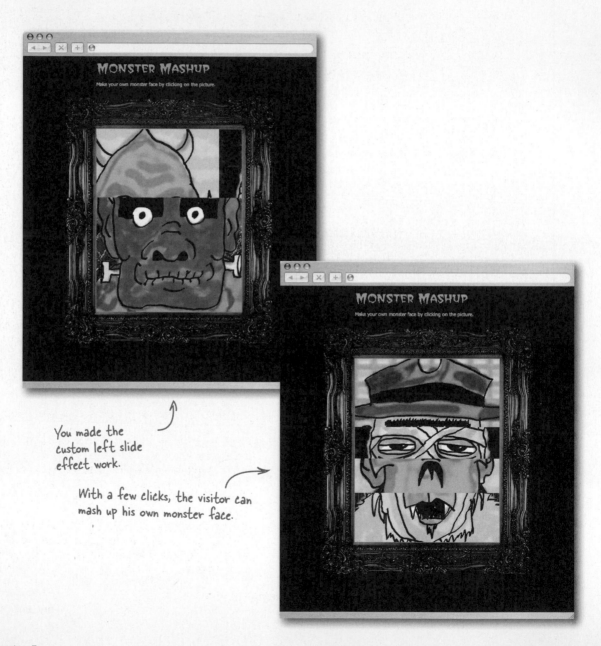

You made the custom left slide effect work.

With a few clicks, the visitor can mash up his own monster face.

jQueryCross

It's time to sit back and give your left brain something to do. It's your standard crossword; all of the solution words are from this chapter.

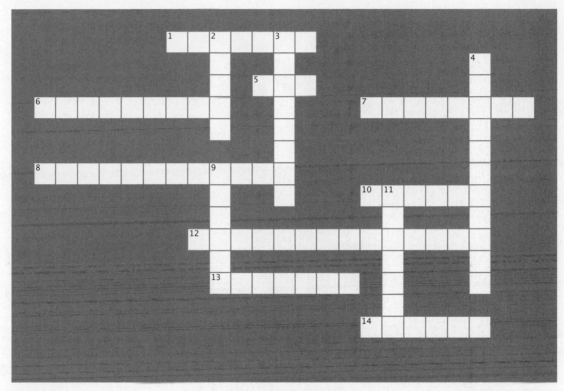

Across

1. `hide`, `show`, and `toggle` animate this CSS property.
5. jQuery effects and animation are about manipulating ___ on the fly.
6. _____ = 1,000 milliseconds.
7. Parameter that controls how long it takes for the effect to complete.
8. Creates the illusion of an element moving on the screen.
10. Effect method that lets you animate the selected element to a specific opacity.
12. jQuery feature that allows you to link together methods you want to run on a returned set of elements.
13. The `animate` method will only work on CSS properties that have _____ values.
14. You can animate CSS _____ and `width` properties to create the illusion of growing or shrinking an element.

Down

2. The effect to use when you want to animate an element's `height` property.
3. When you want to animate elements, you need their position property set to _____, `fixed`, or `relative`.
4. Effects method works like this: if the selected element has a height of 0, the JS interpreter slides it down. If the element is at its full height, the JS interpreter slides the elements up.
9. When you run this jQuery effect, the JS interpreter changes the CSS opacity property for the selected element from 0 to 100.
11. The jQuery library offers this method when you want to build custom effects.

Look, Ma, no Flash!

The web projects director is pleased with the results of Monster Mashup. You used jQuery's out-of-the-box effects combined with your own custom effects tailored to the customer's needs.

Our 6- to 10-year age group loves Monster Mashup. And we don't need to use Flash or browser plug-ins. Wow, jQuery is a good fit for us!

This is awesome! I'm going to scare my little sister with the monster I made!

This is cool! I've made so many monsters, I've lost count!

 **jQueryCross Solution**

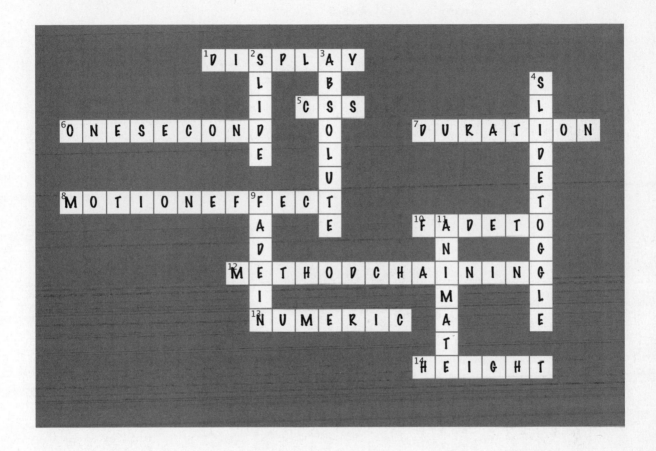

The completed crossword puzzle reads:

1 Across: DISPLAY
5 Across: CSS
6 Across: ONESECOND
7 Across: DURATION
8 Across: MOTIONEFFECT
10 Across: FADETO
12 Across: METHODCHAINING
13 Across: NUMERIC
14 Across: HEIGHT

2 Down: SLIDE
3 Down: ABSOLUTE
4 Down: SLIDETOGGLE
9 Down: FADIN
11 Down: ANIMAT

Your jQuery Toolbox

You've got Chapter 5 under your belt and now you've added jQuery fade and slide effects plus custom animation to your toolbox.

Fade effects

Change the opacity property of CSS elements:

fadeIn

fadeOut

fadeTo

Slide effects

Change the height property of CSS elements:

slideUp

slideDown

slideToggle

animate

Lets you create custom animations when out-of-the-box jQuery effects aren't enough.

Animates CSS properties over time.

Only works with CSS properties that have numerical settings.

Elements can be moved either absolutely or relatively.

Operator combinations (=, +, −) make relative animation much easier.

6 jQuery and JavaScript

~~Luke~~ jQuery, I am your father!

There are just some things you can't do on your own, son...

jQuery can't do it all alone. Although it is a JavaScript library, unfortunately it can't do everything its parent language can do. In this chapter, we'll look at some of the features of JavaScript that you'll need to create really compelling sites, and how jQuery can use them to create custom lists and objects as well as loop through those lists and objects to make your life much easier.

Spicing up the Head First Lounge

Lucky you, news of your jQuery prowess is spreading far and wide. Check out this email from the Head First Lounge asking for some help to increase the entertainment level for its visitors.

From: **Head First Lounge**
Subject: **Blackjack Application**

Hi!

It's your pals over at the Head First Lounge. We're hoping you can help us out with a new application we want to give to our visitors.

We would REALLY like a blackjack application for our site. Can you do that?

Ideally, the player would click and get dealt two cards, with the option to ask for more cards.

Here's the house rules we would want included in the game:

1. Ace is ALWAYS high (equaling 11, never 1).

2. If a player's cards add up to more than 21, then she is bust and must start again. The game is over.

3. If a player's cards add up to exactly 21, then she has gotten a blackjack and the game is over.

4. If a player's cards add up to 21 or less, but she has already been dealt five cards, then the game is over, and she wins.

If none of those conditions is met, players can ask for another card.

If one of the rules/conditions is met, then end the game.

Give the players the option to reset and play again.

But we don't want them to have to reload the page. The game should reset itself.

Can you do that for us? We'd be ever so grateful!

--

Frank

Joe

Jim

Jim: Hey, have you guys read the email from the Head First Lounge folks?

Frank: Yeah, it looks like they want an easy-to-play blackjack game on their site. Should be pretty straightforward, I think.

Jim: Straightforward? But it's blackjack! We need a deck of cards, a dealer, a counter for the hand, and more. Do you think we can do all that?

Joe: It's not going to be *easy*, but I think we can get it done. Like you said, we'll need something to deal the cards. We can write a function to do that. We've already written a random function before, so we can probably use that again.

Jim: Oh yeah… But what about the cards? There are 52 of them in a deck.

Frank: We can just have a big list of them and pick a random one from the list each time.

Jim: But how do we avoid picking the same card twice?

Frank: I think I know how to do that…

Jim: Wow, that's impressive! And what about remembering which cards we have already? And counting them up as we go?

Frank: OK, now you've got me. I'm not too sure how to do that.

Joe: No worries. There are quite a few JavaScript and jQuery features we can use to help us out here.

Jim: Wait, wait, JavaScript? Can't we use variables or jQuery arrays to remember our cards? I thought we really didn't have to get into a bunch of JavaScript if we're using jQuery…

Frank: Variables on their own may not cut it. They can only really store one value at a time, like a number or a string of text, or a particular element on the page. And a jQuery array can hold multiple values, but only of DOM elements returned by a selector…

Joe: That's right. We need something a little more flexible.

Frank: Like *our own* structures or variable types.

Joe: Correct again! And we're going to need JavaScript to create our own structures…

Objects offer even smarter storage

The data structures you've used so far are variables and arrays. Variables offer simple storage: they assign one value to one name. Arrays let you store more data more efficiently by letting you create multiple values with one variable name.

Variable

A variable remembers one value when you assign the value to the variable name.

```
var a = 42;
```

Array

An array remembers multiple values when you assign those values to the variable name.

```
var v = [2, 3, 4]
```

Objects offer even smarter storage. You use objects when you need to store multiple variables about a particular thing. Inside of an object, a variable is called a *property*. An object can also contain functions that let you interact with the object's properties. When you build such a function inside of an object, it's called a *method*.

Object

```
planeObject={
    engines:"4",
    type:"passenger",
    propellor: "No"};
```

An object remembers its data as properties.

The data is now collected under one grouping for a plane.

```
leopardObject={
    num_spots:"23",
    color:"brown"};
```

You associate a property name...   ...with a value.

You can get at any of an object's properties using dot syntax.

```
planeObject.engines;
leopardObject.color;
```

The object   Its property

Use objects when you need to store multiple pieces of data about a particular thing.

What properties might a card object have?

Build your own objects

Objects are essentially a way to create your own custom variables exactly how *you* want them. You can create one-time-use objects, or create your own object blueprint that you can use again and again. We'll look at reusable objects in a little bit, but for now let's discuss how to create a one-time-use object and some of the terms and diagrams associated with an object.

Objects can be described in a standard way, using a UML (Unified Modeling Language) diagram. UML is a general-purpose, worldwide standard for helping to describe objects in object-oriented programming.

When an object has a variable associated with it, we call that a *property* of the object. When an object has a function associated with it, we call that a *method* of the object. You create one-time-use objects using the `var` keyword, just like for all the other variables you've seen so far.

UML diagram of an object

This structure helps you see how your object is structured before you write any code.

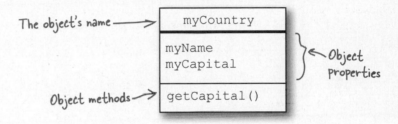

The object's name ⟶ | myCountry
myName
myCapital ⟶ Object properties

Object methods ⟶ getCapital()

And here's how you'd write that object in code:

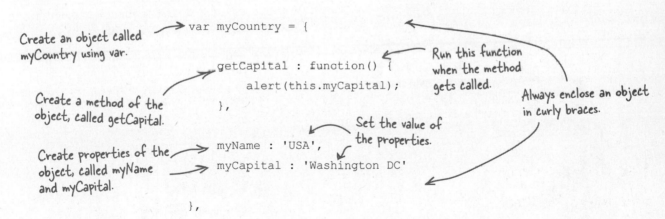

Create an object called myCountry using var. ⟶ `var myCountry = {`

Create a method of the object, called getCapital. ⟶ `getCapital : function() {`
`    alert(this.myCapital);`
`},`

Run this function when the method gets called.

Set the value of the properties.

Create properties of the object, called myName and myCapital. ⟶ `myName : 'USA',`
`myCapital : 'Washington DC'`

Always enclose an object in curly braces.

`},`

Relax

As it turns out, nearly everything in jQuery and JavaScript is an object.

This includes elements, arrays, functions, numbers, even strings—and they all have properties and methods.

Create reusable objects with object constructors

One really nice aspect of objects is that they can have the same structure but hold different values for their properties (or variables). Just like creating reusable functions—like we did in Chapter 3—we can create an object blueprint, or *object constructor*, so we can use it multiple times. An object constructor can also be used to create *instances* of the object.

The constructor is just a function, so in order to create a constructor for an object, you use the keyword `function` instead of the keyword `var`. Then, use the `new` keyword to create a new instance of the object.

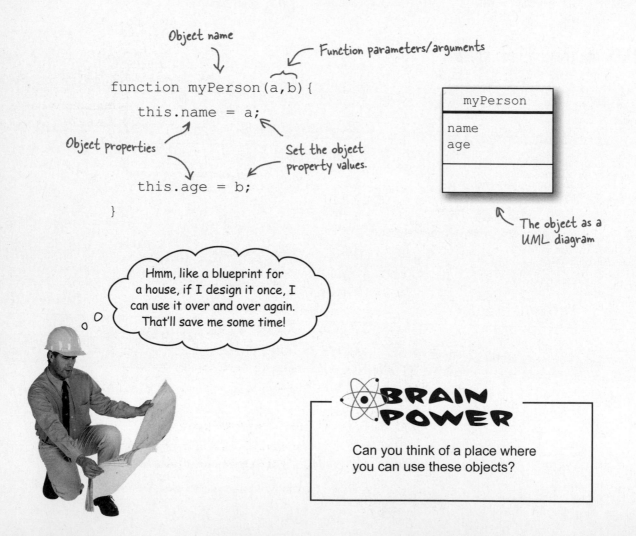

Object name

Function parameters/arguments

```
function myPerson(a,b){
    this.name = a;

    this.age = b;
}
```

Object properties

Set the object property values.

myPerson
name
age

The object as a UML diagram

Hmm, like a blueprint for a house, if I design it once, I can use it over and over again. That'll save me some time!

BRAIN POWER

Can you think of a place where you can use these objects?

Interacting with objects

Objects come in all shapes and sizes. After you *instantiate* (or create an instance of)
an object—whether it is an object you created or one created by someone else—you
interact with it using the dot (.) operator. To get a feel for how this works, let's take a
closer look at the `myCountry` and `myPerson` objects that we just defined.

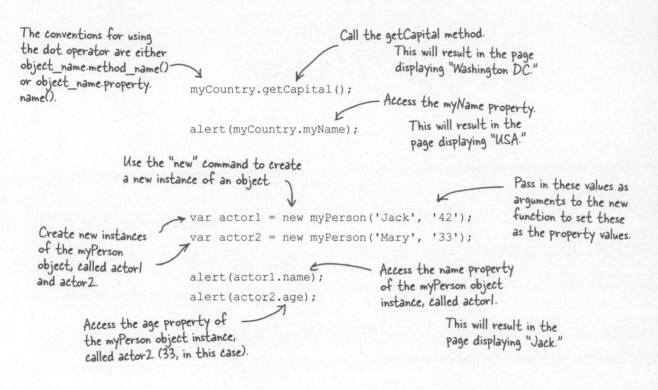

The conventions for using
the dot operator are either
object_name.method_name()
or object_name.property.
name().

```
myCountry.getCapital();
```

Call the getCapital method.
This will result in the page
displaying "Washington DC."

```
alert(myCountry.myName);
```

Access the myName property.
This will result in the
page displaying "USA."

Use the "new" command to create
a new instance of an object.

Pass in these values as
arguments to the new
function to set these
as the property values.

```
var actor1 = new myPerson('Jack', '42');
var actor2 = new myPerson('Mary', '33');
```

Create new instances
of the myPerson
object, called actor1
and actor2.

```
alert(actor1.name);
alert(actor2.age);
```

Access the name property
of the myPerson object
instance, called actor1.

Access the age property of
the myPerson object instance,
called actor2 (33, in this case).

This will result in the
page displaying "Jack."

Ah, I think I get how this works... Could
I create an object to represent cards in
a deck for the Head First Lounge?

Yes! That's a great idea.

Let's set up the HTML page and then have a look at
how we can go about creating a card object.

Set up the page

Create your HMTL and CSS files using the information below.
Don't forget to create a *my_scripts.js* file, too, in your *scripts* folder.
We'll be adding plenty of code to that in the coming pages. You
can download all the image resources for the entire chapter from
http://thinkjquery.com/chapter06/images.zip.

Do this!

```css
#controls{
    clear:both;
}
#my_hand{
    clear:both;
    border: 1px solid gray;
    height: 250px;
    width: 835px;
}
h3 {
    display: inline;
    padding-right: 40px;
}
.current_hand{
    float:left;
}
```

my_style.css

```html
<!DOCTYPE html>
<html>
    <head>
        <title>Head First Black Jack</title>
        <link href="styles/my_style.css" rel="stylesheet">
    </head>
    <body>
        <div id="main">
            <h1>Click to reveal your cards</h1>
            <h3 id="hdrTotal"></h3><h3 id="hdrResult"></h3>
            <div id="my_hand">
            </div>
            <div id="controls">
                <div id="btnDeal">
                    <img src="images/deck_small.jpg">
                </div>
            </div>
        </div>
        <script src="scripts/jquery-1.6.2.min.js"></script>
        <script src="scripts/my_scripts.js"></script>
    </body>
</html>
```

index.html

Am I going to get
to deal these cards
sometime soon??

TEST DRIVE

Open up the *index.html* page you just created in your favorite browser to see the basic structure of the page.

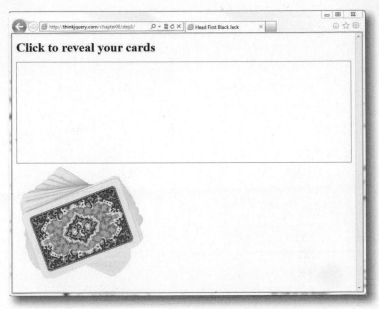

Exercise

Using the UML diagram for a card object given below, create a reusable object called `card` that takes three parameters called `name`, `suit`, and `value`. Set these parameters as the values of the object's properties. This particular object doesn't have any methods. We've filled in some of the code for you already.

card
name
suit
value

```
function card(                          ) {




}
```

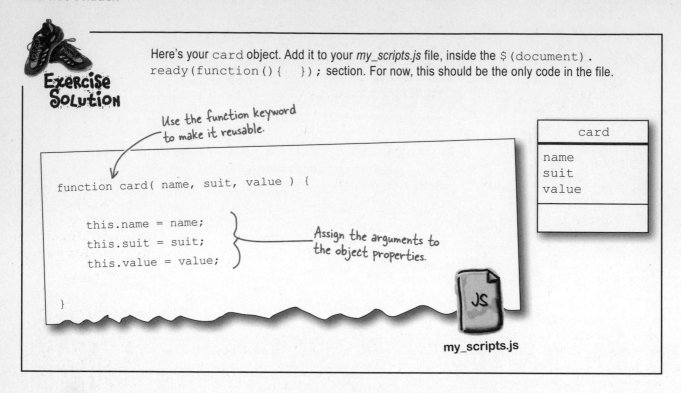

Exercise Solution

Here's your `card` object. Add it to your *my_scripts.js* file, inside the `$(document).ready(function(){ });` section. For now, this should be the only code in the file.

Use the function keyword to make it reusable.

```
function card( name, suit, value ) {

    this.name = name;
    this.suit = suit;
    this.value = value;

}
```

Assign the arguments to the object properties.

card
name
suit
value

my_scripts.js

---

there are no Dumb Questions

Q: What's the difference between one-time and reusable objects?

A: One-time use objects are simply a fancy variable defined to hold multiple pieces of information. Reusable objects are just that—reusable. After you define the template for a reusable object with its properties/methods, you can create as many copies of this object as you want—each with different information describing the object.

Q: It looks like you're using different ways of setting properties. Is that right?

A: Yes, we are, and yes, it is. You can assign the value of properties using the assignment operator (=) or the colon (:) symbol, just as we did for our objects. Both are valid and interchangeable.

Q: Anything else about objects you're not telling me?

A: That's a tough one. They are a pretty complex feature in JavaScript. Later in the book, we'll use JavaScript Object Notation, aka JSON. Using JSON, we'll access properties with a slightly different method, which can also be applied to your JavaScript objects here. That is the "key" notation. Rather than doing:

```
object.my_property
```

you can do the following:

```
object['my_property']
```

and get the same result—access to the value of `my_property`.

Q: Where did UML come from?

A: UML was born in the mid-90s when companies were trying to get a clear method of describing objects. There have been several iterations of it since, with several private companies competing to have their version as the accepted standard. Thankfully, though, there is a standard, and anyone using UML will be able to read and understand diagrams and information from other UML sources.

So that card object is going to be super useful, but we still need some way of keeping track of individual cards as they're played, right?

You're right.

We need a way to store and access cards as they're dealt. Good thing is, we've already seen how to do this…

It's me again! You've already worked with me a bit back in Chapter 4.

The return of arrays

As you've already seen, we can group several items into a single structure called an array. The items in an array are not necessarily related to one another, but accessing their values becomes a lot easier this way. Back in Chapter 4, we saw how a jQuery selector returns items and stores them in an array. Now we're going to use JavaScript to get even more utility out of arrays.

Variables in an array can be any type, including strings, numbers, objects, even HTML elements! There are several different ways of creating your own arrays:

Create an empty array, using the "new" keyword.
```
var my_arr1 = new Array();
```

Create an array, using the "new" keyword, and also say what the values of the array are.
```
var my_arr2 = new Array('USA', 'China', 'Japan', 'Ireland');
```

```
var my_arr3 = ['USA', 'China', 'Japan', 'Ireland'];
```
Create an array, without the "new" keyword, but set the values by enclosing them in square [ ] brackets.

And, as we mentioned earlier, arrays are objects too, which means they have methods and properties. A common array property is `length`. This denotes how many items there are in the array. You can access the `length` property with `array_name.length`.

Watch it!

There is no difference between the various ways of creating arrays.

It's common to mix and match the different ways, depending on the array's purpose. Look up "JavaScript array methods" in your favorite search engine to find all the methods the array object has.

Accessing arrays

Unlike with creating arrays, there is only one way to access the information inside an array. Arrays are *zero-indexed*—that is, their position (or index) in the list starts at 0. We used the index back in Chapter 3, so you can always go back there for a refresher if this isn't clicking.

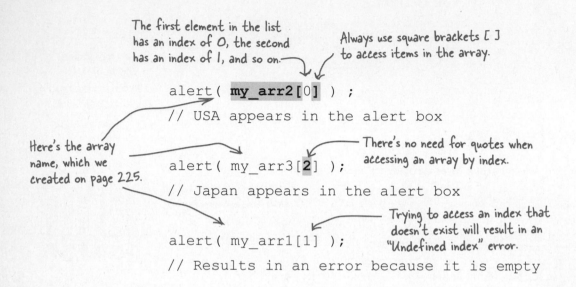

The first element in the list has an index of 0, the second has an index of 1, and so on.

Always use square brackets [ ] to access items in the array.

```
alert( my_arr2[0] ) ;
// USA appears in the alert box
```

Here's the array name, which we created on page 225.

There's no need for quotes when accessing an array by index.

```
alert( my_arr3[2] );
// Japan appears in the alert box
```

Trying to access an index that doesn't exist will result in an "Undefined index" error.

```
alert( my_arr1[1] );
// Results in an error because it is empty
```

The index of an item in a list refers to where it appears in the list.

OK, so now we've got an array with some stuff in it, but are we stuck with what we initially put in there?

Definitely not!

It's easy to add, change, and delete items in an array. Let's take a look at how.

Add and update items in arrays

We can add as many items to an array as we want. In the example on the
previous pages, we prepopulated some items into the `my_arr2` and `my_arr3`
arrays, but we left the `my_arr1` array empty. We can add or update items in
an array, and to do that, it's again all about the index. Here are a few different
approaches to updating an array:

*Set the value of the <u>first</u>
item in the my_arr1 array.*

```
my_arr1[0] = "France";

alert( my_arr1[0] );

// Displays 'France' on the screen
```

*Add a second value to
the my_arr1 array.*

```
my_arr1[1] = "Spain" ;
```

*Update the value of the first
item in the my_arr1 array.*

```
my_arr1[0] = "Italy" ;

alert( my_arr1[0] );

// Displays 'Italy' on the screen
```

*Update the value of the third
item in the my_arr3 array.*

```
my_arr3[2] = "Canada";

alert( my_arr3[2] );

// Displays 'Canada' on the screen
```

Exercise

In your *my_scripts.js* file, after the `card` object code, create an array called
`deck` with all 52 cards in a standard deck in it.

You can use the `card` object you've already created and call the constructor each
time with the correct parameters to create each card—Ace through King, for each of
the four suits (Clubs, Hearts, Diamonds, and Spades)—and the value of each card,
with "Ace" worth 11, "Two" worth 2, "Three" worth 3, and so on.

Exercise Solution

Your *my_scripts.js* file should now contain an array called `deck` with 52 cards from a standard deck in it, as well as the `card` object. You should use the `card` object you've already created and call the constructor each time with the correct parameters to create each card.

Set the name of the array.

Pass in the three parameters for each of the card objects.

```
var deck = [
    new card('Ace', 'Hearts',11),
    new card('Two', 'Hearts',2),
    new card('Three', 'Hearts',3),
    new card('Four', 'Hearts',4),




    new card('King', 'Hearts',10),
    new card('Ace', 'Diamonds',11),
    new card('Two', 'Diamonds',2),
    new card('Three', 'Diamonds',3),



    new card('Queen', 'Diamonds',10),
    new card('King', 'Diamonds',10),
    new card('Ace', 'Clubs',11),
    new card('Two', 'Clubs',2),



    new card('King', 'Clubs',10),
    new card('Ace', 'Spades',11),
    new card('Two', 'Spades',2),
    new card('Three', 'Spades',3),



    new card('Jack', 'Spades',10),
    new card('Queen', 'Spades',10),
    new card('King', 'Spades',10)
];
```

Remember to enclose the values in your array in square brackets.

my_scripts.js

But we have a lot of cards in an array now. It seems like we'd be writing a whole lot of code to get them back out again. What a pain!

Not necessarily.

We will still access each item by its index, but we can use a technique similar to `each`, which we saw back in Chapter 3, to access each item in turn without writing a ton of code for every card.

It's time to take a trip through Loopville…

Perform an action over (and over, and over...)

You're going to be putting cards into and getting info back out of arrays quite a bit for this blackjack game. Thankfully, JavaScript comes prepared for just this scenario with *loops*. And the ***even better*** news is you've already done this before: back in Chapter 3, you used the each jQuery method to loop through elements based on a jQuery selector. But in this case, we've got more options, as JavaScript has several different types of loops, each with a slightly different syntax, and each with its own purpose.

The for loop is great for repeating code a defined number of times. You should know this number before you start your loop, or it could go on forever. It can run zero or many times, depending on variable values.

The do...while loop will run your code once, and then will keep running the same code until a particular condition is met, like a value turns from true to false (or vice versa), or counting to a particular number is reached in the code. A do...while loop can run one or many times.

A for loop repeat cycle:

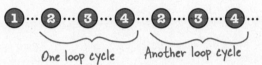

One loop cycle   Another loop cycle

A do...while loop repeat cycle:

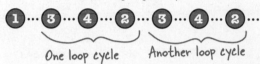

One loop cycle   Another loop cycle

for loops let you repeat code a defined number of times.

do...while loops let you run your code once and then repeat it until a particular condition is met.

Every loop, regardless of type, has four distinct parts:

1 **Initialization**
This takes place one time, at the start of the loop.

2 **Test condition**
This checks to see if the loop should stop or keep going for another round of running code, usually by checking the value of a variable.

3 **Action**
This is the code that is repeated each time we go through the loop.

4 **Update**
This portion updates the variables being used by the test condition to see if we should keep looping or not.

Good thing I like doing things over and over again!

Loops Up Close

Taking an up close look at the different loop types we mentioned, we can see that they each contain the four main elements, but in a slightly different order. This order reflects some of the main differences between the loop types.

for loops

Start with the word "for."

The section between the ( ) defines how long the loop is going to last.

Always enclose loops in curly brackets.

Declare a variable in the loop that you will use to access the index of the array. This variable in only used inside the loop. }

```
for( var i=0 ; i < my_arr2.length ; i++ ){
     ❸ alert( my_arr2[i] );
}
```

❶ ❷ ❹

Increase the index value as you go through the loop.

Access the array using the variable defined in the loop.

.length is a common method for all arrays. It tells you how many items the array has.

Close your loop's curly brackets.

for loop repeat cycle:

❶ ... ❷ ... ❸ ... ❹ ... ❷ ... ❸ ... ❹ ...

One loop cycle   Another loop cycle

do...while loops

Declare a variable in the loop that you will use to access the index of the array.

Remember, this variable is only used inside the loop.

```
var i=0;
```

Start with the word "do."

```
❶ do{
     ❸ alert(my_arr2[i]);
     i++; ❹
}while (i<=5); ❷
```

Remember to enclose loops in curly brackets.

Increase the conditional variable as you go through the loop.

End with the word "while."

Do...while loop repeat cycle:

❶ ... ❸ ... ❹ ... ❷ ... ❸ ... ❹ ... ❷ ...

One loop cycle   Another loop cycle

Wow, these loops should get us moving pretty quickly through all the cards. We'll have this app done in no time. What's next?

Frank

Jim

Joe

Frank: Well, we have our array of `card` objects, but we need to be able to pull out a card at random when we deal, right?

Joe: Yes, and thankfully, we've already written that `getRandom` function back in Chapter 3. That'll give us a random number each time to pull a card out of the array.

Jim: But what will we do with it then?

Frank: We're going to have to remember it. We have to be able to add up the total value of the cards to find out if the players went over 21 or not.

Joe: And for another reason. We can't give them the same card twice, so we also have to make sure it hasn't been dealt already.

Jim: Can we use a variable to remember the cards?

Frank: We can use an array variable…

Joe: Good thinking! We don't even have to store the cards; we can just store their index values. That way we can test if it's in our `used_cards` array.

Jim: Wow, that's impressive! How can we tell if a value is in an array?

Frank: Using a jQuery utility method called `inArray`.

Joe: That sounds handy. But I think we're going to need several functions to do this for us. We have to get a random number between 0 and 51, and we have to check if we've used it already. If we have, we need to try again. If not, we need to get the correct card out of the deck and remember the index of that card. And then we need to show that card to the player.

Jim: Sounds like a lot! How are we going to show the card to the player?

Frank: Well, we already have the images, and they're arranged by suit and named type, so we can use those attributes of the `card` object to put the image on the screen.

Joe: Exactly. We can create a DOM element and append it to the `my_hand div` element already on our page.

Frank: This `card` object is already paying dividends… Let's get to it!

Looking for the needle in a haystack

Often you'll need to see if a variable already exists in an array or not, so you don't end up duplicating data, or to prevent your code from adding the same thing several times to an array. This can be particularly useful if you use arrays to store things like a shopping cart or a wish list.

Create an array for stuff in the haystack.

But what if we want to find <u>where</u> this value is in our haystack array?

```
var haystack = new Array('hay', 'mouse', 'needle', 'pitchfork')
```

jQuery provides a whole host of *utility* methods to help us get particular tasks done more efficiently. These include functions for checking what type of browser the site visitor is using, for returning the current time, for merging arrays, or for removing duplicates from arrays.

The utility method that's useful for this particluar situation is the `inArray` method. It will return where in the array the value you're looking for is located (its index), if at all. If it cannot find the value in the array, it will return −1. Like other utility methods, `inArray` does not require a selector—it's called directly by the jQuery function or jQuery shortcut.

Create a variable to hold the return value of the function.

The value you're looking for

The array in which you want to look

```
var index = $.inArray( value, array );
```

The jQuery shortcut

The inArray utility method call

Here's the value you're looking for.

Here's the array you want to search.

```
var needle_index = $.inArray( 'needle', haystack );
```

BRAIN POWER

Which feature of the blackjack application needs to check if we've already used a value?

jQuery Blackjack Code Magnets

Arrange the magnets to write the code that will complete several functions to help you finish the blackjack game. The completed code should create two functions—`deal` and `hit`—as well as a click event listener for an element with the ID of `btnDeal`, and a new array variable called `used_cards` to remember what cards have been dealt already.

```
var used_cards = new _____();
function _____{
    for(var i=0;i<2;i++){
        hit();
    }
}
function getRandom(num){
    var my_num = Math.floor(_____*num);
    return my_num;
}
function _____{
    var good_card = false;
    do{
        var index = _____(52);
        if( !$.inArray(index, _____ ) > -1 ){
            good_card = true;
            var c = deck[ index ];
            _____[used_cards.length] = index;
            hand.cards[hand.cards.length] = c;
            var $d = $("<div>");
            $d.addClass("current_hand")
              .appendTo(_____);
            $("<img>").appendTo($d)
                    .attr( _____ , 'images/cards/' + c.suit + '/' + c.name + '.jpg'
)
                    .fadeOut('slow')
                    .fadeIn('slow');
        }
    }_____(!good_card);
    good_card = false;
}
$("#btnDeal").click( _____(){
    deal();
    $(this).toggle();
});
```

Magnets: `getRandom`, `deal()`, `used_cards`, `'src'`, `hit()`, `while`, `Array`, `"#my_hand"`, `function`, `used_cards`, `Math.random()`

my_scripts.js

jQuery Blackjack Code Magnets Solution

Here's the code to complete the `deal` and `hit` functions, as well as a click event listener for an element with the ID of `btnDeal`, and a new array variable called `used_cards` to remember what cards have been dealt already.

```javascript
var used_cards = new   Array   ();          Create an array to
function   deal()   {                        hold used cards.
    for(var i=0;i<2;i++){
        hit();                    Use a for loop to call the hit function twice.
    }
               The getRandom
}              function again!
function getRandom(num){
    var my_num = Math.floor(   Math.random()   *num);
    return my_num;
}
function   hit()   {
    var good_card = false;                        Check if you're already using the
    do{                                           card you've picked, by using the
        var index =    getRandom    (52);         inArray function.
The conditional  if( !$.inArray(index,   used_cards   ) > -1 ){
variable for the     good_card = true;
do...while loop.     var c = deck[ index ];       Get the card from
                                                  the deck array.
         used_cards   [used_cards.length] = index;
        hand.cards[hand.cards.length] = c;        Add the array index
        var $d = $("<div>");                      of the card to the
        $d.addClass("current_hand")               used_cards array.
          .appendTo(   "#my_hand"   );
        $("<img>").appendTo($d)
                  .attr(   'src'   , 'images/cards/' + c.suit + '/' + c.name + '.jpg'
                  .fadeOut('slow')     Make the card       Use properties of the
                  .fadeIn('slow');     flash on screen.    card object to build the
        }                                                  path to the image.
    }   while   (!good_card);      Try again, if you've
    good_card = false;            already used the card.
}
$("#btnDeal").click(   function   (){
    deal();              Call the deal function on click.
    $(this).toggle();
});
```

TEST DRIVE

Add all the code from the previous magnets exercise to your *my_scripts.js* file, after your `deck` array, and give it a try in your browser. Click on the deck of cards to deal your next hand of blackjack.

> Hey, I can only give out two cards. As the dealer, I'll nearly always win! But maybe we should make it fair. Can you build a way to give out more cards?

Sure, we can create an option to get more cards from the deck using the `hit` function we've already created.

We just need something to run that function, like a button click or similar. This adds a new wrinkle, too: now we have to remember and count which cards have been dealt out so we can tell if the player goes bust or not.

BRAIN POWER

Can you think of what we could use to remember all this different information?

 **Ready Bake HTML & CSS**

Since you're already a style and structure pro, we'll just give you the updated code for your *index.html* and *my_style.css* files so you can compare. You should see some changes to your page after you add in the new HTML and CSS code. We'll wire it all up in a little bit.

```html
<!DOCTYPE html>
<html>
    <head>
        <title>Head First Black Jack</title>
        <link href="styles/my_style.css" rel="stylesheet">
    </head>
    <body>
        <div id="main">
            <h1>Click to reveal your cards</h1>
            <h3 id="hdrTotal"></h3>
            <h3 id="hdrResult"></h3>
            <div id="my_hand">
            </div>
            <div id="controls">
                <div id="btnDeal">
                    <img src="images/deck_small.jpg">
                </div>
                <div id="btnHit">
                    <img src="images/deck_small.jpg">
                </div>
                <div id="btnStick">
                    <img src="images/stick_small.jpg">
                </div>
            </div>
        </div>
        <script src="scripts/jquery-1.6.2.min.js"></script>
        <script src="scripts/my_scripts.js"></script>
    </body>
</html>
```

Add new controls for the blackjack game.

Add some CSS for the new controls.

index.html

```css
#controls{
    clear:both;
}

.current_hand{
    float:left;
}

#my_hand{
    clear:both;
    border: 1px solid gray;
    height: 250px;
    width: 835px;
}

#btnHit, #btnStick, #btnRestart{
    display:none;
    float:left;
}

h3 {
    display: inline;
    padding-right: 40px;
}
```

my_style.css

there are no Dumb Questions

Q: Are there any other types of loops I should know about?

A: Yes, there are. There's the `while` loop, which is very similar to the `do...while` loop, except it does its conditional check at the start. There's also a `for...in` loop, which will loop through an object's properties and pull out the value of each one.

Q: So, I've started a loop going. Can I stop it in the middle?

A: Yes, you can, with a very simple command: `break`. Calling this anywhere in your loop will cause the loop to stop and proceed to the next piece of code after the loop.

Q: What's `appendTo`? I've only seen `append` before. Is there a difference?

A: With `append`, the selector calling the method is the container into which the content is inserted. With `appendTo`, on the other hand, the content comes before the method, either as a selector expression or as HTML markup created on the fly, and it is inserted into the target container.

Exercise

Using the UML diagram given below, create a one-time object called `hand`. The `cards` property should be a new empty array. The `current_total` property should be set to 0 (zero). The `sumCardTotal` method should loop through all the cards in the `cards` property and add their values together, and set this number as the value of the `current_total` property. Then, use the `current_total` value to set the value of the element with the ID of `hdrTotal`. We've started the object code for you.

```
var hand = {
    cards : new Array(),
    current_total : 0,

    sumCardTotal: function(){



    }
};
```

hand
cards current_total
sumCardTotal()

Exercise Solution

Now you've got a `hand` object with a `card` property (that's an array) and a function that loops through the `card` array, gets the current card, and updates the current total.

hand
cards current_total
sumCardTotal()

```
var hand = {
    cards : new Array(),
    current_total : 0,

    sumCardTotal: function(){
        this.current_total = 0;
        for(var i=0;i<this.cards.length;i++){
            var c = this.cards[i];
            this.current_total += c.value;
        }
        $("#hdrTotal").html("Total: " + this.current_total );
    }
};
```

Set the card property to be a new array.

Set the current_total property to 0.

Loop through the card array.

Get the current card from the array.

Add the value to current_total.

Output the total count to the screen, in the hdrTotal element.

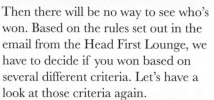

But I don't see anything there that'll tell me if I won. Won't I just get *all* the cards?

We definitely don't want that.

Then there will be no way to see who's won. Based on the rules set out in the email from the Head First Lounge, we have to decide if you won based on several different criteria. Let's have a look at those criteria again.

1 If a player's cards add up to more than 21, then she is bust and must start again. The game is over.

2 If a player's cards add up to exactly 21, then she has a blackjack, and the game is over.

3 If a player's cards add up to 21 or less, but she has already been dealt five cards, then the game is over, and she wins.

4 Otherwise, the player can choose to get another card or stop playing.

Decision making time...again!

Back in Chapter 3, we looked at using conditional logic to run different code based on decisions you want your code to make, given information it already has.

Start the if statement.

The thing we want to check

A JavaScript variable

```
if ( myBool == true ){
    // Do Something!
}else{
    // Otherwise Do something else!
}
```

The equality operator. This can be read as "is equal to."

The code we want to run, if what we check turns out to be true

As it turns out, there's an additional option for making more than a single decision at a time. By combining `if` and `else` statements into a composite statement called `else if`, you can check several conditions all inside one statement. Let's take a look.

The thing we want to check

Another thing we want to check for

```
if ( myNumber < 10 ){
    // Do Something!
}else if ( myNumber > 20 ){
    // Do something else!
}else{
    // Finally, Do something even different!
}
```

Can you think of where in your code you could use a `if` / `else if` / `else` statement?

Comparison and logical operators

For conditional logic statements (like `if/else` or `do...while`) to work properly, they have to be able to make the right decision based on what they are checking for. To do this, they use a series of *comparison* and *logical* operators to help them make the decision. In JavaScript, there are seven different comparison operators and three logical operators, as well as a shorthand operator for the `if/else` statement, called the *ternary* operator. We've seen some of these already, but here's the full list.

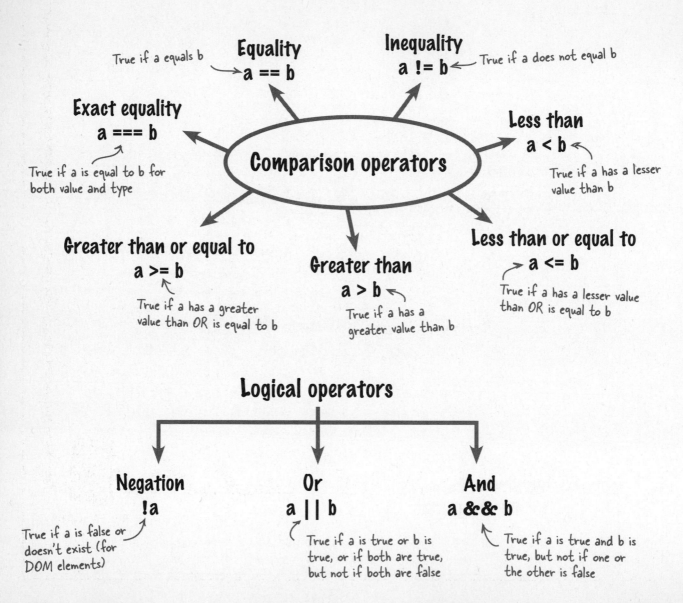

Equality
a == b
True if a equals b

Inequality
a != b
True if a does not equal b

Exact equality
a === b
True if a is equal to b for both value and type

Less than
a < b
True if a has a lesser value than b

Comparison operators

Greater than or equal to
a >= b
True if a has a greater value than OR is equal to b

Greater than
a > b
True if a has a greater value than b

Less than or equal to
a <= b
True if a has a lesser value than OR is equal to b

Logical operators

Negation
!a
True if a is false or doesn't exist (for DOM elements)

Or
a || b
True if a is true or b is true, or if both are true, but not if both are false

And
a && b
True if a is true and b is true, but not if one or the other is false

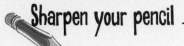
Sharpen your pencil

Update your `hand` object to check if the value of the `current_total` property meets the criteria for the game (go back and check the original email if you don't remember all the rules). Here's the existing object, as well as pieces of the new code you need to write.

```
var hand = {
    cards : new Array(),
    current_total : 0,

    sumCardTotal: function(){
        this.current_total = 0;
        for(var i=0;i<this.cards.length;i++){
            var c = this.cards[i];
            this.current_total += c.value;
        }
        $("#hdrTotal").html("Total: " + this.current_total );
        if(this._____ > 21){
            $("#btnStick").trigger("click");
            $("#hdrResult").html("BUST!");
        } _____ (this.current_total _____ ){
            $("#btnStick").trigger("click");
            $("#hdrResult").html("BlackJack!");
        }else if( ____ .current_total ___ 21 ___ this.cards.length == 5){
            $("#btnStick").trigger("click");
            $("#hdrResult").html("5 card trick!");
        } _____
            // Keep playing! :)
        }
    }
};
```

my_scripts.js

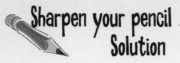

Sharpen your pencil
Solution

You've now updated the `sumCardTotal` method to include logic that checks the value of the dealt hand. There are lots of conditional and logical operators in there, even for this simple application.

```javascript
var hand = {
    cards : new Array(),
    current_total : 0,

    sumCardTotal: function(){
        this.current_total = 0;
        for(var i=0;i<this.cards.length;i++){
            var c = this.cards[i];
            this.current_total += c.value;
        }
        $("#hdrTotal").html("Total: " + this.current_total );
        if(this.current_total > 21){
            $("#btnStick").trigger("click");
            $("#hdrResult").html("BUST!");
        }else if(this.current_total == 21){
            $("#btnStick").trigger("click");
            $("#hdrResult").html("BlackJack!");
        }else if(this.current_total <= 21 && this.cards.length == 5){
            $("#btnStick").trigger("click");
            $("#hdrResult").html("BlackJack - 5 card trick!");
        }else{
            // Keep playing! :)
        }
    }
};
```

Check if current_total is greater than 21.

Check if current_total is equal to 21.

Check if current_total is less than or equal to 21, and if 5 cards have been dealt already.

Otherwise, do nothing!

my_scripts.js

But we still can't get at these new functions because we've got nothing to call them with, right?

Yeah, we're not quite done yet.

You already have all the pieces in your HTML code for dealing the initial cards, asking for another card, and ending the game. You just haven't wired them up yet. And don't forget, you need to call the method to add up the card totals each time you deal a new card.

jQuery Blackjack Code Magnets

Move the magnets to write the code for a function that will add several event listeners to the blackjack application. The listeners should be on the elements with the IDs of `btnHit` and `btnStick`. The `btnHit` event should deal another card. The other should stop the game. Also, call the `sumCardTotal` method after any card is dealt out. We've included some code from the end of the `hit` function for you to update too.

```
        }while(!_____);
        good_card = false;
        hand._____();
    }
    $("#btnDeal").click( _____(){
        deal();
        $(this).toggle();
        $("#btnHit")._____();
        $("#btnStick").toggle();
    });
    $("_____").click( function(){
        hit();
    });
    $("#btnStick").click( function(){
        $("#hdrResult").html(_____);
    });
```

my_scripts.js

function

toggle

good_card

'Stick!'

#btnHit

sumCardTotal

jQuery Blackjack Code Magnets Solution

This code creates a function that will add several event listeners on the hit and stick buttons, and also calls the `sumCardTotal` method after any card is dealt out.

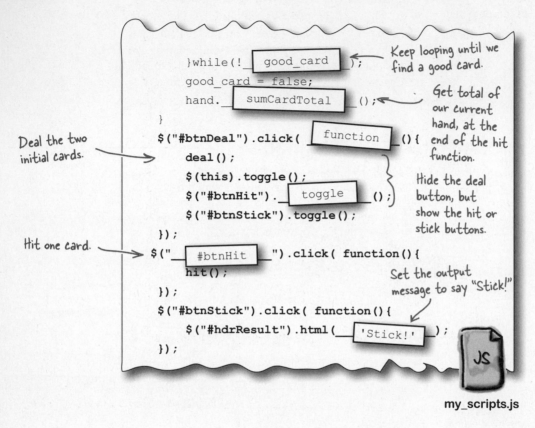

```
        }while(!_ good_card __);        ← Keep looping until we
        good_card = false;                find a good card.
        hand._ sumCardTotal __();←
                                           Get total of
        }                                  our current
$("#btnDeal").click( function ()(        hand, at the
    deal();                               end of the hit
    $(this).toggle();                     function.
    $("#btnHit"). toggle ();
    $("#btnStick").toggle();              Hide the deal
});                                       button, but
$("_ #btnHit __").click( function(){      show the hit or
    hit();                                stick buttons.
});
$("#btnStick").click( function(){         Set the output
    $("#hdrResult").html(_ 'Stick!' _);   message to say "Stick!"
});
```

Deal the two initial cards.

Hit one card.

my_scripts.js

there are no Dumb Questions

Q: Are there any other ways to compare values in JavaScript?

A: Not compare values, *per se*, but there is another method used to make decisions based on the values of variables. That method is called the `switch` method, and can have many different conditions. Often, if you find yourself writing large `if/else if/else` statements, a `switch` statement might be easier.

Q: You said there was a shortcut for the `if/else` statement. What is it?

A: It's called the ternary operator, and it uses a question mark to separate the logic operation from the resulting actions, like this:

```
a > b ? if_true_code : if_false_code
```

Test Drive

Add all the code you've just created to your *my_scripts.js* file, after your `hit` function—including an update to the end of the `hit` function itself—and give it a runthrough in your favorite browser.

So that's it? Are we done now?

Frank: Not so fast. We still have to add in the reset feature they asked for. So, once a game is over, the players can start again without reloading the page.

Joe: We also need to make sure that people aren't getting cards from previous games. We have to be sure we're removing everything.

Jim: But how do we do that? We have HTML elements that we added dynamically and new items in arrays. We have to clear it all?

Frank: Yes. We'll have to use slightly different techniques for each, but yes, we have to clear it all.

Joe: I know just the tricks! For jQuery, have a look at the `empty` method. For the arrays, there are a few ways, but not all are cross-browser. Let's see what the best options are.

Clearing things up with jQuery...

Remember back in Chapter 2 when we used the jQuery `remove` method to eliminate a particular element and all its child elements from the DOM, never to be seen again? That approach is great if you want to remove the parent element. However, if you want to keep the main element around and you just want to empty out its contents, you can use the jQuery `empty` method, which—like `remove`—requires a selector, but will leave the calling element in place.

```
$("#my_hand").empty();
```

The current page structure

body

div id="main"

div id="my_hand"

~~div class= "current_hand"~~   ~~div class= "current_hand"~~

The elements we want to remove

...is even easier in JavaScript

Often we find ourselves writing jQuery to avoid having to write multiple lines of JavaScript. Thankfully, there are a few occasions where doing something in JavaScript is as easy as it is in jQuery, and this is one of those times. While the syntax is a little different, the end result is the same and you don't have to keep track of where you are in the DOM. To truly empty an array in JavaScript, you simply set its length to 0 (zero):

```
used_cards.length = 0;
```

Things can't get much easier than that, right?

So, all we have to do now is figure out what needs clearing, and we're done, right?

Yes, but the order in which you clear stuff is important.

Since we also have to deal the next hand from a restart, we should clear everything first, *then* deal the new hand. We also have to make another element clickable to call our code.

Sharpen your pencil

Update your *index.html* file with an element, similar to all the other elements in the controls `div` element. Give the clickable `div` an ID of `btnRestart`. Inside the `div`, put an image with a source of *restart_small.jpg*, from the *images* folder.

Also, update your *my_scripts.js* file with an click event listener for the `btnRestart` element. This should empty the `my_hand` element, the `used_cards` array, and the `cards` array in the `hand` object. It should also toggle a new `div` element with the IDs of `result` and `itself`. It should also clear the `html` of the `hdrResult` elements. Finally, it should toggle and trigger the click event on the `btnDeal` element.

```
<div id="btnStick">
    <img src="images/stick_small.jpg">
</div>

    _____

    _____

    _____
    <div id="_____"><img src="" id="imgResult">_____
</div>
</div>
<script src="scripts/jquery-1.6.2.min.js"></script>
```

index.html

```
        $("#hdrResult").html('Stick!');
});
$("#btnRestart").click( function(){
    _____.toggle();
    $(this)._____
    $("#my_hand")._____
    $("#hdrResult").html('');
    used_cards. _____ = 0;
    _____.length = 0;
    hand._____  = 0;

    $("#btnDeal").toggle()
                ._____('click');
});
```

my_scripts.js

Sharpen your pencil
Solution

Now you've got a reset button to start the game over, which resets all the elements back to what they were before the game started. Add a little JavaScript magic with the `length` property, and you're good to go.

```html
<div id="btnStick">
    <img src="images/stick_small.jpg">
</div>
<div id="btnRestart">
    <img src="images/restart_small.jpg">
</div>
<div id="result"><img src="" id="imgResult"></div>
</div>
</div>
<script src="scripts/jquery-1.6.2.min.js"></script>
```

A reset button to start the game over again

index.html

Make the result more obvious in here.

```javascript
$("#hdrResult").html('Stick!');
$("result").toggle();
});
$("#btnRestart").click( function(){
    $("#result").toggle();
    $(this).toggle();
    $("#my_hand").empty();
    $("#hdrResult").html('');
    used_cards.length = 0;
    hand.cards.length = 0;
    hand.current_total = 0;

    $("#btnDeal").toggle()
                .trigger('click');
});
```

my_scripts.js

Reset all the elements back to the way they were.

Simulate a click of the btnDeal element.

Test Drive

Add a click event for the `btnRestart` element to your *my_scripts.js* file. Also, don't forget to include the additional HTML code in your *index.html* file.

Oh man, this is so close to what I wanted, but there's just one more thing: can we make the win and lose more obvious or exciting? Sorry to keep messing with ya.

Add some extra excitement

Update your *my_scripts.js* file with a new end function, which gets called by btnStick, and some other updates to the computational logic in sumCardTotal. Also, grab the latest *my_style.css* file here: *http://thinkjquery.com/chapter06/end/styles/my_style.css*.

Do this!

```javascript
        if(this.current_total> 21){
            $("#btnStick").trigger("click");
            $("#imgResult").attr('src','images/x2.png');
            $("#hdrResult").html("BUST!")
                        .attr('class', 'lose');
        }else if(this.current_total == 21){
            $("#btnStick").trigger("click");
            $("#imgResult").attr('src','images/check.png');
            $("#hdrResult").html("BlackJack!")
                        .attr('class', 'win');
        }else if(this.current_total <= 21 && this.cards.length == 5){
                $("#btnStick").trigger("click");
                $("#imgResult").attr('src','images/check.png');
                $("#hdrResult").html("BlackJack - 5 card trick!")
                            .attr('class', 'win');
        }else{}
        $("#hdrTotal").html("Total: " + this.current_total );
    }
};
function end(){
    $("#btnHit").toggle();
    $("#btnStick").toggle();
    $("#btnRestart").toggle();
}
$("#btnStick").click( function(){
    $("#hdrResult").html('Stick!')
                .attr('class', 'win');
    $("#result").toggle();
    end();
});
```

Set the src of imgResult to a different image, depending on the result.

Set a different class for the header, depending on the result.

Toggle all the controls to end the game.

Call the end function to end the game, after you stick.

my_scripts.js

Test Drive

Update the `sumCardTotal` method of the `hand` function in your *my_scripts.js* file. Also, don't forget to grab the new *my_style.css* file and replace your current one with the new version.

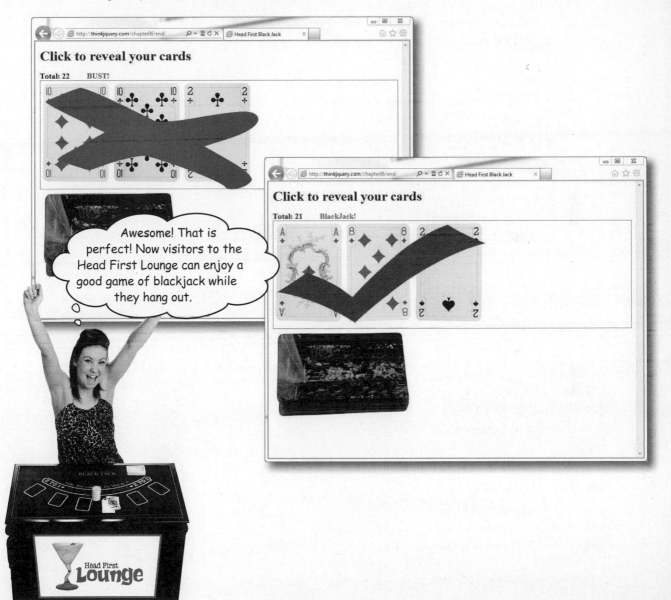

Awesome! That is perfect! Now visitors to the Head First Lounge can enjoy a good game of blackjack while they hang out.

Your jQuery/JavaScript Toolbox

You've got Chapter 6 under your belt and now you've added JavaScript objects, arrays, and loops to your toolbox.

JavaScript object

Creating standalone and creating a constructor

Using objects and calling the constructor

Arrays

Creating arrays

Assigning values to an array

Adding more elements to an array

Updating existing array elements

Loops

for Loop

do...while loop

Logical operators

Comparison operators

jQuery

.empty

$.inArray — Utility method

.attr

.trigger

7 custom functions for custom effects

What have you done for me lately?

I could really use a doHousework function.

When you combine jQuery's custom effects with JavaScript functions you can make your code—and your web app—more efficient, more effective, and more *powerful*. In this chapter, you'll dig deeper into improving your jQuery effects by handling **browser events**, working with **timed functions**, and improving the **organization and reusability** of your custom JavaScript functions.

A storm is brewing

The Monster Mashup web app you built in Chapter 5 was a big hit with kids and their parents. But it sounds like there might be a bug that's making the lightning go haywire. DoodleStuff's quality assurance manager contacts you with some issues and a feature request for making Monster Mashup better.

Jill, who runs QA for DoodleStuff

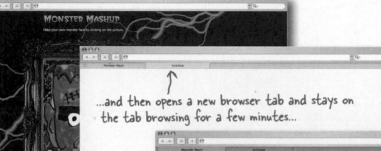

We've discovered that when a user opens a new tab in his browser and leaves Monster Mash open in another tab, when he comes back the lightning goes off in rapid succession with no pause in between. It seems like the app is just going haywire!

When a visitor starts up Monster Mashup...

...and then opens a new browser tab and stays on the tab browsing for a few minutes...

...and then returns to the tab the Monster Mashup app is running in, the lightning goes off in rapid succession as if the effects are crashing into one another.

BRAIN POWER

Try reproducing the issue. Then think about what's going wrong with the lightning functions. Why do they all crash together when someone switches from one tab to another?

We've created a monster...function

The lightning function we created in Chapter 5 has turned out to be a bit of a monster. It runs and runs, even if the user navigates away from the page. When the user returns to the tab, the timer has to catch up, and it tries to redraw the lightning on screen in rapid succession. It seems that the timer doesn't work the way we wanted it to, so what happened?

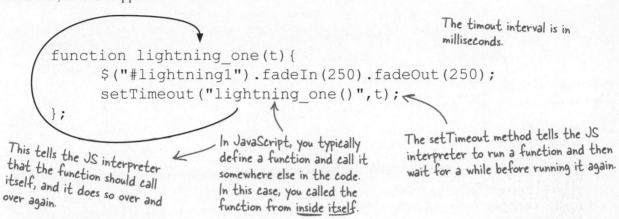

The timout interval is in milliseconds.

```
function lightning_one(t){
    $("#lightning1").fadeIn(250).fadeOut(250);
    setTimeout("lightning_one()",t);
};
```

This tells the JS interpreter that the function should call itself, and it does so over and over again.

In JavaScript, you typically define a function and call it somewhere else in the code. In this case, you called the function from <u>inside itself</u>.

The setTimeout method tells the JS interpreter to run a function and then wait for a while before running it again.

In Chapter 5, we needed a way to call the method again and again, with a timeout in between those calls. In solving that problem, we unknowingly created a new problem: the function continues to run when the window loses the visitor's *focus* (i.e., when the visitor opens a new tab and moves away from the active window).

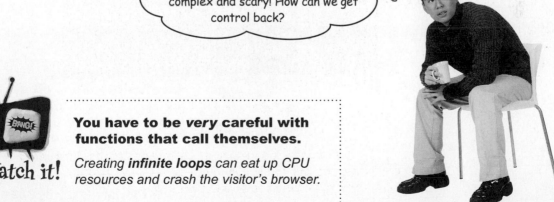

> A function that runs infinitely *and* is out of our control? That's complex and scary! How can we get control back?

You have to be *very* careful with functions that call themselves.

Watch it! *Creating **infinite loops** can eat up CPU resources and crash the visitor's browser.*

Get control of timed effects with the window object

Fortunately, you have a way to get control of your lightning animation using JavaScript's `window` object. The `window` object is created every time the visitor opens a new window in his browser, and it offers a lot of jQuery and JavaScript power. In the world of JavaScript, the `window` object is the *global* object. In other words, `window` is the *topmost object* of the JavaScript world.

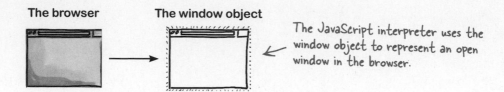

The browser → **The window object**

The JavaScript interpreter uses the window object to represent an open window in the browser.

Let's say you've opened three tabs in your browser. The browser creates one `window` object for each of those tabs. The `window` object is an object just like the ones you worked with in Chapter 6, so it has properties, event handlers, and methods. And they're super handy—we can use the `window` object's `onblur` and `onfocus` event handlers to find out what the visitor is doing at the browser level.

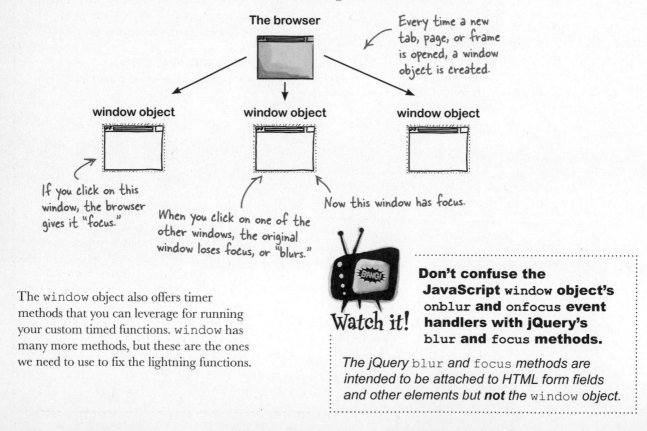

The browser

Every time a new tab, page, or frame is opened, a window object is created.

window object   **window object**   **window object**

If you click on this window, the browser gives it "focus."

When you click on one of the other windows, the original window loses focus, or "blurs."

Now this window has focus.

The `window` object also offers timer methods that you can leverage for running your custom timed functions. `window` has many more methods, but these are the ones we need to use to fix the lightning functions.

Watch it!

Don't confuse the JavaScript `window` object's `onblur` and `onfocus` event handlers with jQuery's `blur` and `focus` methods.

*The jQuery `blur` and `focus` methods are intended to be attached to HTML form fields and other elements but **not** the `window` object.*

WHO DOES WHAT?

Match each property, event handler, or method for the `window` object to what it does.

`window.name`

Detects when the window receives a click, keyboard input, or some other kind of input.

`window.history`

A property of the `window` object that refers to the main content of the loaded document.

`window.document`

Detects when the window loses focus.

`window.onfocus`

A method of the `window` object used to set a period of time to wait before calling a function or other statement.

`window.setTimeout()`

A method of the `window` object used to cancel the period of time to wait between repetitions.

`window.clearTimeout()`

A method of the `window` object used to set a period of time to wait between repetitions of a function call or other statement.

`window.setInterval()`

A property of the `window` object that lets you access the different URLs that the window has loaded over time.

`window.clearInterval()`

A method of the `window` object used to cancel the period of time to wait.

`window.onblur`

A property of the `window` object that lets us access or set the name of the window.

WHO DOES WHAT? SOLUTION

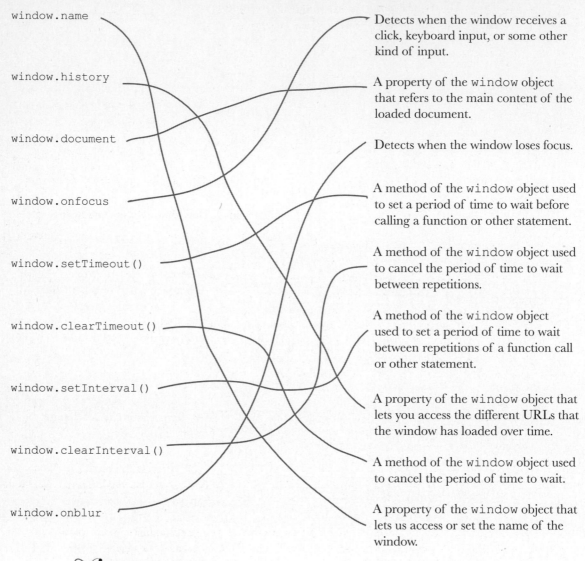

`window.name`

`window.history`

`window.document`

`window.onfocus`

`window.setTimeout()`

`window.clearTimeout()`

`window.setInterval()`

`window.clearInterval()`

`window.onblur`

Detects when the window receives a click, keyboard input, or some other kind of input.

A property of the `window` object that refers to the main content of the loaded document.

Detects when the window loses focus.

A method of the `window` object used to set a period of time to wait before calling a function or other statement.

A method of the `window` object used to cancel the period of time to wait between repetitions.

A method of the `window` object used to set a period of time to wait between repetitions of a function call or other statement.

A property of the `window` object that lets you access the different URLs that the window has loaded over time.

A method of the `window` object used to cancel the period of time to wait.

A property of the `window` object that lets us access or set the name of the window.

BRAIN POWER

The `window` object's `onfocus` and `onblur` event handlers can detect a change to the window's focus, but what can you do in response to those events?

Respond to browser events with onblur and onfocus

So we know that with `window.onfocus,` you can tell when the window gains focus (i.e., a visitor activates the page or directs mouse or keyboard input to the window), and with `window.onblur,` you can tell when the active browser window loses focus. But what can you do in response to these events? You can *assign a function reference* to `onfocus` or `onblur`.

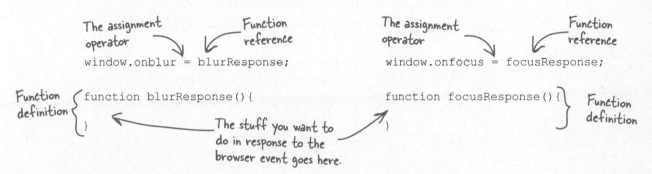

The assignment operator → Function reference

```
window.onblur = blurResponse;
```

Function definition {
```
function blurResponse(){

}
```

The assignment operator → Function reference

```
window.onfocus = focusResponse;
```

```
function focusResponse(){

}
```
} Function definition

The stuff you want to do in response to the browser event goes here.

And here's where the power of writing your own custom functions really starts to come into play. Now you've got a `window` object that gives you a ton of information about what your user is doing in the browser, and you can assign your own custom functions based on what that object tells you. So, really, you can do just about *anything* you want, as long as you can write your own custom function for it…

Test Drive

Let's test-drive the window object's `onfocus` and `onblur` event handlers. In the code files you downloaded for Chapter 7, you'll find a folder called *window_tester*. Open the *window_tester.html* file in that folder in your favorite browser. Open a second tab and play with clicking between the two browser windows.

Test Drive

Here's what you should see when you open the *window_tester.html* file, open a second tab, and switch between the two windows by clicking on them alternately.

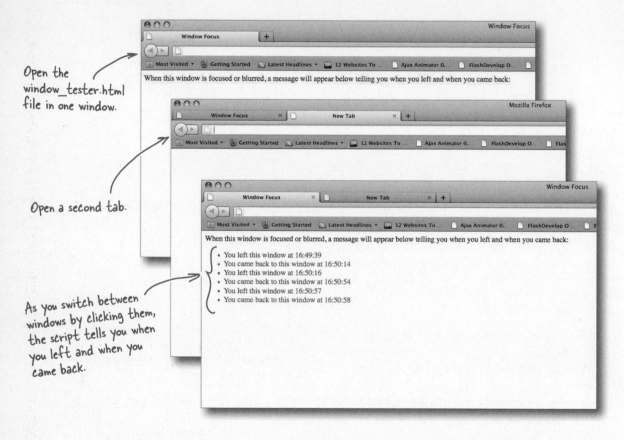

Open the window_tester.html file in one window.

Open a second tab.

As you switch between windows by clicking them, the script tells you when you left and when you came back.

Using the information you get from the `window` **object, you can stop the lightning when the visitor wanders away from the Monster Mashup window and then restart it when she returns.**

jQuery Magnets

Put the code magnets in the right order to assign function definitions to the `onblur` and `onfocus` handlers. One function definition will stop the lightning when the browser loses focus (call this one `stopLightning`). The other function definition will start the lightning back up when the browser regains focus (call this one `goLightning`). You won't write the code for the functions just yet, so for now, just put the magnets with comments (starting with //) inside each function.

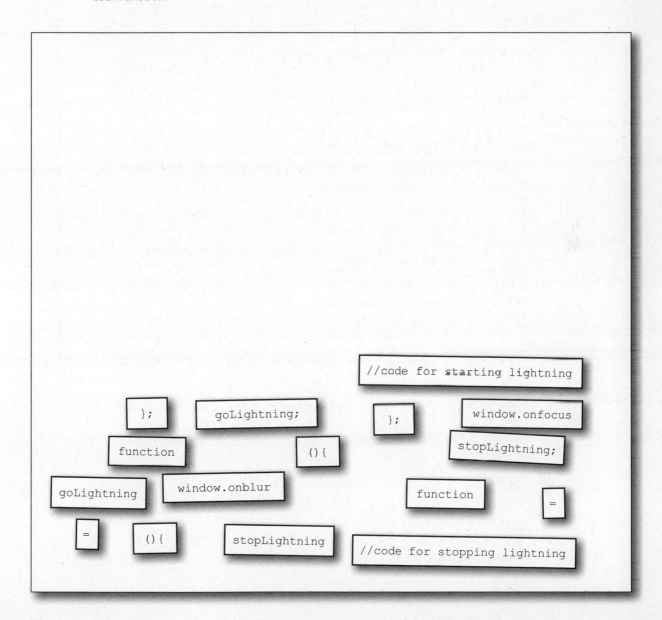

```
//code for starting lightning

};          goLightning;          };          window.onfocus

function                    (){          stopLightning;

goLightning      window.onblur              function        =

=       (){       stopLightning       //code for stopping lightning
```

jQuery Magnets Solution

Now you're ready to go with function declarations for both `window` object event handlers.

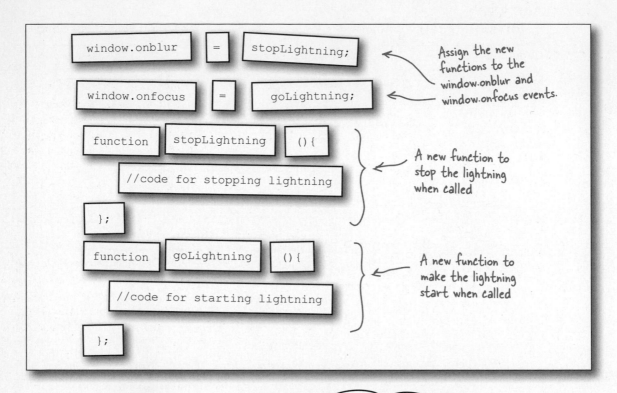

```
window.onblur        =        stopLightning;
```
Assign the new functions to the window.onblur and window.onfocus events.

```
window.onfocus       =        goLightning;
```

```
function   stopLightning   (){
    //code for stopping lightning
};
```
A new function to stop the lightning when called

```
function   goLightning   (){
    //code for starting lightning
};
```
A new function to make the lightning start when called

But those are just comments inside the functions. The functions need to **do something**! Should we just copy and paste the timed lightning functions in there?

Right. The functions don't do anything...yet.

Instead of copying and pasting our old code, let's look at one of the `window` object's methods—a timer method— that might give us a better way of handling the timing effects for the lightning.

Timer methods tell your functions *when* to run

Both JavaScript and jQuery offer us timer methods that call functions to run based on time passing. JavaScript's `window` object has four timer methods for timed control: `setTimeout`, `clearTimeout`, `setInterval`, and `clearInterval`. jQuery offers us the `delay` method. Let's take a closer look at these methods and what they offer us.

JavaScript timer methods

setTimeout

Use me when you want to set a period of time to wait until telling a function to run.

```
setTimeout(myFunction, 4000);
```

The function to call when the timeout duration has passed

The timer delay (in milliseconds)

setInterval

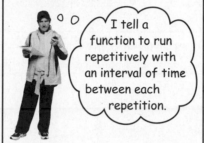

I tell a function to run repetitively with an interval of time between each repetition.

```
setInterval(repeatMe, 1000);
```

The function to repeat after each interval is up.

The interval of time between function calls (in milliseconds)

jQuery's delay method

delay

I add a pause between effects that are queued up in a chain of effects.

```
slideDown().delay(5000).slideUp();
```

When this chain runs, it's known in jQuery as an effects queue.

In this example, the delay method puts a five-second pause in between the slideUp and slideDown effects.

Sharpen your pencil

Which of these timer methods will work best for fixing the `goLightning` function? For each timer method, answer whether it will help and explain why you chose or didn't choose it.

Timer	Should we use it?	Why?
setTimeout		
setInterval		
delay		

Sharpen your pencil
Solution

Which of these timer methods will work best for fixing the lightning function? Here are our answers.

Timer	Should we use it?	Why?
setTimeout	No	The setTimeout method is intended for situations where you want to wait a specific amount of time before running a function.
setInterval	Yes	The setInterval method is specifically intended for situations where you want a function to run on a repeating schedule. That's what you need the lightning to do.
delay	No	The delay method works well for sequenced effects, but it has no mechanism for running on a repeating schedule.

So **setInterval** will be the best solution for the **goLightning** function, but the **stopLightning** function needs to stop the timer. Will the **clearInterval** method do that for us?

Great question!

You can use the clearInterval method to stop the repeating schedule of function calls created by setInterval. To do so, you need to pass a variable to clearInterval as a parameter. Let's take a closer look at how that works.

Assign a variable that identifies the setInterval method.

```
myInterval = setInterval(repeatMe, 1000);
```

```
clearInterval(myInterval);
```

Pass the variable to clearInterval as a parameter.

The clearInterval method tells the setInterval to wipe out its timer and stops the repeating action.

there are no
Dumb Questions

Q: Do all browsers process the `setTimeout` method the same way?

A: No. Mozilla Firefox and Google Chrome display the behavior we encountered earlier (stacking up the function calls). Internet Explorer 9 keeps calling the function as it was intended from Chapter 5. This shows that not just web designers have issues with cross-browser compatibility.

Q: Can the timing functions like0 `setInterval` and `setTimeout` be used with things other than the window object?

A: That's a great question. Unfortunately, they can't. They are specific methods of the `window` object, and can only be called in reference to the `window` object. They can, however, be called without the prefix "window," and the browser will know you intend for this to be attached to the current `window` object. It's good practice to include the prefix, though.

WHO DOES WHAT?

Match each timer method to what it does when it runs.

```
window.clearInterval(int1);
```

```
window.onfocus = goLightning;
```

```
setTimeout(wakeUp(),4000);
```

```
$("#container #lightning1").
fadeIn(250).delay(5000).fadeOut(250).;
```

```
int1 = setInterval( function() {
        lightning_one();
    },
    4000
);
```

```
window.onblur = stopLightning;
```

Detects when the current window gains focus and calls the `goLightning` method.

Sets the `lightning_one` function to run every four seconds and assigns it to the variable `int1`.

Detects when the current window loses focus and calls the `stopLightning` function.

Wipes out the timer and stops the repeating `setInterval` for `int1`.

Sets a four-second wait before calling a function named `wakeUp`.

Creates a five-second pause between a `fadeIn` and `fadeOut` effect.

WHO DOES WHAT? SOLUTION

Match each timer method to what it does when it runs.

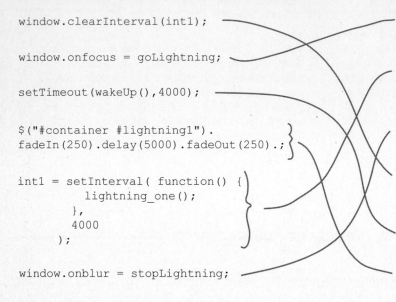

```
window.clearInterval(int1);

window.onfocus = goLightning;

setTimeout(wakeUp(),4000);

$("#container #lightning1").
fadeIn(250).delay(5000).fadeOut(250).;

int1 = setInterval( function() {
        lightning_one();
    },
    4000
);

window.onblur = stopLightning;
```

Detects when the current window gains focus and calls the `goLightning` method.

Sets the `lightning_one` function to run every four seconds and assigns it to the variable `int1`.

Detects when the current window loses focus and calls the `stopLightning` function.

Wipes out the timer and stops the repeating `setInterval` for `int1`.

Sets a four-second wait before calling a function named `wakeUp`.

Creates a five-second pause between a `fadeIn` and `fadeOut` effect.

Write the stopLightning and goLightning functions

Now that you know more about timer methods, let's review where we need them.

```
goLightning();
```
← Start the lightning when the page loads.

```
window.onblur = stopLightning;
```
← Call the stopLightning function when the browser loses focus.

```
window.onfocus = goLightning;
```
← Call the goLightning function when the browser regains focus.

```
function stopLightning (){
  //code for stopping lightning
};
```
← Clear the timers for the three lightning intervals. We need <u>three</u> clearIntervals here. Know why?

```
function goLightning (){
  //code for starting lightning
};
```
← Set three timers for the three lightning intervals. And yep, we need <u>three</u> setIntervals here.

For each blank line in the file, write in the variable, function, or method that will help fix the Monster Mashup app. When in doubt, look at the previous two pages for guidance. We've done a few for you.

```javascript
goLightning();
window.onblur = stopLightning;
window.onfocus = goLightning;
var int1, int2, int3 ;
function goLightning(){
    int1 = .................( function() {

        }, .....................
        4000
    );

    ......... = .................( function() {

        }, .....................
        5000
    );
    ......... = .................( function() {
            lightning_three();
        },
        7000
    );
}

function stopLightning()
{
    window......................( int1 );
    window......................(.......);
    window......................(.......);
}
function lightning_one() {
  $("#container #lightning1").fadeIn(250).fadeOut(250);
};

function ..................... {
  $("#container #lightning2").fadeIn(250).fadeOut(250);
};

function ..................... {
  $("#container #lightning3").fadeIn(250).fadeOut(250);
};
```

my_scripts.js

Exercise
Solution

Now you've got two custom functions—each with references to the lightning functions you wrote back in Chapter 5—that respond to the window object's onfocus and onblur events.

```
goLightning();
window.onblur = stopLightning;
window.onfocus = goLightning;
var int1, int2, int3 ;
function goLightning(){
    int1 = setInterval ( function() {
        lightning_one();
    },
    4000
    );

    int2 = setInterval ( function() {
        lightning_two();
    },
    5000
    );
    int3 = setInterval ( function() {
        lightning_three();
    },
    7000
    );
}

function stopLightning()
{
    window.clearInterval ( int1 );
    window.clearInterval (int2 );
    window.clearInterval ( int3 );
}
function lightning_one() {
  $("#container #lightning1").fadeIn(250).fadeOut(250);
};

function lightning_two() {
  $("#container #lightning2").fadeIn(250).fadeOut(250);
};

function lightning_three()    {
  $("#container #lightning3").fadeIn(250).fadeOut(250);
};
```

Declare three variables for remembering our timers so the browser can clear them again.

Here, you call the lightning_one function.

Set three different timers for the three lightning intervals.

And then call the lightning_two function.

Now call the lightning_three function.

Clear the timers for the three lightning intervals.

Our three lightning function definitions.

JS

my_scripts.js

Do this!

You'll be updating a bunch of code to fix and improve on what you built in Chapter 5, so let's start with a blank script file. The code files you downloaded for this book contain a folder for Chapter 7. In the folder, you'll find a *begin* folder structured like this:

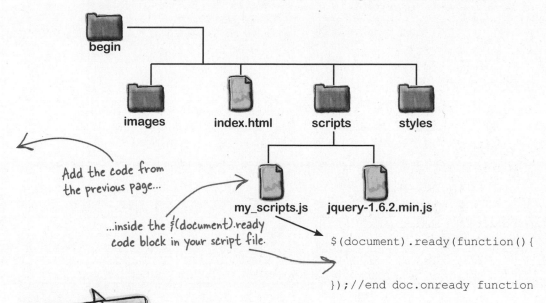

Add the code from the previous page...

...inside the $(document).ready code block in your script file.

```
$(document).ready(function(){



});//end doc.onready function
```

Test Drive

Once you've added the code from the previous page to the script file, open the page up in your favorite browser to see if your lightning effect fix was successful.

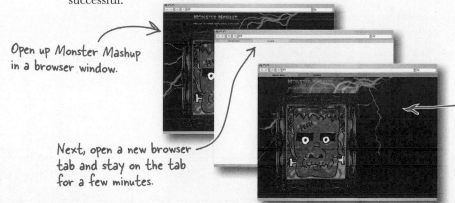

Open up Monster Mashup in a browser window.

Next, open a new browser tab and stay on the tab for a few minutes.

Then return to the original tab the Monster Mashup app is running in. When you return, the first effect should not be running. It should start up after four seconds.

> Since we're fixing stuff, shouldn't we go back and fix those repetitive functions we built in Chapter 5?

A different data structure would work better here, one that handles <u>multiple</u> variables.

Great idea. We have a bunch of click-related functions for that face that we could likely combine into **one** multipurpose function.

Can you write <u>one function</u> that will work for each of these?

```javascript
var headclix = 0, eyeclix = 0, noseclix = 0, mouthclix = 0;

        $("#head").click(function(){
            if (headclix < 9){
                    $("#head").animate({left:"-=367px"},500);
                    headclix+=1;
            }
            else{
                    $("#head").animate({left:"0px'},500);
                    headclix = 0;
            }
        });

        $("#eyes").click(function(){
            if (eyeclix < 9){
                    $("#eyes").animate({left:"-=367px"},500);
                    eyeclix+=1;
            }
            else{
                    $("#eyes").animate({left:"0px"},500);
                    eyeclix = 0;
            }
        });

        $("#nose").click(function(){
            if (noseclix < 9){
                    $("#nose").animate({left:"-=367px"},500);
                    noseclix+=1;
            }
            else{
                    $("#nose").animate({left:"0px"},500);
                    noseclix = 0;
            }
        });//end click

        $("#mouth").click(function(){
            if (mouthclix < 9){
                    $("#mouth").animate({left:"-=367px"},500);
                    mouthclix+=1;
            }
            else{
                    $("#mouth").animate({left:"0px"},500);
                    mouthclix = 0;
            }
        });//end click
```

my_scripts.js

jQuery Magnets

From the previous page, identify which snippets of code are common to all of the different aspects of the application. Use the magnets below to create a generic function, called moveMe, that will be called whenever a user clicks on any of the moveable images. For the moveMe function, the first parameter is the corresponding index in the clix array, and the second is a reference to whatever was clicked.

```
var clix = _____;  // head,eyes,nose,mouth

    $("#head").click( function(){


        _____
    });//end click function

    $("#eyes").click( function(){


        _____
    } );//end click function

    $("#nose").click( function(){


        _____
    });//end click function

    $("#mouth").click( function(){


        _____
    });//end click function

    function moveMe(_____){

        if (_____ < 9){
            $(obj).animate({left:"-=367px"},500);
            clix[i] = clix[i]+1;
        }else{
            clix[i] = 0;
            $(_____).animate({left:"0px"},500);
        }
    }
```

Magnets:

```
moveMe(2, this);
obj
moveMe(0, this);
i, obj
moveMe(3, this);
clix[i]
[0,0,0,0]
moveMe(1, this);
```

jQuery Magnets Solution

Now that you've got one reusable function that leverages an array, you'll have less code to maintain, and it will be easier to track down and debug any issues you might run into.

```javascript
var clix = [0,0,0,0]; // head,eyes,nose,mouth

    $("#head").click( function(){

        moveMe(0, this);
    });//end click function

    $("#eyes").click( function(){

        moveMe(1, this);
    } );//end click function

    $("#nose").click( function(){

        moveMe(2, this);
    });//end click function

    $("#mouth").click( function(){

        moveMe(3, this);
    });//end click function

    function moveMe( i, obj ){

        if ( clix[i] < 9){
            $(obj).animate({left:"-=367px"},500);
            clix[i] = clix[i]+1;
        }else{
            clix[i] = 0;
            $( obj ).animate({left:"0px"},500);
        }
    }
```

Turning clix into an array helps economize your code.

You pass the moveMe function a reference to the slot for the clix array. Then you can use that slot to keep track of how many times each element has been clicked.

You also pass the moveMe function the current object so that it can be animated.

By creating a more multipurpose moveMe function, you've reduced the possibility of code errors and the number of functions to maintain.

The repetitive logic you had before is now in one place, which makes it easier to fix if something goes wrong.

JS

my_scripts.js

Test Drive

Add the code from the magnets exercise on the previous page to your *my_scripts.js* file and save it. Then, open up the *index.html* page in your favorite browser to make sure your function rewrite didn't introduce any problems when all the various face parts are clicked.

The Mashup page shouldn't look any different than before, but you'll know that your code is more efficient, less repetitive, and easier to maintain.

Feature request for Monster Mashup

Jill and the QA team are really happy with your fixes, and since
they like your work, they want to pass along a feature request for
Monster Mashup from the product team.

We've had several requests
from kids who want a button that will
create a random monster face. Can you
build that into the app, along with a way
to start over from the beginning again?

I like the monster
faces I make, but it
would be fun to see the
computer mix them all
up for me.

Let's get (more) random

You've been building random functions throughout the book, so you're likely a pro at that by now. In this case, you need to create a function that randomly animates the monster faces. Let's divide and conquer the problem by breaking it down into smaller steps. Let's start with figuring out the current position for each image strip.

You need to keep track of the current position for each monster image strip. Let's say the visitor is on this one.

The current position is the number of clicks multiplied by the distance between face parts (367 pixels). For our example, the current position is 2 * 367, which is 734.

From the current position, we need to figure out the target position, which is essentially a random position on the screen. It helps to think of this in two parts:

1 **Get a random number.**

Here's what we did in Chapters 2 and 3 to get a random number.

```
var my_num = Math.floor((Math.random()*5) + 5);
```

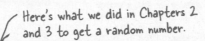

But now we need a number between 1 and 10 (because each monster strip has 10 monster face parts).

2 **Move each face part to a random position based on that random number.**

For each monster face part, you need to move it to the random position multiplied by the width of each face on each strip. For a random number of 7, the target position is 7 * 367, which is 2,569.

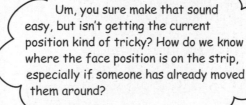

Um, you sure make that sound easy, but isn't getting the current position kind of tricky? How do we know where the face position is on the strip, especially if someone has already moved them around?

It's not as hard as you think.

In fact, just turn the page to find out how.

the more you know...

You already know the current position...

Fortunately, you don't have to come up with all new variables or functions here. The index value of the `clix` array provides the current position because it tells us how many times the user has clicked on each monster face part. So all you need is one line of code:

Set the current position to
the value of clix[index].

```
var current_position = clix[index] ;
```

...and the getRandom function too

We built a function for getting random numbers in Chapters 2, 3, and 6.
We can reuse that function here with minimal tweaks.

```
function getRandom(num) {
    var my_random_num = Math.floor(Math.random()*num);
    return my_random_num;
}
```

You can pass a number as an argument to the getRandom function...

...to generate and return a whole number. Here, we'd get a number between 0 and 10.

By multiplying Math.random and the number passed as input, you can create a number between 0 and whatever the value of the num variable is.

1 **Set your variable and pass it to the function:**

Passing a value
to the function

```
num = 10;
getRandom(num);
```

2 **Here's the core operation of the function:**

Some folks would refer to this as a utility function. It does one thing and does it well.

```
var my_random_num = Math.floor(Math.random()*num);
```

3 **And the result (or output) of the function:**

```
return my_random_num;
```

Some folks refer to functions that return values as "getters" because they get you a value.

Next up: the `target_position` (i.e., the random face part) we want to slide to.

 **Ready Bake Code**

Add the bolded code to your *index.html* and *my_scripts.js* files. This will get your randomize function set up, along with some alerts that will show you the target position (which uses a random number) and the current position (which is determined by the number of times the visitor clicked).

```
<header id="top">
    <img src="images/Monster_Mashup.png" />
    <button id="btnRandom">Randomize</button>
    <button id="btnReset">Reset</button>
    <p>Make your own monster face by clicking on the picture.</p>
</header>
```

You need some interface buttons for both the randomize and reset behaviors.

index.html

```
var w = 367; //width of the face strip
var m = 10; //number of the monster face strip we're on


$("#btnRandom").click( randomize );
$("#btnReset").click(  );


function getRandom(num){
        var my_random_num = Math.floor(Math.random()*num);
        return my_random_num;
}
function randomize(){
        $(".face").each(function(index){
                var target_position = getRandom(m);
                var current_position = clix[index] ;
                clix[index] = target_position;
                var move_to = target_position * w;
                $(this).animate({left:"-="+move_to+"px"},500);
        });
};
```

Randomize the position of each face part.

Set the target_position to the result of the getRandom function.

Update clix[index] so the user can still click to advance the monster face parts.

Set move_to to the random position multiplied by the width of the face strip sections.

Run your custom animation code to move the strip left.

my_scripts.js

Test Drive

After entering the code from the previous page to your files, open up the *index.html* page in your favorite browser to test the `randomize` function. Click the Randomize button 10 to 20 times to make sure you do a full test.

The randomizer works...

On the first few clicks, the randomizer function does what you asked it to do.

...for the first few clicks

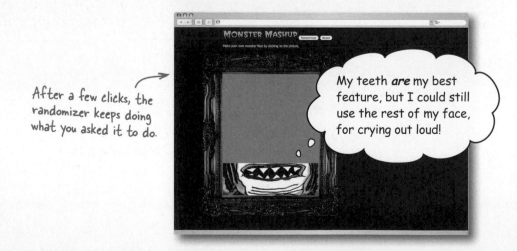

After a few clicks, the randomizer keeps doing what you asked it to do.

My teeth *are* my best feature, but I could still use the rest of my face, for crying out loud!

We didn't code it to make the face's parts go blank. We set it to go to a random position! Did we go too far somehow?

You're right.

Those custom functions had unintended effects, but they likely did exactly what we wrote in the code. Let's have a look at what we might not have thought about.

The animate statement keeps sliding the image strip to the left, and it eventually moves it past what the user can see inside the picture frame. It's gone "off the grid," so to speak.

```
$(this).animate({left:-="+move_to+"px"},500);
```

Help! We fell off our picture frame!

If the user keeps clicking the Randomize button, it eventually pushes the image strip so far to the left, it won't appear on screen anymore.

BRAIN BARBELL

What do you need to do to keep the image strip from going off the grid, and instead landing on a random monster face part?

Move <u>relative</u> to the current position

To keep the image strip from going off the grid—but still falling correctly on a random monster face part—you need to move it *relative* to the *current position*, which means including the current position and some conditional logic. Let's break it down.

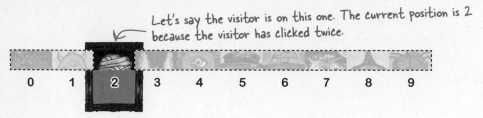

Let's say the visitor is on this one. The current position is 2 because the visitor has clicked twice.

Then the user clicks on the Randomize button, which comes up with a random number between 0 and 9. Let's look at two different scenarios that could happen as a result.

Scenario 1: target > current

The `getRandom` function returns a value of 5. So the `target_position` variable gets set to 5, which means that it's *greater than* the `current_position` variable. We need to write conditional logic to handle this situation.

How many positions do we have to move the strip?

Subtract current_position from target_position, and you get 3. We need to move three positions to the left.

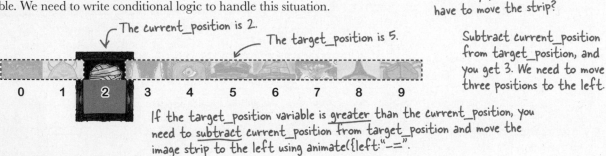

The current_position is 2.

The target_position is 5.

If the target_position variable is <u>greater</u> than the current_position, you need to <u>subtract</u> current_position from target_position and move the image strip to the left using animate({left:"−="}.

Scenario 2: target < current

The `getRandom` function returns a value of 1. The `target_position` variable is 1, which means that it's *less than* the `current_position` variable. Based on the conditional logic from Scenario 1, can you figure out what logic you need here?

Subtract target_position from current_position, and you get 1. You need to move one position to the right.

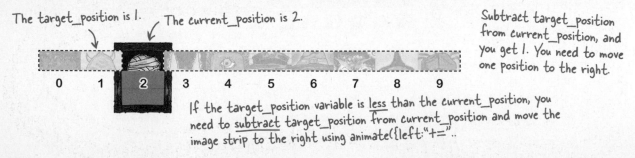

The target_position is 1.

The current_position is 2.

If the target_position variable is <u>less</u> than the current_position, you need to <u>subtract</u> target_position from current_position and move the image strip to the right using animate({left:"+="}..

Pool Puzzle

Your job is to take code snippets from the pool and place them into the blank lines in the code. You may **not** use the same snippet more than once, and you won't need to use all the snippets. Your **goal** is to make the randomizer function work the way it is intended to, so parts of the face doesn't go blank.

```
var w = 367;
var m = 10;

function getRandom(num){
        var my_random_num = Math.floor(Math.random()*num);
        return my_random_num;
}
function randomize(){
        $(".face")......................................{
                var target_position = getRandom(m);
                        var current_position = clix[index] ;
                        clix[index] = target_position;

                        if(.................................................) {
                                var move_to = (.............................................................) * w;
                                $(this).animate(................................................);
                        }else if(........................................................){
                                var move_to = (.............................................................) * w;
                                $(this).animate(................................................);
                        }else{
                                // They are the same - Don't move it.
                        }
                });
        };
```

Note: each thing from the pool can only be used once!

```
{left:"-="+move_to+"px"},500

{left:"+="+move_to+"px"},500

target_position > current_position        {left:"="+move_to+"px"},500

target_position - current_position        target_position + current_position
current_position - target_position
target_position == current_position        target_position < current_position

                                each(function(index)
```

Pool Puzzle Solution

Your job is to take code snippets from the pool and place them into the blank lines in the code. You may **not** use the same snippet more than once, and you won't need to use all the snippets. Your **goal** is to make the randomizer function work the way it is intended to, so parts of the face doesn't go blank.

```
var w = 367;
var m = 10;

function getRandom(num) {
    var my_random_num = Math.floor(Math.random()*num);
    return my_random_num;
}
function randomize(){
    $(".face").each(function(index)    {
        var target_position = getRandom(m);
        var current_position = clix[index] ;
        clix[index] = target_position;

        if( target_position > current_position    ) {
            var move_to = ( target_position - current_position ) * w;
            $(this).animate( {left:"-="+move_to+"px"},500 );
        }else if( target_position < current_position    ){
            var move_to = ( current_position - target_position ) * w;
            $(this).animate( {left:"+="+move_to+"px"},500 );
        }else{
            // They are the same - Don't move it.
        }
    });
};
```

Run the following code for each element that's a member of the face class.

If the target_position variable is <u>more</u> <u>than</u> the current_position...

...subtract target_position from current position.

Move the image strip to the left. That means we need to use animate({left:"-=".

If the target_position variable is <u>less</u> <u>than</u> the current_position.

subtract target_position from current position and...

...move the image strip to the right. That means we need to use animate({left:"+="...

```
{left:"="+move_to+"px"},500

          target_position + current_position

target_position == current_position
```

You didn't need these snippets.

The randomizer is working great now. I assume we'll need another custom function to reset everything, right?

Exactly.

Remember that reset button in the *index.html* file a few pages back? Now you just need to wire it up to a custom `reset` function.

jQuery Magnets

Put the code magnets in proper order to write the code for the reset button and build your custom reset function. We've done some of them for you.

```
$("#btnReset").click( reset );



function reset(){




}
```

```
$(".face")
                        });
$(this)
                .each(function(index){
            .animate({left:"0px"},500);
clix[index] = 0;
```

jQuery Magnets Solution

And voilà! Just a couple of quick lines puts everything back in place to start over.

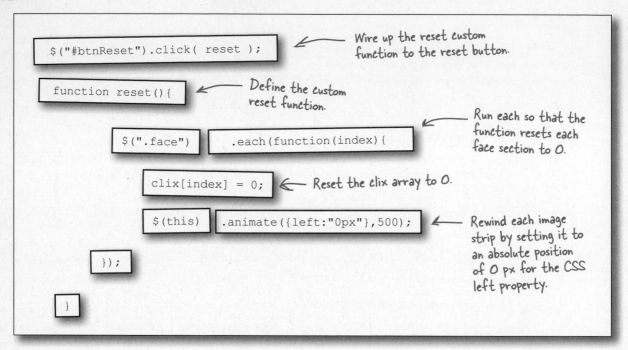

```
$("#btnReset").click( reset );
```
Wire up the reset custom function to the reset button.

```
function reset(){
```
Define the custom reset function.

```
$(".face")    .each(function(index){
```
Run each so that the function resets each face section to 0.

```
clix[index] = 0;
```
Reset the clix array to 0.

```
$(this)    .animate({left:"0px"},500);
```
Rewind each image strip by setting it to an absolute position of 0 px for the CSS left property.

```
    });
```

```
}
```

there are no Dumb Questions

Q: Do all browsers have the window object?

A: Yes, all modern browsers have a window object you can interact with. Each window object, per tab on your browser, will also have a separate document object, into which your web page will get loaded.

Q: So, why do I have to move relative to the current position? Can't I just move to wherever the random number tells me to go?

A: That could work, except you'd have to reset your image back to the starting position, and then move it to wherever the random function says to move it to. That'll double the amount of code you'll have to write and maintain, and will slow down your application considerably.

Q: How does the reset function work?

A: The reset function simply loops through each element with the class of face and sets its left CSS property to 0. It sets each item in the clix array to be 0 as well—just as it was when we loaded the page.

Do this!

Below, you'll find all the code you've built in the last few pages. If you haven't done so already, add the bolded code to your *my_scripts.js* file and get ready to test all the new functionality you've built.

```javascript
var w = 367; //width of the face strip
var m = 10; //number of the monster face strip we're on
$("#btnRandom").click( randomize );
$("#btnReset").click( reset );

function getRandom(num){
        var my_random_num = Math.floor(Math.random()*num);
        return my_random_num;
}
function randomize(){
        $(".face").each(function(index){
                var target_position = getRandom(m);
                var current_position = clix[index] ;
                clix[index] = target_position;
                        if( target_position > current_position ) {
                        var move_to = (target_position - current_position) * w;
                                $(this).animate({left:"-="+move_to+"px"},500);
                        }else if( target_position < current_position ){
                                var move_to = (current_position - target_position) * w;
                                $(this).animate({left:"+="+move_to+"px"},500);
                        }else{
                                // They are the same - Don't move it.
                        }
        });
}


function reset(){
        $(".face").each(function(index){
                clix[index] = 0;
                $(this).animate({left:"0px"},500);
        });
}
```

my_scripts.js

TEST DRIVE

After entering the code from the previous page, open the *index.html* page up in your favorite browser to test the `randomize` and `reset` functions. Click the Randomize button 10 to 20 times to make sure you do a full test. Click the reset button intermittently too to make sure that's also working how you want it to.

It all works!

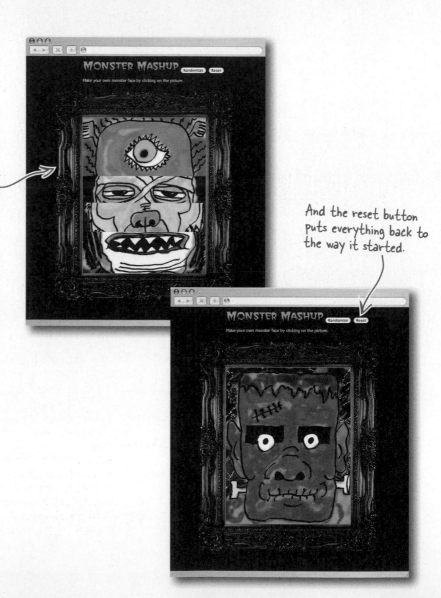

The monster face sections should fly both right and left now, which adds even more visual interest for your users.

And the reset button puts everything back to the way it started.

 # jQuerycross

It's time to sit back and give your left brain something to do. It's your standard crossword; all of the solution words are from this chapter.

Across

6. Tells a function to run repeatedly with an interval of time between each repetition.

7. JavaScript event handler that detects when the window loses focus.

9. A JavaScript method used to cancel the period of time to wait between repetitions.

10. Used to "pass" variables or objects to a function. Hint: Think parentheses.

11. jQuery method that adds a pause between effects in a method chain.

Down

1. Event handler that detects when the window receives a click, keyboard input, or some other kind of input.

2. Functions that return values are sometimes referred to as _____ functions.

3. A property of the `window` object that lets you access the different URLs that the window has loaded over time.

4. The global object that's created every time the visitor opens a new window in her browser.

5. Use this JavaScript timer method when you want to set a period of time to wait until telling a function to run.

8. What some folks call a function that does one thing and does it well: a _____ function.

 jQuerycross Solution

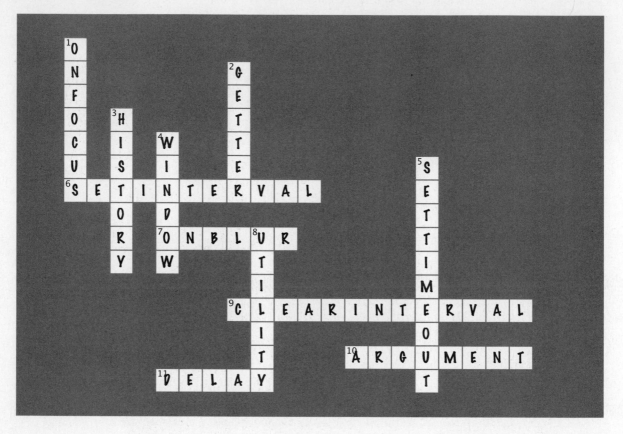

Monster Mashup v2 is a hit!

Your jQuery Toolbox

You've got Chapter 7 under your belt and now you've added the window object, timed functions, and custom functions to your toolbox.

window object

This is the topmost object in JavaScript.

It has properties, event handlers, and methods that help you detect and respond to browser events.

onFocus tells you when a browser window is active.

onBlur detects when a window loses focus.

Timed functions

Methods available for the window object.

setTimeout waits a set period of time before telling a function to run.

setInterval runs a function repeatedly, with a certain amount of time in between.

clearInterval wipes clean the schedule of repeated function calls.

Optimized custom functions

Writing your own custom functions allows you to really start making interactive web pages that people will want to use.

But you can also get carried away, and it's important to look at how best to combine and optimize your functions so you're writing less code that is easier to maintain and debug.

8 jQuery and Ajax

Please pass the data

A dash of Ajax, a drop of jQuery, and *seven* cups of heavy cream. Are you sure you wrote down that recipe right, darling?

Using jQuery to do some cool CSS and DOM tricks is fun,

but soon you'll need to read information (or data) from a server and display it. You may even have to update small pieces of the page with the information from the server, without having to reload the page. Enter Ajax. Combined with jQuery and JavaScript, it can do just that. In this chapter, we'll learn how jQuery deals with making Ajax calls to the server and what it can do with the information returned.

Bring the Bit to Byte race into this century

From: **Webville MegaCorps Marketing**
Subject: **42nd Annual Bit to Byte Race results page**

Hey Web Design Team,

As you're all aware, every year we sponsor Webville's Annual Bit to Byte 10K run by providing the race results page. But our page is *way* behind the times, as we only update it after all the results are in. People want instant gratification, and with Twitter and Facebook, folks attending the race are beating us at providing real-time results.

So we've got a challenge for you with a sweet payoff. If you can update our Webville Results page by next week to provide real-time results, you'll get to hang out in the VIP section at the end of the race. (Oh, and did we mention the race is in Maui this year?)

Here's what we need:

1) The page should provide the option to show either male or female runners, or all participants at once.

2) It should provide automatic updates as runners cross the finish line.

3) People shouldn't have to refresh the page as the results update.

4) Lastly, we want to indicate on the page when it was last updated and the frequency of the updates, and to enable people the ability to start and stop the updates if they want.

It doesn't look super different from last year's page, so that would be a good place to start. This is a great event, so we can't wait to see what you come up with!

--
Dionah C. Housney
  Head of Marketing
  Webville MegaCorp

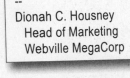

It looks like the web team is already set to go to Hawaii... guess it's time to figure this out!

Dude, Maui! It'll be sweet if we get to go to the VIP party!

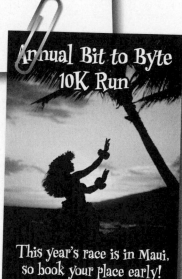

Annual Bit to Byte 10K Run

This year's race is in Maui, so book your place early!

Looking at last year's page

Let's have a look at last year's page to see how it was set up and what it looked like, so we can understand better what is being asked by the marketing department.

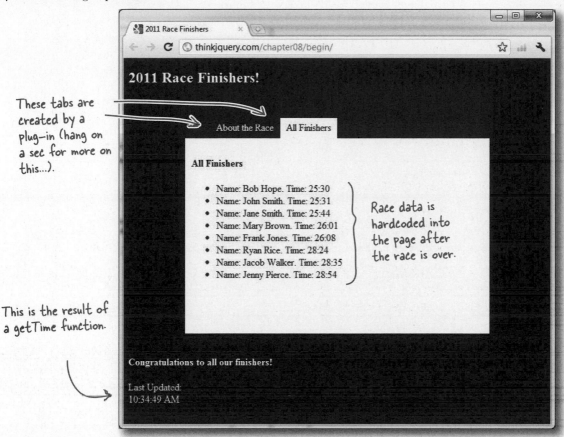

These tabs are created by a plug-in (hang on a sec for more on this...).

This is the result of a getTime function.

All Finishers

- Name: Bob Hope. Time: 25:30
- Name: John Smith. Time: 25:31
- Name: Jane Smith. Time: 25:44
- Name: Mary Brown. Time: 26:01
- Name: Frank Jones. Time: 26:08
- Name: Ryan Rice. Time: 28:24
- Name: Jacob Walker. Time: 28:35
- Name: Jenny Pierce. Time: 28:54

Race data is hardcoded into the page after the race is over.

Configuring a plug-in

Plug-ins are *extensions* to the base jQuery library that improve functionality, or make specific functions or tasks easier. In the example above, in combination with our CSS, the `idTabs` plug-in converts our `ul` element into clickable tabs and tells the `a` links in our `li`s which `div` elements to show when they are clicked. This particular plug-in gives us a very easy-to-use navigation structure for our page, so we can keep different types of information visually separate but still use the same display area.

Don't worry too much about the plug-in.

Plug-ins provide additional functionality to the default jQuery library. We'll look more at these in Chapter 10, but for now let's see what this one can do to speed up our project for us...

Ready Bake Download

Before we go on, let's look at last year's files to see how they set things up. The code should be in the *last_year.zip* file (along with all the other files you can download for this chapter from *http://thinkjquery.com/chapter08*). Here's a partial look at the three main files we'll need: *my_style.css*, *index.html*, and *my_scripts.js*.

```css
body{
    background-color: #000;
    color: white;
}

/* Style for tabs */
#main {
    color:#111;
    width:500px;
    margin:8px auto;
}
#main > li, #main > ul > li
{ list-style:none; float:left; }
#main ul a {
    display:block;
    padding:6px 10px;
    text-decoration:none!important;
    margin:1px 1px 1px 0;
    color:#FFF;
    background:#444;
}
```

A CSS comment

From here, the rest of the CSS is dedicated to building tabs on the page.

```css
#main ul a:hover {
    color:#FFF;
    background:#111;
}
#main ul a.selected {
    margin-bottom:0;
    color:#000;
    background:snow;
    border-bottom:1px solid snow;
    cursor:default;
}
#main div {
    padding:10px 10px 8px 10px;
    *padding-top:3px;
    *margin-top:-15px;
    clear:left;
    background:snow;
    height: 300px ;
}
#main div a {
    color:#000;  font-weight:bold;
}
```

my_style.css

Create the links that will be converted into tabs by the plug-in.

The div elements to hold the Tab content

```
<div id="main">
    <ul class="idTabs">
        <li><a href="#about">About the Race</a></li>
        <li><a href="#finishers">All Finishers</a></li>
    </ul>
    <div id="about">
        <h4>About the race</h4>This race Bit to Byte Campaign!
    </div>
    <div id="finishers">
        <h4>All Finishers</h4>
            <ul id="finishers_all">
                <li>Name: Bob Hope. Time: 25:30</li>
                <li>Name: John Smith. Time: 25:31</li>
                <li>Name: Jane Smith. Time:  25:44</li>
                ...
            </ul>
    </div>
...
<script src="scripts/jquery-1.6.2.min.js"></script>
<script src="scripts/my_scripts.js"></script>
<script src="scripts/jquery.idTabs.min.js"></script>
```

A portion of last year's runners, hardcoded into the page. This must have been a pain to update...

Include the JavaScript files, as per usual. We use the same method for including plug-ins.

index.html

```
$(document).ready(function(){
    getTime();
    function getTime(){
        var a_p = "";
        var d = new Date();
        var curr_hour = d.getHours();
        (curr_hour < 12) ? a_p = "AM" : a_p = "PM";
        (curr_hour == 0) ? curr_hour = 12 : curr_hour = curr_hour;
        (curr_hour > 12) ? curr_hour = curr_hour - 12 : curr_hour = curr_hour;
        var curr_min = d.getMinutes().toString();
        var curr_sec = d.getSeconds().toString();
        if (curr_min.length == 1) { curr_min = "0" + curr_min; }
        if (curr_sec.length == 1) { curr_sec = "0' + curr_sec; }
        $('#updatedTime').html(curr_hour + ":" + curr_min + ":" + curr_sec + " " + a_p );
    }
});
```

Call our custom getTime function.

A new instance of the JavaScript Date object

Methods of the Date object

A JavaScript ternary operator (more on this in a bit)

my_scripts.js

Getting dynamic

The marketing team wants the page to update in almost real time, so those hardcoded results in the HTML file have to go. And they only used JavaScript to update the time on the page! This is the perfect opportunity to take your jQuery to the next level. Welcome to the next generation of web *apps*, where jQuery, JavaScript, and a little bit of Ajax and XML can make your applications feel like *dynamic* (basically, the opposite of *static*), responsive desktop apps.

Ajax, which stands for "Asynchronous JavaScript and XML," is a way of passing data in a structured format between a web server and a browser, without interfering with the website visitor. With Ajax, your pages and applications only ask the server for what they really need—just the parts of a page that need to change, and just the data for those parts that the server has to provide. That means less traffic, smaller updates, and less time sitting around waiting for page refreshes.

And best of all, an Ajax page is built using standard Internet technologies, things you have already seen in this book, or already know how to use, like:

- **HTML**
- **CSS**
- **JavaScript**
- **The DOM**

To use Ajax, we'll look at a data format that's been around for a while (XML) and jQuery's method of handling Ajax requests, `ajax`.

When you use Ajax, your web pages only ask the server for what they really need, when (and where) they need it.

OLD web, meet the NEW web

Despite knowing some jQuery now, dealing with data threatens to drag us back
into the days of the old web, where we had to refresh the whole page, or link
to a completely separate page, in order to get some or all of the data to update.
And then we'd be back to websites that seem sluggish, as the whole page has to
be requested from the server each time. What's the point of learning a bunch
of cool jQuery if handling data is just going to slow us down again?

Enter Ajax

Ajax allows you to exchange data with a server in a dynamic way. Using Ajax
and some DOM maipulation, you can load or reload only a *portion* of the page
with jQuery and JavaScript.

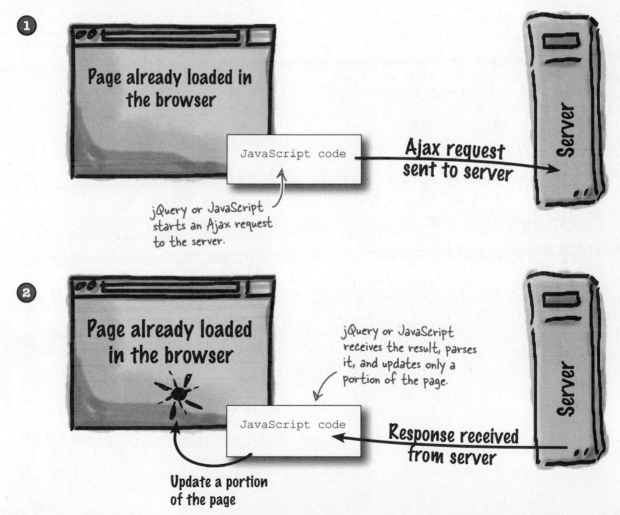

1

Page already loaded in
the browser

JavaScript code

jQuery or JavaScript
starts an Ajax request
to the server.

Ajax request
sent to server

Server

2

Page already loaded
in the browser

jQuery or JavaScript
receives the result, parses
it, and updates only a
portion of the page.

JavaScript code

Update a portion
of the page

Response received
from server

Server

Understanding Ajax

As we mentioned earlier, Ajax is a way of passing data in a structured format between a web server and a browser, without interfering with the website visitor. But, really, it isn't one thing—it is a combination of different technologies used to build exciting, interactive web applications. The JavaScript portion allows it to interact with the DOM structure of your page. *Asynchronous* means it can happen in the background, without interfering with your page or a user interacting with your page. And the X is all about the data.

What is Ajax?

Asynchronous

JavaScript makes a request to the server, but you can still interact with the page by typing in web forms, and even click buttons—all while the web server is still working in the background. Then, when the server's done, your code can update just the part of the page that's changed. But you're never waiting around. That's the power of asynchronous requests!

XML

XML, or eXtensible Markup Language, is a specification for storing information. It is also a specification for describing the structure of that information. And while XML is a markup language (just like HTML), XML has no tags of its own. It allows the person writing the XML to create whatever tags he needs.

JavaScript

JavaScript, as you already know well by now, is a scripting language used in web content development, primarily to create functions that can be embedded in or included from HTML documents and interact with the DOM.

But can't we just use HTML? Why do we need *another* markup language?

Yes, you could use HTML. But for the *transfer* of information, XML offers some unique benefits over its sister language, HTML. Let's have a look to see what those benefits are.

The X factor

XML is an acronym for e**X**tensible **M**arkup **L**anguage. It offers a widely adopted, standard way of representing text and data in a format that can be processed without much human interaction. Information formatted in XML can be exchanged across platforms, applications, and even across both programming and written languages. It can also be used with a wide range of development tools and utilities. XML is easy to create and edit; all you need is a simple text editor, and the XML declaration at the top of the file. The rest is up to you!

XML doesn't DO anything

It may sound a little strange, but XML doesn't really *do* much itself. XML structures and stores information for transportation. In fact, XML is really a metalanguage for describing markup languages. In other words, XML provides a facility to define tags and the structural relationships between them. It is important to understand that XML is not a replacement for HTML. XML is a *complement* to HTML. In many web applications, XML is used to format data for transport, while HTML is used to format and display the data. Let's take a closer look at an XML file that contains data about some books.

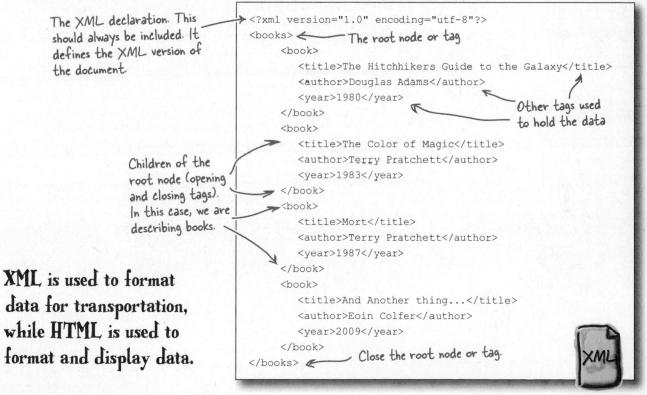

The XML declaration. This should always be included. It defines the XML version of the document.

The root node or tag

Other tags used to hold the data

Children of the root node (opening and closing tags). In this case, we are describing books.

```
<?xml version="1.0" encoding="utf-8"?>
<books>
    <book>
        <title>The Hitchhikers Guide to the Galaxy</title>
        <author>Douglas Adams</author>
        <year>1980</year>
    </book>
    <book>
        <title>The Color of Magic</title>
        <author>Terry Pratchett</author>
        <year>1983</year>
    </book>
    <book>
        <title>Mort</title>
        <author>Terry Pratchett</author>
        <year>1987</year>
    </book>
    <book>
        <title>And Another thing...</title>
        <author>Eoin Colfer</author>
        <year>2009</year>
    </book>
</books>
```

Close the root node or tag.

books.xml

XML is used to format data for transportation, while HTML is used to format and display data.

there are no
Dumb Questions

Q: So the big deal about XML is that you can create your own tags?

A: Exactly! It's pretty convenient to be able to define elements and structure that's suited to your business. Even better, XML is a standard, so tons of people know how to work with it. That means your vocabulary is usable by lots of programmers, in client-side and server-side programs.

Q: Wouldn't it be easier to just make up our own data format?

A: It might seem that way at first, but proprietary data formats—ones that you make up for your own use—can really cause a lot of problems. If you don't document them, people may forget how they work. And if anything changes, you need to make sure everything is up-to-date: the client, the server, the database, the documentation… that can be a real headache.

Q: So are people really using XML as much as you make it seem?

A: Given its flexibility for creating whatever data structures you need, XML is used as a basis for many different types of markup languages around the Web. There are more than 150 different types of languages that use XML, ranging from RSS (RDF Site Summary aka Real Simple Syndication) for news or audio/video feeds; to KML (Keyhole Markup Language) for geographical information used in Google Earth; to OOXML (Office Open XML), a standard submitted by Microsoft for word processing files; spreadsheets, presentations etc.; to SVG (scalable vector graphics), which describes two-dimensional images; to SOAP (Simple Object Access Protocol), which defines methods of exchanging information over Web Services. Wow, that really is a lot of uses for XML!

Q: OK, I get why we should use XML, but doesn't it become a "proprietary data format" when we start declaring element names?

A: No, not at all. That's the beauty of XML: it's flexible. The server and the client need to be looking for the same element names, but you can often work that out at runtime.

Q: But aren't all web pages asynchronous, like when a browser loads an image while I'm already viewing the page?

A: *Browsers* are asynchronous, but the standard web page isn't. Usually, when a web page needs information from a server-side program, everything comes to a complete stop until the server responds… unless the page makes an asynchronous request. And that is what Ajax is all about.

Q: How do I know when to use Ajax and asynchronous requests, and when not to?

A: Think of it like this: if you want something to go on while your user's still working, you likely want an asynchronous request. But if your user needs information or a response from your app before continuing, then you want to make her wait. That usually means a synchronous request.

Q: Shouldn't I use XHTML to interact with XML?

A: Funny story: XHTML *is* XML. At its core, XHTML is not as similar to HTML as people think. XHTML is a stricter language when it comes to parsing, and originates from the same family as XML. But that doesn't mean it can parse it or interact with it any better than HTML can. This book's markup is actually using HTML5, which will encompass XHTML5 whenever the standard specifications get released.

I'm game to get going with Ajax, but we need to get our structure set up for that first, don't we? It's been that way every time before…

You're right.

Let's get that out of the way, so we can get on to adding some Ajax to our page…

HTML Code Magnets

Rearrange the magnets to complete to code to create two new tabs that can display different pieces of information: one for male finishers (with the ID of `male`) and one for female finishers (with the ID of `female`). You can remove the **About** tab, but keep the **All Finishers** tab. In each section, put an empty `ul` element that will contain your runners. Also, remove all the existing content from the `finishers_all ul` element.

```html
<body>
    <header>
        <h2>_____</h2>
    </header>
    <div id="main">
        <ul class="idTabs">
            <li><a href="_____">Male Finishers</a></li>
            <li><a href="#female">_____</a></li>
            <li><a href="#all">All Finishers</a></li>
        </ul>
        <div id="male">
            <h4>Male Finishers</h4>
            <ul id="_____"></ul>
        </div>
        <div _____>
            <h4>Female Finishers</h4>
            <ul id="finishers_f"></ul>
        </div>
        <div _____>
            <h4>All Finishers</h4>
            <ul id=_____></ul>
        </div>
    </div>
    <footer>
        <h4>Congratulations to all our finishers!</h4>
        <br>Last Updated: <div id=_____></div>
    </footer>
    <script src="scripts/jquery-1.6.2.min.js"></script>
    <script src=_____></script>
    <script src="scripts/jquery.idTabs.min.js"></script>
</body>
```

index.html

Magnets:

- `"scripts/my_scripts.js"`
- `#male`
- `"finishers_all"`
- `2011 Race Finishers!`
- `"updatedTime"`
- `Female Finishers`
- `finishers_m`
- `id="female"`
- `id="all"`

HTML Code Magnets Solution

Now you should have two new tabs, one each for male and female runners.

```html
<body>
    <header>
        <h2> 2011 Race Finishers! </h2>
    </header>
    <div id="main">
        <ul class="idTabs">
            <li><a href=" #male ">Male Finishers</a></li>
            <li><a href="#female"> Female Finishers </a></li>
            <li><a href="#all">All Finishers</a></li>
        </ul>
        <div id="male">
            <h4>Male Finishers</h4>
            <ul id=" finishers_m "></ul>
        </div>
        <div id="female" >
            <h4>Female Finishers</h4>
            <ul id="finishers_f"></ul>
        </div>
        <div id="all" >
            <h4>All Finishers</h4>
            <ul id= "finishers_all" ></ul>
        </div>
    </div>
    <footer>
        <h4>Congratulations to all our finishers!</h4>
        <br>Last Updated: <div id= "updatedTime" ></div>
    </footer>
    <script src="scripts/jquery-1.6.2.min.js"></script>
    <script src= "scripts/my_scripts.js" ></script>
    <script src="scripts/jquery.idTabs.min.js"></script>
</body>
```

index.html

Our list of finishers

Include a jQuery plug-in to build our tabs.

TEST DRIVE

Update your *index.html* file with the code you completed in the magnets exercise and open it up in your favorite browser.

Nice work!

The page is starting to take shape. Now let's look at how we can go about getting data from the server so we can populate each of those tabs with some real race information.

GETting data with the ajax method

You want data? jQuery and Ajax are primed to provide it for you. The jQuery Ajax method returns an object (you remember those from Chapter 6, right?) with data about the particular action you are trying to perform. The `ajax` method can accept many different parameters, and can POST data *to* or GET data *from* a server.

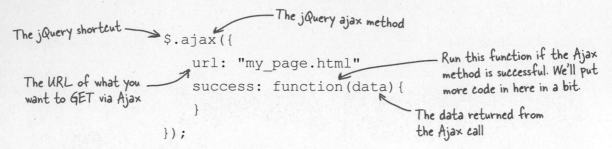

The jQuery shortcut →

The jQuery ajax method

```
$.ajax({
    url: "my_page.html"
    success: function(data){

    }
});
```

The URL of what you want to GET via Ajax

Run this function if the Ajax method is successful. We'll put more code in here in a bit.

The data returned from the Ajax call

For a complete list of all the parameters available on this method, visit the jQuery docs site at *http://api.jquery.com/jQuery.ajax/*. There are also a series of jQuery convenience methods for dealing with Ajax calls. We'll get to those a bit later, we promise.

For now, just update your *my_scripts.js* file with this code, only including the new code in bold below.

```
$(document).ready(function(){
    $.ajax({
        url: "finishers.xml",
        cache: false,
        dataType: "xml",
        success: function(xml){

        }
    });

    getTime();

    function getTime(){
        var a_p = "";
        var d = new Date();
```

Load the finishers.xml file via Ajax.

This parameter caches the results locally. That can cut down on calls to the server.

The data type we're expecting to get back from the server

JS

my_scripts.js

Test Drive

Update your *my_scripts.js* file with the code from the previous page. Then, download the sample XML file for this chapter from *http://thinkjquery.com/chapter08/step2/finishers.xml*, and save it in the same directory as your *index.html* file. When you've done this, open *index.html* in your browser, and open up the "Network" tab (in the developer tools in Google Chrome), or the "Net" tab (in Firebug for Firefox). Your XML file should be listed there, along with the other files from your page.

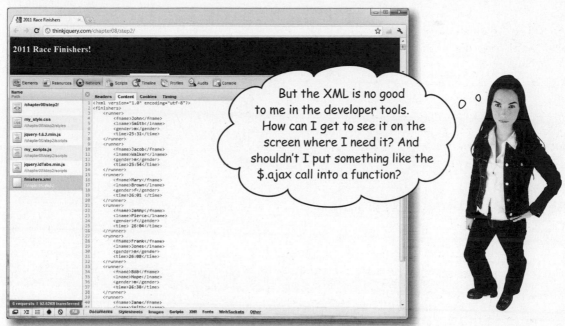

> But the XML is no good to me in the developer tools. How can I get to see it on the screen where I need it? And shouldn't I put something like the $.ajax call into a function?

Good point.

Now that we know we can load the XML file into the browser, we need to pick out the necessary text and display it on screen. We'll need a way to find *each* runner in order to add him or her to the correct list on the page. And yes, it's good practice to put the `ajax` calls into functions, so you can call them whenever you need them.

Ajax calls are subject to the same-origin policy!

The *same-origin policy* is a security concept for JavaScript and other client-side scripting languages. It allows scripts running on the page to access resources, like element properties and methods, that **originate from the same server**. It prevents scripts from accessing elements on pages that did not come from the same server. Due to legacy compatibility, JavaScript includes are not subject to these checks, but the XML file in the example is. That means the XML file **must be on the same server as the page loading it**.

Parsing XML data

We need a method to pick out each runner from our XML file and be able to display it on the screen. Luckily, jQuery supplies us with the `find` method, whose job it is to seek out elements that match whatever criteria we give it. `find` allows us to search through the descendants of elements in a structured, hierarchical set of information, like the DOM tree or an XML document, and construct a new array with the matching elements. The `find` and `children` methods are similar (we looked at the `children` method back in Chapter 4, when we were building the menu for the Webville Eatery), except that the latter only travels a single level down the DOM tree. And we might need to go further...

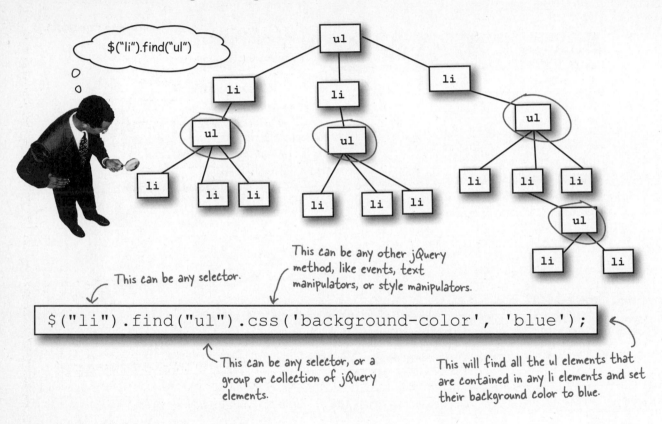

$("li").find("ul")

This can be any selector.

This can be any other jQuery method, like events, text manipulators, or style manipulators.

```
$("li").find("ul").css('background-color', 'blue');
```

This can be any selector, or a group or collection of jQuery elements.

This will find all the ul elements that are contained in any li elements and set their background color to blue.

By combining the find method with the each method, we can search for a group of elements and interact with each one individually, using a loop.

BRAIN POWER

Can you think of which pieces of our XML document we would need to interact with in order to display the individual runners on the screen?

jQuery Code Magnets

Rearrange the code magnets to create a function called getXMLRacers that will call the ajax method and load the *finishers.xml* file. Once the load is successful, empty all the lists that will hold the information, and then find each runner in the XML file and determine whether the runner is male or female. Append the runners to the appropriate list for their gender, and always add them to the finishers_all list. Then, call the getTime function to update the time on the page.

```
function _____
    $.ajax({
        url: _____,
        cache: false,
        dataType: "xml",
        _____ function(xml){
            $(_____).empty();
            $('#finishers_f')_____;
            $('#finishers_all').empty();
            $(xml).find_____(function() {
            var info = '<li>Name: ' + $(this).find_____ + ' ' + $(this).
find("lname").text() + '. Time: ' + _____.text() + '</li>';
            if( $(this).find("gender").text() == "m" ){
                $('#finishers_m').append_____
            }else if ( $(this).find("gender").text() == "f" ){
                _____.append(info);
            }else{   }
                _____.append(info);
            });
            _____
        }
    });
}
```

Code magnets:

`"finishers.xml"`

`getXMLRacers(){`

`getTime();`

`success:`

`(info)`

`$('#finishers_all')`

`'#finishers_m'`

`("runner").each`

`$('#finishers_f')`

`.empty()`

`("fname").text()`

`$(this).find("time")`

my_scripts.js

jQuery Code Magnets Solution

Using `find` and `each`, you can loop through the *finishers.xml* file, check the gender, and add each runner to the appropriate tab in your web app.

```
function getXMLRacers(){
    $.ajax({
        url: "finishers.xml",
        cache: false,
        dataType: "xml",
        success: function(xml){
            $('#finishers_m').empty();
            $('#finishers_f').empty();
            $('#finishers_all').empty();
            $(xml).find("runner").each(function() {
                var info = '<li>Name: ' + $(this).find("fname").text() + ' ' + $(this).
find("lname").text() + '. Time: ' + $(this).find("time").text() + '</li>';
                if( $(this).find("gender").text() == "m" ){
                    $('#finishers_m').append(info);
                }else if ( $(this).find("gender").text() == "f" ){
                    $('#finishers_f').append(info);
                }else{  }
                    $('#finishers_all').append(info);
            });
            getTime();
        }
    });
}
```

Empty all the ul elements so they can get updated data.

Loop through each runner element in the XML file.

Check the gender of each runner, so you can add it to the correct list.

Also, add each runner to the finishers_all list.

Call the getTime function to update the page with the last time the getXMLRacers function was called.

my_scripts.js

In this example, the line starting with "var info = ..." was too long for the page, so we had to let it run onto the next line. You won't need to do that in your code.

Test Drive

Update your *my_scripts.js* file with the `getXMLRacers` function. Also, replace the call to the `getTime` function (in the `document.ready` section) with a call to the `getXMLRacers` function instead. The `getTime` function is now called inside this new function. Make sure you run all your code through your web server, so the URL should say *http://*, not *file://*. Again, make sure your XML file is on the same server as your HTML file, or you will encounter those pesky same-origin permission issues.

Awesome, I have a function I can call to get my XML data. But shouldn't it run more than once if the page is to be automatically updated?

Yes, it should.

Luckily, in the previous chapter, we've already seen how to schedule events to happen regularly on a page. Let's have a quick look at how to do that again, and what options we have this time…

Scheduling events on a page

In the last chapter, we saw that both JavaScript and jQuery offer timer methods that call functions that run based on time passing. JavaScript's window object has four timer methods for timed control: `setTimeout`, `clearTimeout`, `setInterval`, and `clearInterval`. jQuery provides the `delay` method, but it focuses on effects and offers no option for scheduling or repeating actions. So, that one won't help us here…

JavaScript timer methods		jQuery's delay method

setTimeout

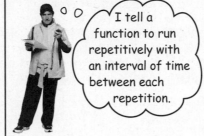

> Use me when you want to set a period of time to wait until telling a function to run.

setInterval

> I tell a function to run repetitively with an interval of time between each repetition.

delay

> I add a pause between effects that are queued up in a chain of effects.

```
setTimeout(myFunction, 4000);
```

The function to call when the timeout duration has passed.

The timer delay (in milliseconds)

```
setInterval(repeatMe, 1000);
```

The function to repeat after each interval is up.

The interval of time between function calls (in milliseconds)

```
slideDown().delay(5000).slideUp();
```

When this chain runs, it's known in jQuery as an effects queue.

In this example, the delay method puts a five-second pause between the slideUp and slideDown effects.

> It's obvious, isn't it? We use **setInterval**, just like last time. Right?

Not so fast!

We can't always be so sure. `setInterval` normally would work to schedule regular events on a page, but when dependent on outside resources (like our data file), it can cause problems.

Watch it!

`setInterval` will run even if the function it is calling isn't finished yet.

If you're waiting on information from another server, or waiting on user interaction, `setInterval` could call your function again before you're ready. Your functions may not always return in the order that you called them.

Self-referencing functions

A *self-referencing* function calls itself during its normal operations. Such functions can be particularly useful when you need to wait for the function's currently running operation to complete before running it again. Combine this with a `setTimeout` call, and you can schedule a function to run but only keep going if the previous call to the function was successful. Otherwise, it won't reach the call to itself in the code, and hence it won't be called again.

Sharpen your pencil

Create a function called `startAJAXcalls` that gets called when the page is loaded and which will call the `getXMLRacers` function every 10 seconds. Define a variable at the start of the script file, inside the `$(document).ready` function, called `FREQ` and set it to the number of milliseconds we will need as a parameter for the frequency of our repeated calls to the `getXMLRacers` function. Use `setTimeout` to call the `startAJAXcalls` function to make it self-referencing, after the `getXMLRacers` function is complete. You'll also need to call the `startAJAXcalls` function directly in your code to start the timer.

```
$(document).ready(function(){

    .........................................

    function startAJAXcalls(){

        .........................................
                .............................................
                .............................................
                ..............
                ...............
        .............
    }
    getXMLRacers();

    .........................................


    function getXMLRacers(){
        $.ajax({
            url: "finishers.xml",
            cache: false,
```

my_scripts.js

Sharpen your pencil
Solution

This solution uses setTimout inside the startAJAXcalls function to call the getXMLRacers function to get our XML, plus a call to itself. This self-call will ensure that the next call will only happen when the last one has completed. This will guarantee that there is not a buildup of requests to the server if the network is slow, or if a response from the server does not come back before the next call is scheduled to be made.

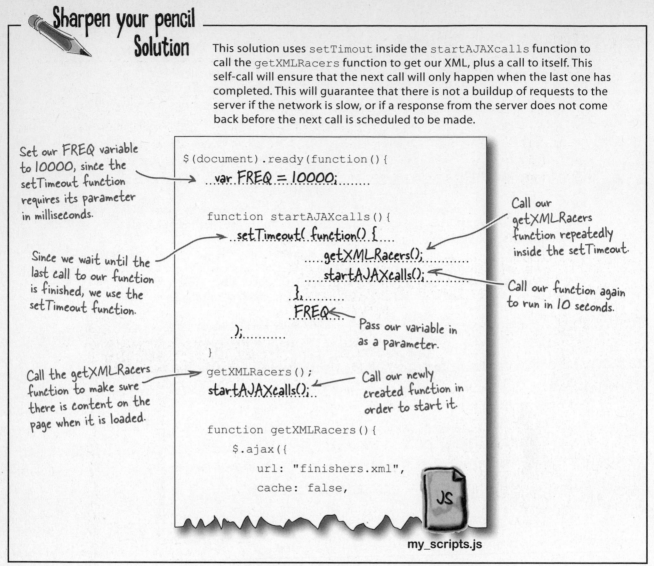

Set our FREQ variable to 10000, since the setTimeout function requires its parameter in milliseconds.

Since we wait until the last call to our function is finished, we use the setTimeout function.

Call the getXMLRacers function to make sure there is content on the page when it is loaded.

Call our getXMLRacers function repeatedly inside the setTimeout.

Call our function again to run in 10 seconds.

Pass our variable in as a parameter.

Call our newly created function in order to start it.

```
$(document).ready(function(){
    var FREQ = 10000;

    function startAJAXcalls(){
        setTimeout( function() {
                getXMLRacers();
                startAJAXcalls();
        },
        FREQ
        );
    }
    getXMLRacers();
    startAJAXcalls();

    function getXMLRacers(){
        $.ajax({
            url: "finishers.xml",
            cache: false,
```

my_scripts.js

there are no
Dumb Questions

Q: Everything I've read about Ajax says I need to use the **XMLHttpRequest** object; is that right?

A: Yes, but not with jQuery. As a web programmer, you don't need to use that object. jQuery does it for you when you use the ajax method. Also, since Ajax calls can differ per browser, jQuery figures out the best way to do an Ajax request for each of your site visitors.

Q: What happens if the server returns an error or doesn't respond? Will it sit and wait forever?

A: No, the request won't wait forever. You can set a timeout as one of your parameters in your ajax call. Also, just like the success event parameter, which can run a function, there are others to handle error, complete, and many more. These events can be set as local events, when the ajax method is called, or as global events to trigger any handlers that may be listening for them.

Test Drive

Update your *my_scripts.js* file with the new code you just created. Also, don't forget to add a call to the new function just after your call to the `getXMLRacers` function at the bottom of your script. Then, view the page in your browser, and use the "Network" feature of Google Chrome or the "Net" feature of Firefox's Firebug to see the file get loaded every 10 seconds. Once you see this happening, update your XML file, using your favorite text editor, with the entry listed below and see your new runner appear on your page... (Don't forget to save the XML file after you've updated it!)

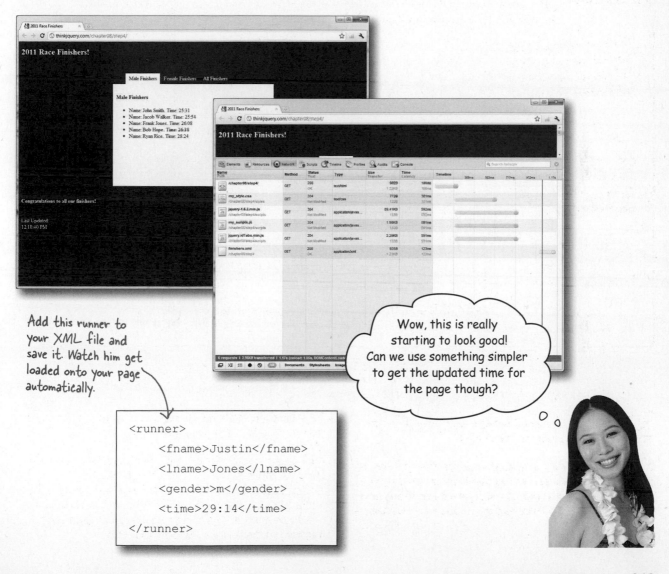

Add this runner to your XML file and save it. Watch him get loaded onto your page automatically.

```
<runner>
    <fname>Justin</fname>
    <lname>Jones</lname>
    <gender>m</gender>
    <time>29:14</time>
</runner>
```

Wow, this is really starting to look good! Can we use something simpler to get the updated time for the page though?

Getting more from your server

As we've seen so far, HTML is great for *displaying* information on a page and XML is great for *formatting data for transportation* to a page, but what if you need your page to actually **do** something, like tell the time or get data from a database? Sure, we could probably do some more fun things with jQuery and JavaScript, but why not use something designed for the job?

Server-side languages to the rescue!

There are several different types of server-side languages—like JSP, ASP, or Cold Fusion—but we're only going to focus on one for our purposes: PHP.

PHP (which stands for PHP: Hypertext Processor—yes, that's an acronym within an acronym; don't ask us why!) is a free, general-purpose, server-side scripting language used to produce dynamic web pages. Files that contain PHP code are run on the server, and produce HTML that is then provided to a browser to render. We'll look at PHP in a little more detail in the next chapter, but for now we'll see how it can help us with our "updated time" feature.

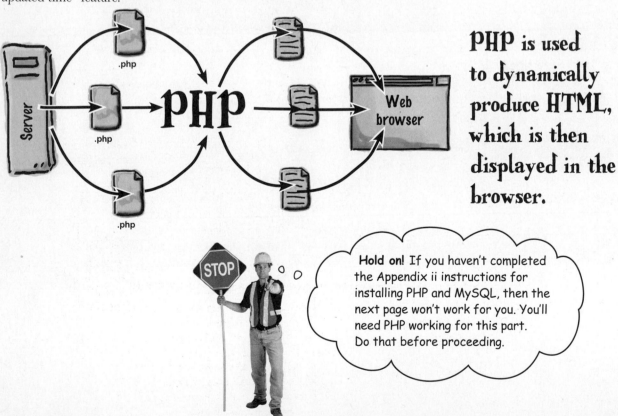

PHP is used to dynamically produce HTML, which is then displayed in the browser.

Hold on! If you haven't completed the Appendix ii instructions for installing PHP and MySQL, then the next page won't work for you. You'll need PHP working for this part. Do that before proceeding.

What time is it?

OK, we'll confess, there *is* already a JavaScript function we could use to get the time. But it is a large, complicated function for doing something so simple. Luckily, PHP gives us a very easy way of getting the time, using the date function. Just like the functions you have created up to this point, it takes multiple parameters and returns a different version of the date, depending on what parameters you pass in. The main parameter determines how you want the date to be displayed. Let's have a closer look:

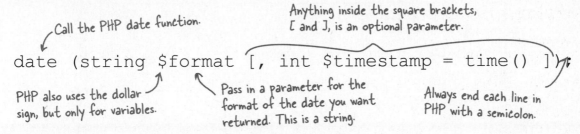

Call the PHP date function.

Anything inside the square brackets, [and], is an optional parameter.

```
date (string $format [, int $timestamp = time() ]);
```

PHP also uses the dollar sign, but only for variables.

Pass in a parameter for the format of the date you want returned. This is a string.

Always end each line in PHP with a semicolon.

For a complete listing of the parameters of the date function, visit *http://php.net/manual/en/function.date.php*.

Do this!

Create a new file in the same folder as your *index.html* file, and call it *time.php*. Add the following code to your new *time.php* file.

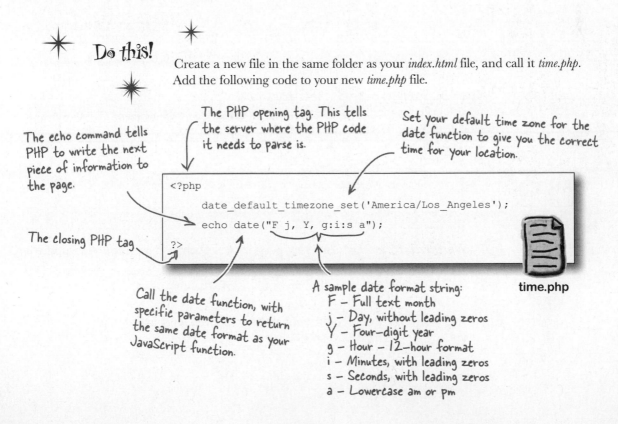

The echo command tells PHP to write the next piece of information to the page.

The PHP opening tag. This tells the server where the PHP code it needs to parse is.

Set your default time zone for the date function to give you the correct time for your location.

```php
<?php
    date_default_timezone_set('America/Los_Angeles');
    echo date("F j, Y, g:i:s a");
?>
```

The closing PHP tag

time.php

Call the date function, with specific parameters to return the same date format as your JavaScript function.

A sample date format string:
F – Full text month
j – Day, without leading zeros
Y – Four-digit year
g – Hour – 12-hour format
i – Minutes, with leading zeros
s – Seconds, with leading zeros
a – Lowercase am or pm

Test Drive

After you save your *time.php* file, bring it up in your browser to make sure the date is in the correct format. PHP code **must** run through your web server, so the URL should say *http://*, not *file://*. Also, make sure the URL is pointing to the server where you are developing your code.

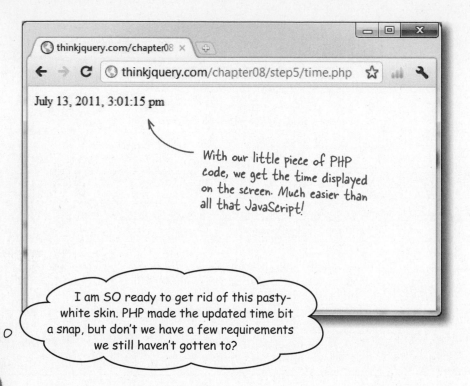

With our little piece of PHP code, we get the time displayed on the screen. Much easier than all that JavaScript!

I am SO ready to get rid of this pasty-white skin. PHP made the updated time bit a snap, but don't we have a few requirements we still haven't gotten to?

Yeah, we're not getting on that plane quite yet. Let's see what's left to do:

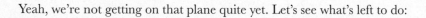

1 We want to indicate on the page how recently the page was updated.

2 We want to indicate the frequency of the updates.

3 We want to give people the ability to stop and start the updates, should they so choose.

Let's have a go at the first and second items on the list. We'll tackle them together since they are related.

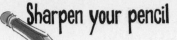

Sharpen your pencil

Add a `<span>` tag, with the ID of `freq`, in the footer of your *index.html* page. This will be used to indicate the result of a new function called `showFrequency`, which should display how often the page is updated. Also, create another function, called `getTimeAjax`, which will load the *time.php* file using the `load` method—a jQuery convenience method for Ajax. This method will take a URL as a parameter and write the result automatically into the `div` with the ID of `updatedTime`. Last, replace the call to the `getTime` function in `getXMLRacers` with this new `getTimeAjax` function.

```
<footer>
    <h4>Congratulations to all our finishers!</h4>
    ...........................................
    <br><br>
    Last Updated: <div id="updatedTime"></div>
</footer>
<script src="scripts/jquery-1.6.2.min.js"></script>
<script src="scripts/my_scripts.js"></script>
```

index.html

```
function ............................
    ....................... "Page refreshes every " + FREQ/1000 + " second(s).");
}
.
.
.
.
function ....................
    $(.................).load(...................);
}
```

my_scripts.js

Sharpen your pencil Solution

Now you'll have added a `<span>` tag with the ID of `freq` in the footer of your *index.html* page to display how often the page is updated. You've also created a new `getTimeAjax` function, which loads the *time.php* file using the `load` Ajax convenience method, which will then write the result into the `updatedTime` div. You've also updated the `getXMLRacers` function to use the new `getTimeAjax` function instead of the JavaScript `getTime` function.

```
<footer>
    <h4>Congratulations to all our finishers!</h4>
    <span id="freq"></span>        ⟵——  Add the span element to
                                          display the frequency.
    <br><br>
    Last Updated: <div id="updatedTime"></div>
</footer>
<script src="scripts/jquery-1.6.2.min.js"></script>
<script src="scripts/my_scripts.js"></script>
```

index.html

```
function showFrequency(){
    $("#freq").html( "Page refreshes every " + FREQ/1000 + " second(s).");
}
.
.
.
.
function getTimeAjax(){
    $( '#updatedTime' ).load(  "time.php"  );
}
```

Create two new functions, one to show the frequency, and the other to get the time from the server via Ajax.

Divide by 1,000 to convert milliseconds to seconds.

Load the time.php file using Ajax.

Output the result to the screen in the element updatedTime.

my_scripts.js

TEST DRIVE

Update your *my_scripts.js* file with the new code you just created. Also, don't forget to add the new `span` element to your *index.html* file, and replace the call to the `getTime` function with the `getTimeAjax` function.

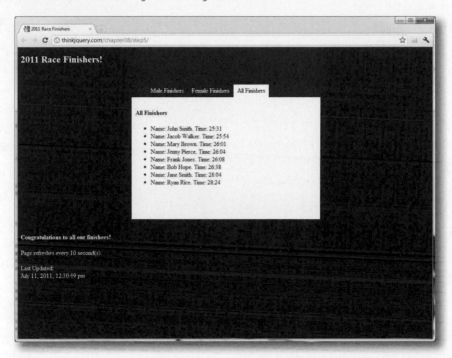

1. ~~We want to indicate on the page how recently the page was updated.~~

2. ~~We want to indicate the frequency of the updates.~~

3. We want to give people the ability to stop and start the updates, should they so choose.

> But how are we going to stop a function that calls itself?

That's a tricky one.

We'll need to change the function to only run when certain conditions are met.

BRAIN POWER

What feature have we seen so far that checks if conditions are met?

Turning off scheduled events on your page

Back in Chapters 5 and 7, we created a "monster" function by using `setTimeout` to continuously call the functions that produced the lightning effects. This led to some unexpected consequences—the page lost focus and the visual effects piled on top of one another when someone returned to the app.

Need some more monsters??

However, since we already determined that we need to wait until the previous call to the function is finished, we can't switch to using `setInterval` for these calls.

We need to come up with a better solution. And what better solution than one we've already seen? We can't use the `window.onblur` and `window.onfocus` browser events, since we don't want people to have to leave in order to stop the updating. But we have already seen, across several chapters, how to run code based on *conditional logic*, so let's use that for our solution here as well.

BRAIN POWER

Can you think of which conditional logic structure we could use for this? (Hint: We've used it already to check the gender of the runners in the XML file.)

there are no Dumb Questions

Q: What other stuff, besides XML, can Ajax load into the page?

A: Using jQuery, you can load all sorts of information into the page. Like you've just seen, using the `load` method, you can load the results of a PHP file directly into your HTML element. Also, you can load other HTML files, JavaScript files, plain text, and JSON (JavaScript Object Notation) objects. We'll look at JSON in the next chapter.

Q: What other convenience methods are there for Ajax in jQuery?

A: jQuery has five convenience or shorthand methods for Ajax: `get`, `getJSON`, `getScript`, `post`, and `load`. The first four are called using the jQuery object. But `load` can be called from any element—which will be the destination of the returned data.

Q: When should I use the `load` method and when should I use `ajax`?

A: The `load` method is designed for loading a particular piece of data into a specific place, like we do with our `getTimeAjax` function. The `ajax` method is much more complex and has many more purposes and parameters. It can be used to load other information or send data to the server for processing. We'll see that more in the next chapter.

Sharpen your pencil

Create a global variable called `repeat`, with a default value of `true`. Create a function that will alter the repeat variable with the click of a new button, giving it the ID of `btnStop`. Set the HTML of the `span` element with the ID of `freq` to say "Updates paused." Also, create a button called `btnStart` that will set the `repeat` global variable to `true`, as well as call both the `startAJAXcalls` and the `setTimeout` functions if the `repeat` variable is true. Add the new buttons to the footer area of the page.

```
$(document).ready(function(){

    ......................
    var FREQ = 10000;
    function startAJAXcalls(){

        ..................
            setTimeout( function() {
                getXMLRacers();
                startAJAXcalls();
            },
            FREQ

        .............
    );
 .
 .
    $("#btnStop").click(function(){

        ......................
        $("#freq").html( .......................... );
    });
    ..........................,,, function(){

        ......................
        startAJAXcalls();

        ......................
    });
```

my_scripts.js

```
<footer>
    <h4>Congratulations to all our finishers!</h4>
    ...............................................
    ...............................................
    <br>
    <span id="freq"></span> <br><br>
```

index.html

Sharpen your pencil
Solution

When finished, you should have a variable called `repeat` that will control whether or not the function will call itself again to get the XML file for updating. The value of this variable should be controlled by the `btnStop` and `btnStart` buttons, which are added to the footer area of the page. These buttons also set the text of the `freq` span element to show different messages depending on whether or not the page is being updated.

Set the variable to a default value of true so it'll update when the page loads.

Check if the repeat variable is true.

```
$(document).ready(function(){
    var repeat = true;
    var FREQ = 10000;
    function startAJAXcalls(){
        if(repeat) {
            setTimeout( function() {
                getXMLRacers();
                startAJAXcalls();
            },
            FREQ
            )
        }
    );
    .
    .
```

Set the variable to false when the btnStop button is clicked.

Set the variable back to true when the btnStart button is clicked. Also call the startAJAXcalls function to start getting the file again.

```
    $("#btnStop").click(function(){
        repeat = false;
        $("#freq").html( "Updates paused.");
    });
    $("#btnStart").click(function(){
        repeat = true;
        startAJAXcalls();
        showFrequency();
    });
```

my_scripts.js

Add the new buttons to the footer area of the page.

```
<footer>
    <h4>Congratulations to all our finishers!</h4>
    <button id="btnStart">Start Page Updates</button>
    <button id="btnStop">Stop Page Updates</button>
    <br>
    <span id="freq"></span> <br><br>
```

index.html

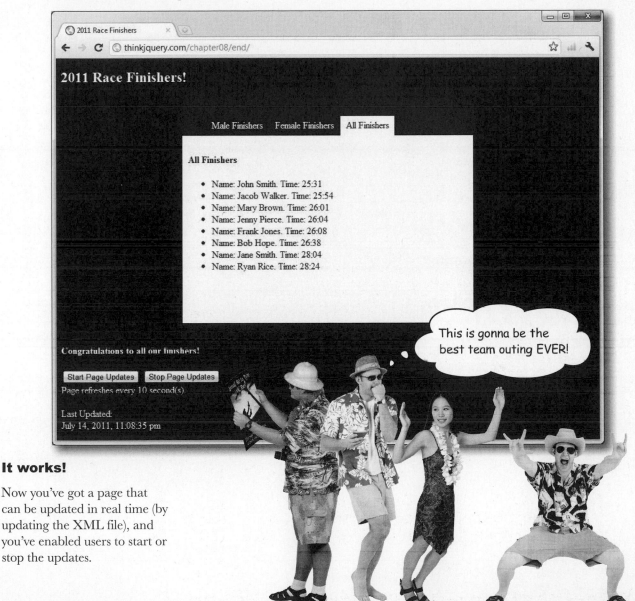

TEST DRIVE

Update your *my_scripts.js* file and your *index.html* file with the new code you just created. Then, load the page in your favorite browser to make sure it all still works. Try out the new buttons to make sure they stop the Ajax requests. You will be able to tell in the "Network" tab in Google Chrome, or the "Net" tab in Firebug for Firefox.

2011 Race Finishers

← → C 🔒 thinkjquery.com/chapter08/end/ ☆ ⚒ 🔧

2011 Race Finishers!

Male Finishers   Female Finishers   All Finishers

All Finishers

- Name: John Smith. Time: 25:31
- Name: Jacob Walker. Time: 25:54
- Name: Mary Brown. Time: 26:01
- Name: Jenny Pierce. Time: 26:04
- Name: Frank Jones. Time: 26:08
- Name: Bob Hope. Time: 26:38
- Name: Jane Smith. Time: 28:04
- Name: Ryan Rice. Time: 28:24

Congratulations to all our finishers!

Start Page Updates   Stop Page Updates
Page refreshes every 10 second(s)

Last Updated:
July 14, 2011, 11:08:35 pm

> This is gonna be the best team outing EVER!

It works!

Now you've got a page that can be updated in real time (by updating the XML file), and you've enabled users to start or stop the updates.

Your jQuery/Ajax Toolbox

You've got Chapter 8 under your belt and you've added a little PHP, some XML, and a bunch of Ajax to your toolbox.

Ajax

A combination of technologies that allow you to update a portion of a web page without having to reload the whole page.

Makes calls to a backend server that can process data before sending it back.

jQuery implements Ajax functionality through the ajax method.

XML

A strict yet flexible markup language used to describe data and data structure.

Can be used for information storage or for formatting data for transfer.

Used in many common web technologies like RSS, SOAP/Web Services, and SVG.

ajax() shortcuts

There are five shortcuts for ajax in jQuery, all configured to have different parameters by default, but ultimately calling the ajax method:

$.get

$.getJSON

$.getScript

$.post

$.load

PHP

A server-side scripting language that lets you manipulate web page content on the server before a page is delivered to the client browser.

9 Handling JSON data

✳ Client, meet server ✳

Flowers? I hope there's some data to follow those. But this could be the beginning of a beautiful friendship.

As useful as reading data from an XML file was, that won't always cut the mustard. A more efficient data interchange format (JavaScript Object Notation, aka JSON) will make it easier to get data from the server side. JSON is easier to generate and read than XML, too. Using jQuery, PHP, and SQL, you'll learn how to create a database to store information so you can retrieve it later, using JSON, and display it on the screen using jQuery. A true web application superpower!

Webville MegaCorp's Marketing Department doesn't know XML

From: **Webville MegaCorps Marketing**
Subject: **Re: 42nd Annual Bit to Byte Race results page**

Hey Web Design Team,

We really like the updates you've made to the website.

We have a problem though: nobody in our office knows XML! So we don't know how to add new finishers to the race website.

We've tried, but every time we get it wrong, it makes the website do some strange things... Finishers don't show, or fields disappear from the page even though they're in the XML file. It's very odd.

What we'd really like is some way to just type into a few boxes and click a button to add a finisher. Can you make this happen?

And if we make a mistake, can you make it so we don't break the whole site?

I know it's only three days until we all fly out to Hawaii, but we'd really like this working before we go. Do you think you can make it in time?

--
Dionah C. Housney
   Head of Marketing
   Webville MegaCorp

XML errors break the page

When there are errors in the XML, the logic that we wrote to read and parse that XML fails. These errors mainly happen when there are issues with the tags, like forgetting to close a tag or having the wrong case in the tag name. However, data in the tags can also cause XML some problems if it's not encoded for use in XML properly.

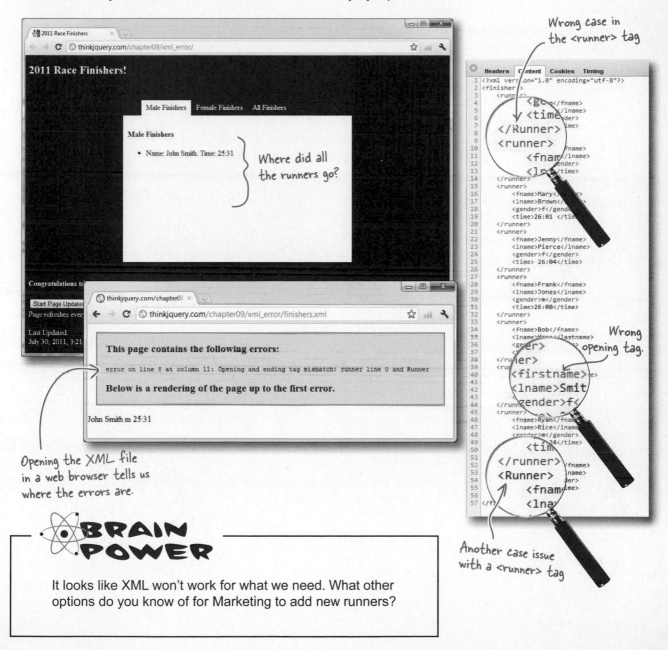

Wrong case in the `<runner>` tag

Where did all the runners go?

Opening the XML file in a web browser tells us where the errors are.

Wrong opening tag.

Another case issue with a `<runner>` tag

BRAIN POWER

It looks like XML won't work for what we need. What other options do you know of for Marketing to add new runners?

Collect data from a web page

Odds are, you've already thought of using an HTML **form**. With a form, you can collect all sorts of data and send it to the server for processing. Forms have several different types of elements used to collect various types of data. We'll look at forms in much more detail in Chapter 10, but for now, let's just use two of the most basic form elements: a text box and a drop-down list. You may be a pro at forms already, but let's just take a quick look so we know what we're dealing with here.

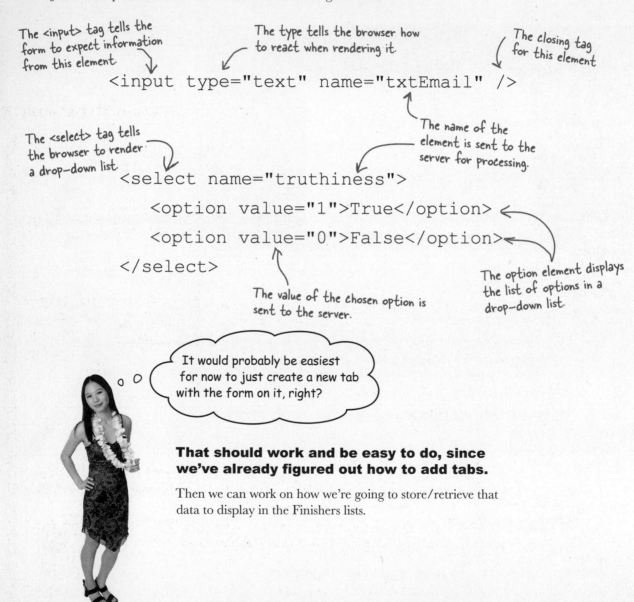

The <input> tag tells the form to expect information from this element.

The type tells the browser how to react when rendering it.

The closing tag for this element

```
<input type="text" name="txtEmail" />
```

The name of the element is sent to the server for processing.

The <select> tag tells the browser to render a drop-down list.

```
<select name="truthiness">
    <option value="1">True</option>
    <option value="0">False</option>
</select>
```

The value of the chosen option is sent to the server.

The option element displays the list of options in a drop-down list.

It would probably be easiest for now to just create a new tab with the form on it, right?

That should work and be easy to do, since we've already figured out how to add tabs.

Then we can work on how we're going to store/retrieve that data to display in the Finishers lists.

 Ready Bake
HTML & CSS

Update your *index.html* file with an additional tab to add new finishers via a form. Also update the entry in your *my_style.css* file to make the element with the ID of main wider.

```
#main {                    my_style.css
    background:#181818;
    color:#111;
    padding:15px 20px;
    width:600px;
    border:1px solid #222;
    margin:8px auto;
}
```

```
<ul class="idTabs">
    <li><a href="#male">Male Finishers</a></li>
    <li><a href="#female">Female Finishers</a></li>
    <li><a href="#all">All Finishers</a></li>
    <li><a href="#new">Add New Finisher</a></li>
</ul>
<div id="male">
    <h4>Male Finishers</h4><ul id="finishers_m"></ul>
</div>
<div id="female">
    <h4>Female Finishers</h4><ul id="finishers_f"></ul>
</div>
<div id="all">
    <h4>All Finishers</h4>  <ul id="finishers_all"></ul>
</div>
<div id="new">
    <h4>Add New Finisher</h4>
    <form id="addRunner" name="addRunner" action="service.php" method="POST">
        First Name: <input type="text" name="txtFirstName" id="txtFirstName" /> <br>
        Last Name: <input type="text" name="txtLastName" id="txtLastName" /> <br>
        Gender: <select id="ddlGender" name="ddlGender">
            <option value="">--Please Select--</option>
            <option value="f">Female</option>
            <option value="m">Male</option>
        </select><br>
        Finish Time:
        <input type="text" name="txtMinutes" id="txtMinutes" size="10" maxlength="2" />(Minutes)
        <input type="text" name="txtSeconds" id="txtSeconds" size="10" maxlength="2" />(Seconds)
        <br><br>
        <button type="submit" name="btnSave" id="btnSave">Add Runner</button>
        <input type="hidden" name="action" value="addRunner" id="action">
    </form>
</div>
```

Add the new tab, called "Add New Finisher."

Add a new HTML form for collecting and posting data to the server.

The action tells the form <u>where</u> to be sent for processing.

The method determines <u>how</u> the data will be sent to the server.

A hidden HTML field. We'll use this more in a little bit.

index.html

Test Drive

Open up *index.html* in your browser and select the **Add New Finisher** tab to see the new form and fields added to your page.

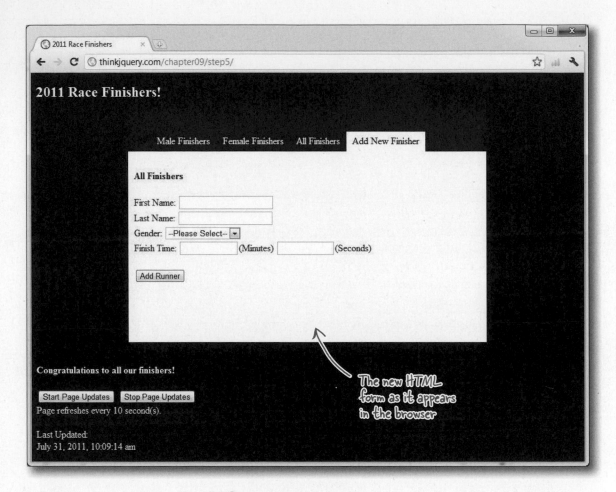

The new HTML form as it appears in the browser

BRAIN POWER

Now that you've got a form in place to collect the data, how do you think we should go about storing and retrieving it?

What to do with the data

Now we need to send the data collected by the form to the server and store it somehow. To do that, we're going to use another language, PHP, to insert the data into a *database*. Don't worry! We'll get you up to speed on PHP and databases in a bit, but first let's focus on how we get our form data to the server.

There are two methods of sending the data to the server using HTTP: GET and POST. The main difference between GET and POST is how the data is sent to the server. GET will append the form field names and values onto the end of the URL as key/value pairs. PHP can read this information out of an associative array called $_GET[], which is sent to the server when the form is submitted. The data is visible after the **?** in the URL.

POST sends the data—also in an associative array, but encoded differently—and is not visible to the end user in the URL. The $_POST[] associative array contains all the information from the form elements. This, like the $_GET[] array, is a series of key/value pairs of the form element names and values.

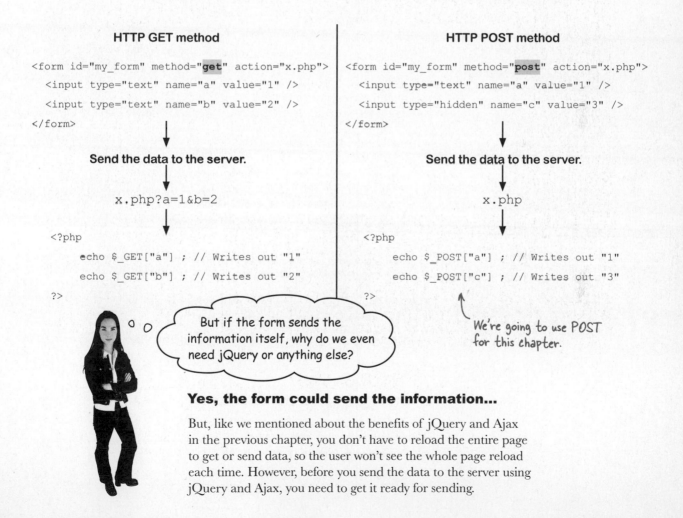

HTTP GET method

```
<form id="my_form" method="get" action="x.php">
   <input type="text" name="a" value="1" />
   <input type="text" name="b" value="2" />
</form>
```

Send the data to the server.

```
x.php?a=1&b=2
```

```php
<?php
    echo $_GET["a"] ; // Writes out "1"
    echo $_GET["b"] ; // Writes out "2"
?>
```

HTTP POST method

```
<form id="my_form" method="post" action="x.php">
   <input type="text" name="a" value="1" />
   <input type="hidden" name="c" value="3" />
</form>
```

Send the data to the server.

```
x.php
```

```php
<?php
    echo $_POST["a"] ; // Writes out "1"
    echo $_POST["c"] ; // Writes out "3"
?>
```

We're going to use POST for this chapter.

> But if the form sends the information itself, why do we even need jQuery or anything else?

Yes, the form could send the information...

But, like we mentioned about the benefits of jQuery and Ajax in the previous chapter, you don't have to reload the entire page to get or send data, so the user won't see the whole page reload each time. However, before you send the data to the server using jQuery and Ajax, you need to get it ready for sending.

Format the data before you send it

Before we can send information to the server (using Ajax), we need to do a little prepping to get it into a format that the Ajax call can send and the server will understand. To do this, we *serialize* our data into a single object, so the Ajax call can send it as one single package. jQuery offers two form helper methods for serializing data: `serialize` and `serializeArray`. The former will join all the inputs of your form into a single string of key/value pairs, separated by ampersands (**&**). The latter will create an associative array of key/value pairs, which is still a single object but is much more structured than the result of the simple `serialize` method. We'll take a look at both, but we're going to use `serializeArray` for our marathon data.

serialize	**serializeArray**

```
<form id="my_form">
  <input type="text" name="a" value="1" />
  <input type="text" name="b" value="2" />
  <input type="hidden" name="c" value="3" />
</form>
```

```
$("#my_form").serialize();
```

↖ The form ID selector ↗ The serialize method

```
<form id="my_form">
  <input type="text" name="a" value="1" />
  <input type="hidden" name="c" value="3" />
</form>
```

```
$("#my_form:input").serializeArray();
```

The form's ID selector, followed by the HTML element input filter. This tells the selector to only look at HTML elements of type "input."

↖ Call the serializeArray method.

End result

a=1&b=2&c=3

End result

```
[
  {
    name: "a",
    value: "1"
  },
  {
    name: "c",
    value: "3"
  }
]
```

Send the data to the server

jQuery provides a shortcut method, post, dedicated to sending data to the server. The post method takes several parameters, including the URL you want to send your information to, the information you want to send, and a handler function that will run when the POST is complete.

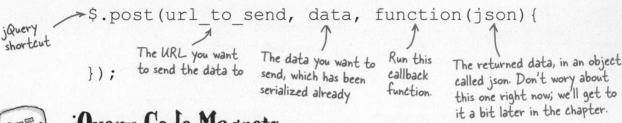

jQuery shortcut

```
$.post(url_to_send, data, function(json){

});
```

The URL you want to send the data to

The data you want to send, which has been serialized already

Run this callback function.

The returned data, in an object called json. Don't wory about this one right now; we'll get to it a bit later in the chapter.

jQuery Code Magnets

Create a click event listener on #btnSave that takes all the data in the form and serializes it. Then send this information to the server using a jQuery post method. Get the URL to post to from the action attribute of the form. Also, create a clearInputs function that sets all values of the form fields to blank, if the post is **successful**. You will also need to cancel the default submit action of the form (by returning false), using a .submit listener on the form with the ID of addRunner.

```javascript
$('_____').click(function() {
    var data = $("#addRunner :input")._____();
    $.post($("#addRunner").attr('action'), _____ , _____(json){
        if (json.status == "fail") {
            alert(json._____);
        }
        if (json.status == _____) {
            alert(json.message);
            clearInputs();
        }
    }, "json");
});
function _____{
    $("#addRunner :input").each(function(){
        $(this).val('');
    });
}
$("#addRunner")._____(function(){
    return false;
});
```

serializeArray

"success"

message

data

#btnSave

function

submit

clearInputs()

JS

my_scripts.js

jQuery Code Magnets Solution

Create a `btnSave` click action that takes all the data in the form and serializes it. Then send this information to the server using a jQuery `post` method. Get the URL to post to from the `action` attribute of the form. Also, create a `clearInputs` function that sets all values of the form fields to blank if the post is successful. You will also need to cancel the default submit action of the form, using a `.submit` listener on the form, with the ID of `addRunner`.

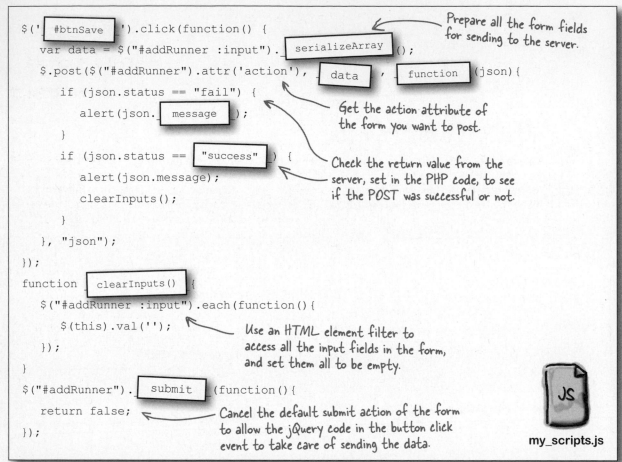

```
$(' #btnSave ').click(function() {
    var data = $("#addRunner :input"). serializeArray ();
    $.post($("#addRunner").attr('action'), data , function (json){
        if (json.status == "fail") {
            alert(json. message );
        }
        if (json.status == "success" ) {
            alert(json.message);
            clearInputs();
        }
    }, "json");
});
function clearInputs() {
    $("#addRunner :input").each(function(){
        $(this).val('');
    });
}
$("#addRunner"). submit (function(){
    return false;
});
```

Prepare all the form fields for sending to the server.

Get the action attribute of the form you want to post.

Check the return value from the server, set in the PHP code, to see if the POST was successful or not.

Use an HTML element filter to access all the input fields in the form, and set them all to be empty.

Cancel the default submit action of the form to allow the jQuery code in the button click event to take care of sending the data.

my_scripts.js

Test Drive

Your page isn't going to look any different with these recent additions. You should, however, update your *my_scripts.js* file with the code you just created. Then, open up your *index.html* page in a browser, open the "Network" tab (Chrome) or "Net" tab (Firebug); you should see the POST to the *service.php* file happening each time you press the `btnSubmit` button. There will be a **POST** listed in the **Request Method** section of the **Headers** tab. The **Form Data** will also be listed there. Now we just need a place to put it…

Store your data in a MySQL database

Relational Database Management Systems (RDBMS) are extremely organized applications designed to store, organize, and remember relationships between your various pieces of data.

Often called *database servers*, they come in various shapes and sizes (and costs). For our purposes, we'll use a free database server called **MySQL**. You communicate with a database server in a language it can understand, which in our case is **SQL**. A database server typically runs alongside a web server, sometimes on the same server, and they work in concert to read and write data and deliver web pages.

The "SQL" in MySQL stands for Structured Query Language.

MySQL stores data inside of database tables.

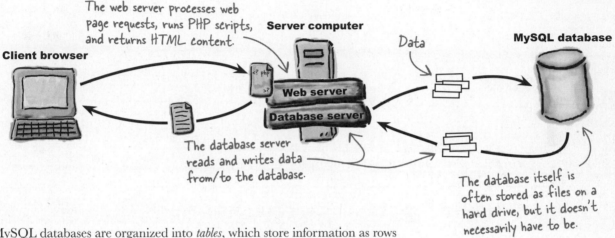

The web server processes web page requests, runs PHP scripts, and returns HTML content.

Client browser

Server computer

Web server

Database server

Data

MySQL database

The database server reads and writes data from/to the database.

The database itself is often stored as files on a hard drive, but it doesn't necessarily have to be.

MySQL databases are organized into *tables*, which store information as rows and columns of related data. Most web applications use one or more tables inside a single database, sort of like different file folders within a file cabinet.

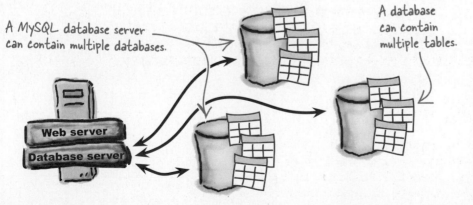

A MySQL database server can contain multiple databases.

A database can contain multiple tables.

Web server

Database server

SQL is the query language used to communicate with a MySQL database.

Create your database to store runner info

Hey! Have you configured MySQL and PHP yet? Make sure you go through Appendix ii for installing and configuring PHP and MySQL before continuing.

All right, carry on. You'll be able to complete the chapter now.

Ready Bake SQL

To get your database, table, and users set up, we've written the SQL for you. Open up MySQL Workbench, open a new connection, and run the following SQL.

```sql
create database hfjq_race_info;
```
Create a database called hfjq_race_info.

```sql
CREATE USER 'runner_db_user'@'localhost' IDENTIFIED BY 'runner_db_password';
GRANT SELECT,INSERT,UPDATE,DELETE ON hfjq_race_info.* TO 'runner_db_user'@'localhost';
```
Create a user, called runner_db_user, give it a password to log in with and allow that user to get, set, update, and remove data in the database.

```sql
use hfjq_race_info;
```
Tell the script that the next piece relates to your new database.

```sql
CREATE TABLE runners(
    runner_id INT not null AUTO_INCREMENT,
    first_name VARCHAR(100) not null,
    last_name VARCHAR(100) not null,
    gender VARCHAR(1) not null,
    finish_time VARCHAR(10),
    PRIMARY KEY (runner_id)
);
```
Create a table called runners that holds all the information we want to remember about the people who finished the race.

Test Drive

Open up MySQL Workbench and open a connection to the server. Paste the SQL from the previous page into the Query pane and press the lightning icon to run the SQL code. You should get success messages in the Output pane at the bottom.

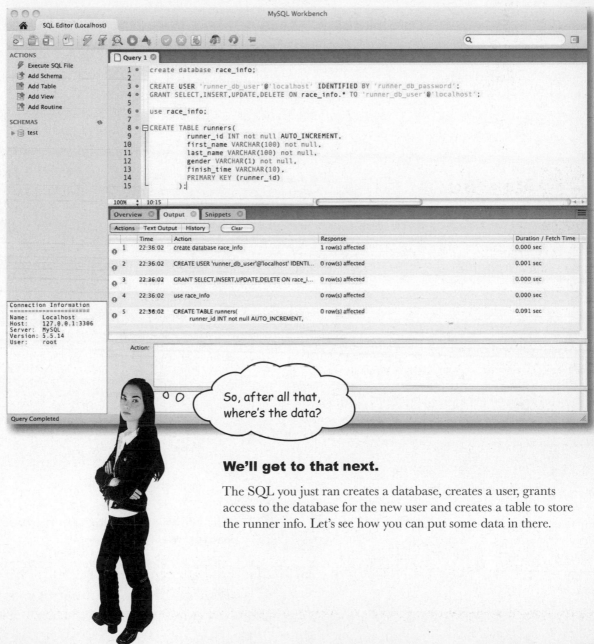

So, after all that, where's the data?

We'll get to that next.

The SQL you just ran creates a database, creates a user, grants access to the database for the new user and creates a table to store the runner info. Let's see how you can put some data in there.

Anatomy of an insert statement

There is one primary way of putting data into our database, another way to change/update it, and a third to get it back out again. We'll look at getting data out in a bit, but for now, let's focus on putting data ***into*** our database tables.

To put data into database tables, we use an `insert` statement.

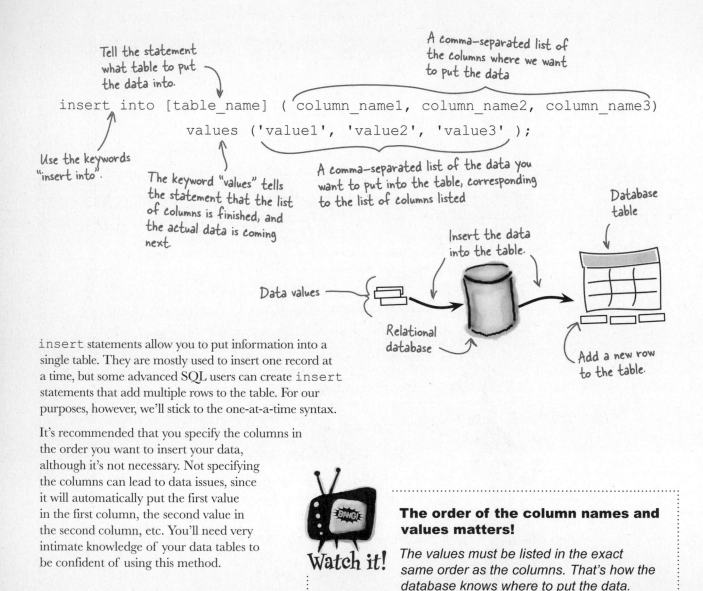

Tell the statement what table to put the data into.

A comma-separated list of the columns where we want to put the data

```
insert into [table_name] ( column_name1, column_name2, column_name3)
              values ('value1', 'value2', 'value3' );
```

Use the keywords "insert into".

The keyword "values" tells the statement that the list of columns is finished, and the actual data is coming next.

A comma-separated list of the data you want to put into the table, corresponding to the list of columns listed

Database table

Insert the data into the table.

Data values

Relational database

Add a new row to the table.

`insert` statements allow you to put information into a single table. They are mostly used to insert one record at a time, but some advanced SQL users can create `insert` statements that add multiple rows to the table. For our purposes, however, we'll stick to the one-at-a-time syntax.

It's recommended that you specify the columns in the order you want to insert your data, although it's not necessary. Not specifying the columns can lead to data issues, since it will automatically put the first value in the first column, the second value in the second column, etc. You'll need very intimate knowledge of your data tables to be confident of using this method.

Watch it!

The order of the column names and values matters!

The values must be listed in the exact same order as the columns. That's how the database knows where to put the data.

Exercise

Write the SQL `insert` statements to insert the data you already have in your XML file into your database. You should insert one record at a time into the runners table you created earlier. We've done the first one for you.

```
insert into runners (first_name, last_name, gender, finish_time)
   values ('John','Smith','m','25:31') ;
```

Exercise Solution

Now that you've written all the SQL necessary for inserting the runners into your database tables, open up MySQL Workbench and run your code.

```
insert into runners (first_name, last_name, gender, finish_time)
    values ('John','Smith','m','25:31') ;
```

insert into runners (first_name, last_name, gender, finish_time)
    values ('Jacob','Walker','m','25:54') ;

insert into runners (first_name, last_name, gender, finish_time)
    values ('Mary','Brown','f','26:01') ;

insert into runners (first_name, last_name, gender, finish_time)
    values ('Jenny','Pierce','f','26:04') ;

insert into runners (first_name, last_name, gender, finish_time)
    values ('Frank','Jones','m','26:08') ;

insert into runners (first_name, last_name, gender, finish_time)
    values ('Bob','Hope','m','26:38') ;

insert into runners (first_name, last_name, gender, finish_time)
    values ('Jane','Smith','f','28:04') ;

insert into runners (first_name, last_name, gender, finish_time)
    values ('Ryan','Rice','m','28:24') ;

insert into runners (first_name, last_name, gender, finish_time)
    values ('Justin','Jones','m','29:14') ;

But now that we have the runners in the database, how do we get them out again for our web app?

Time for a new language: PHP.

Don't worry! We'll give you just enough PHP chops to do all the server-side communication you need—including talking to a database server—and that's it.

Use PHP to access the data

PHP is a programming language, and it needs an environment to run in: a web server with PHP support. PHP scripts and web pages that rely on the scripts **must be placed on a real web server**, as opposed to just opening a script directly from a local filesystem.

If you do have a web server installed locally and it has PHP support, then you can test out PHP scripts directly on your local computer.

Web browsers know nothing about PHP and, therefore, have no ability to run PHP scripts.

Unlike HTML web pages, which can be opened locally in a web browser, PHP scripts must always be "opened" through a URL from a web server.

This PHP script is just a bunch of meaningless code to the web browser.

The web server understands this PHP code and runs the script!

Web servers with PHP support are equipped to run PHP scripts and turn them into HTML web pages that browsers can understand.

A quick way to tell if a web page is being delivered by a web server is to look for the URL starting with "http:". Web pages opened as local files always start with "file:".

PHP scripts must be run <u>on</u> <u>a</u> <u>web</u> server or they won't work.

PHP and MySQL? I thought we were learning jQuery here! What gives?

There will be jQuery, we promise.

But first, let's look at how we get our PHP file to handle POST data, too, so it can write it into the database. We'll also look at some of the important things to remember when dealing with sending information to your server.

Handle POST data on the server

We've already looked at the special object created to handle the transportation of information from the form in the browser to the server: the $_POST object. It's an associative array of all the information you sent, using the *name* (not the IDs) of the HTML elements as the *key* for the associative array, and the information in the HTML element as the *value* of the associative array. The PHP code on the server reads the $_POST object and determines what information has been sent to the server.

You can get the information back *out* of this array by using the key you sent with it (the name of the HTML element). This will return the value in your PHP script.

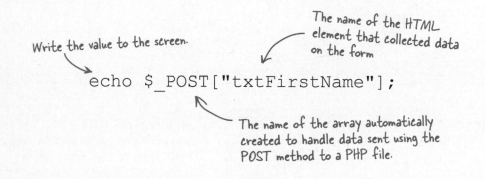

Write the value to the screen.

The name of the HTML element that collected data on the form

```
echo $_POST["txtFirstName"];
```

The name of the array automatically created to handle data sent using the POST method to a PHP file.

Hey, what's left to do? I want to hit the beach!

We're almost at the point where we can grab the data back out of the database and figure out how to display it in our Finishers lists. But first, we need a little more PHP to get us connected to the database...

Connect to a database with PHP

Remember how when you went through the PHP installation process, you selected a particular library near the end of the process?

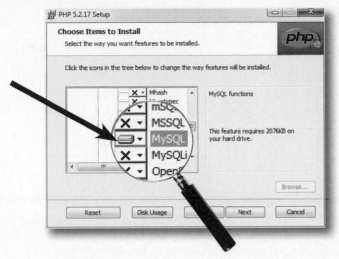

This library will enable PHP to talk to the MySQL database. We'll use this library to connect to the database we've created so we can start reading out the runner data.

Open the PHP tags.

mysql_connect is a function in the PHP library that we included during the install of PHP.

The server name where the MySQL database is

The MySQL user you want to connect as

The MySQL password for this user

The die command outputs a message and ends the PHP script.

```php
<?php

    mysql_connect('127.0.0.1', 'runner_db_user', 'runner_db_password')
    OR die( 'Could not connect to database.');
    mysql_select_db('hfjq_race_info');

    echo "Connected!";

?>
```

mysql_select_db tells PHP what database to use.

Close the PHP tags.

Write to the screen if the database connection is successful. If it is not, the script will not reach this point.

service.php

TEST DRIVE

Open up your favorite text editor and add the code from the previous page. Save the file as *service.php* in the same directory as your *index.html* file for this chapter. Open *service.php* in your browser to see the results of your database query.

Don't forget, the PHP code **must** run through your web server, so the URL should say *http://*, not *file://*.

Well, that doesn't look very exciting. Sure, we can connect... but I'm still not seeing any data!

You're right.

Just like INSERT-ing, there's a special syntax for reading the data back out again. Let's look at how that works.

there are no Dumb Questions

Q: Is MySQL Workbench the only way to interact with or manage a MySQL database?

A: No! There are other ways and other tools. PHPMyAdmin is a common, web-based tool used to manage MySQL databases. You can also use a terminal window to manage the database and the data from the command line.

Q: What other kinds of PHP libraries are there?

A: There are many different PHP libraries, for a wide variety of purposes. These range from SSL, Emailing (SMTP or IMAP), Compression, Authentication, other database connections, and many more. Type "PHP libraries" into your favorite search engine to see a list of available libraries.

Use select to read data from a database

To read data from databases, we use a select statement, and the data is returned in a *resultset*. The resultset is a collection of all the data you asked for in your select query. Using a select statement, you can also join several tables, so you can get data from more than one table in the same resultset.

For plenty more info on PHP, SQL, databases, and tables, pick up a copy of Head First PHP & MySQL.

A comma-separated list of the columns that we want to pull the data from.

Tell the statement what table to pull the data from.

The "asc" keyword tells "order by" how to order the results (asc for ascending, desc for decending).

```
select column_name1, column_name2 from table_name order by column_name1 asc
```

The "select" keyword kicks off the statement

The "from" keyword tells the statement that the list of desired columns is finished, and where to get the data that comes next.

The "order by" keyword, followed by one or more column names, sorts the returned data in whatever order we tell it.

The SQL select statement retrieves columns of data from one or more tables and returns a resultset.

Sharpen your pencil

Create a select statement for the data we need to display the runners on the website. You'll need to read out the first_name, last_name, gender, and finish_time from the runners table. Sort the data so it comes back ordered by finish_time, lowest to highest. If you need to, look back to page 336, where you created the table, so you can get the column names right.

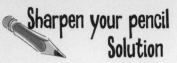

Sharpen your pencil
Solution

You've just created your very own SQL statement to retrieve the runners from your database.

The list of columns you need to select

How you want the data ordered

SELECT first_name, last_name, gender, finish_time FROM runners order by finish_time ASC

The table where you want to get the data from

TEST DRIVE

Using MySQL Workbench, run your `select` statement to see all your data as it will be returned to you in the resultset.

It's great that I can see the data in Workbench, but don't we need it on the web page?

Yeah, we do.

Let's look at how we can get information from the database for display on our page.

Get data with PHP

Up to now, we've looked at some very basic PHP and some not-so-basic PHP. We've seen how to write some basic information to the screen and how to connect to a database and write a `select` statement to get information out of a database. Now let's see how we can **_get_** information from a database and write that information to the screen.

PHP Code Magnets

Rearrange the magnets below to complete the PHP code that creates a function called `db_connection`, which manages the database connections. Also create a `$query` variable and set its value to be the `select` statement you wrote earlier that selects all the runners from the database. Then create a `$result` variable that will call the `db_connection` function, which passes the `$query` variable as a parameter. Last, using a `while` loop, go through each row of the resultset—which is an associative array—and print it to the screen.

```php
<?php

  $query = "SELECT first_name, last_name, gender, finish_time _____ runners
order by _____ASC ";
  $result = _____($query);


  while ($row = mysql_fetch_array(_____, MYSQL_ASSOC)) {
    print_r(_____);
  }



  _____db_connection(_____) {
    mysql_connect('127.0.0.1', 'runner_db_user', 'runner_db_password')
      OR _____ ('Could not connect to database.');
      _____('hfjq_race_info');



  return mysql_query($query);
  }
?>
```

`$row`

`die`   `mysql_select_db`

`FROM`   `db_connection`   `$query`

`$result`   `function`   `finish_time`

PHP service.php

PHP Code Magnets Solution

With just a little bit of PHP, you're now grabbing the data from the database and getting the
results returned in an array that can be displayed on your web page.

```php
<?php

   $query = "SELECT first_name, last_name, gender, finish_time FROM runners
order by finish_time ASC ";
   $result = db_connection ($query);

   while ($row = mysql_fetch_array( $result , MYSQL_ASSOC)) {
      print_r( $row );
   }


   function db_connection( $query ) {
      mysql_connect('127.0.0.1', 'runner_db_user', 'runner_db_password')
         OR die ('Could not connect to database.');
      mysql_select_db ('hfjq_race_info');

      return mysql_query($query);
   }
?>
```

service.php

there are no Dumb Questions

Q: So, can a `select` only pull all my
information from a table? I see I can limit
the columns I get back, but what about
the rows?

A: Yes, you can limit the rows you get back,
by using a `where` clause. We'll look at this a
little bit more in Chapter 11, but you can pass
in a filter condition in the `where` clause, and
only get the rows that match your condition
returned to you in a `select` statement.

Q: Can I only get data from one table
at a time?

A: No, you can join as many tables as
you'd like in your query, often by a common
identifier, and also in the `where` clause.
Joining many tables together can slow your
database queries down a lot, so you need to
be careful when doing it. For more information
on this, look at Chapter 8 of *Head First PHP &
MySQL* or Chapter 2 of *Head First SQL*.

Q: What database is on 127.0.0.1? I
see my website on "localhost." What's
the difference?

A: Good question, and the answer is
nothing. 127.0.0.1 and localhost refer to the
same thing—the computer/server you are
currently working on.

TEST DRIVE

Update your *service.php* file with the code you just created and then open it in your browser to see the results of your database query. Don't forget, the PHP code **must** run through your web server, so the URL should say *http://*, not *file://*.

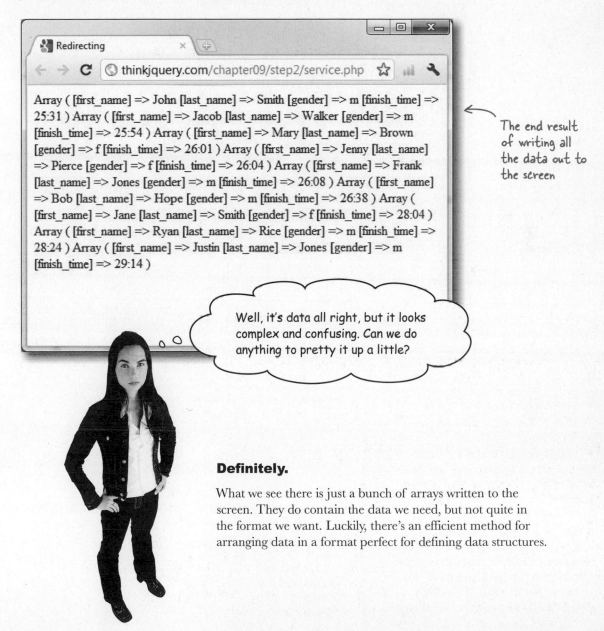

Array ([first_name] => John [last_name] => Smith [gender] => m [finish_time] => 25:31) Array ([first_name] => Jacob [last_name] => Walker [gender] => m [finish_time] => 25:54) Array ([first_name] => Mary [last_name] => Brown [gender] => f [finish_time] => 26:01) Array ([first_name] => Jenny [last_name] => Pierce [gender] => f [finish_time] => 26:04) Array ([first_name] => Frank [last_name] => Jones [gender] => m [finish_time] => 26:08) Array ([first_name] => Bob [last_name] => Hope [gender] => m [finish_time] => 26:38) Array ([first_name] => Jane [last_name] => Smith [gender] => f [finish_time] => 28:04) Array ([first_name] => Ryan [last_name] => Rice [gender] => m [finish_time] => 28:24) Array ([first_name] => Justin [last_name] => Jones [gender] => m [finish_time] => 29:14)

The end result of writing all the data out to the screen

Well, it's data all right, but it looks complex and confusing. Can we do anything to pretty it up a little?

Definitely.

What we see there is just a bunch of arrays written to the screen. They do contain the data we need, but not quite in the format we want. Luckily, there's an efficient method for arranging data in a format perfect for defining data structures.

JSON to the rescue!

JSON, short for JavaScript Object Notation, is a lightweight data-interchange format. It is easy for humans to read and write. It is easy for machines to parse and generate. That's what makes it perfect for structuring and transferring data. It's based on a subset of the standard used to define JavaScript, and is language independent. That means it can be used with pretty much any programming language. It is more efficient at transferring data than XML, and is based on name/value pairs, like associative arrays. The values in JSON can be strings, numbers, arrays, objects, Boolean values (true or false) or null.

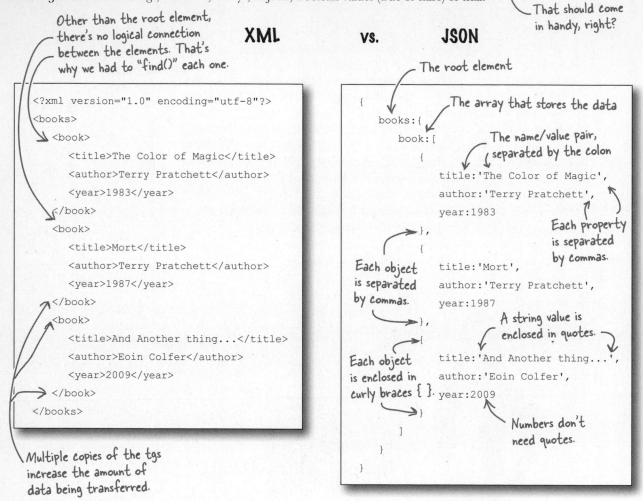

That should come in handy, right?

XML   vs.   JSON

Other than the root element, there's no logical connection between the elements. That's why we had to "find()" each one.

```
<?xml version="1.0" encoding="utf-8"?>
<books>
    <book>
        <title>The Color of Magic</title>
        <author>Terry Pratchett</author>
        <year>1983</year>
    </book>
    <book>
        <title>Mort</title>
        <author>Terry Pratchett</author>
        <year>1987</year>
    </book>
    <book>
        <title>And Another thing...</title>
        <author>Eoin Colfer</author>
        <year>2009</year>
    </book>
</books>
```

Multiple copies of the tgs increase the amount of data being transferred.

The root element

The array that stores the data

The name/value pair, separated by the colon

```
{
    books:{
        book:[
            {
                title:'The Color of Magic',
                author:'Terry Pratchett',
                year:1983
            },
            {
                title:'Mort',
                author:'Terry Pratchett',
                year:1987
            },
            {
                title:'And Another thing...',
                author:'Eoin Colfer',
                year:2009
            }
        ]
    }
}
```

Each property is separated by commas.

Each object is separated by commas.

A string value is enclosed in quotes.

Each object is enclosed in curly braces { }.

Numbers don't need quotes.

To access the information in the JSON object, you can use the same notation that you do for any other object: the dot (.) notation. Arrays inside the JSON object are like other JavaScript arrays and have the same properties, like `length`. In our example JSON object above, you would find out how many books were returned by using `books.book.length`. Different JSON objects will have different structures, so you might not need as many dots to access the array object.

jQuery + JSON = Awesome

Since JSON is so prevalent and easy to use, the good folks at jQuery built a special shortcut just for dealing with getting JSON data: the getJSON method.

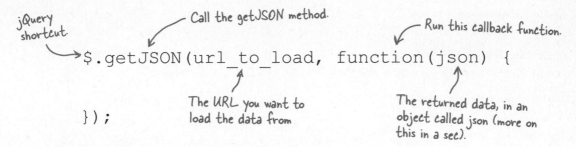

jQuery shortcut.

Call the getJSON method.

Run this callback function.

```
$.getJSON(url_to_load, function(json) {

});
```

The URL you want to load the data from

The returned data, in an object called json (more on this in a sec).

If this seems familiar, that's because it's almost the same as the post method we used earlier to get the data from the form. This simple method is a *shortcut* for the ajax method, with several parameters already set for you. To make this call without the shortcut, it would look like this:

```
$.ajax({
    url: url_to_load,
    dataType: 'json',
    data: json,
    success: function(json){

    };
});
```

But the data we have isn't in JSON format, just a series of arrays. Can we turn those arrays into JSON ?

Yes, we can.

As luck would have it, the PHP folks thought of this already. Let's have a look at a few more PHP basics, and then see how to combine those with other PHP functions to get our data in JSON.

A few PHP rules...

Let's face it, nobody really likes a bunch of coding rules, but there are just a few more things about PHP—much of which are syntax—that we should take a look at to help you wrangle your data for jQuery. Thankfully, we've already seen many of these concepts in relation to JavaScript, so we'll keep this as quick and painless as possible...

PHP basics

1. All PHP code needs to be wrapped with `<?php` and `?>` tags.

2. You can **intersperse PHP with HTML**, using the `<?php` and `?>` tags around your PHP code

3. All lines of PHP code must **end with a semicolon (;)**.

```
<div><span> Hello
<?php
    echo "Bob";
?>
</span></div>
```

Rules for variables

1. All variables *must* start with a **dollar sign ($).**

2. After that, they must contain **at least** one letter or underscore, and then any combination of letters, numbers, or underscores.

3. Dashes (-), spaces ( ), and **all special characters** (except for $ and _) are *not* **allowed** in variable names.

```
<?php
$u = "USA"; // OK
$home_country = "Ireland"; // OK
$another-var = "Canada"; // Causes an error
?>
```

Rules for loops

1. PHP also contains `for`, `while`, and `do...while` loops—all with the **same syntax as JavaScript**.

2. PHP also contains an extra loop mechanism called the `foreach` loop, which will go through all the elements of an array one by one, using the `as` keyword until it reaches the end, and then stopping automatically.

```
<?php
for ($i = 1; $i <= 10; $i++) {
    echo $i;
}
while ($j <= 10) {
    echo $j++;
}
$a = array(1, 2, 3, 17);
foreach ($a as $v) {
    echo "Current value: $v.\n";
}
?>
```

A few (more) PHP rules...

There are a few more rules that will help us get the data we need,
format it correctly, and get it onto our web pages.

Rules for arrays

1. You can create new arrays using the `array` keyword,
   similar to JavaScript.

2. You can access the array values using the index of the
   item, in **square brackets [ ]**, like JavaScript. They
   are also **zero-indexed**, like JavaScript.

3. Arrays can also be **associative**, which means you can
   use a key to access the item in the array, instead of the
   index. These are called **key/value pairs**.

4. To assign a value to a key in an associative array, you
   use the **=> operator**.

```php
<?php
$my_arr2 = array('USA', 'China',
'Ireland');
echo $my_arr2[2]; // Prints "Ireland"


$arr = array("foo" => "bar", 12 => true);
echo $arr["foo"]; // Prints "bar"
echo $arr[12]; // Prints true
?>
```

Rules for conditionals

1. The `if` statement has the **same syntax as
   JavaScript,** as does the `else` clause, and the `else
   if` clause.

2. The **comparison operators** are all the same as
   JavaScript.

3. **Logical operators** are also the same as in
   JavaScript, with the addition of descriptive words—
   and, or, and `not`—which can be used in place of
   the operators.

```php
<?php
if ($x > $y){
    echo "x is greater than y";
}
elseif ($x == $y) {
    echo "x is equal to y";
}
else {
    echo "x is smaller than y";
}
?>
```

Rules for writing to the screen

1. The keywords `echo` and `print` write to
   the screen.

2. You can write out the contents of an **array** using the
   `print_r` command.

```php
<?php
    echo "Bob";
    print_r($my_arr2);
?>
```

Format the output using PHP

OK, now that we've got that out of the way, let's see what PHP can do for us! The `json_encode` function in PHP allows you to take an associative array and convert it into a JSON-encoded string of values.

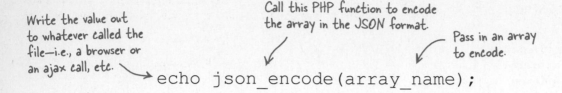

Write the value out to whatever called the file—i.e., a browser or an ajax call, etc.

Call this PHP function to encode the array in the JSON format.

Pass in an array to encode.

```php
echo json_encode(array_name);
```

But before we can encode the data, it must be in a single associative array. We've already seen a method to loop through the resultset and see each associative array in there. What we need is a way to take each of these arrays and combine them into a single one. Using the PHP function `array_push`, we can add new items onto the end of an array.

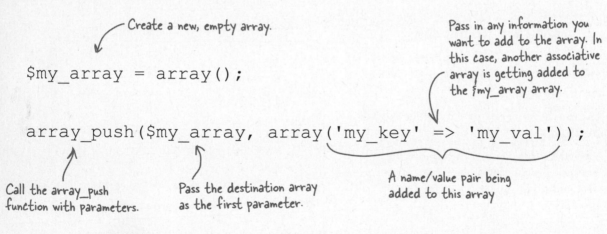

Create a new, empty array.

Pass in any information you want to add to the array. In this case, another associative array is getting added to the $my_array array.

```php
$my_array = array();

array_push($my_array, array('my_key' => 'my_val'));
```

Call the array_push function with parameters.

Pass the destination array as the first parameter.

A name/value pair being added to this array

Geek Bits

The `json_encode` function only became available in PHP version 5.2. If you're using a version earlier than that, either update your version of PHP or type "json_encode PHP alternatives" into your favorite search engine, and you'll find out just how the folks at PHP created that function. That way, you can create your own so you can take advantage of its cool features.

Dumb Questions

Q: Did the jQuery folks come up with JSON?

A: No. Douglas Crockford, Yahoo!'s JavaScript architect, invented JSON to be what he calls a "fat-free alternative to XML." He explains his reasons for that designation here: *http://www.json.org/fatfree.html*.

Q: Isn't JSON just JavaScript??

A: Yes and no. JSON is based on a subset of JavaScript, ECMA 262 Third Edition, but can be used by a multitude of languages for data transfer. To see the list of languages that use JSON, visit *http://www.json.org/*.

Q: So, if JavaScript and PHP have such a similar syntax, why can't I just use JavaScript to do what I need??

A: Like we've mentioned, PHP is a *server-side* scripting language, and can interact with the web server and databases on your behalf. The code is executed on the server, generating HTML, which is then sent to the client. JavaScript, on the other hand, only lives in your browser, and interacts *client* side.

Q: All right. What is PHP again?

A: PHP (recursive acronym for PHP: Hypertext Preprocessor) is a widely used, open source, general-purpose scripting language that is especially suited for web development and can be embedded into HTML.

Q: So where did PHP come from, then?

A: Good question. PHP first appeared back in 1994. It was created by Rasmus Lerdorf as a way of displaying his resumé online. He released the the source in June 1995, which allowed other developers to update and fix bugs. It has since taken off and is used in over 20 million websites around the world.

Relax

You've just put a bunch of new learning about PHP, MySQL, and JSON into your brain. We're about to dive into a big exercise to pull everything together, so take a quick break and have a cup of coffee, take a walk, or do something else to give your brain a rest and get ready for what's to come. When you're done, turn the page and dive in.

Long Exercise

Update your *my_scripts.js* file with new function, called `getDBRacers`, which calls the *service.php* file. This call should return a JSON object and then should alert out the number of runners that were returned. Also update the `startAJAXCalls` timer to call this new function instead of the `getXMLRunners` function. Then, update *service.php* to send back the runners' retrieved data from the database, JSON-encoded.

```
function startAJAXcalls(){
   if(repeat){
      setTimeout( function() {
      ..................
      startAJAXcalls();
      },
      FREQ
   );
   }
}


function getDBRacers(){
   $.getJSON(.......... function(.....) {
      .....(json.runners........);
   });
   getTimeAjax();
}
```

my_scripts.js

```php
<?php

    $query = "SELECT first_name, last_name, gender, finish_time FROM runners
order by finish_time ASC ";
    $result = .................($query);


    $runners = array();


    while ($row = mysql_fetch_array($result, MYSQL_ASSOC)) {
        .............($runners, array('fname' => $row['first_name'], 'lname' =>
$row['last_name'], 'gender' => $row['gender'], 'time' => $row['finish_time']));
    }
    echo ...........(array("runners" => ............));
    exit;


    function db_connection($query) {
        mysql_connect('127.0.0.1', 'runner_db_user', 'runner_db_password')
          OR die(fail('Could not connect to database.'));
        mysql_select_db.................

        return mysql_query($query);
    }


    function fail($message) {
        die(json_encode(array('status' => 'fail', 'message' => $message)));
    }
    function success($message) {
        die(json_encode(array('status' => 'success', 'message' => $message)));
    }
?>
```

service.php

Long Exercise Solution

Your *my_scripts.js* file now has a new function, called getDBRacers, which calls the *service.php* file. There is no need for the old getXMLRunners function anymore, so you can get rid of that. The new function accepts JSON returned from the *service.php* file and alerts out the number of runners that was returned. The startAJAXCalls timer function has also been updated to call the new function. The *service.php* file has been updated to send back the runners retrieved from the database, JSON-encoded and ordered by finish_time, starting with the lowest first.

```
function startAJAXcalls(){
    if(repeat){
        setTimeout( function() {
            getDBRacers();                    ← Call the new function on a
                                                 scheduled basis.
            startAJAXcalls();
        },
        FREQ
        );
    }
}


                                         The data returned from
                                         the getJSON call
function getDBRacers(){                           ↓
    $.getJSON("service.php",  function(json) {
        alert(json.runners.length);    Like other arrays,
    });                                this also has a
    getTimeAjax();                     length property.
}
```

Use the getJSON jQuery method to call the service.php file. →

The json object contains an array called runners. It got this name from the json_encode method in PHP.

JS

my_scripts.js

```php
<?php
                    The database query to
                    get the runners
   $query = "SELECT first_name, last_name, gender, finish_time FROM runners
order by finish_time ASC ";
   $result = db_connection($query);

                              Create a new array to
   $runners = array();        hold our returned values.

                                                            Loop through the
                                                            resultset, getting
                                                            associative arrays back.

   while ($row = mysql_fetch_array($result, MYSQL_ASSOC)) {
       array_push.($runners, array('fname' => $row['first_name'], 'lname' =>
$row['last_name'], 'gender' => $row['gender'], 'time' => $row['finish_time']));
   }
                                                            Put the returned
   echo json_encode(array("runners" => $runners));          data into our own
                                                            associative array.
   exit;                      Encode our associative array in
                              the JSON format and write it
                              to whatever called it.
   function db_connection($query) {
       mysql_connect('127.0.0.1', 'runner_db_user', 'runner_db_password')
          OR die(fail('Could not connect to database.'));
       mysql_select_db ('hfjq_race_info');
                                                A function to handle the
                                                database communication

       return mysql_query($query);       Return the resultset to
   }    Handler functions to deal with   whatever called this function.
        errors or successes in our scripts
   function fail($message) {
       die(json_encode(array('status' => 'fail', 'message' => $message)));
   }
   function success($message) {
       die(json_encode(array('status' => 'success', 'message' => $message)));
   }
?>
```

PHP

service.php

Test Drive

Update your *service.php* and *my_scripts.js* file with the code you just created, and open *index.html* in your browser. Open the "Network" tab in the Developer tools, and you'll see the JSON information getting loaded in.

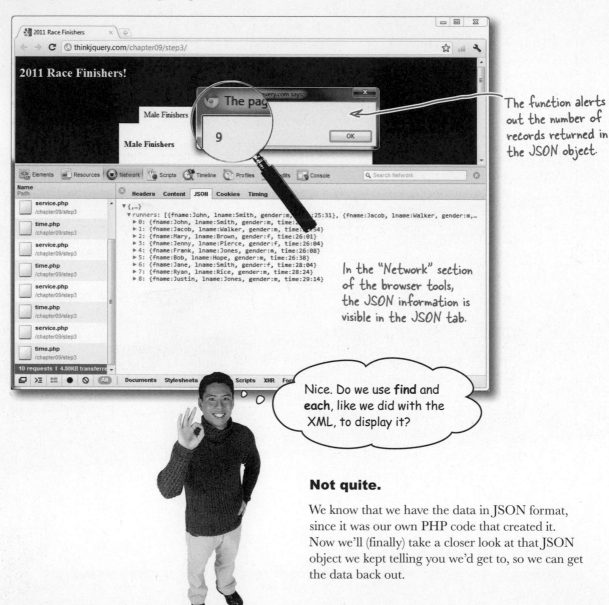

The function alerts out the number of records returned in the JSON object.

In the "Network" section of the browser tools, the JSON information is visible in the JSON tab.

Nice. Do we use **find** and **each**, like we did with the XML, to display it?

Not quite.

We know that we have the data in JSON format, since it was our own PHP code that created it. Now we'll (finally) take a closer look at that JSON object we kept telling you we'd get to, so we can get the data back out.

Access data in the JSON object

The `json_encode` function in PHP allows us to convert an associative array into a JSON-encoded string of values. These values can then be accessed in JavaScript as associative arrays too, so we can loop through them and interact with them in the same way we interact with other arrays.

When we were using XML, we had to scan through the data to `find` the next runner. Then, once we found a runner, we again had to `find` if the runner was male or female. Remember that JSON object that gets returned from `json_encode`? With the JSON object, we can directly access its properties, using the dot (.) notation. It contains a single array, called `runners`, as a property. And, once we have the array, we can use the key of the associative array to know if the runner is male or female—which is much more efficient than looking for it each time.

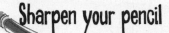

Sharpen your pencil

Update your `getDBRunners` function to read the JSON object from *service.php*. Then, use conditional logic to decide which list the runner goes in. But watch out! Only do that if there are actually runners returned in the JSON object.

```
function getDBRacers(){
    $.getJSON(..................., function(json) {
        if (json.runners............. > 0) {
            $('#finishers_m').empty();
            $('#finishers_f').empty();
            $('#finishers_all').empty();
            $.......... (json.runners,function() {
                var info = '<li>Name: ' + this['fname'] + ' ' + this['lname'] + '. Time: ' +
this[..........] + '</li>';
                if(this['gender'] == 'm'){
                    $('.....................').append( info );
                }else if(this['gender'] == 'f'){
                    $('#finishers_f').append(..........);
                }else{}
                $('.....................').append( info );
            });
        }
    });
    getTimeAjax();
}
```

my_scripts.js

Sharpen your pencil
Solution

Using conditional logic and the information returned in the JSON object, you can determine which list the runner should go in. Like before, the runners should also always be added to the `all_finishers` list.

```
function getDBRacers(){                 Get the information from
                                        the service.php file.
    $.getJSON("service.php", function(json) {
                                             Check if there is data in
        if (json.runners.length> 0) {        the runners array.
            $('#finishers_m').empty();
            $('#finishers_f').empty();            Empty out the lists again.
            $('#finishers_all').empty();

            $.each(json.runners,function() {
                var info = '<li>Name: ' + this['fname'] + ' ' + this['lname'] + '. Time: ' +
this['time'] + '</li>';
                if(this['gender'] == 'm'){          Check if the current
                    $('#finishers_m').append( info );   object property of
                                                        gender is m or f.
                }else if(this['gender'] == 'f'){
                    $('#finishers_f').append(info);
                }else{}
                $('finishers_all').append( info );
            });                        Add the runner to the
        }                              all_runners list.
    });
getTimeAjax();
}
```

my_scripts.js

Geek Bits

We can use `each` method to loop through all the elements in the array returned in the JSON object. This method is slightly different from the `(selector).each` method, since it can iterate over non-jQuery arrays, like our `runners` array.

Test Drive

Update the `getDBRacers` function in your *my_scripts.js* file. Then open up *index.html* and see your runners get loaded from a MySQL database, using Ajax, JSON, and PHP.

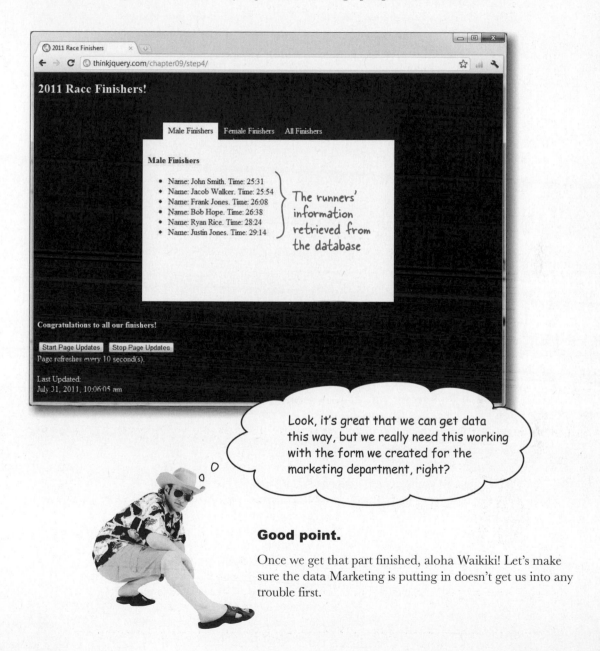

The runners' information retrieved from the database

Look, it's great that we can get data this way, but we really need this working with the form we created for the marketing department, right?

Good point.

Once we get that part finished, aloha Waikiki! Let's make sure the data Marketing is putting in doesn't get us into any trouble first.

Data sanitization and validation in PHP

With the increase of spam bots and hackers trying to get ownership of your dataset for nefarious purposes, you should never trust the data that is entered into a web form. It's **always** a good idea to *validate* and *sanitize* any data sent to your server before you insert it into your database. This ensures that you got the type of data you expected for a particular field (validation) **and** that the data you received doesn't contain anything that could be potentially dangerous to your server or database (sanitization). This can help protect you against issues like SQL injections, drive-by cross-site scripting issues, and lots of other nasty things you can find out more about online. For our application, we'll use some nifty PHP methods to clean up our data and make sure the correct data is used.

Converts some special HTML entities in a format that is safe for the database

```php
<?php

    htmlspecialchars($_POST["a"]) ; // Encode the strings into safer web and database values

    empty($_POST["b"]) ; // The "empty" method checks if the value is empty

    preg_match('',$var); //This is a "Regular Expression". It checks $var against a set pattern

?>
```

Check if a string is empty or not.

A regular expression matching function. The pattern matching using regular expressions can be very specific, so you can really control the type of data entered.

There are many other functions you could also look at for data sanitization; these include `htmlentities`, `trim`, `stripslashes`, `mysql_real_escape_string`, and many more. You can find a bunch more of these in Chapter 6 of *Head First PHP & MySQL*.

Use the same PHP file for multiple purposes

We've looked at the two ways of sending data to the server to be processed by PHP: POST and GET. In combination with some conditional logic, we can detect if there was a POST or a GET request to our PHP file and act accordingly. Remember that hidden field we added to our form a few pages ago?

```html
<input type="hidden" name="action" value="addRunner" id="action">
```

We can watch for this value in the POST, and know that we posted a form. Then, we can run some data validation and sanitization functions to make sure we got all the data we want. Similarly, if we update the `getJSON` call to get the runners from the database with a URL parameter (for the `$_GET` PHP object), we can target just that code in the PHP file to run. That way, we'll only have one PHP file to maintain.

```php
$.getJSON("service.php?action=getRunners", function(json) {
```

Use this to tell the PHP function to run the code associated with getting the runners from the database.

Ack! Everyone's clearing their desks and heading to the airport! So, we know how to complete the form now, right?

Ready Bake PHP

Update your *service.php* file with the following code. It will handle both the GET and POST of information. You'll also need to include the `db_connection`, `success`, and `fail` functions from before.

```php
<?php
   if ($_POST['action'] == 'addRunner') {
      $fname = htmlspecialchars($_POST['txtFirstName']);
      $lname = htmlspecialchars($_POST['txtLastName']);
      $gender = htmlspecialchars($_POST['ddlGender']);
      $minutes = htmlspecialchars($_POST['txtMinutes']);
      $seconds = htmlspecialchars($_POST['txtSeconds']);
      if(preg_match('/[^\w\s]/i', $fname) || preg_match('/[^\w\s]/i', $lname)) {
         fail('Invalid name provided.');
      }
      if( empty($fname) || empty($lname) ) {
         fail('Please enter a first and last name.');
      }
      if( empty($gender) ) {
         fail('Please select a gender.');
      }
      $time = $minutes.":".$seconds;
      $query = "INSERT INTO runners SET first_name='$fname', last_name='$lname',
gender='$gender', finish_time='$time'";
      $result = db_connection($query);
      if ($result) {
         $msg = "Runner: ".$fname." ".$lname." added successfully" ;
         success($msg);
      } else {   fail('Insert failed.');} exit;
   }elseif($_GET['action'] == 'getRunners'){
      $query = "SELECT first_name, last_name, gender, finish_time FROM runners order by
finish_time ASC ';
      $result = db_connection($query);
      $runners = array();
      while ($row = mysql_fetch_array($result, MYSQL_ASSOC)) {
         array_push($runners, array('fname' => $row['first_name'], 'lname' => $row['last_name'],
'gender' => $row['gender'], 'time' => $row['finish_time']));
      }
      echo json_encode(array("runners" => $runners));
      exit;
   }
```

Check if there was a value of addRunner POSTed to the server. This is our hidden field from earlier.

Data sanitization of the information in the $_POST array

Data validation ensures that something was entered.

Call the fail function, if the validation fails.

Tell the database to insert a new record...

...and check if it was successful or not.

Check if the getRunners value was sent in the URL string.

Get and return the runners.

PHP

service.php

hawaii, here you come...

```
function getDBRacers(){
    $.getJSON("service.php?action=getRunners", function(json) {
        if (json.runners.length > 0) {
            $('#finishers_m').empty();
    .
    .
        }
    });
    getTimeAjax();
}
```

Do this!

Update the getJSON call to include a URL parameter called action with a value of getRunners to tell the *service.php* file to return the runners.

my_scripts.js

Test Drive

After updating your *service.php* and *my_scripts.js* files, open up *index.html* in your browser. You should see runners getting loaded in. You should also be able to add new runners to the list using the form on the new tab you created.

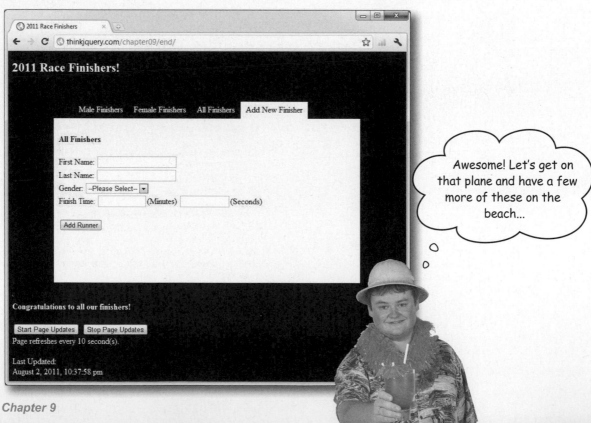

Awesome! Let's get on that plane and have a few more of these on the beach...

jQuerycross

It's time to sit back and give your left brain
something to do. It's your standard crossword; all of
the solution words are from this chapter.

Across

2. _____ _____ Management Systems (RDBMS)
are extremely organized applications designed to store,
organize, and remember relationships between your various
pieces of data.

5. A jQuery shortcut method that's dedicated to
sending data to the server. The method takes several
parameters: URL, the information you want to send,
and a handler function that will run after the data
is sent.

6. Server-side scripting language often used to send data
collected in a form to the server.

10. JSON = Java Script _____ _____.

12. Popular, open source database server that you can
download for free.

14. The jQuery shortcut for getting JSON information from a
server.

15. Another jQuery form helper method that will create an
associative array of key/value pairs (which happens to make for
great structured stoarge).

16. SQL = _____ _____ Language.

Down

1. A special type of array that holds its information in name/
value pairs.

3. JSON and XML are two types of data-_____ formats
that jQuery and PHP can pass back and forth to each other.

4. One of two methods used to send data to the server from an
HTML form. This one will append the form field names and their
values onto the end of the URL.

7. One of two methods used to send data to the server from an
HTML form. This one also sends data, but doesn't make that data
visible in the URL string.

8. The jQuery form helper method that will join all the inputs of
your form into a single string of key/value pairs, separated by
ampersands (&).

9. HTML element to use when you want to collect data on a web
page and send it to a server for processing.

11. The SQL command used to put data *into* a table.

13. The SQL command to retrieve data *from* a database table.

jQuerycross Solution

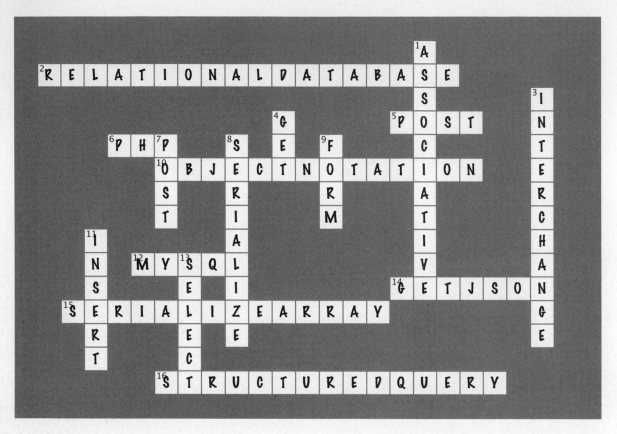

CHAPTER 9

Your jQuery/Ajax/PHP/MySQL Toolbox

You've got Chapter 9 under your belt, and now you've added some basic PHP, MySQL, JSON, and more Ajax to your toolbox.

MySQL
Lets you store data in databases and tables and insert and retrieve information using the SQL language.

SQL
A query language for interacting with database applications like MySQL.

JSON
Use the getJSON function to get JSON-encoded data from a server. This returns a JSON object.

Data can be sent from a form using the post method. Before you send the data, you need to format it using serializeArray.

PHP
A server-side scripting language that lets you manipulate web page content on the server before a page is delivered to the client browser.

PHP script
A text file that contains PHP code to carry out tasks on a web server.

<?php ?>
These tags must surround all PHP code in your PHP scripts.

echo
The PHP command for sending output to the browser window. Its syntax is:

echo 'Hello World';

$_POST
A special variable that holds form data.

json_encode
This command takes an array and converts it to JSON-encoded data, requested by jQuery.

10 jQuery UI

Extreme form makeover

The Web lives and dies by users and their data.

Collecting data from users is a big business and can be a time-consuming challenge for a web developer. You've seen how jQuery can help make Ajax, PHP, and MySQL web apps work more effectively. Now let's look at how jQuery can help us build the user interface for the forms that collect data from users. Along the way, you'll get a healthy dose of jQuery UI, the official user interface library for jQuery.

Cryptozoologists.org needs a makeover

Dr. Pattersby and Dr. Gimli are dedicated to collecting as much *cryptid* sighting data as possible from users around the world. Their website, cryptozoologists.org, is revered by professional and amateur cryptozoologists worldwide. The good doctors have another gig for you: update their very outdated Cryptid Sightings form.

Cryptids are creatures unknown or unrecognized by the scientific community. Collecting good data from users is crucial for our research.

Some famous cryptids include Bigfoot, chupacabras, and the Loch Ness Monster. We need a better form to capture when and where people see them.

I wish I could get the paparazzi off my back!

Dr. Pattersby

Dr. Gimli

The cryptozoologists want to say good riddance to their old, clunky HTML form.

The look and feel of the form is not engaging. It looks like it's from the late 90s.

There's nothing visual that assists the user in entering quality data, and HTML doesn't offer a lot of options for that. As a result, the doctors get a lot of junk data.

Submit a Cryptid Sighting

Please ... the ... of your crytpid sighting below along ...
your ... t inform...

Fi... the form below ... lick "Enter" to Submit

D... f Sighting:

Wh... You Saw the Creature:

Cre... Type: ○ Mammal ○ Re... ○ Bird

Desc... Creature:

Pimp your HTML form

Below is a mockup of what our cryptozoologists want the new form to look like, along with a few extra notes.

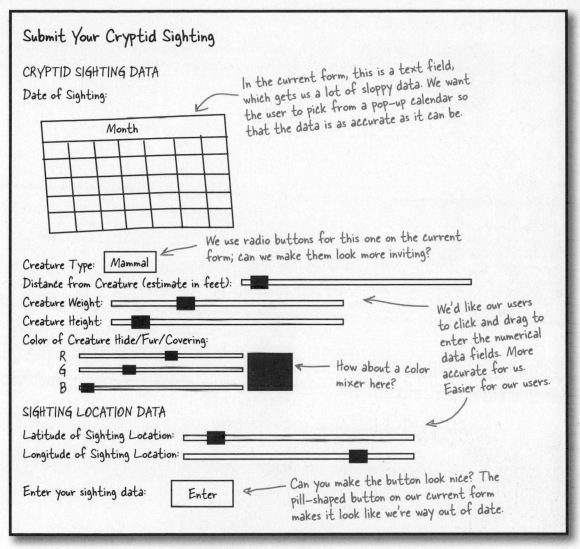

Submit Your Cryptid Sighting

CRYPTID SIGHTING DATA

Date of Sighting:

Month

In the current form, this is a text field, which gets us a lot of sloppy data. We want the user to pick from a pop-up calendar so that the data is as accurate as it can be.

Creature Type: Mammal

We use radio buttons for this one on the current form; can we make them look more inviting?

Distance from Creature (estimate in feet):

Creature Weight:

Creature Height:

Color of Creature Hide/Fur/Covering:

R
G
B

We'd like our users to click and drag to enter the numerical data fields. More accurate for us. Easier for our users.

How about a color mixer here?

SIGHTING LOCATION DATA

Latitude of Sighting Location:

Longitude of Sighting Location:

Enter your sighting data: Enter

Can you make the button look nice? The pill-shaped button on our current form makes it look like we're way out of date.

BRAIN POWER

The crytozoologists have asked for a tall order here. They want you to build a user interface like you would find in a desktop application. What do you think jQuery offers that can accomplish this?

Did you guys check out the sketchup of the "Submit Your Cryptid Sighting" form?

Frank

Jim

Joe

Frank: I saw it. The current form is an HTML form, but HTML and CSS aren't going to cut it for the new form the cryptozoologists want.

Jim: Tell me about it. Have you ever tried to style form elements with CSS? I'd rather have a root canal.

Frank: Yeah, and jQuery…well, I haven't seen anything in jQuery that will help us build interface components like *that*.

Joe: We've got to figure this out, guys. Folks are used to fancy components like this, so we're going to have to find a way to build them.

Frank: We'll probably need a combination of JavaScript, jQuery, and CSS to pull this one off.

Jim: That's a lot of logic to write. Just the calendar pop up they want will be lines and lines of code and a bunch of complex CSS.

Joe: Hmmm. There may be a jQuery plug-in for this kind of stuff, actually.

Jim: A plug-in, right! We used one a couple chapters back to create tabs for the Bit to Byte race results page. So there's more to plug-ins, huh?

Joe: Yeah, if jQuery doesn't offer something a developer needs, that developer can build a plug-in and release it to the jQuery community for it to use. This saves other developers tons of hours.

Jim: So some developer or dev team out there may have already dealt with this?

Frank: That would really save us some headaches.

Joe: Let's go poke around out at jQuery.com and see what we can find.

Save coding headaches (and time) with jQuery UI

Fortunately for developers everywhere, jQuery has an official library of user interface plug-ins for just this kind of project. That library is called jQuery UI, and it offers three main types of plug-ins for the jQuery core: effects, interactions, and widgets.

Effects plug-ins

jQuery UI extends jQuery by adding more effects. Make your elements bounce, explode, pulsate, or shake. jQuery UIs also includes *easing functions*, complex mathematical operations that make animations look more realistic.

Interaction plug-ins

Interactions add more complex behavior to web apps. You can enable users to interact with elements by making those elements draggable, droppable, or sortable, just to name a few of the options.

Widget plug-ins

A web widget is a self-contained component that adds functionality to your web app. Widgets save you tons of coding time and complexity while creating usable and responsive user interface elements.

We're going to focus mostly on widgets for our UI work in this chapter.

jQuery offers a plug-in architecture that allows web developers to extend (or add onto) the core jQuery library.

Test Drive

Try out some jQuery UI effects, interactions, and widgets by visiting the following URLs and doing what the instructions say.

URL	Instructions
http://jqueryui.com/demos/animate/#default	Click the Toggle Effect button.
http://jqueryui.com/demos/effect/default.html	Choose an effect from the drop-down list. Then click Run Effect.
http://jqueryui.com/demos/draggable/#default	Click and hold on the box that says "Drag me around." Then, drag your mouse to drag the box within the screen area provided.
http://jqueryui.com/demos/accordion/#default	Click on the different sections to see the accordion expand and contract.
http://jqueryui.com/demos/dialog/#animated	Click the Open Dialog button to see a custom jQuery UI dialog box. A lot better than a boring, old JavaScript alert box, no?

WHO DOES WHAT?

Match each jQuery UI plug-in to what type of plug-in it is and
what it does. Hint: If you're not sure, spend some more time poking
around the demo site from the Test Drive on the facing page.

Puff   Interaction: Makes a DOM element a
                                   target for draggable elements.

Autocomplete   Widget: Displays the current percentage
                                   of completion for some event.

Droppable   Effect: Makes an element appear to
                                   expand and dissipate into transparency,
                                   like smoke.

Explode   Widget: Provides a list of possible values
                                   when a user types into an input field.

Sortable   Effect: Makes an element appear to slide
                                   up or down like a window treatment.

Progressbar   Widget: Creates stacked and collapsible
                                   areas to organize web content.

Resizable   Effect: Makes an element appear to
                                   break into pieces and spread out in
                                   several directions.

Blind   Interaction: Makes an element
                                   sortable by dragging.

Accordion   Interaction: Gives an element
                                   draggable handles that allow a user
                                   to scale it.

WHO DOES WHAT? SOLUTION

Match each jQuery UI plug-in to what type of plug-in it is and what it does.

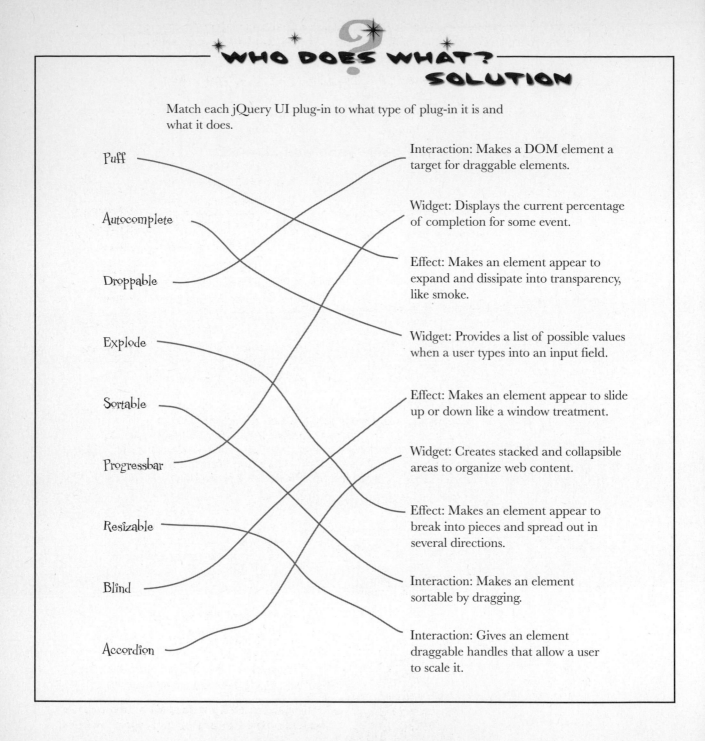

Puff

Autocomplete

Droppable

Explode

Sortable

Progressbar

Resizable

Blind

Accordion

Interaction: Makes a DOM element a target for draggable elements.

Widget: Displays the current percentage of completion for some event.

Effect: Makes an element appear to expand and dissipate into transparency, like smoke.

Widget: Provides a list of possible values when a user types into an input field.

Effect: Makes an element appear to slide up or down like a window treatment.

Widget: Creates stacked and collapsible areas to organize web content.

Effect: Makes an element appear to break into pieces and spread out in several directions.

Interaction: Makes an element sortable by dragging.

Interaction: Gives an element draggable handles that allow a user to scale it.

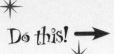

Before we can do anything with jQuery UI, we need to configure the components we want, choose a theme, and download a copy of it. Follow the steps below:

1 **Point your browser to the jQuery UI download page:**

http://jqueryui.com/download

2 **Choose the components you want to download.**

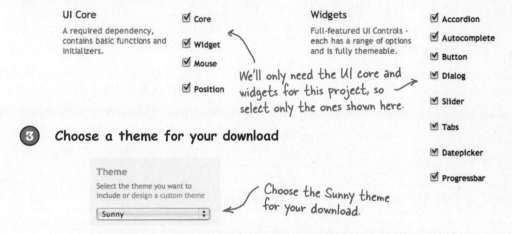

We'll only need the UI core and widgets for this project, so select only the ones shown here.

3 **Choose a theme for your download**

Choose the Sunny theme for your download.

One of the best things about jQuery UI are its themes. The dev team for jQuery UI included all of the CSS for making a nice-looking interface. You can even create your own theme with jQuery UI's "theme roller." For a gallery of all the jQuery UI themes, visit the following URL:

http://jqueryui.com/themeroller/#themeGallery

4 **Press the Download button.**

So I'm all loaded up with jQuery UI! How do I start using it?

You just need to unzip the folder and include the library in a project folder.

Turn the page, and we'll have a look inside jQuery UI.

What's inside the jQuery UI package

After downloading and unzipping jQuery, you'll find that it's structured like this:

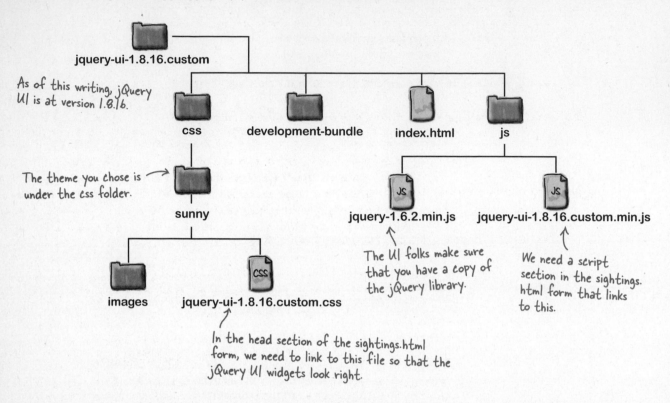

As of this writing, jQuery UI is at version 1.8.16.

The theme you chose is under the css folder.

In the head section of the sightings.html form, we need to link to this file so that the jQuery UI widgets look right.

The UI folks make sure that you have a copy of the jQuery library.

We need a script section in the sightings.html form that links to this.

We've included the jQuery UI folder in the code folder you downloaded at the beginning of the book. You'll find it in the *end* folder inside the *ch10* folder.

Our project checklist

jQuery UI does a lot for you, but we've still got quite a few items to tackle in order to build the new form. Here's a checklist of what we need to do:

☐ 1. Build a datepicker for users to enter the date of the sighting.

☐ 2. Build more engaging radio buttons for users to choose the creature type.

☐ 3. Build number-entry sliders for users to enter distance from creature, creature weight, creature height, latitude, and longitude.

☐ 4. Build a color mixer interface component for the user to enter creature color.

☐ 5. Build a nicer-looking submit button for the sightings form.

Build a date picker into the sightings form

It's amazing how easy it is to put a jQuery UI widget into an HTML form.
Let's start with the calendar datepicker:

1 **Create a link to the jQuery UI CSS file:**

```
<link type="text/css" href="jquery-ui-1.8.16.custom/css/sunny/
jquery-ui-1.8.16.custom.css" rel="stylesheet" />
```

2 **Create a `<script>` tag that points to jQuery UI.**

```
<script src="jquery-ui-1.8.16.custom/js/jquery-ui-1.8.16.
custom.min.js"></script>
```

3 **Take a plain old HTML `input` field.**

```
<input type="text" name="sighting_date">
```

CRYPTID SIGHTING DATA

Date of Sighting:

4 **Add an ID of `datepicker` to the `<input>` tag.**

```
<input type="text" name="sighting_date" id="datepicker">
```

5 **Create a JavaScript file and put the following code between the curly braces of the `$(document).ready(function(){}`.**

```
$('#datepicker').datepicker();
```

6 **Open the file in your favorite browser and click into the `input` field.**

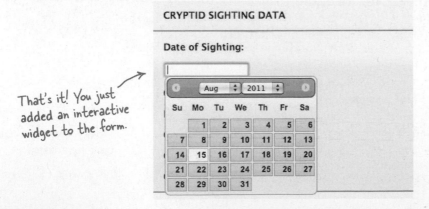

That's it! You just added an interactive widget to the form.

jQuery UI behind the scenes

It may seem a bit like magic, but jQuery UI is really just a lot of well-designed and well-written jQuery code—code that *you* didn't have to write. Let's take a closer look at how it works.

1 Just like all the other jQuery code you've written, the datepicker uses a selector and a method.

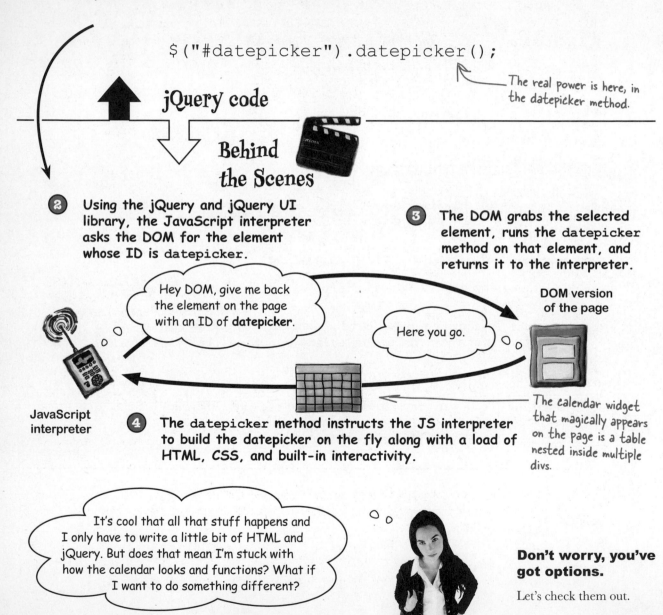

```
$("#datepicker").datepicker();
```

The real power is here, in the datepicker method.

jQuery code

Behind the Scenes

2 Using the jQuery and jQuery UI library, the JavaScript interpreter asks the DOM for the element whose ID is datepicker.

*Hey DOM, give me back the element on the page with an ID of **datepicker**.*

Here you go.

3 The DOM grabs the selected element, runs the datepicker method on that element, and returns it to the interpreter.

DOM version of the page

JavaScript interpreter

4 The datepicker method instructs the JS interpreter to build the datepicker on the fly along with a load of HTML, CSS, and built-in interactivity.

The calendar widget that magically appears on the page is a table nested inside multiple divs.

It's cool that all that stuff happens and I only have to write a little bit of HTML and jQuery. But does that mean I'm stuck with how the calendar looks and functions? What if I want to do something different?

Don't worry, you've got options.

Let's check them out.

Widgets have customizable options

If you dig into the datepicker widget, you'll find that it's got a lot of rich features and options you can configure.

The "previous" button takes you to the previous month.

The current date will be highlighted in a different color.

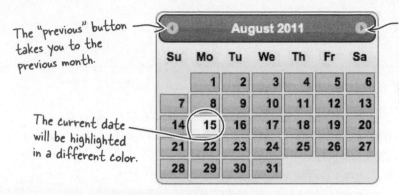

The "next" button takes you to the next month. Every time you click, a new table for that month is generated on the fly.

Customize the datepicker with options

Because jQuery UI is built on jQuery, you don't have to write much code to customize the datepicker widget to fit your needs. At the time of this writing, the datepicker has 46 different options you can set.

```
$("#datepicker").datepicker({
    stepMonths: 3
});
```

The datepicker widget comes with tons of configurable options. The stepMonths option lets you change how many months you want to hop.

If you start on August, when you press the "previous" or "next" button, you'll hop three months backward or three months forward.

```
$("#datepicker").datepicker({
    changeMonth: true
});
```

If you set the changeMonth option to true, the user can choose the month from a drop-down list.

Exercise

Write the code that will let the user change both the month and the year of the datepicker widget using a drop-down. Hint: Put a comma between the options when you're setting more than one.

....

....

....

Exercise Solution

Write the code that will let the user change both the month and the year of the datepicker widget using a drop-down. Hint: Put a comma between the options when you're setting more than one.

```
$('#datepicker').datepicker({
        changeMonth: true, changeYear: true
});
```

Ready Bake Code

Find the file called *sightings_begin.html* in the *begin* folder under *ch10*. Save it as *sightings_end.html* into the *end* folder for Chapter 10. Add the bolded code below to your *sightings_end.html* and *my_scripts.js* files.

```html
<head>
    <title>Submit Your Cryptid Sighting</title>
    <link rel="stylesheet" type="text/css" href="style/form.css" />
    <link type="text/css" href="jquery-ui-1.8.16.custom/css/sunny/jquery-ui-1.8.16.
custom.css" rel="stylesheet" />
</head>
```

Near the top of the sightings_end.html file

We need to link to the jQuery UI CSS file so the widgets look right.

```html
<h3>Date of Sighting:</h3>
        <input  type="text" name="sighting_date" id="datepicker" />
```

sightings_end.html

```html
<script src="scripts/jquery-1.6.2.min.js"></script>
<script src="scripts/my_scripts.js"></script>
<script src="jquery-ui-1.8.16.custom/js/jquery-ui-1.8.16.custom.min.js"></
script>
    </body>
</html>
```

We need to include the jQuery UI library to make all the cool UI features available.

Near the bottom of the sightings_end.html file

```javascript
$(document).ready(function(){

    $('#datepicker').datepicker({ changeMonth: true, changeYear: true});

});//end doc ready
```

The datepicker code

JS

my_scripts.js

TEST DRIVE

After entering the code from the previous page, open *sightings_end.html* in your favorite browser to test the datepicker widget. Click the "next" and "previous" buttons and the month and year drop-down lists to make sure everything works.

The datepicker works!

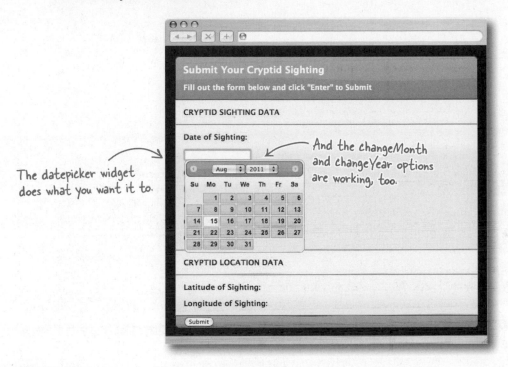

The datepicker widget does what you want it to.

And the changeMonth and changeYear options are working, too.

Check it off

Checklist item 1 is done. Let's move on to checklist item 2.

☑ 1. Build a datepicker for users to enter the date of the sighting.

☐ 2. Build more engaging radio buttons for users to choose the creature type.

☐ 3. Build number-entry sliders for users to enter distance from creature, creature weight, creature height, latitude, and longitude.

☐ 4. Build a color mixer interface component for the user to enter creature color.

☐ 5. Build a nicer-looking submit button for the sightings form.

Styling up your buttons

What does "more engaging" really mean? It's mostly a question of style: make a better-looking button, and people are going to want to click it. One super-useful widget in the jQuery UI library is the button widget. The button widget offers a `button` method to help you make more appealing form elements like submit buttons, radio buttons, and checkboxes.

Here's the HTML for a single button.

This input will be updated when the user clicks.

```
<input type="radio" id="radio1" name="radio" />
        <label for="radio1">Choice 1</label>
```

The button widget styles the label to appear as a button.

And the corresponding jQuery statement.

```
$( "#radio1" ).button();
```

The button method turns a plain old HTML radio button into a nice-looking, more interactive button.

Don't forget that the markup code for input buttons needs to be inside an HTML form tag.

Grouping button widgets

For building a grouped set of buttons, jQuery UI offers the `buttonset` method, which turns individual button elements into a group by referencing the container element for that group.

```
<div id="radio">
        <input type="radio" id="radio1" name="radio" />
            <label for="radio1">Choice 1</label>
        <input type="radio" id="radio2" name="radio" />
            <label for="radio2">Choice 2</label>
        <input type="radio" id="radio3" name="radio" />
            <label for="radio3">Choice 3</label>
</div>
```

Put your radio button group inside a container element.

In your jQuery code, select the container element.

```
$( "#radio" ).buttonset();
```

The buttonset method groups the buttons for you and runs the button method on each element.

jQuery UI Magnets

Put the code magnets in proper order to create a set of buttons for users to select the creature type that they saw. We put a few in for you.

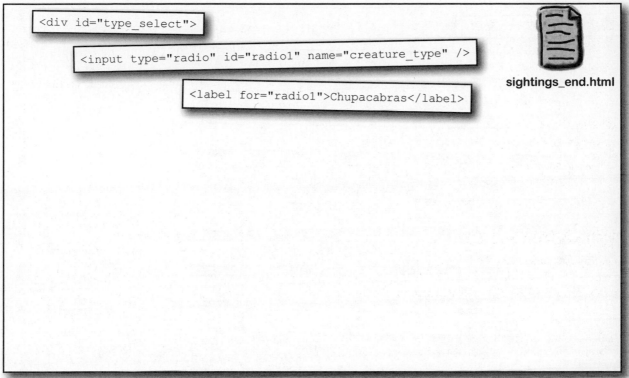

```
<div id="type_select">

        <input type="radio" id="radio1" name="creature_type" />

            <label for="radio1">Chupacabras</label>
```

sightings_end.html

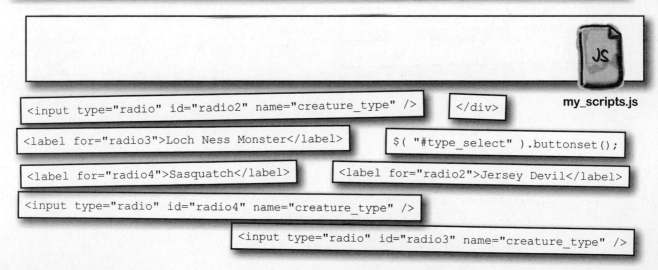

my_scripts.js

```
<input type="radio" id="radio2" name="creature_type" />          </div>

<label for="radio3">Loch Ness Monster</label>          $( "#type_select" ).buttonset();

<label for="radio4">Sasquatch</label>          <label for="radio2">Jersey Devil</label>

<input type="radio" id="radio4" name="creature_type" />

        <input type="radio" id="radio3" name="creature_type" />
```

jQuery UI Magnets Solution

Now you've got a nice-looking set of buttons that match the overall theme for your form.

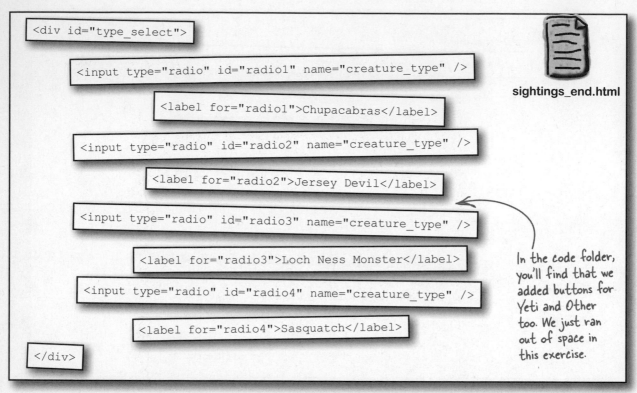

```html
<div id="type_select">

    <input type="radio" id="radio1" name="creature_type" />

        <label for="radio1">Chupacabras</label>

    <input type="radio" id="radio2" name="creature_type" />

        <label for="radio2">Jersey Devil</label>

    <input type="radio" id="radio3" name="creature_type" />

        <label for="radio3">Loch Ness Monster</label>

    <input type="radio" id="radio4" name="creature_type" />

        <label for="radio4">Sasquatch</label>

</div>
```

sightings_end.html

In the code folder, you'll find that we added buttons for Yeti and Other too. We just ran out of space in this exercise.

```javascript
$( "#type_select" ).buttonset();
```

my_scripts.js

Test Drive

Add the lines of code above to your *sightings_end.html* and *my_scripts.js* file. Then, open the page up in your favorite browser to make sure everything's working.

Creature Type:

⊙ Chupacabras ⊙ Jersey Devil ⊙ Loch Ness Monster ⊙ Sasquatch ⊙ Yeti ⊙ Other

You took these plain old HTML radio buttons...

...and turned them into a nice-looking set of push buttons.

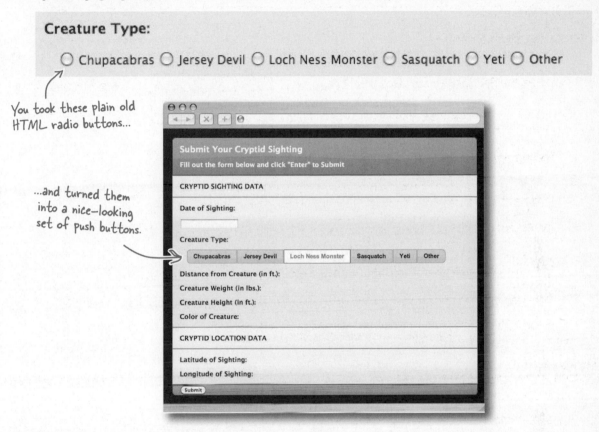

Wow, that was pretty easy. What's next on our list for the form?

☑ 1. Build a datepicker for users to enter the date of the sighting.

☑ 2. Build more engaging radio buttons for users to choose the creature type.

☐ 3. Build number-entry sliders for users to enter distance from creature, creature weight, creature height, latitude, and longitude.

☐ 4. Build a color mixer interface component for the user to enter creature color.

☐ 5. Build a nicer-looking submit button for the sightings form.

Control numerical entries with a slider

The plug-in for the jQuery UI slider gives you the power to build a slider interface that users can control with their mouse or keyboard. Sliders also help you control the numbers that users enter. As you've already seen, building widgets is a snap once you have the jQuery UI library. Building a slider widget is just as easy.

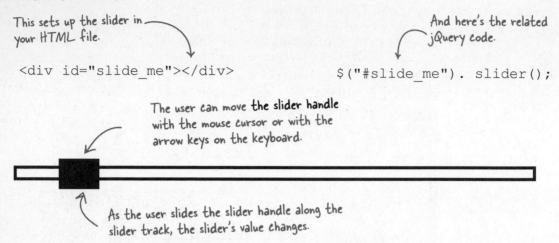

This sets up the slider in your HTML file.

And here's the related jQuery code.

```
<div id="slide_me"></div>
```

```
$("#slide_me"). slider();
```

The user can move **the slider handle** with the mouse cursor or with the arrow keys on the keyboard.

As the user slides the slider handle along the slider track, the slider's value changes.

Sliders offer a bunch of customization options too. Let's say we need the user to enter a set of numbers. The lowest value we want users to enter is 0; the maximum value is 100. And we want the users to enter values in increments of 5. Here's how we can do that with the slider widget's options:

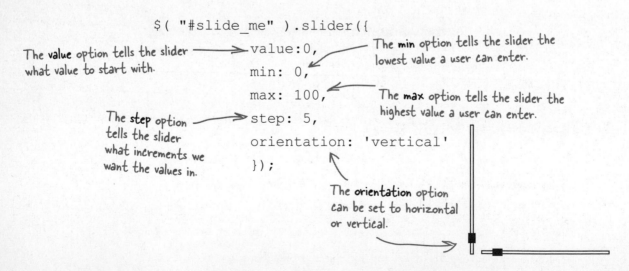

```
$( "#slide_me" ).slider({
    value:0,
    min: 0,
    max: 100,
    step: 5,
    orientation: 'vertical'
});
```

The **value** option tells the slider what value to start with.

The **min** option tells the slider the lowest value a user can enter.

The **max** option tells the slider the highest value a user can enter.

The **step** option tells the slider what increments we want the values in.

The **orientation** option can be set to horizontal or vertical.

> The slider widget's got some great options, but how do we get the value from the slider into a form input?

We have to connect the slider with one of the slider widget's event handlers.

We've seen some widget options, but we haven't yet explored another powerful feature of jQuery UI. Many jQuery components offer event handlers, and the slider is one of them. At the time of this writing, jQuery UI's slider widget offers five event handlers: `create`, `start`, `slide`, `change`, and `stop`. To connect the slider to a form input, let's try out the `slide` event handler.

If you don't want the user to be able to type to enter a number, set the input to "readonly."

The HTML for a slider widget

```html
<input type="text" id="my_value" readonly="readonly"/>
        <div id="slide_me"></div>
```

The input "my_value"

The slider "slide_me"

The JQuery script for a slider widget

```javascript
$( "#slide_me" ).slider({
    slide: function( event, ui ) {
        $( "#my_value" ).val( ui.value);
    }
});
$( "#my_value" ).val( $( "#slide_me" ).slider( "value" ));
```

*This is the **slide event** handler. The user triggers the slide event when she moves the slide handle.*

The slide event is attached to a function callback. When the function runs, this sets the input with the jQuery val method.

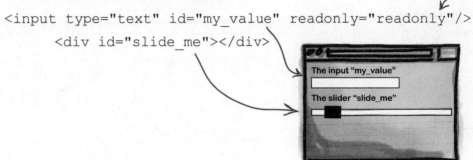

When the user slides the slide handle, the function is called and the input is updated to the slider's value.

Long Exercise

Fill in the blanks for the code for each input field the cryptozoologists want. They've left some notes on the slider options for you to set.

> Distance from Creature (in ft.):
>
> Starting value should be 0.
>
> Minimum distance should be 0.
>
> Maximum distance should be 500.
>
> Use increments of 10 feet.

```
<h3>Distance from Creature (in ft.):</h3>
<input type="text" id="..............." class="just_display" name="creature_distance"
                                              readonly="readonly"/>
            <div id="..............."></div>
        </div>
</div>
```

sightings_end.html

```
$( "#slide_dist" ).slider({
            ...............
            ...............
            ...............
            ...............
            slide: function( event, ui ) {
                    $( "#distance" ...............  )
            }
});
```

my_scripts.js

Creature Weight (in lbs.):

Starting value should be 0,

Minimum weight should be 0.

Maximum weight should be 5,000.

Use increments of 5 pounds.

Creature Height (in ft.):

Starting value should be 0.

Minimum height should be 0.

Maximum height should be 20.

Use increments of 1 foot.

```html
<h3>Creature Weight (in lbs.):</h3>
        <input  type="text" id="weight" class="just_display" name="creature_weight"
                                                readonly="readonly"/>

                    <div id="              "></div>


<h3>Creature Height (in ft.):</h3>
        <input  type="text" id="height" class="just_display" name="creature_height"
                                                readonly="readonly"/>

                    <div id="slide_height"></div>
```

sightings_end.html

```javascript
$( "              " ).slider({
    ......................

                ...............

                ...............

                ...............

                ...............
    slide: function( event, ui ) {
      $( "        " ).val( ui.value);
             ...............
      }
});
```

my_scripts.js

```javascript
$( "#slide_weight" ).slider({

                ...............

                ...............

                ...............

                ...............

    ...............................................
            $( "#weight" ).val( ui.value);
        }
});
```

my_scripts.js

LONG EXERCISE SOLUTION

Fill in the blanks for the code for each input field the cryptozoologists want. They've left some notes on the slider options for you to set.

> Distance from Creature (in ft.):
>
> Starting value should be 0.
>
> Minimum distance should be 0.
>
> Maximum distance should be 500.
>
> Use increments of 10 feet.

```html
<h3>Distance from Creature (in ft.):</h3>
<input type="text" id=" distance " class="just_display" name="creature_distance"
                                                readonly="readonly"/>
            <div id="slide_dist "></div>
    </div>
</div>
```

sightings_end.html

```javascript
$( "#slide_dist" ).slider({
                value:0,
                min:0,
                max:500,
                step: 10,
                slide: function( event, ui ) {
                        $( "#distance".val( ui.value); )
                }
});
```

my_scripts.js

Creature Weight (in lbs.):

Starting value should be 0.

Minimum weight should be 0.

Maximum weight should be 5,000.

Use increments of 5 pounds.

Creature Height (in ft.):

Starting value should be 0.

Minimum height should be 0.

Maximum height should be 20.

Use increments of 1 foot.

```html
<h3>Creature Weight (in lbs.):</h3>
        <input   type="text" id="weight" class="just_display" name="creature_weight"
                                                            readonly="readonly"/>
                        <div id=" slide_weight "></div>

<h3>Creature Height (in ft.):</h3>
        <input   type="text" id="height" class="just_display" name="creature_height"
                                                            readonly="readonly"/>
                        <div id="slide_height"></div>
```

sightings_end.html

```javascript
$( " #slide_height " ).slider({
                    value:0,
                    min:0,
                    max:20,
                    step: 1,
        slide: function( event, ui ) {
            $( "#height " ).val( ui.value);
        }
});
```

my_scripts.js

```javascript
$( "#slide_weight" ).slider({
                    value:0,
                    min:0,
                    max:5000,
                    step: 10,
        slide: function( event, ui ) {
            $( "#weight" ).val( ui.value);
        }
});
```

my_scripts.js

Test Drive

Add the code from the long exercise on the previous pages to your files. Then, open *sightings_end.html* in your favorite browser. Make sure to test the sliders using your mouse and keyboard (the left and right arrow keys should advance the slider by its increments).

Users can now enter the data by sliding the handles, and the cryptozoologists have much better data quality control.

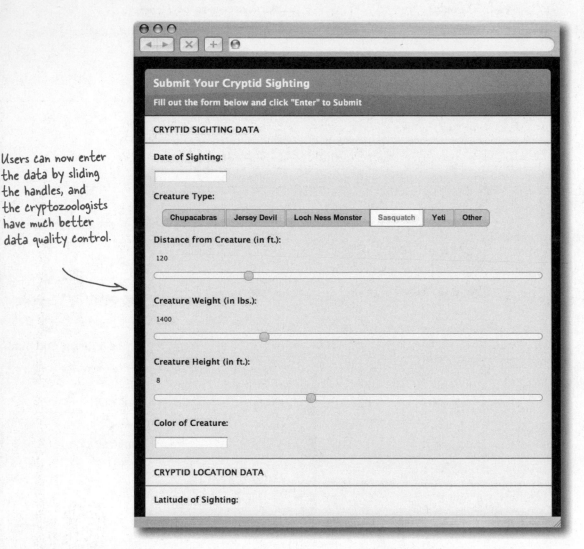

You've got two more number sliders to build: latitude and longitude. Then you can check off another item from your project checklist!

> But latitude and longitude have negative values and decimal intervals like 0.00001. Can the slider widget handle those kinds of numbers?

jQuery UI has you covered there, too.

The slider widget can deal with negative numbers and decimal numbers. You can enter negative numbers as values, as minimums, and as maximums. Give that a try below to see it in action.

Sharpen your pencil

Fill in the jQuery code to make the sliders for latitude and longitude work. The latitude slider should have a range of –90 to 90 with increments of 0.00001. The longitude slider should have a range of –180 to 180 with increments of 0.00001.

```
...........................          value:0,
                             .................
                             .................
                             .....................
                             slide: function( event, ui ) {
                                     $( " ................ " ).val( ui.value);
                             }
                     });


    ..............................................          value:0,
                             .................
                             .................
                             ............................
                             slide: function( event, ui ) {
                                     $( " ................. " ).val( ui.value);
                             }
                     });
```

my_scripts.js

Sharpen your pencil
Solution

Fill in the jQuery code to make the sliders for latitude and longitude work. The latitude slider should have a range of –90 to 90 with increments of 0.00001. The longitude slider should have a range of –180 to 180 with increments of 0.00001.

```
$( "#slide_lat" ).slider({
                    value:0,
                    min: -90,
                    max: 90,
                    step: 0.00001,
                    slide: function( event, ui ) {
                            $( " latitude " ).val( ui.value);
                    }
        });


$( "#slide_long" ).slider({
                    value:0,
                    min: -180,
                    max: 180,
                    step: 0.00001,
                    slide: function( event, ui ) {
                            $( " longitude " ).val( ui.value);
                    }
        });
```

my_scripts.js

So far, you've checked off quite a few items from the list:

☑ 1. Build a datepicker for users to enter the date of the sighting.

☑ 2. Build more engaging radio buttons for users to choose the creature type.

☑ 3. Build number-entry sliders for users to enter distance from creature, creature weight, creature height, latitude, and longitude.

What's up next? Now you need to build the cryptozoologists an interface that will allow users to enter the color of the creature they saw by using sliders that represent red, green, and blue.

☐ 4. Build a color mixer interface component for the user to enter creature color.

Computers mix color using red, green, and blue

The values of red, green, and blue each have a minimum of 0 and a maximum of 255. When each color is at its minimum—in other words, when red's value is 0, green's is 0, and blue's is 0—you get black. When each color is at its maximum—when red's value is 255, green's is 255, and blue's is 255—you get white.

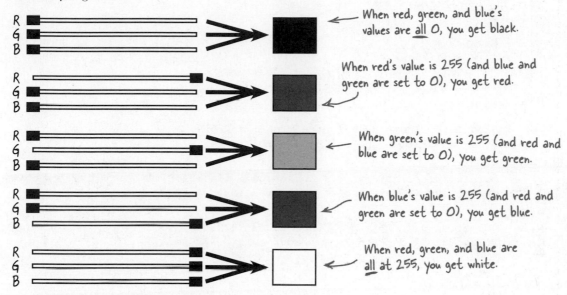

When red, green, and blue's values are all 0, you get black.

When red's value is 255 (and blue and green are set to 0), you get red.

When green's value is 255 (and red and blue are set to 0), you get green.

When blue's value is 255 (and red and green are set to 0), you get blue.

When red, green, and blue are all at 255, you get white.

Your sliders need to do the same

So you need to build three different sliders: one for red, one for green, and one for blue. Then you'll combine each of the slider's values to become one color. Let's look at what we need each slider widget to do.

The CSS ID for the inputs will be red_val, green_val, and blue_val.

We need the values from each slider to be concatenated to create the div#swatch's color.

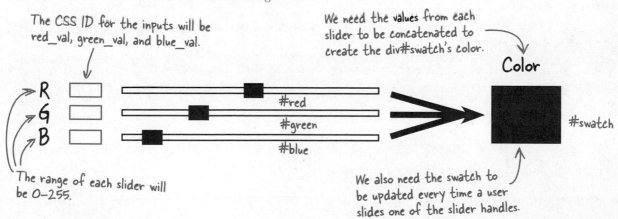

The range of each slider will be 0–255.

We also need the swatch to be updated every time a user slides one of the slider handles.

Ready Bake Code

Add the bolded code to your *sightings_end.html* and your *form.css* file. This will get your files set up to build the color picker.

```css
//color slider styles
  #slide_dist, #slide_weight, #slide_height {
  margin-bottom:14px;
  }

  #swatch {
    width: 75px;
    height: 75px;
    background-image: none;
}

#red .ui-slider-range { background: #ef2929; }
#red .ui-slider-handle { border-color: #ef2929; }

#green .ui-slider-range { background: #8ae234; }
#green .ui-slider-handle { border-color: #8ae234; }

#blue .ui-slider-range { background: #729fcf; }
#blue .ui-slider-handle { border-color: #729fcf; }
```

This CSS ID style defines the swatch that will show the color as the user changes the slider.

form.css

Each of these styles puts the color of the slider in the slider track.

```html
<h3>Color of Creature (use the color sliders to enter):</h3>

Color (in hexadecimal):<input  type="text" class="just_display"
name="creature_color" id="color_val" readonly="readonly"/><br /><br />
  <div id="swatch" class="ui-widget-content ui-corner-all"></div>

Red:<input  type="text" class="just_display" name="creature_color" id="red_val"
readonly="readonly"/>
  <div id="red"></div>

Green:<input type="text" class="just_display" name="creature_color" id="green_val"
readonly="readonly"/>
  <div id="green"></div>

Blue:<input type="text" class="just_display" name="creature_color" id="blue_val"
readonly="readonly"/>
  <div id="blue"></div>
```

The input field that will hold the hex value of the color

The div for the color swatch

The div for the red slider

The div for the green slider

The div for the blue slider

sightings_end.html

Sharpen your pencil

The script below sets up the red, green, and blue color sliders. Read each line and think about what it might do based on what you already know about jQuery and jQuery UI. Then, write down what you think the code does. If you're not sure what a line does, it's perfectly OK to guess. We did one for you.

```
$( "#red, #green, #blue" ).slider({
     orientation: "horizontal",
     range: "min",                         Sets the slider range so the user can only select a maximum.
     max: 255,
     value: 127,
     slide: refreshSwatch,
     change: refreshSwatch
});
```

there are no
Dumb Questions

Q: **What's all that CSS that comes with jQuery UI?**

A: The great thing about jQuery UI is that the developers have thought out a lot of the complex CSS so that you don't have to. You can learn about the CSS by looking through the file in the jQuery UI package under *jquery-ui-1.8.16.custom/css/sunny/ jquery-ui-1.8.16.custom.css*. To read more about those CSS classes, visit jQuery UI's documentation at the following URL: *http://jqueryui.com/docs/Theming/API*.

Q: **You said we can make our own theme for jQuery UI. How do I do that?**

A: You can easily create your own theme by using jQuery UI's theme roller. First, point your browser to the theme roller application here:

http://jqueryui.com/themeroller/

Then, click on the "Roll your own" tab. You'll see settings for things like font, click states, drop shadows, and overlay screen. Make your own custom changes, and the UI elements will change to reflect your design settings.

When you have your theme set how you want it, just click the Download Theme button, and you'll be taken to the Build Your Download page to create your own jQuery UI package. If you want to save your theme for later, just bookmark that Build Your Download page.

Q: **I don't get the interactions widgets. What would I use those for?**

A: Interactions allow you to create the kind of interactive functionality you would find in a desktop application.

Using the Draggable widgets, you can turn your elements into draggable components.

The Droppable widget can be a target for a droppable widget.

The Resizable widget turns your element into a scalable object whose size you can change by dragging on its corner, its right border, or its bottom border.

Selectables are widgets that turn your elements into selectable components. A site visitor can drag his mouse over those elements to select them just like he might select files on his desktop.

Sortables are widgets that can be interactively reordered by the user.

Sharpen your pencil Solution

The script below sets up the red, green, and blue color sliders. Read each line and think about what it might do based on what you already know about jQuery and jQuery UI. Then, write down what you think the code does. If you're not sure what a line does, it's perfectly OK to guess. Here are our answers.

```
$( "#red, #green, #blue" ).slider({        Turns each of the divs for R,G,B into slider widgets.
    orientation: "horizontal",             Makes them into horizontal sliders rather than vertical.
    range: "min",                          Sets the slider range so the user can only select a maximum.
    max: 255,                              Sets the max value to 255 to stick within the color limits.
    value: 127,                            Sets the value so the slider handles are roughly in the middle.
    slide: refreshSwatch,                  Calls a function named refreshSwatch when the user slides.
    change: refreshSwatch                  Calls the same function when any value changes.
});
```

Build the refreshSwatch function

To finish our color mixer, we need a JavaScript function that will set and refresh the swatch. Here's a skeleton version of that function, along with some of the key questions to consider before fleshing it out to get it to do what you want.

```
function refreshSwatch() {
    var red = ???
    var green = ???                How will you get the
                                   values of each slider into
    var blue = ???                 each of these variables?

    var my_rgb = ???               We need to concatenate the RGB
                                   values in this variable so that we
                                   can set the color swatch.

    $( "#swatch" ).???;            What jQuery method will let us
                                   set the color swatch's color?

    $( "#red_val" ).val(red );
    $( "#blue_val" ).val( blue);       No big questions here. We can
                                       simply use jQuery's val method
    $( "#green_val" ).val( green);     to set the input fields to show
                                       the value of the sliders as they
    $( "#color_val" ).val(my_rgb);     change. That way, the user will
                                       know what the values are.
}
```

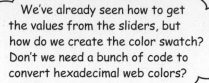

We've already seen how to get the values from the sliders, but how do we create the color swatch? Don't we need a bunch of code to convert hexadecimal web colors?

Good catch! We *could* write a decimal-to-hexadecimal conversion function, or we could use the decimal values straight from the sliders.

Remember that the CSS background-color property allows us to specify colors like this:

R   G   B

```
background-color:rgb(255,0,255)
```

But that's just a hint for one of the questions. To write the whole function, you'll have to do a little brain workout.

Exercise

Fill in the blank lines of code to finish off the refreshSwatch function.

```
function refreshSwatch() {
        var red = ........................................................
        var green = ......................................................
        var blue = .......................................................
        var my_rgb = .....................................................
        $( "#swatch" ). ...........................................;
        $( "#red_val" ).val(red );
        $( "#blue_val" ).val( blue);
        $( "#green_val" ).val( green);
        $( "#color_val" ).val(my_rgb);
}
```

Exercise Solution

Fill in the blank lines of code to finish off the `refreshSwatch` function.

```
function refreshSwatch() {
        var red =   $( "#red" ).slider( "value" );
        var green =  $( "#green" ).slider( "value" );
        var blue =   $( "#blue" ).slider( "value" );
        var my_rgb =   "rgb(" + red + "," + green + "," + blue + ")";
        $( "#swatch" ).  $( "#swatch" ).css( "background-color", my_rgb );
        $( "#red_val" ).val(red );
        $( "#blue_val" ).val( blue);
        $( "#green_val" ).val( green);
        $( "#color_val" ).val(my_rgb);

}
```

By concatenating the RGB values into this variable...

...we can set the CSS for the swatch to the combined values of the three colors.

Ready Bake Code

Update your *my_scripts.js* file to include the code for the color slider and `refreshSwatch` function on the previous pages. Add the lines below too. They will trigger the slider values to run the `refreshSwatch` function when the web page loads, which will start the web page with a colored swatch rather than an empty one.

```
$( "#red" ).slider( "value", 127 );
$( "#green" ).slider( "value", 127 );
$( "#blue" ).slider( "value", 127 );
```

Test Drive

Open *sightings_end.html* in your favorite browser. Make sure to test the sliders using your mouse and keyboard (the left and right arrow keys should advance the slider by its increments).

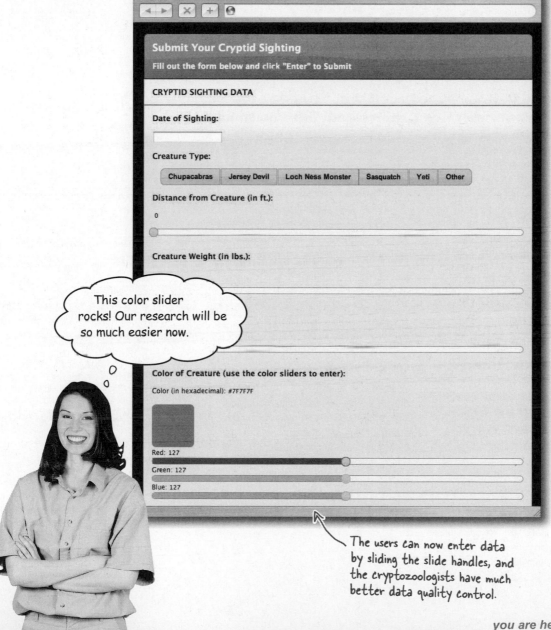

This color slider rocks! Our research will be so much easier now.

The users can now enter data by sliding the slide handles, and the cryptozoologists have much better data quality control.

One last little thing...

There's just one item left on your checklist:

☑ 1. Build a datepicker for users to enter the date of the sighting.

☑ 2. Build more engaging radio buttons for users to choose the creature type.

☑ 3. Build number-entry sliders for users to enter distance from creature, creature weight, creature height, latitude, and longitude.

☑ 4. Build a color mixer interface component for the user to enter creature color.

☐ 5. Build a nicer-looking submit button for the sightings form.

You've used buttons already in this chapter and you've been using buttons since Chapter 1, so this one should be pretty easy for you!

---

there are no Dumb Questions

Q: We used the `rgb` setting for `background-color` for the color slider we built. What if I want to make a color slider that uses standard hex notation for colors?

A: We tried to create the most elegant and simple code possible for the color slider. If you need a color slider that will collect data in hex color format, you're in luck.

You can use the sample code for a simple color picker provided at the jQuery UI site. Point your browser to the following URL:

http://jqueryui.com/demos/slider/#colorpicker

Now, find the View Source link under the demo color picker. Select and copy the HTML, CSS, and jQuery code in the text field and save it into a new document. Make sure to link that document up to the appropriate CSS and jQuery files in your copy of the jQuery bundle. Voilà—you have a color picker that uses hex values for color.

Q: I need a form field that will suggest search terms as a user types. Does jQuery UI have anything for that?

A: Yes! One of jQuery's newest features, at the time of this writing (August 2011), is the Autocomplete widget, which displays suggestions for search terms as a user types into a form field.

Where do the search terms come from? You provide them in a JavaScript array, from a URL, or using a callback function that can grab the data from a server using the Ajax methods you learned in Chapters 8 and 9. For more information on this widget, visit jQuery UI's demo page here:

http://jqueryui.com/demos/autocomplete/

Q: Does jQuery UI provide any sort of form validation?

A: No. Unfortunately, jQuery UI does not provide form validation, but there is a jQuery plug-in that works well for validation. You can find the plug-in here:

http://bassistance.de/jquery-plugins/jquery-plugin-validation/

We talk more about that plug-in in Appendix i. Check there for more information.

Wait. Sure, we've used buttons since Chapter 1, but this is a jQuery UI button *and* an HTML form element.

OK, good point.

We've used jQuery's click method and jQuery UI's button method, but we haven't done much with *selecting form elements* like input submit buttons. Here's a quick guide on how to select those.

BULLET POINTS

- `$(":input")` = Select all input elements
- `$(":text")` = Select all elements of type text
- `$(":radio")` = Select all input elements of type radio
- `$(":checkbox")` = Select all elements of type checkbox
- `$(":submit")` = Select all input elements of type submit
- `$(":reset")` = Select all input elements of type reset

- `$(":checked")` = Select all inputs that have been checked
- `$(":selected")` = Select all inputs that have been selected
- `$(":enabled")` = Select all inputs that are enabled
- `$(":disabled")` = Select all inputs that are disabled
- `$(":password")` = Select all inputs that are intended for passwords

Exercise

Write the single line of code you need to add to *my_scripts.js* that will transform the pill button into a themed jQuery UI button.

....

Exercise Solution

Be sure to add this to your *my_scripts.js* file and test it out by opening *sightings_end.html* in your favorite browser.

```
$( "button:submit" ).button();     ;
```

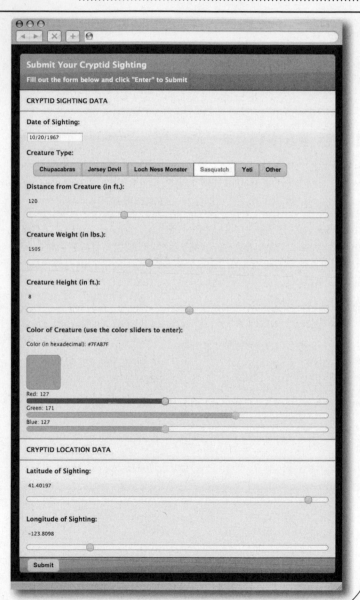

Submit Your Cryptid Sighting
Fill out the form below and click "Enter" to Submit

CRYPTID SIGHTING DATA

Date of Sighting:

10/20/1967

Creature Type:

Chupacabras | Jersey Devil | Loch Ness Monster | Sasquatch | Yeti | Other

Distance from Creature (in ft.):

120

Creature Weight (in lbs.):

1505

Creature Height (in ft.):

8

Color of Creature (use the color sliders to enter):

Color (in hexadecimal): #7FAB7F

Red: 127
Green: 171
Blue: 127

CRYPTID LOCATION DATA

Latitude of Sighting:

41.40197

Longitude of Sighting:

~123.8098

Submit

We're so happy with your work that we're calling you back to help us in the next chapter.

Yeah, thanks a lot! Now we won't get *any* peace and quiet!

**Bonus
Exercise**

Your form looks great, but it doesn't actually *submit* any data at this point. However, you learned everything you need to do that back in Chapter 9, so take some time to think through how you could make this stylish form truly functional.

The *end* folder in the code you downloaded for this chapter contains all the code you need to get this up and working: *sightings.html*, *service.php*, and *sightings.sql*. You will have to do some work on your own to get it set up, but that's what being a web developer is all about, isn't it? We included the Ajax and JSON methods you learned in Chapter 9 so that the form you just built can submit data.

You need to do all of the setup on your own (i.e., run the *sightings.sql* script or create the database with the fields in that script yourself, and add the Ajax and JSON methods to your *my_scripts.js* file). You also need to add some records to the database before going on to Chapter 11. If you need a refresher on MySQL, PHP, and AJAX, feel free to go back to Chapters 8 and 9.

There's no solution to this exercise, but if you're having any issues, you can always jump on the forum for this book at www.headfirstlabs.com, and chat with the authors and other readers.

Your jQuery Toolbox

You've got Chapter 10 under your belt and now you've added jQuery UI to your toolbox.

CHAPTER 10

jQuery UI

An official jQuery library that offers three main types of plug-ins for the jQuery core: effects, interactions, and widgets.

Widget

A self-contained component that adds functionality to your web app.

Saves you tons of coding time and complexity while creating usable and responsive user interface elements.

Button widget

Provides a button method to help you make more appealing form elements like submit buttons, radio buttons, and checkboxes.

Datepicker widget

The datepicker method instructs the JS interpreter to build the datepicker on the fly, along with a load of HTML, CSS, and built-in interactivity.

Comes with a host of customizable options, too.

Sliders

UI elements that users can manipulate with their mouse or keyboard, controlling the data that they enter.

Include five event handlers that you use to connect the slider to a form input: create, start, slide, change, and stop.

11 jQuery and APIs

Objects, objects everywhere

I wonder what I'll get this year? I hope it's another API...

As talented a developer as you are, you can't do it all alone...

We've seen how we can include jQuery plug-ins, like jQuery UI or the tabs navigation to help boost our jQuery app, without much effort. To take our applications to the next level, apply some of the really cool tools out there on the Internet, and use information provided by the big hitters—like Google, Twitter, or Yahoo!—we need something…more. Those companies, and many others, provide APIs (application programming interfaces) to their services so you can include them in your site. In this chapter, we'll look at some API basics and use a very common one: the Google Maps API.

Where's ~~Waldo~~ Sasquatch?

Dr. Pattersby and Dr. Gimli want to add some more cool features to their website—think you're up to the task?

From: **Dr. Gimli [gimli@cryptozoolologists.org]**
Subject: **Some more updates to our site**

Hey guys,

Thank you so much for helping make our website more user-friendly and easier to collect data about sightings. We've had a substantial increase in traffic, so we're really excited to look at all the data we're collecting.

We've had several requests to make the information more accessible to the masses. Lots of people are interested in the sightings data, so we'd like to give them a way to see what we've collected.

Here's what we need:

1) We'd like to be able to select a single sighting and view the information associated with it. Along with the information about the cryptid, we'd like to see the latitude/longitude information appear on a Google map.

2) When a point is displayed on the Google map, we'd like to be able to click it to see more information about the sighting.

3) We'd like to be able to select the creature type from a list and display all the creatures associated with that type from our database. We'd also like to see all the creatures with that type on a Google map, so we can find some sighting hotspots to examine more closely. Can all these points be clickable, as well as the list of creatures, so users can see more information about each one?

Not too much to ask, right, since we already have all the information stored?

Looking forward to hearing from you!

--

Dr. Gimli and Dr. Pattersby
cryptozoologists.org

This should be a piece of cake. It looks like the crypto doctors are only asking for a few things.

Jim

Frank

Joe

Joe: Are you talking about the Google map we need to build?

Frank: Yep. Pretty straightforward…

Jim: Straightforward? They want a whole Google map!

Frank: Yep.

Jim: Multiple points on the map—one for each of their cryptids—each being clickable for more information…

Frank: Yeah, I think I know how to do that.

Jim: And custom click on the list to interact with the points and show the "more information" pop ups on the map.

Frank: Yeah, uh, I'm not too sure how to do that.

Joe: No worries on that part. The Google Maps folk provide an API we can use to get the job done.

Jim: AP what?

Frank: API. It's short for *application programming interface*. It's how companies like Google, Netflix, and Yahoo! enable us to use some of their cool tools on our own sites.

Jim: That does sound pretty cool, but will it give us all the pop ups and whatever else we need to put on the map?

Joe: Well, it *should*. Maybe we should look at the Google Maps API to see how it works.

The Google Maps API

For any API you want to use, you can look up documentation and get sample code online. We grabbed this sample from *http://code.google.com/apis/maps*.

```javascript
var map;
function initialize() {
  var myLatlng = new google.maps.LatLng(40.720721,-74.005966);
  var myOptions = {
    zoom: 13,
    center: myLatlng,
    mapTypeId: google.maps.MapTypeId.ROADMAP
  }

  map = new google.maps.Map(document.getElementById("map_canvas"), myOptions);

  google.maps.event.addListener(map, 'zoom_changed', function() {
    setTimeout(moveToNewYork, 3000);
  });

  var marker = new google.maps.Marker({
      position: myLatlng,
      map: map,
      title:"Hello World!"
  });
  google.maps.event.addListener(marker, 'click', function() {
    map.setZoom(8);
  });
}

function moveToNewYork() {
  var NewYork = new google.maps.LatLng(45.526585, -122.642612);
  map.setCenter(NewYork);
}
```

OK, I recognize some variables and functions in there, but what's all that other stuff?

That's Google's code.

It's not as bad as it looks. Let's see what's going on in the code in a little more detail.

APIs use objects

Back in Chapter 6, we created our own JavaScript objects with properties and methods to store and use information as we saw fit. Many companies—like Google, Netflix, Microsoft, and Yahoo!—also create API objects to allow us to interact with their data. If you need a little reminder, feel free to hop back there to reacquaint yourself with objects and how they work.

Declare variables.

Assign this variable to a new Google LatLng object..

```
var map;
var myLatlng = new google.maps.LatLng(40.720721,-74.005966);
var myOptions = {
    zoom: 13,
    center: myLatlng,
    mapTypeId: google.maps.MapTypeId.ROADMAP
}
map = new google.maps.Map(document.getElementById("map_canvas"), myOptions);

google.maps.event.addListener(map, 'zoom_changed', function() {
    setTimeout(moveToNewYork, 3000);
});
```

Create an array to store some options for the map.

Pass in some latitude and longitude values as parameters of our object.

Set the map variable to be a new Google Maps object.

Tell the map to go in the map_canvas element.

Add an event listener to our Google map.

Declare a variable as a Marker object.

Pass in values as parameters.

```
var marker = new google.maps.Marker({
    position: myLatlng,
    map: map,
    title:"Hello World!"
});

function moveToNewYork() {
    var NewYork = new google.maps.LatLng(45.526585, -122.642612);
    map.setCenter(NewYork);
}
```

The LatLng object we declared above

The Map object we declared above

Declare a function to call some more Google code.

Create another LatLng object.

Tell the map where to center itself.

So APIs do everything with objects? Why would we use objects created by somebody else?

Because it speeds everything up.

Like we saw back in Chapter 6, objects offer smarter storage. You use objects when you need to *store multiple variables* about a particular thing. An API is just a series of object *constructors* that allow you to create your own instances of other people's objects. Then, once you have an instance, you can use all the properties and methods associated with those objects in your code!

The complexities of creating a mapping application for everyone to use are exactly why Google uses objects in its API. That way, it can create objects with many different methods and properties for all the different elements you'd need to build a map.

From the code on the previous page, you can see that the map object has properties of `zoom`, `center`, and `mapTypeId`—plus many more that we haven't shown here. The map also has many methods, like `setCenter`.

 Do this!

Create a new page called *display_one.html* and save it in your project folder for this chapter.

```html
<!DOCTYPE html>
<html>
   <head>
      <title>View Cryptid Sightings</title>
      <link type="text/css" href="style/form.css" rel="stylesheet"/>
      <link type="text/css" href="jquery-ui-1.8.16.custom/css/sunny/jquery-ui-1.8.16.custom.css" />
   </head>
   <body>
      <div class="ui-widget-header ui-corner-top form_pad">
         <h2>View Cryptid Sightings</h2>
      </div>
      <div class="ui-widget-content form_pad">
         <div id="map_canvas"></div>
      </div>
      <script src="http://maps.google.com/maps/api/js?sensor=false"></script>
      <script src="scripts/jquery-1.6.2.min.js"></script>
      <script src="scripts/maps.js"></script>
   </body>
</html>
```

display_one.html

Create a place for our map to go.

Include the Google Maps API.

Include the jQuery library.

Include a new maps.js file.

Include Google maps in your page

First, make a copy of all the files you have from the end of the previous chapter. We'll use all the same files in this solution too, so we might as well pick up where we left off. All that code plus your new *display_one.html* file will give us two important new things:

A `div` with the ID of `map_canvas`.

The Google Maps API code, by adding `<script type="text/javascript" src="http://maps.google.com/maps/api/js?sensor=false"></script>`.

To include a Google map on that page, you'll need to create a *maps.js* file and add a function to it that calls the API code to build a map on the page.

jQuery Code Magnets

Rearrange the magnets to complete the code to create a function called `initialize`. This function will then create a new instance of the Google Maps `map` object, using some parameters defined in the code. The new `map` object will then be applied to the `map_canvas` element on the page. Also, update your existing *form.css* file to include some style definition for the map container.

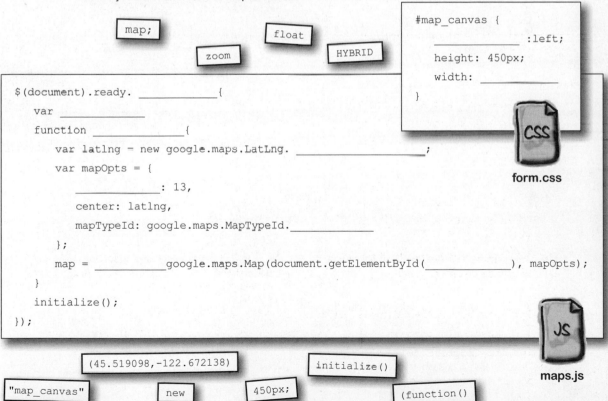

```
map;

zoom          float          HYBRID

#map_canvas {
    _____ :left;
    height: 450px;
    width: _____
}
```

form.css

```
$(document).ready. _____ {
    var _____
    function _____ {
        var latlng = new google.maps.LatLng. _____;
        var mapOpts = {
            _____: 13,
            center: latlng,
            mapTypeId: google.maps.MapTypeId._____
        };
        map = _____ google.maps.Map(document.getElementById(_____), mapOpts);
    }
    initialize();
});
```

maps.js

```
(45.519098,-122.672138)          initialize()

"map_canvas"          new          450px;          (function()
```

jQuery Code Magnets Solution

Rearrange the magnets to complete the code to create a function called `initialize`. This function will then create a new instance of the Google Maps `map` object, using some parameters defined in the code. The new `map` object will then be applied to the `map_canvas` element on the page. Also, update your existing *form.css* file to include some style definition for the map container.

```css
#map_canvas {
    float  :left;
    height: 450px;
    width: 450px;
}
```

form.css

```javascript
$(document).ready.(function() {
    var map;
    function initialize() {
        var latlng = new google.maps.LatLng.(45.519098,-122.672138);
        var mapOpts = {
            zoom : 13,
            center: latlng,
            mapTypeId: google.maps.MapTypeId.HYBRID
        };
        map = new google.maps.Map(document.getElementById("map_canvas"), mapOpts);
    }
    initialize();
});
```

maps.js

---

there are no Dumb Questions

Q: What about that `LatLng` object and `mapOpts` property?

A: You can find more information about the API's objects, methods, and more at *http://code.google.com/apis/maps/documentation/javascript/reference.html*. This website offers some example code and more details about all the different objects and methods you'll need to interact with.

Q: Is Google Maps my only option for creating a map?

A: Definitely not! It is probably the most popular though, which is why we're using it here. Other companies like Yahoo!, Microsoft, MapQuest, and OpenLayers also offer Mapping APIs.

TEST DRIVE

Update your *maps.js* file with the `initialize` function you put together with the magnets. Also, ensure that the *maps.js* file is included in *display_one.html*. Then, open up *display_one.html* in your browser. You should run all your code through your web server, so the URL should say *http://*, not *file://*.

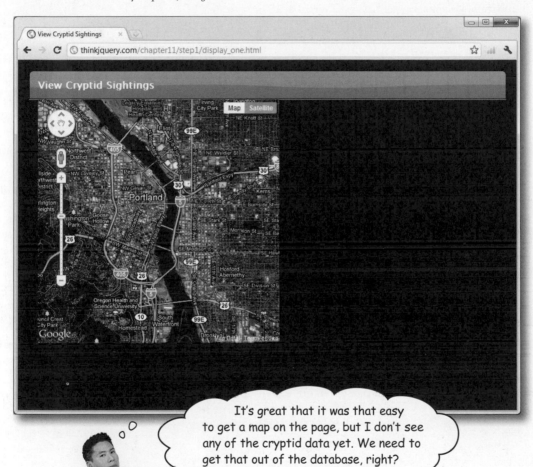

> *It's great that it was that easy to get a map on the page, but I don't see any of the cryptid data yet. We need to get that out of the database, right?*

Exactly.

Back in Chapter 9, you learned how we can get information from a MySQL database, using jQuery, Ajax, JSON, PHP, and MySQL. Although that's quite a list of technologies, it did exactly what we needed it to. Let's see how we can apply that here again.

Getting JSON data with SQL and PHP

Chapter 9 showed how a SQL `select` statement could pull the information you wanted out of the database so that a PHP file could turn it into JSON and return it to our page, using Ajax.

You also learned how to use Ajax to get JSON-encoded information from a PHP file. For PHP to return JSON data, it was easy—the `json_encode` function, which accepted an array, gave back JSON-encoded data so that jQuery could interact with it.

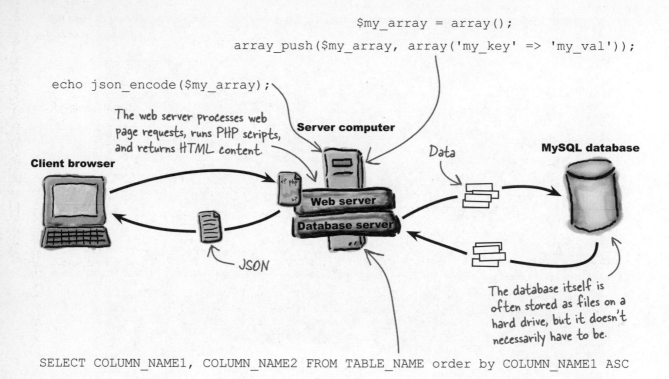

```
                                              $my_array = array();
                        array_push($my_array, array('my_key' => 'my_val'));

echo json_encode($my_array);
```

The web server processes web page requests, runs PHP scripts, and returns HTML content.

Server computer

Data

MySQL database

Client browser

Web server

Database server

JSON

The database itself is often stored as files on a hard drive, but it doesn't necessarily have to be.

```
SELECT COLUMN_NAME1, COLUMN_NAME2 FROM TABLE_NAME order by COLUMN_NAME1 ASC
```

For this chapter, we've written all of the PHP and SQL for you. As long as you've got the MySQL database from Chapter 10, you're good to go! The rest of the SQL and PHP code are in the downloads for this chapter. Feel free to run them on your own server. You can download all the PHP and SQL in a single file from *http://thinkjquery.com/chapter11/end/service.zip.*

jQuery, HTML, and CSS Code Magnets

Rearrange the magnets to update your *display_one.html*, *forms.css*, and *maps. js* files to get your data via JSON and display it on the screen. Add a `div` and a `ul` element to hold the data, some CSS to style the list, and a function to get the data, via JSON, to add each cryptid to the list.

```
function getAllSightings(){
    $.getJSON("service.php?action=getAllSightings",_____ {
    if (_____length > 0) {
        $("#sight_list")_____;
        _____(json.sightings,function() {
            var info = 'Date: ' + this['date'] + ', Type: ' + this['type'];
            var $li = $("<li />");
            _____
            $li.addClass(_____);
            $li.attr('id', this['id']) ;
            $li.appendTo(_____);
        });
    }
    });
}
```

maps.js

```
"map_canvas"
```

```
"sightings"
```

```
json.sightings.
```

```
li.sightings:hover {
```

```
$li.html(info);
```

```
#sight_nav{
    float:left;
}
ul#sight_list{
    width:150px;
    padding:0px;
    margin:0px;
}
li.sightings {
    padding:4px;
    background:#7B7382;
    border:1px #000 solid;
    color:#fff;

    _____

}

    _____
    background:#eee;
    color:#000;
}
```

form.css

```
<div class="ui-widget-content form_pad">
    <div id= _____></div>
    <div id="sight_nav">
        <ul id= _____>
        </ul>
    </div>
</div>
```

```
.empty()
```

```
$.each
```

display_one.html

```
list-style:none;
```

```
"sight_list"
```

```
"#sight_list"
```

```
function(json)
```

jQuery, HTML, and CSS Code Magnets Solution

Rearrange the magnets to update your *display_one.html*, *forms.css*, and *maps.js* files to get your data, via JSON, and display it on the screen. Add a `div` and a `ul` element to hold the data, some CSS to style the list, and a function to get the data, via JSON, and add each cryptid to the list.

```js
function getAllSightings(){
    $.getJSON("service.php?action=getAllSightings", function(json) {
        if ( json.sightings. length > 0) {
            $("#sight_list") .empty() ;
            $.each (json.sightings,function() {
                var info = 'Date: ' + this['date'] + ', Type: ' + this['type'];
                var $li = $("<li />");
                $li.html(info);
                $li.addClass( "sightings" );
                $li.attr('id', this['id']) ;
                $li.appendTo( "#sight_list" );
            });
        }
    });
}
```

maps.js

```html
<div class="ui-widget-content form_pad">
    <div id= "map_canvas" ></div>
    <div id="sight_nav">
        <ul id= "sight_list" >
        </ul>
    </div>
</div>
```

display_one.html

```css
#sight_nav{
    float:left;
}
ul#sight_list{
    width:150px;
    padding:0px;
    margin:0px;
}
li.sightings {
    padding:4px;
    background:#7B7382;
    border:1px #000 solid;
    color:#fff;
    list-style:none;
}
li.sightings:hover {
    background:#eee;
    color:#000;
}
```

form.css

Test Drive

Update your *maps.js* file with the `getAllSightings` function you just completed. Also, add a call to this new function at the end of the `initialize` function. Then open up *display_one.html* in your browser. This assumes you've added some creatures to your database, back in Chapter 10; if not, be sure to do so now. Remember, you should run all your code through your web server, so the URL should say *http://*, not *file://*.

That's nice looking and all, but all this code still doesn't actually display anything **on** our map.

Right. We need to be able to add our cryptid data to the map.

Google Maps provides a very easy method to do this. Let's have a look at how that works.

423

Points on a map are markers

When it comes to putting points on a map, Google's got it down.
However, Google doesn't call them points. It calls them *markers*.
Markers are objects—just like everything else in the Google Maps
API—and have their own methods and properties for interaction
and manipulation.

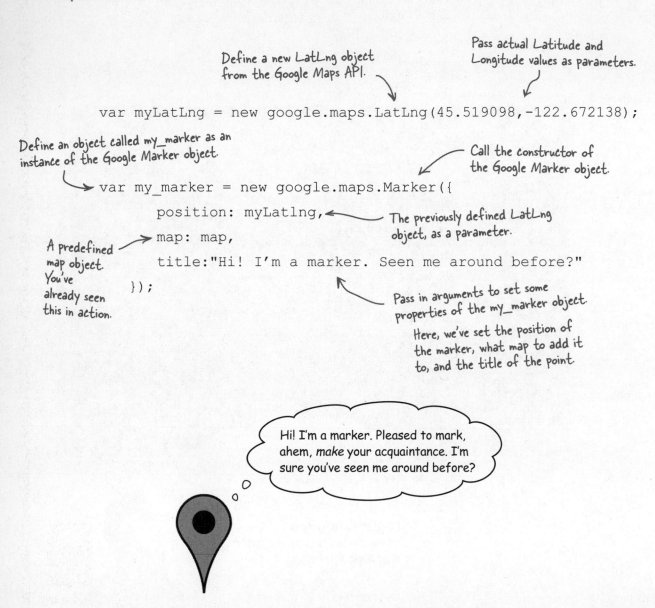

Define a new LatLng object
from the Google Maps API.

Pass actual Latitude and
Longitude values as parameters.

```
var myLatLng = new google.maps.LatLng(45.519098,-122.672138);
```

Define an object called my_marker as an
instance of the Google Marker object.

Call the constructor of
the Google Marker object.

```
var my_marker = new google.maps.Marker({
        position: myLatlng,
        map: map,
        title:"Hi! I'm a marker. Seen me around before?"
});
```

The previously defined LatLng
object, as a parameter.

A predefined
map object.
You've
already seen
this in action.

Pass in arguments to set some
properties of the my_marker object.

Here, we've set the position of
the marker, what map to add it
to, and the title of the point.

Hi! I'm a marker. Pleased to mark,
ahem, *make* your acquaintance. I'm
sure you've seen me around before?

Sharpen your pencil

Update your `getAllSightings` function to add a click event listener to the list item, *before* it gets added to the list. This click event should call a custom function, called `getSingleSighting`, which take a single parameter—the ID of the clicked sighting. This new function should then load information about the clicked item and add it as a marker on the map, using its latitude and longitude properties.

```
function getAllSightings(){
   $.getJSON("service.php?action=getAllSightings", function(json) {
      if (json.sightings.length > 0) {
         $("#sight_list").empty();
         $.each(json.sightings,function() {
            var info = 'Date: ' + this['date'] + ', Type: ' + this['type'];
            var $li = $("<li />");
            $li.html(info);
            $li.addClass("sightings");
            $li.attr('id', this['id']) ;
            $li.click(function(){
                            _____ this['id'] );
            });
            $li.appendTo("#sight_list");
         });
      }
   });
}

function getSingleSighting(_____){
   $.getJSON("service.php?action=getSingleSighting&id="+id, function(json) {
      if (json.sightings.length > 0) {

         _____
         var loc = new google.maps.LatLng(this['lat'], this['long']);
         var my_marker = new google.maps_____({
            _____loc,
            map: map,
            title:this['type']
         });
         _____setCenter(loc, 20);
      });
   }
   });
}
```

maps.js

Sharpen your pencil
Solution

After you've completed the code, your list items will be clickable, which will then load data about the clicked cryptid and put it on the map.

```javascript
function getAllSightings(){
    $.getJSON("service.php?action=getAllSightings", function(json) {
        if (json.sightings.length > 0) {
            $("#sight_list").empty();
            $.each(json.sightings,function() {
                var info = 'Date: ' + this['date'] + ', Type: ' + this['type'];
                var $li = $("<li />");
                $li.html(info);
                $li.addClass("sightings");
                $li.attr('id', this['id']) ;
                $li.click(function(){
                    getSingleSighting(this['id'] );
                });
                $li.appendTo("#sight_list");
            });
        }
    });
}

function getSingleSighting( id ){
    $.getJSON("service.php?action=getSingleSighting&id="+id, function(json) {
        if (json.sightings.length > 0) {
            $.each(json.sightings,function() {
                var loc = new google.maps.LatLng(this['lat'], this['long']);
                var my_marker = new google.maps.Marker({
                    position: loc,
                    map: map,
                    title:this['type']
                });
                map.setCenter(loc, 20);
            });
        }
    });
}
```

maps.js

Test Drive

Update your *maps.js* file with the `getAllSightings` and `getSingleSighting` functions you just completed. Then open up *display_one.html* in your browser, using *http://* like before.

Wow! That's looking really impressive. How's the other piece of what we asked for coming along? You know, where we have multiple creatures displayed at the same time.

You've already nailed the first two requirements, so let's have a look at the final thing the doctors asked for.

3) We'd like to be able to select the creature type from a list and display all the creatures associated with that type from our database. We'd also like to see all the creatures with that type on a Google map so we can find some sighting hotspots to examine more closely. Can all these points be clickable, as well as the list of creatures, so users can see more information about each one?

Multicreature checklist

Here's what we need in order to nail this last request:

1. A drop-down list with the list of creature types (selected from the database).
2. When the drop-down list changes, get a list of creatures from the database that match the selected type.
3. Display all the creatures returned from the database in the list and on the map.
4. Both the list and the map pointers should be clickable so users can get more information on the map to pop up.

 **Ready Bake Code**

Create a new page called *display_type.html* and save it in the same directory as the other HTML files for this project. This new file will display the list of creature types that can be selected. Then, once selected, all the creatures of that type will be displayed on the map. The structure and style of this new page is very similar to our old page, except for the addition of a `select` element with the ID of `ddlTypes`.

```html
<!DOCTYPE html>
<html>
    <head>
        <title>View Cryptid Sightings</title>
        <link type="text/css" href="style/form.css" rel="stylesheet" />
        <link type="text/css" href="jquery-ui-1.8.16.custom/css/sunny/
jquery-ui-1.8.16.custom.css"/>
    </head>
    <body>
        <div class="ui-widget-header ui-corner-top form_pad">
            <h2>View Cryptid Sightings</h2>
        </div>
        <div class="ui-widget-content form_pad">
            <div id="map_canvas"></div>
            <div id="sight_nav">
                <select id="ddlTypes">          Add a drop-down list, to be
                                                 populated with creature types.
                    <option value="">-- Please Select --</option>
                </select>
                <ul id="sight_list"></ul>
            </div>
        </div>
                                    Include the Google Maps API.
        <script src="http://maps.google.com/maps/api/js?sensor=false"></script>
        <script src="scripts/jquery-1.6.2.min.js"></script>
        <script src="scripts/maps.js"></script>
    </body>                                          Include the jQuery library.
</html>
              Include the maps.js file.
```

display_type.html

jQuery Code Magnets

Rearrange the magnets to complete the `getAllTypes` function. This function will call the *service.php* file (which should be included in your downloads for this chapter) to get a list of the different creature types in the database. These creature types should then be added to the drop-down list, with the ID of `ddlTypes`. Also, create an event listener on the drop-down list to listen for a `change` event and alert the selected value. Finally, since we're using the same *maps.js* file for our two HTML files, add some logic to the `initialize` function to check if the drop-down list exists. If it does, call the `getAllTypes` function. Otherwise, call the `getAllSightings` function.

```javascript
function initialize(){
.

.
map = new google.maps.Map(document.getElementById(_____), mapOpts);
    if ( $('#ddlTypes').length ) {

        _____

    }else{

        _____

    }
}
function getAllTypes(){
    $.getJSON("service.php?action=getSightingsTypes", function(json_types) {
        if (_____creature_types.length > 0) {
            $.each(json_types.creature_types,_____
                var info = this['type'];
                var $li = _____
                $li.html(info);
                $li_____("#ddlTypes");
            });
        }
    });
}

_____change(function() {
    if($(this).val() != ""){
        alert( $(this).val() );
    }
});
```

Magnets:

```
$("<option />");
```
```
getAllSightings();
```
```
"map_canvas"
```
```
getAllTypes();
```
```
.appendTo
```
```
json_types.
```
```
function() {
```
```
$('#ddlTypes').
```

maps.js

jQuery Code Magnets Solution

Now you've got a drop-down list associated with your Google map, a function to grab the data (in JSON) on the selected creature types from the database, and an alert showing which creature type was selected.

```
function initialize(){
    .
    .
    map = new google.maps.Map(document.getElementById( "map_canvas" ), mapOpts);
        if ( $('#ddlTypes').length ) {
            getAllTypes();
        }else{
            getAllSightings();
        }
    }
    function getAllTypes(){
        $.getJSON("service.php?action=getSightingsTypes", function(json_types) {
            if ( json_types. creature_types.length > 0) {
                $.each(json_types.creature_types, function() {
                    var info = this['type'];
                    var $li = $("<option />");
                    $li.html(info);
                    $li.appendTo ("#ddlTypes");
                });
            }
        });
    }

    $('#ddlTypes'). change(function() {
        if($(this).val() != ""){
            alert( $(this).val() );
        }
    });
```

Use the .length property to check for the existence of an element.

Get the types from the database, using JSON and PHP.

Set the text of the item in the dropdown list.

Append the option item to the drop-down list.

Add a listener for the change event on the drop-down list.

The value of the selected item on the list

maps.js

TEST DRIVE

Update your *maps.js* file with the `getAllTypes` function and the event listener for the `change` event on the drop-down list. Also, update your `initialize` function with this new logic. Then open up *display_type.html* in your browser, again using *http://*.

You're really cookin' now. You'll have this map finished up in no time!
Time to cross off a couple of those requirements.

1. ~~A drop-down list with the list of creature types (selected from the database).~~

2. ~~When the drop-down list changes, get a list of creatures from the database that match the selected type.~~

3. Display all the creatures returned from the database in the list and on the map.

4. Both the list and the map pointers should be clickable so users can get more information on the map to pop up.

Hey! Not so fast! When I select an item from the drop-down list, I don't see creatures. I only see an alert pop up. I don't think we're done with the second item yet!

You've got us there.

We need to update our code so we can get information from the database when the drop-down list is changed, instead of just showing the creature type in an alert box.

Then we can mark that one off the list. But while we're at it, we should be able knock off the third item on the list too. Roll up your sleeves—we're about to dive in and put this all together.

 LONG Exercise

Fill in the missing lines of code to create a `getSightingsByType` function. This function should accept one parameter: the creature type you are viewing. This function should get its data in JSON format, loop through all the returned creatures (if there are any), and add points for each one on the map. Also, create two more global variables: an array called `markerArray` and a new Google Maps `LatLngBounds` object called `bounds`. Also, create a function that clears the previous points, before adding any new ones, if the drop-down list is changed.

```
var markersArray = [];
var bounds = new google.maps_____;
function getSightingsByType(type){
   $.getJSON("service.php?action=getSightingsByType&type="+type, function(json)
{
      if (_____sightings.length > 0) {
         $('#sight_list').empty();
         $.each(json.sightings,function() {
            var loc = new google.maps_____(this['lat'], this['long']);
            var opts = {
               map: map,
               position:_____
            };
```

```
                var marker = new google.maps_____(opts);
                markersArray.push(_____);
                var $li = $("<li />");
                $li.html('Date: ' + this['date'] + ', Type: ' + this['type']);
                $li_____("sightings");
                $li.appendTo("#sight_list");
                bounds.extend(loc);
            });
          map.fitBounds(bounds);
       }
    });
}
$('#ddlTypes').change(function() {
  if($(this).val() != ""){
     clearOverlays();
     _____( $(this).val() );
  }
});
function _____ {
  if (markersArray) {
     for (i in markersArray) {
        markersArray[i].setMap(null);
     }
     markersArray.length = 0;
     bounds = null;
     bounds = new_____LatLngBounds();
  }
}
```

maps.js

LONG EXERCISE Solution

With the addition of the two new global variables and some other Google Maps functions, you can now add and remove markers from the map when the drop-down list is changed. As the markers are being added to the map, they are also added to the `markerArray` array and used to extend the map's `bounds`. This way, the map can autozoom to fit all the points, using the `fitBounds` function. The `getSightingsByType` function, now called on any change of the drop-down list, adds the markers to the map and adds the creature to the list on the page.

```
var markersArray = [];
var bounds = new google.maps.LatLngBounds()( ;          ← A new LatLngBounds object
function getSightingsByType(type){
   $.getJSON("service.php?action=getSightingsByType&type="+type, function(json)
{
                                                          Get our data, with JSON.
     if (json.sightings.length > 0) {
        $('#sight_list').empty();
        $.each(json.sightings,function() {
           var loc = new google.maps.LatLng(this['lat'], this['long']);
           var opts = {
              map: map,
              position: loc
           };
                                                          Create a new Marker
                                                          object for each point
                                                          on the map.

           var marker = new google.maps.Marker(opts);
           markersArray.push(marker);
           var $li = $("<li />");
           $li.html('Date: ' + this['date'] + ', Type: ' + this['type']);
           $li.addClass("sightings");
           $li.appendTo("#sight_list");            Add the current
           bounds.extend(loc);              ←      Lat/Long value to
        });                                         our bounds object.
        map.fitBounds(bounds);
     }                                 ←      Tell the map to use our bounds
   });                                        to zoom to the correct level
}                                             so we see them all.
```

```
$('#ddlTypes').change(function() {
    if($(this).val() != ""){
        clearOverlays();
        getSightingsByType ( $(this).val() );
    }
});
function clearOverlays() {
    if (markersArray) {
        for (i in markersArray) {
            markersArray[i].setMap(null);
        }
        markersArray.length = 0;
        bounds = null;
        bounds = new .google.maps.LatLngBounds();
    }
}
```

Before we get the data to add the markers to the map, remove all the old markers.

Pass the value of the drop-down list as a parameter to our function.

Remove the Marker from the map.

Reset the bounds variable too.

maps.js

 Geek Bits

We've included a function called `clearOverlays` that will remove the previously added markers before adding the new ones. Google refers to anything added to a base map as an *overlay*, which can be a **Marker**, a **Line**, a **Polyline**, a **Polygon**, or many other types of objects.

TEST DRIVE

Update your *maps.js* file with the new code you just created. Then, open up *display_type.html* in your browser and select some creatures from the list.

1. ~~A drop-down list with the list of creature types (selected from the database).~~
2. ~~When the drop-down list is changed, get a list of creatures from the database that match the selected type.~~
3. ~~Display all the creatures returned from the database in the list and on the map.~~
4. Both the list and the map pointers should be clickable so users can get more information on the map to pop up.

So close...just one more item to go!

BRAIN POWER

You already know how to make things clickable with jQuery. How will this help complete the final requirement on the list?

there are no
Dumb Questions

Q: So, is the Google Maps API free for me to use on my website?

A: Yes! Google makes the API freely available to everyone who wants to use it—personal or commercial—as long as they comply with the Terms of Service.

Q: I don't know if I comply or not. Where can I see the Terms of Service?

A: Simply browse to *http://www.google.com/apis/maps/terms.html* to view the full Terms of Service.

Q: Does the Google Maps API cover the whole world?

A: Not quite, but it's close. There are only a few countries that are not covered. Check out the Google Maps API site to find the list.

Q: Can I show maps on a mobile device, using the Google Maps API?

A: Yes, you can. At the time of publishing, version 3 of the Google Maps API has been released. It has been developed to cater to mobile devices with browsers capable of running JavaScript.

Q: But I'd rather write an app for that. Is the Google Maps API for me?

A: If you're writing for the Android or iPhone platforms, then yes. Google provides specific frameworks for both of these platforms for you to include in your app. If you're writing for another mobile platform, there is no specific framework yet, so you'll have to use the same as on your website.

Q: The full version of Google Maps lets me get directions. Can this API do that?

A: No, you cannot do that with this API. There is another API produced by Google, called the Google Directions API, that you can use to find the directions.

Q: What about finding places on a map by address?

A: In the business, they call this *geocoding*. Google has yet another API to do that: the Geocoding API. These are all part of the Google Maps API family. Also, luckily for you, whenever you request data from Google, it will return JSON data to you, which you already know how to handle!

Q: What else is in the Google Maps API family?

A: Both the Directions and Geocoding APIs belong to a subsection called the Maps API Web Service. Also in that sub-section are the Distance API, the Elevation API, and the Places API.

Q: There's even more?

A: Yup. There's also the Static Maps API for browsers that don't fully support JavaScript; Maps API for Flash; and even an Earth API, which lets you load a Google Earth viewer into your page to get 3D images of the globe, as well as take virtual tours and draw shapes over the terrain. This one requires the Google Earth plug-in to be installed too, though.

Q: So JavaScript aside, can I get APIs for any other languages?

A: Yes! There are countless numbers of APIs available—some free, some that require licensing. Chances are, if you're looking for a specific piece of functionality you don't want to write, there's probably an API for it somewhere.

Listening for map events

We're almost at the end here, and by now you've seen a whole variety of events that jQuery and JavaScript provide for making fun, interactive web apps. Since the Google Maps API is just JavaScript (albeit very well written and efficient JavaScript), it too can utilize the browser's ability to listen for events and act accordingly.

And for the same reasons that jQuery added its own event listener creation functions, the folks on the Google Maps end of things have provided the capability to add event listeners through the API. This is because not all browsers deal with event listeners in the same way, so this ensures that the API can control how the listeners are added to the page. Let's have a look at adding an event listener for the **click** event to create a Google Maps pop up (also called an *InfoWindow*):

Define a variable with the content we would like to show.

```
var contentString = "This is an InfoWindow";

var my_infowindow = new google.maps.InfoWindow({
        content: contentString
});
```

Create an instance of the Google Maps InfoWindow object.

Set the value of the content property of the InfoWindow object.

Tell the map to listen out for a click event on our marker object.

```
google.maps.event.addListener(my_marker, 'click', function() {
    my_infowindow.open(map,my_marker);
});
```

Run this code when the marker is clicked (open a pop-up window on the map).

Geek Bits

In the Google Maps API, almost all the different object types (**Map**, **Marker**, **Line**, **InfoWindow**, **TrafficOverlay**, **Polygon**, and more) have events associated with them. However, even if the events for the different objects have the same event *name*, they may take different *parameters*! Be sure to check the documentation for the object you want to use.

Sharpen your pencil

Fill in the missing pieces of code to complete the `getSightingsByType` function, which will add the click functionality to both the markers on the map and the items on the list. Also, create a global variable called `info_window`, which will be a new instance of the Google Maps `InfoWindow` object with the default content set to an empty string.

```
var info_window = new google.maps_____({content: ''});
function_____(type){
  $.getJSON("_____ action=getSightingsByType&type="+type, function(json) {
    if (json.sightings.length > 0) {
      $('#sight_list').empty();
      $.each(json.sightings,function() {
        var info = 'Distance: ' + this[_____] + '<br>' + ' Height: ' + this['height'];
        info += ', Weight: ' + this['weight'] + ', Color: ' + this['color'] + '<br>';
        info += 'Latitude: ' + this['lat'] + ', Longitude: ' + this[_____];
        var loc = new _____(this['lat'], this['long']);
        var opts = {
          map: map,
          position:_____
        };
        var marker = new google.maps _____(opts);
        markersArray.push(marker);
        google.maps.event_____(marker, 'click', function() {
          info_window.content = info;
          info_window.open(map, marker);
        });
        var $li = $("<li />");
        $li.html('Date: ' + this['date'] + ', Type: ' + this['type']);
        $li.addClass("sightings");
        $li_____(function(){
          info_window.content = info;
          info_window.open(map, _____);
        });
        $li.appendTo("#sight_list");
        _____ extend(loc);
      });
      map _____ (bounds);
    }
  });
}
```

maps.js

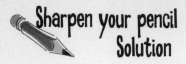

Sharpen your pencil Solution

You've now updated the getSightingsByType function to display in list format and on the map, along with making the map markers and the list clickable.

```javascript
var info_window = new google.maps.InfoWindow({content: ''});
function getSightingsByType(type){
  $.getJSON("service.php?action=getSightingsByType&type="+type, function(json) {
    if (json.sightings.length > 0) {
      $('#sight_list').empty();
      $.each(json.sightings,function() {
        var info = 'Distance: ' + this['distance'] + '<br>' + ' Height: ' + this['height'];
        info += ', Weight: ' + this['weight'] + ', Color: ' + this['color'] + '<br>';
        info += 'Latitude: ' + this['lat'] + ', Longitude: ' + this['long'];
        var loc = new google.maps.LatLng(this['lat'], this['long']);
        var opts = {
          map: map,
          position: loc
        };
        var marker = new google.maps.Marker(opts);
        markersArray.push(marker);
        google.maps.event.addListener(marker, 'click', function() {
          info_window.content = info;
          info_window.open(map, marker);
        });
        var $li = $("<li />");
        $li.html('Date: ' + this['date'] + ', Type: ' + this['type']);
        $li.addClass("sightings");
        $li.click(function(){
          info_window.content = info;
          info_window.open(map, marker);
        });
        $li.appendTo("#sight_list");
        bounds.extend(loc);
      });
      map.fitBounds.(bounds);
    }
  });
}
```

Add an event listener to the Marker, on the map, for the click event.

Add an event listener item on the list to open the InfoWindow on the map.

maps.js

Test Drive

Update your *maps.js* file with the new code you created on the previous page. Then, open up *display_type.html* in your browser and select a creature from the list. Click on the markers or the list to view more information about the creature.

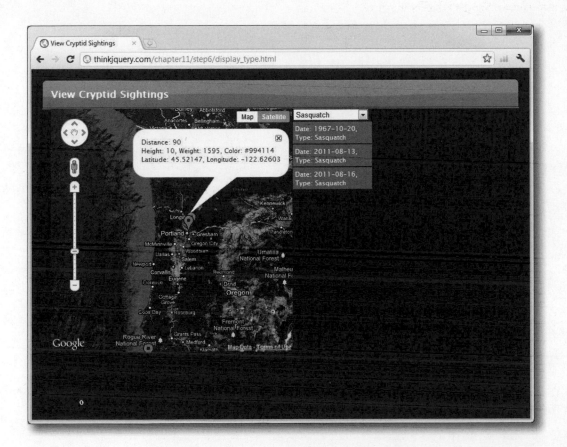

1. A drop-down list with the list of creature types (selected from the database, if possible).

2. When the drop-down list is changed, get a list of creatures from the database that match the selected type.

3. Display all the creatures returned from the database in the list and on the map.

4. Both the list and the map pointers should be clickable so users can get more information on the map to pop up.

You did it!

In just a few short pages, you managed to put together a fully functional website, using code from several different languages—PHP, SQL, JavaScript, and jQuery—as well as pairing up the the Google Maps API with Ajax and JSON to display some pretty complex data. No small feat!

The site looks awesome. It's exactly what we wanted! Thank you!

Can't a guy just get some peace and quiet?

APIcross

It's time to sit back and give your left brain something to do. It's your standard crossword; all of the solution words are from this chapter.

Across

1. The code for a Google Maps API constructor that lets you put a point on a Google Map: `google.maps: new google.maps._____()`.
2. The Google Maps API we used in Chapter 11 is written in this language.
7. Once you have an instance of an API object, you can use all the properties and _____ associated with those objects in your code.
8. API = Application Programming _____.
9. We used this jQuery method to get data from the sightings database using JSON and PHP.
10. Google Maps API object that has the following properties: `zoom`, `center`, and `mapTypeId`.

Down

1. To include the GoogleMaps API in your web page, use this script tag: `<script src="http://____._____.___maps/api/js?sensor=false"></script>`.
3. Google Maps API method that listens for a click event on a marker: `google.maps.event._____`.
4. The jQuery event listener you used in this chapter. When the value of data in a field changes, this listener is triggered.
5. An API is a series of object _____, allowing you to create your own instances of the API provider's objects.
6. The Google Maps API object constructor that lets you pass the latitude and longitude as a parameter.

 # APIcross Solution

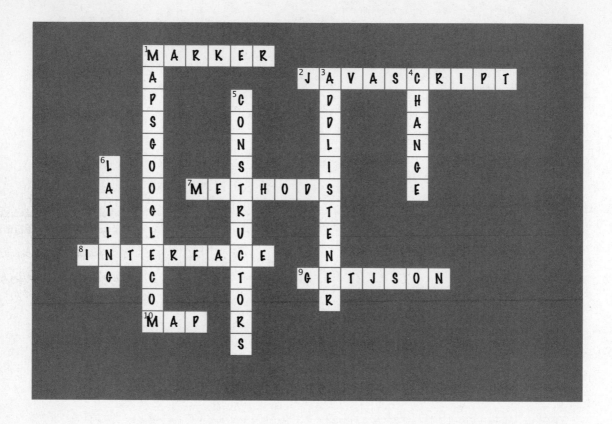

Your jQuery API Toolbox

You've got Chapter 11 under your belt and now you've learned how to pull together jQuery with APIs (plus JavaScript, PHP, MySQL, Ajax, JSON, and more!).

APIs

Application programming interfaces are really just code provided by other people (or companies) that you can tap into for their data, objects, and other services.

They provide a series of object constructors, allowing you to create your own instances of other objects. Once you have an instance, you can use all the properties and methods associated with those objects in your code.

Leaving town...

It's been great having you in jQueryville!

We're sad to see you leave, but now that you have all the skills
you need to build your own cool jQuery-powered websites, we're sure you'd rather be
doing that than hanging around here. It's been great showing you around the world of
jQuery. Feel free to drop us a line or tell us about your cool new site at the Head First Labs:
http://headfirstlabs.com.

appendix i: leftovers

The Top Ten Things *(we didn't cover)*

You have even more goodies to share with me?

Even after all that, there's still plenty we didn't get around to. There are lots of other jQuery and JavaScript goodies we didn't manage to squeeze into the book. It would be unfair not to tell you about them, so you can be more prepared for any other facet of jQuery you might encounter on your travels.

#1. Every single thing in the jQuery library

You probably realize by now that jQuery is a massive library. We tried to cover the main stuff that a person new to jQuery would need. You are now armed with all of this knowledge so you can go and check the rest of the library out.

jQuery methods

.add()
.addClass()
.after()
jQuery.ajax()
.ajaxComplete()
.ajaxError()
jQuery.ajaxPrefilter()
.ajaxSend()
jQuery.ajaxSetup()
.ajaxStart()
.ajaxStop()
.ajaxSuccess()
.andSelf()
.animate()
.append()
.appendTo()
.attr()
.before()
.bind()
.blur()
jQuery.browser
.change()
.children()
.clearQueue()
.click()
.clone()
.closest()
jQuery.contains()
.contents()
.context
.css()
jQuery.cssHooks
.data()
jQuery.data()
.dblclick()
deferred.always()
deferred.done()

deferred.fail()
deferred.isRejected()
deferred.isResolved()
deferred.pipe()
deferred.promise()
deferred.reject()
deferred.rejectWith()
deferred.resolve()
deferred.resolveWith()
deferred.then()
.delay()
.delegate()
.dequeue()
jQuery.dequeue()
.detach()
.die()
jQuery.each()
.each()
.empty()
.end()
.eq()
.error()
jQuery.error
event.currentTarget
event.data
event.isDefaultPrevented()
event.
isImmediatePropagationStopped()
event.isPropagationStopped()
event.namespace
event.pageX
event.pageY
event.preventDefault()
event.relatedTarget
event.result
event.stopImmediatePropagation()
event.stopPropagation()

event.target
event.timeStamp
event.type
event.which
jQuery.extend()
.fadeIn()
.fadeOut()
.fadeTo()
.fadeToggle()
.filter()
.find()
.first()
.focus()
.focusin()
.focusout()
jQuery.fx.interval
jQuery.fx.off
jQuery.get()
.get()
jQuery.getJSON()
jQuery.getScript()
jQuery.globalEval()
jQuery.grep()
.has()
.hasClass()
jQuery.hasData()
.height()
.hide()
jQuery.holdReady()
.hover()
.html()
jQuery.inArray()
.index()
.innerHeight()
.innerWidth()
.insertAfter()
.insertBefore()

#1. Every single thing in the jQuery library (continued)

jQuery methods (continued)

```
.is()
jQuery.isArray()
jQuery.isEmptyObject()
jQuery.isFunction()
jQuery.isPlainObject()
jQuery.isWindow()
jQuery.isXMLDoc()
jQuery()
.jquery
.keydown()
.keypress()
.keyup()
.last()
.length
.live()
.load()
.load()
jQuery.makeArray()
.map()
jQuery.map()
jQuery.merge()
.mousedown()
.mouseenter()
.mouseleave()
.mousemove()
.mouseout()
.mouseover()
.mouseup()
.next()
.nextAll()
.nextUntil()
jQuery.noConflict()
jQuery.noop()
.not()
jQuery.now()
.offset()
.offsetParent()
.one()
.outerHeight()
.outerWidth()
```

```
jQuery.param()
.parent()
.parents()
.parentsUntil()
jQuery.parseJSON
jQuery.parseXML()
.position()
jQuery.post()
.prepend()
.prependTo()
.prev()
.prevAll()
.prevUntil()
.promise()
.prop()
jQuery.proxy()
.pushStack()
.queue()
jQuery.queue()
.ready()
.remove()
.removeAttr()
.removeClass()
.removeData()
jQuery.removeData()
.removeProp()
.replaceAll()
.replaceWith()
.resize()
.scroll()
.scrollLeft()
.scrollTop()
.select()
.serialize()
.serializeArray()
.show()
.siblings()
.size()
.slice()
.slideDown()
```

```
.slideToggle()
.slideUp()
.stop()
jQuery.sub()
.submit()
jQuery.support
.text()
.toArray()
.toggle()
.toggle()
.toggleClass()
.trigger()
.triggerHandler()
jQuery.trim()
jQuery.type()
.unbind()
.undelegate()
jQuery.unique()
.unload()
.unwrap()
.val()
jQuery.when()
.width()
.wrap()
.wrapAll()
.wrapInner()
```

#1. Every single thing in the jQuery library (continued)

jQuery selectors

All Selector ("*")
Attribute Contains Prefix Selector
[name|="value"]
Attribute Contains Selector [name*="value"]
Attribute Contains Word Selector [name~="value"]
Attribute Ends With Selector [name$="value"]
Attribute Equals Selector [name="value"]
Attribute Not Equal Selector [name!="value"]
Attribute Starts With Selector [name^="value"]
:animated Selector
:button Selector
:checkbox Selector
:checked Selector
Child Selector ("parent > child")
Class Selector (".class")
:contains() Selector
Descendant Selector ("ancestor descendant")
:disabled Selector
Element Selector ("element")
:empty Selector
:enabled Selector
:eq() Selector
:even Selector
:file Selector
:first-child Selector
:first Selector
:focus selector
:gt() Selector

Has Attribute Selector [name]
:has() Selector
:header Selector
:hidden Selector
ID Selector ("#id")
:image Selector
:input Selector
:last-child Selector
:last Selector
:lt() Selector
Multiple Attribute Selector [name="value"]
[name2="value2"]
Multiple Selector ("selector1, selector2,
selectorN")
Next Adjacent Selector ("prev + next")
Next Siblings Selector ("prev ~ siblings")
:not() Selector
:nth-child() Selector
:odd Selector
:only-child Selector
:parent Selector
:password Selector
:radio Selector
:reset Selector
:selected Selector
:submit Selector
:text Selector
:visible Selector

#2. jQuery CDNs

CDNs (*content delivery networks*, or *content distribution networks*) are large networks of servers, designed to store and deliver information—data, software, API code, media files or videos, etc.—making it easily accessible on the Web. Each server in the node contains a copy of the data that is being served out. When these nodes are strategically placed around a network—like the Internet—they can increase the speed of information delivery to many more people consuming this data. Windows Azure and Amazon CloudFront are examples of traditional CDNs.

A number of large enterprises provide hosted copies of jQuery on CDN networks that are available for public use. Below are links to the CDN-hosted copies of jQuery that you may hotlink to.

- **Google Ajax API CDN**

  - *http://ajax.googleapis.com/ajax/libs/jquery/1.6.2/jquery.min.js*

- **Microsoft CDN**

  - *http://ajax.aspnetcdn.com/ajax/jQuery/jquery-1.6.2.min.j*s

- **jQuery CDN (via Media Temple)**

  - *http://code.jquery.com/jquery-1.6.2.min.js* (Minified version)

  - *http://code.jquery.com/jquery-1.6.2.js* (Source version)

You can include these in your jQuery applications instead of downloading jQuery every time.

#3. The jQuery namespace: noConflict method

Many JavaScript libraries use $ as a function or variable name, just as jQuery does. In jQuery's case, $ is just an alias for jQuery, so all functionality is available without using $. If we need to use another JavaScript library alongside jQuery, we can return control of $ back to the other library with a call to $.noConflict:

```
<script type="text/javascript" src="other_lib.js"></script>
<script type="text/javascript" src="jquery.js"></script>
<script type="text/javascript">

        $.noConflict();
        //Code that uses other libraries $ can follow here.

</script>
```

This technique is especially effective in conjunction with the .ready method's ability to alias the jQuery object, as within a callback passed to .ready we can use $ if we wish without fear of conflicts later:

```
<script type="text/javascript" src="other_lib.js"></script>
<script type="text/javascript" src="jquery.js"></script>
<script type="text/javascript">
        $.noConflict();

        jQuery(document).ready(function($) {
                // Code that uses jQuery's $ can follow here.
        });
        // Code that uses other libraries $ can follow here.

</script>
```

You'll only need to use this if you plan to use other JavaScript libraries that use the $ as a reference. You will **not** need this if you are only using jQuery on your page. Even if you include several plug-ins, you will **not** need this.

#4. Debugging your jQuery code

It is always useful to debug your code—especially if you're working on a large-scale project, with many different types of objects, includes, or APIs. Oftentimes, you'll need to know the content of an object or variable sent back to you, but don't want to alert it out, or figure out how to get at all the properties of an object.

Enter some debugging plug-ins. These can help you look inside your objects so you can see when their properties change values, or track the changes of a variable over time. You can also see how it evolves throughout your application, or if it ever gets null values unintentionally. This can be very useful when you're troubleshooting JavaScript or jQuery code.

Two of the debugging plug-ins we've found useful when coding in JavaScript and jQuery are Dump and VariableDebugger.

> *http://plugins.jquery.com/project/Dump* (For seeing what your object contains.)
> *http://plugins.jquery.com/project/VariableDebugger* (Similar, but displays info in pop up.)

There are several others, and there will be more and more over time, as well as improvements to these. We found these useful, but to look for some more that you might like better, go to the jQuery Plug-ins site (*http://plugins.jquery.com/*) and search for "debug."

Of course, for everything else, there's always the browser tools we've been using throughout the book.

#5. Advanced animation: queues

Queues in jQuery are mostly used for animations. You can use them for any purpose you like. They are an **array of functions stored on a per-element basis**, using jQuery.data. They are first-in-first-out (FIFO). You can **add a function to the queue** by calling .queue, and you remove (by calling) the functions using .dequeue.

Every element can have **one to many queues of functions** attached to it by jQuery. In most applications, only one queue (called **fx**) is used. Queues allow a **sequence of actions to be called on an element asynchronously**, without halting program execution. The typical example of this is calling multiple animation methods on an element. For example:

```
$('#my_element').slideUp().fadeIn();
```

When this statement is executed, the element begins its sliding animation immediately, but the fading transition is placed on the fx queue to be called only once the sliding transition is complete.

The .queue method allows us to **directly manipulate this queue of functions**. Calling .queue with a callback is particularly useful; it allows us to place a new function at the end of the queue.

This feature is similar to providing a callback function with an animation method, but does not require the callback to be given at the time the animation is performed.

```
$('#my_element').slideUp();
$('#my_element').queue(function() {
    alert('Animation complete.');
    $(this).dequeue();
});
```

This is equivalent to:

```
$('#my_element').slideUp(function() {
    alert('Animation complete.');
});
```

Note that when adding a function with .queue, we should ensure that .dequeue is eventually called so that the next function in line executes.

In jQuery 1.4, the function that's called is passed in another function, as the first argument, that when called automatically dequeues the next item and keeps the queue moving. You would use it like so:

```
$("#test").queue(function(next) {
    // Do some stuff...
    next();
});
```

The default queue in jQuery is fx. It is used by .animate and all functions that call it by default.

NOTE: If you are using a custom queue, you must manually .dequeue the functions—they will not autostart like the default fx queue!

#6. Form validation

One *very* important feature we didn't have room for is **form validation**, on the **client/browser side**, using jQuery. In Chapters 9, 10, and 11, we saw a small piece of **server-side** validation, using PHP, before our data was inserted into our databases. This is also very important, and strongly advised. A malformed `insert` or `select` statement to your database could end up revealing much more about your data than you intended.

But back to the client-side validation…

There are many jQuery plug-ins dedicated to form validation. One of our favorites is the aptly named "validation" plug-in, found here: *http://docs.jquery.com/Plugins/validation*.

This plug-in will allow you to create a **series of rules** for each element on your form, so you can customize the validation, and **refine the data you want to accept in your form**. This includes everything from **minimum** or **maximum** field lengths, check for **required** fields, check if a **valid email address** is entered, and more. Here's some examples from the jQuery website:

Specifies a name element as required and an email element as required (using the shortcut for a single rule) and a valid email address (using another object literal).

```
$(".selector").validate({
      rules: {
            // simple rule, converted to {required:true}
            name: "required",
            // compound rule
            email: {
                  required: true,
                  email: true
            }
      }
});
```

Adds `required` *and a* `minlength` *of 2 to an element and specifies custom messages for both.*

```
$("#myinput").rules("add", {
      required: true,
      minlength: 2,
      messages: {
            required: "Required input",
            minlength: jQuery.format("Please, at least {0} characters
are necessary")
      }
});
```

#7. jQuery UI effects

The jQuery UI Effects library comes with some **extra animations**, not available in the regular jQuery library. These can be broken down into **three separate types of functionality**:

1 ### Color animations

Color animations extend the `animate` function to be able to animate colors as well. It's heavily used by the class transition feature, and it's able to color-animate the following properties:

```
backgroundColor
borderBottomColor
borderLeftColor
borderRightColor
borderTopColor
color
outlineColor
```

2 ### Class transitions

Class transitions extend the base class API to be able to animate between two different classes. The following jQuery methods are modified by jQuery UI to accept three additional parameters: `speed`, `easing` (optional), and `callback`.

```
addClass(class)
```
Adds the specified class(es) to each set of matched elements.
```
removeClass(class)
```
Removes all or the specified class(es) from the set of matched elements.
```
toggleClass(class)
```
Adds the specified class if it is not present; removes the specified class if it is present.
```
switchClass(currentClass, newClass)
```
Allows you to visually transition from one class to another.

3 ### Advanced easing

Advanced easing is included in the Effects core, and is a jQuery port of the easing functions written by Robert Penners, which were originally written in ActionScript for Flash. They are a series of mathematical equations designed to make the animation of objects smoother and more accurate. Here's a list of all the easing functions:

linear	easeInQuart	easeInExpo	easeInBack
swing	easeOutQuart	easeOutExpo	easeOutBack
jswing	easeInOutQuart	easeInOutExpo	easeInOutBack
easeInQuad	easeInQuint	easeInCirc	easeInBounce
easeOutQuad	easeOutQuint	easeOutCirc	easeOutBounce
easeInOutQuad	easeInOutQuint	easeInOutCirc	easeInOutBounce
easeInCubic	easeInSine	easeInElastic	
easeOutCubic	easeOutSine	easeOutElastic	
easeInOutCubic	easeInOutSine	easeInOutElastic	

#8. Creating your own jQuery plug-ins

Extending jQuery with plug-ins and methods is very powerful and can save you and your peers a lot of development time by abstracting your most clever functions into plug-ins.

Rather than writing a whole bunch of text about how to create a jQuery plug-in, we think it's best left to the experts over at jQuery. They have a very substantial and informative tutorial here: *http://docs.jquery.com/Plugins/Authoring*.

Here's a brief summary of what to keep in mind when developing your next jQuery plug-in:

● Always wrap your plug-in in `(function ( $ ) { // plugin goes here }) ( jQuery );`.

● Don't redundantly wrap the `this` keyword in the immediate scope of your plug-in's function.

● Unless you're returning an intrinsic value from your plug-in, always have your plug-in's function return the `this` keyword to maintain chainability.

● Rather than requiring a lengthy amount of arguments, pass your plug-in settings in an object literal that can be extended over the plug-in's defaults.

● Don't clutter the `jQuery.fn` object with more than one namespace per plug-in.

● Always namespace your methods, events, and data.

● `jQuery.fn` is pronounced "jQuery effin."

#9. Advanced JavaScript: closures

Closures are a very complex topic within **JavaScript**, and were quite close to making it into the book proper. Although they didn't, we feel strongly about you needing to know about them, so we wanted to mention them here.

Closures are not hard to understand once you grasp the core concept. However, if you read some of the more detailed, technical descriptions, you might get very confused.

First, a definition (or two):

● **A closure is the local variable for a function, kept alive after the function has returned.**

● **Whenever you see the `function` keyword within another function, the inner function has access to variables in the outer function.**

Crazy, right?

Closures fully rely on the **scope** of variables and objects. The scope refers to where objects, variables, and functions are **created and accessible**, and in what **context** they are being called. Basically, objects, variables, and functions can be defined in either a **local** or **global** scope.

Local scope: The local scope is when something is defined and accessible only in a certain part of the code, like inside a function.

Global scope: As opposed to the local scope, when something is global is accessible from anywhere in your code.

Consider the following code:

```
function func1(x) {
    var tmp = 3;
    function func2(y) {
        alert(x + y + (++tmp));
    }
    func2(10);
}
func1(2);
```

#9. Advanced JavaScript: closures (continued)

The tmp variable is declared in **local** scope, inside the func1 function. This will always alert 16, because func2 can access the x (which was defined as an argument to func1), and it can also access tmp from func1.

That is **not a closure.** A closure is when you return the inner function. The inner function will close over the variables of func1 before leaving.

Now consider:

```
function func1(x) {
     var tmp = 3;
     return function (y) {
          alert(x + y + (++tmp));
     }
}
var func2 = func1(2);   // func2 is now a closure.
func2(10);
```

Again, tmp is in the **local scope**, but the func2 function is in the **global scope**. The above function will also alert 16, because func2 can still refer to x and tmp, even though it is no longer directly inside the scope.

However, since tmp is still hanging around inside func2's closure, it is also being incremented. It will be incremented each time you call func2.

It is possible to create more than one closure function, either by returning a list of them or by setting them to global variables. All of these will refer to the same x and the same tmp; they don't make their own copies.

#10. Templates

jQuery templates are still in beta, but are a cool, upcoming feature that might help you build a more flexible site, without much HTML or jQuery. They are designed to **take data and bind it to some template markup**, so you can consistently use the same markup to display similarly related data.

Check them out here: *http://api.jquery.com/category/plugins/templates/*.

Get ready for the big times

If I learn this early, I'll be way ahead of everyone else...

You need a place to practice your newfound PHP skills without making your data vulnerable on the Web. It's always a good idea to have a safe place to develop your PHP application before unleashing it on the world (wide web). This appendix contains instructions for installing a web server, MySQL, and PHP to give you a safe place to work and practice.

Create a PHP development environment

Before you can put your finished application on the Web with your newfound jQuery and AJAX skills, you need to develop it. And it's never a good idea to develop your web application on the Web where everyone can see it. You can **install software locally that lets you build and test your application before you put it online.**

There are three pieces of software you'll need on your local computer to build and test PHP and MySQL applications:

1. A web server

2. PHP

3. A MySQL database server

PHP isn't a server; it's a set of rules that your web server understands that allow it to interpret PHP code. Both the web server and the MySQL server are executable programs that run on a computer.

Keep in mind that we're talking about setting up your **local computer** as a web server for PHP development. You'll ultimately still need an **online web server** to upload your finished application to so that other people can access and use it.

Web server software such as Apache or IIS is required to serve up PHP scripts as web pages.

The MySQL database server is often installed on the same computer as the web server software—in this case, your local computer!

In a PHP development environment, your local computer acts as a server computer for the purposes of running PHP scripts.

PHP is installed as part of the web server and allows the web server to run PHP scripts.

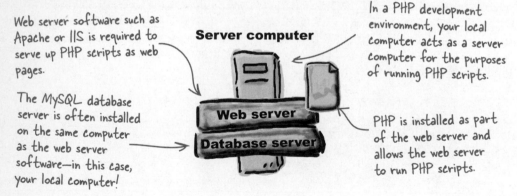

Server computer

Web server

Database server

Find out what you have

Before trying to install any of the pieces of the PHP development puzzle, your best bet is to first evaluate what you already have installed. Let's take a look at the three pieces and how you can tell what's already on your system.

The platform of your local computer makes a big difference when it comes to what's already installed. For example, Mac OS X has a web server installed by default, while most Windows computers do not.

NOTE: This appendix covers Windows XP, Vista, Windows 7, and Windows Server 2003/2008. For Mac, it applies to Mac OS X 10.3.x or newer.

Do you have a web server?

You probably already have a web server if you are using a newer PC or Mac. To find out quickly on either system, open a brower window and type **http://localhost** in the address bar. If you get an introductory page, that means your web browser is alive and well on your local machine.

If you have a Mac or Windows machine with the Apache web server installed, you might see something like this.

If you have a Windows machine with IIS, you might see something like this.

Do you have PHP? Which version?

If you have a web server, you can check to see if you have PHP installed very easily, as well as which version you have. Create a new script named *info.php* and type this in it:

```
<?php phpinfo(); ?>
```

Save this file to the directory your web server uses. On Windows, it's typically:

   C:\inetpub\wwwroot (for IIS)

or:

   C:\Program Files (x86)\Apache Software Foundation\Apache2.2\htdocs (for Apache)

On the Mac, it's usually something like:

   /Users/yourname/sites/

If you try to open this file in your browser by typing **http://localhost/info.php**, you'll see something like this if you have PHP installed:

Here's the version of PHP you have installed.

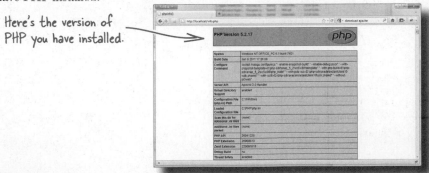

Do you have MySQL? Which version?

On Windows, you can tell by right-clicking on the Windows taskbar, selecting **Task Manager**, and selecting the **Services** tab. For more information, you can click the services button on Windows 7.

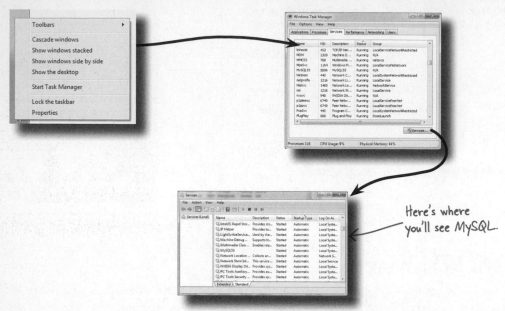

Here's where you'll see MySQL.

To determine whether you have MySQL on the Mac, open your terminal and type:

    cd /user/local/mysql

If the command works, you have MySQL installed. To check the version, type:

    mysql

The MySQL terminal is also known as the MySQL "monitor."

If this command succeeds, it means MySQL is installed.

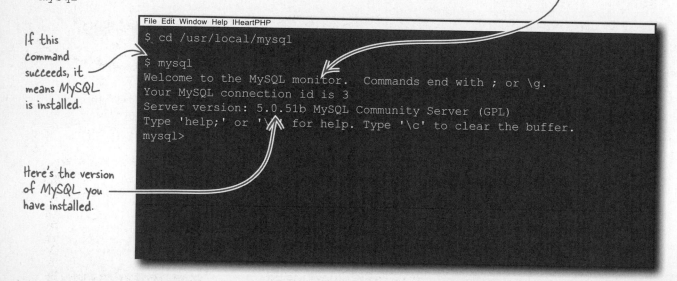

```
File Edit Window Help IHeartPHP
$ cd /usr/local/mysql

$ mysql
Welcome to the MySQL monitor.  Commands end with ; or \g.
Your MySQL connection id is 3
Server version: 5.0.51b MySQL Community Server (GPL)
Type 'help;' or '\h' for help. Type '\c' to clear the buffer.
mysql>
```

Here's the version of MySQL you have installed.

Start with the web server

Depending on the version of Windows you have, you can download Microsoft's Internet Information Server (IIS), or the open source Apache web server. If you need a server on the Mac, you should probably go with Apache since it's already installed.

Here's a brief overview of installing Apache on Windows:

Head over to *http://httpd.apache.org/download.cgi*.

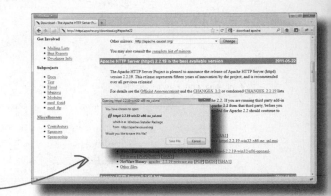

If you're using Windows, we suggest you download the *apache_2.2.19-win32-x86-no_ssl.msi* file. This will automatically install Apache for you after you download and double-click it.

Grab this version and double-click it after you've downloaded it.

Next you'll see the Installation Wizard. Most of the instructions are straightforward, and you can accept the default choices.

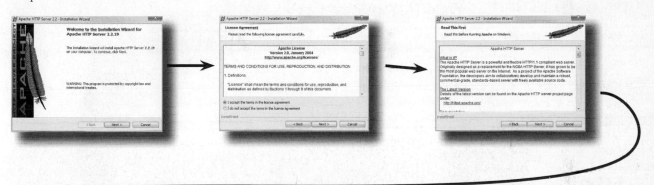

Choose the domain your computer is on. If you don't have one, you can enter `localhost`.

Your best bet is to choose the typical installation option.

You can usually choose the default directory for installation of the software.

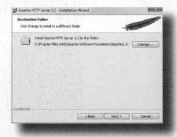

Apache installation...concluded

You're nearly finished. Click **Install** and wait a minute or so for the installation to complete. That's it!

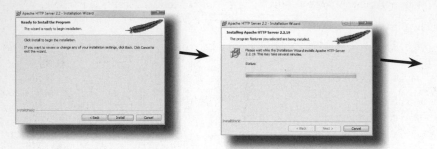

Your web server is set to start automatically when you start up your computer. But you can control it using the **Services** panel by stopping and starting it in the **Control Panel** → **Administrative Tools** → **Services** dialogue, where it will now show up as **Apache2.2**.

If these instuctions don't work for you, try again, or type "Installing Apache on Windows" into your favorite search engine for more help.

PHP installation

Go to *http://www.php.net/downloads.php*, or *http://windows.php.net/download/*, if you are using Windows.

Just as with Apache, if you're using Windows, we suggest you download the Windows installer version. If you're using Apache, download the *php-5.2.17-Win32-VC6-x86.msi* file. If you're using IIS, download the *php-5.3.6-Win32-VC9-x86.msi* file. This will automatically install PHP for you after you download and double-click it.

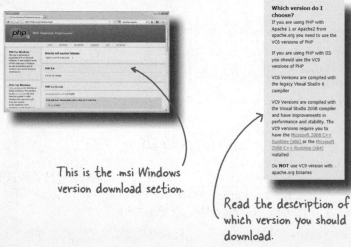

This is the .msi Windows version download section.

Read the description of which version you should download.

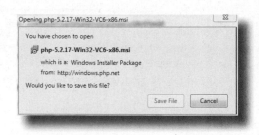

After you've downloaded the file, double-click it. Click the **Run** button to begin the installation.

PHP installation steps

It starts with a basic setup.

Accept the License Agreement to continue.

Selecting the default installation folder is usually a good idea, but it depends on preference. Here, we choose *C:\PHP*.

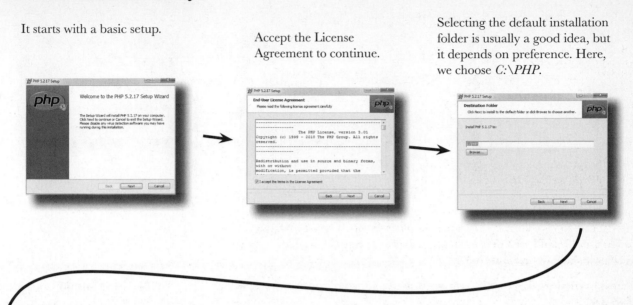

Be careful on this screen. If you're using Apache, select the right version. If you're using IIS, you will probably select the IISAPI module. Check with your particular software to determine exactly what you need. Here, we've chosen Apache 2.2, and need to give the path to our Apache install in the next screen.

This next screen is also tricky. You need to scroll down under **Extensions** and choose **MySQL**. This will enable you to use the built-in PHP MySQL functions that we use throughout this book!

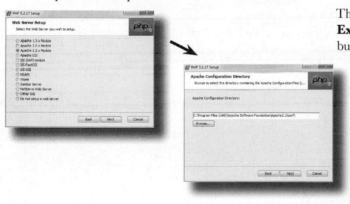

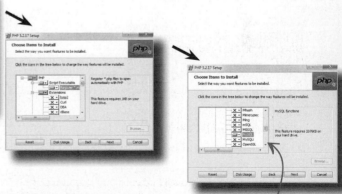

Scroll down below Extensions and click on
MySQL. Click on the "Entire feature" choice.

PHP installation steps...concluded

That's it. Click on **Install** and then **Done** to close the installer.

If you haven't done so already, create a new script named *info.php* and type this in it:

```
<?php phpinfo(); ?>
```

Save this file to the directory your web server uses. On Windows, it's typically:

C:\inetpub\wwwroot (for IIS)

or:

C:\Program Files (x86)\Apache Software Foundation\Apache2.2\htdocs (for Apache)

On the Mac, it's usually something like:

/Users/yourname/sites/

If you try to open this file in your browser by typing
`http://localhost/info.php`,
you'll see something like this if you have PHP installed:

If these instuctions don't work for you, try again, or type "Installing PHP for Apache [or IIS] on Windows" into your favorite search engine for more help.

Installing MySQL

Instructions and troubleshooting

You still need MySQL, so let's work through downloading and installing it. The official name for the free version of the MySQL RDBMS server these days is **MySQL Community Server**.

The following is a list of steps for installing MySQL on Windows and Mac OS X. This is **not** meant to replace the excellent instructions found on the MySQL website, and **we strongly encourage you to go there and read them!** For much more detailed directions, as well as a troubleshooting guide, go here:

— Get version 5.5 or newer.

`http://dev.mysql.com/doc/refman/5.5/en/windows-installation.html`

You'll also like the MySQL query browser, where you can type your queries and see the results inside the software interface, rather than in a console window.

Steps to install MySQL on Windows

1 **Go to:**

http://dev.mysql.com/downloads/

and click on the **MySQL Installer for Windows "Download the Beta"** download button. (Note: It was "Beta" at the time of this writing.)

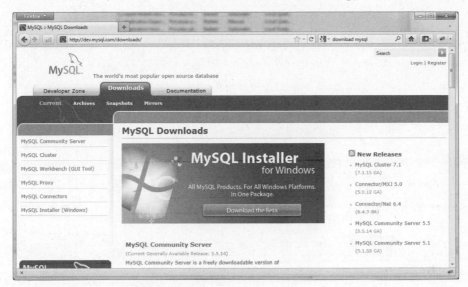

2 Choose **Microsoft Windows** from the list.

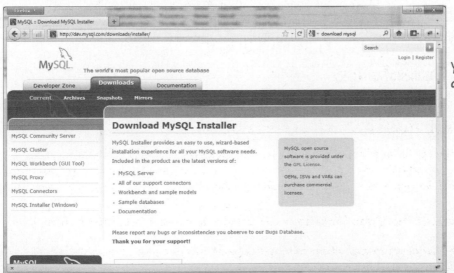

You may have to scroll down a little.

Download your installer

3 Choose **Windows(x86, 32-bit), MSI Installer** from the list.

Get version 5.5.13 or newer.

The top one!

Click on **No thanks, just take me to the downloads!** unless you want to register for an account on the site, or already have one.

Continue without registering.

4 You'll see a list of locations that have a copy you can download; choose the one closest to you.

5 When the file has finished downloading, right-click on it and choose "Run as Administrator" to launch it, if you have Windows UAC enabled. At this point, you will be walked through the installation with the **Setup Wizard**. Click **Next**.

When the Setup Wizard dialog appears, click the Install MySQL Products button.

Pick a destination folder

6 Read and agree to the license terms and and click **Next**.

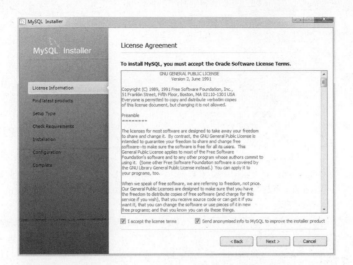

7 The next step will run an automatic update to make sure there are no newer versions. You can skip this by selecting the Skip Check box, but it is good practice to make sure your applications are up to date. After the update is complete, click **Next** to continue.

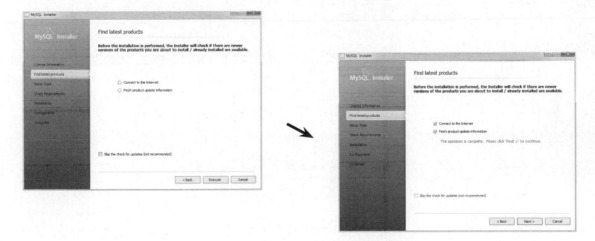

8 You'll be asked to choose a setup type for your installation. For your purposes, the **Developer Default** will be perfect. Also, leave the installation paths as the default ones set for you already and click **Next**.

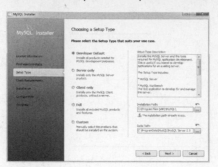

9 Next, the installer will check your compatibility with the Microsoft .NET Framework 4 Client Profile. This is to run the MySQL Workbench application. If you are missing this, update your Windows instance at *http://update.microsoft.com/*.

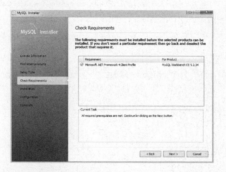

10 The next screen will list all the features to be installed. Click **Execute** to start the installation.

11 After all the services show a successful installation, click **Next** to access the configuration options for the MySQL service. Choose **Developer Machine** and click **Next**.

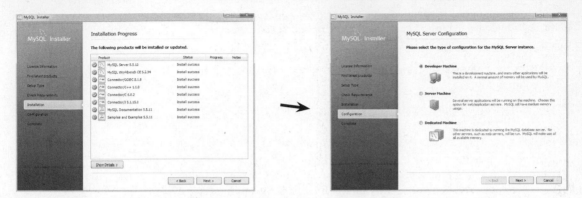

12 Make sure both the **Enable TCP/IP Networking** and **Create Windows Service** options are selected, and leave the default values in place. Enter a password for the root MySQL user into the boxes at the bottom and click **Next**.

13 The installation should now be complete. If it doesn't start up automatically, open the MySQL Workbench from the **Start → All Programs → MySQL** menu.

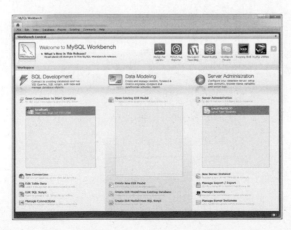

Enabling PHP on Mac OS X

PHP is included on Macs with OS X version 10.5+ (Leopard), but it's not enabled by default. You have to access the main Apache configuration file and comment out a line of code in order to get PHP going. This file is called *http.conf*, and is hidden inside the Apache install folder.

You're looking for the following line of code, which has a pound symbol (#) in front of it to comment it out:

```
#LoadModule php5_module          libexec/apache2/libphp5.so
```

You need to remove the pound symbol and restart the server to enable PHP. The *http.conf* document is owned by "root," which means you'll have to enter your password to change it. You'll probably also want to tweak the *php.ini* file so that Apache uses it. For more detailed information about how to carry out these steps and enable PHP, visit *http://foundationphp.com/tutorials/php_leopard.php*.

Steps to install MySQL on Mac OS X

If you are running Mac OS X server, a version of MySQL should already be installed.

Before you begin, check to see if you already have a version installed. Go to *Applications/Server/MySQL Manager* to access it.

 Go to:

> *http://dev.mysql.com/downloads/*

and click on the **MySQL Community Server** link.

For these instructions, we're downloading the 32-bit version. Make sure you download the version relevant to your operating system.

You may have to scroll down a bit.

② Click on the **Mac OS X v10.6 (x86, 32-bit), DMG Archive** download
button.

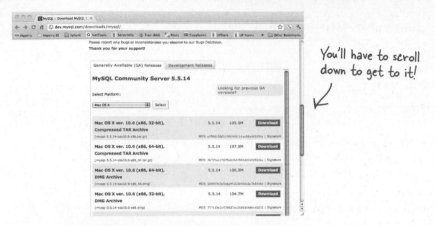

You'll have to scroll
down to get to it!

③ Click on **No thanks, just take me to the downloads!** unless you want to register for an
account on the site, or already have one.

Continue without
registering.

Click on a mirror that is nearest you, for faster downloads.

Download your installer

4 **Return to:**

> *http://dev.mysql.com/downloads/*

and click on **MySQL Workbench** (GUI tool).

Click on **No thanks, just take me to the downloads!** unless you want
to register for an account on the site, or already have one, and choose a
mirror again.

Continue without
registering.

5 When both files have finished downloading, double-click on the *mysql-5.5.14-
osx10.6-x86.dmg* file to mount the installer and then double-click on the *mysql-
5.5.14-osx10.6-x86.pkg* file to start the package installer.

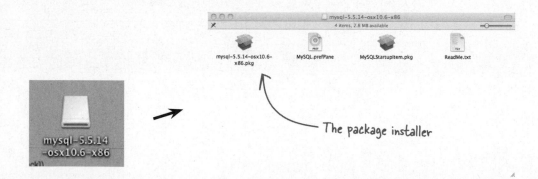

The package installer

Run the package installer

6 The package installer should start. Click **Next** to continue to the **Read Me** page, and **Continue** to get to the **License** page.

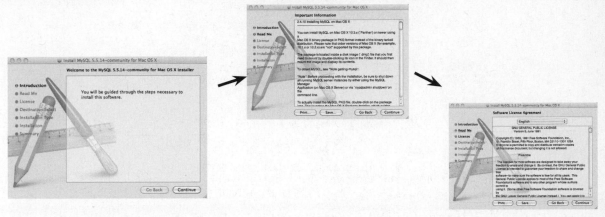

7 The next step will display this licensing information for MySQL. If you agree to the terms, click **Continue**, and then **Agree**. Select **Continue** again to install it in the default location.

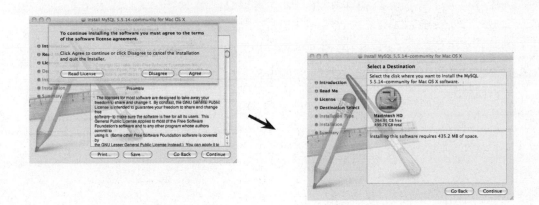

8 Click **Install**, enter the username and password of an admin user, and press **OK** to begin the installation.

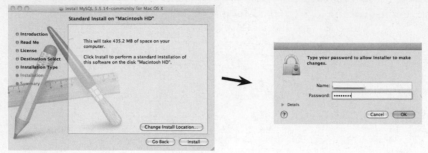

The installation should start, and give a success message when complete.

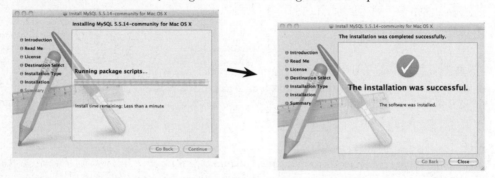

9 Repeat the same steps for the *MySQLStartupItem.pkg* file.

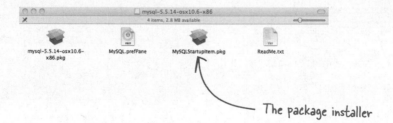

The package installer

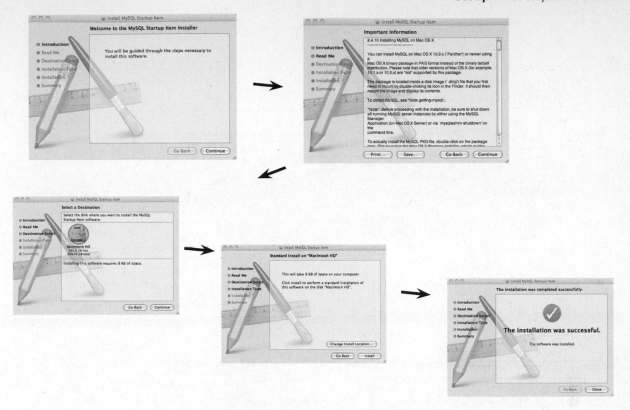

10 Double-click on the **MySQL.prefPane**, also found in the *mysql-5.5.14-osx10.6-x86.dmg*, to install the MySQL Preference pane; then, click on **Start MySQL Server**.

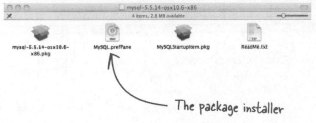

The package installer

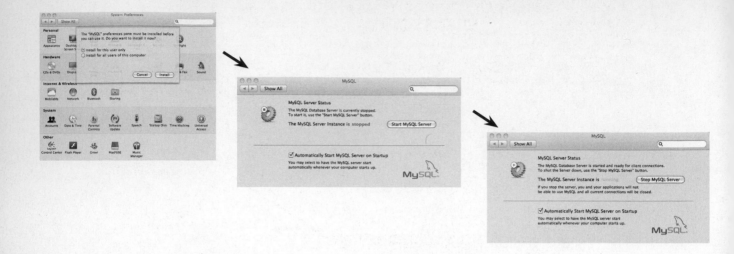

(11) Double-click on the *mysql-workbench-gpl-5.2.34.osx-i686.dmg* file that you also downloaded to start the installer for the MySQL Workbench tool.

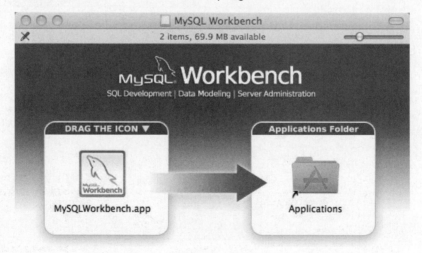

Drag the *MySQLWorkbench.app* into your *Applications* folder.

Open up the Workbench tool from your **Applications** list.

⓬   Using the **Server Administration** panel, ensure that your server is running. If the panel is empty, click the **New Server Instance** option and select your running server.

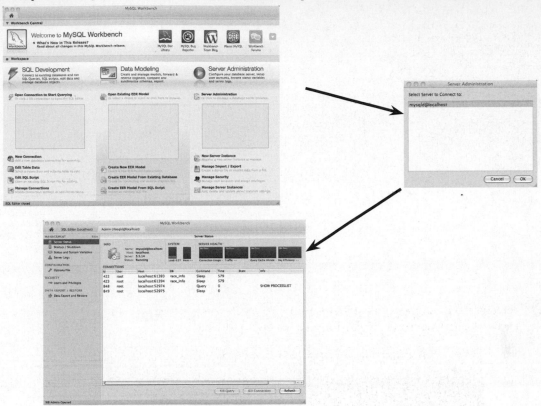

⓭   Create a new connection in the SQL Development section by clicking **New Connection** and completing the screen that pops up. Then, double-click on your new connection to open it.

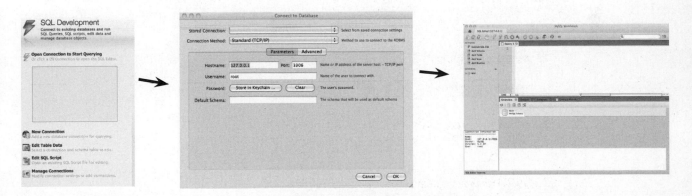

For more help on MySQL or MySQL Workbench, visit *http://dev.mysql.com/doc/*.

Index

Symbols

$.contains() method 114

$ (dollar sign)
    and array names 151
    for PHP variables 352
    for jQuery function shortcut 12, 19, 33
    for variable storing elements 150

$_GET[ ] associative array 331

$_POST[ ] associative array 331

$_POST object 342

$_POST variable 369

$(this) selector 63–64, 74, 88

&& (and) operator 240

{ } (curly braces)
    for code block 25, 42
    for function block 101
    for loops 230

. (dot) operator 221. *See also* . (period)

== (equality operator) 109, 240
    and if statement 239

= (equals sign), for setting variable value 56, 105, 207

=== (exact equality operator) 240

> (greater than) operator 240

>= (greater than or equal to) operator 240

(hash mark)
    for CSS id 13
    for id selector 49

!= (inequality) operator 240

<= (less than or equal to) operator 240

! (negation) operator 240

-= operator 207

*= operator 207

/= operator 207

+= operator 207

=> operator, in PHP 353

|| (or) operator 240

( ) (parentheses), for click method 42

. (period)
    to separate selector from method 25
    to start CSS class 13, 48

<?php and ?> tags 343, 352, 369

+ (plus), for concatenation 57

" " (quotation marks)
    for text or HTML value 57
    for selectors 15

; (semicolon)
    to end jQuery statement 16, 25
    to end PHP line 315, 352

[ ] (square brackets)
    for array 225
    for array item index 226
    in PHP function 315

A

absolute movement of elements 206

absolute positioning of elements 180

Accordion widget 378

actions
    of forms 329
    repeating 229–230

active state, for anchor element 21

addClass() method 117, 118, 172

addition operator (+=) 207

advanced easing 456

a element. *See* anchor element (HTML)

lists
of elements, index of 110
unordered 128–129
.live() method 91
loading information, using Ajax for 320
local files, for web pages, vs. web server 341
localhost 348, 463
local scope 458
logical operators 240–242
longitude, slider for 397–398
loops 229–230, 252
to change multiple elements 9, 90
declaring variables in 230
each() method for 168
and array elements 362
infinite 255
in PHP 352
syntax 230
types 237

M

Mac OS X
default web server 462
determining MySQL install status 464
enabling PHP 474
installing MySQL on 474–482
many-to-one substitution 158
map_canvas element 417–418
map events, listening for 438
map object
creating instance 417–418
properties and methods 416
mapOpts property 418
MapQuest 418
Marker object (Google) 424
markup languages 299
max option for slider widget 390
menus. *See* interactive menu

messages
append() to insert 59
concatenation when creating 57
displaying for user 55–60
removing 66
methods
chaining 142
for combining effects 193
for CSS changes 115–116
of objects 219
static 114
Microsoft CDN 451
Microsoft IIS (Internet Information Server) 462
downloading 465
Microsoft Internet Explorer 84, 265
layout engine 182
Microsoft, maps 418
Microsoft .NET Framework 4 Client Profile 472
milliseconds setting, for fade effect 192
min option for slider widget 390
mobile device, maps on 437
Monster Mashup
click event 182–184
do-it-yourself effects 199
layout and positioning 178–180
lightning effect 187
testing 269
troubleshooting 254–255
project blueprint 177
randomize feature request 274–277
testing 278–280
testing 273, 286
motion effects
with animate() method 199
relative to current position 280
mouseenter event 117
mouse events 82
mouseleave event 117
moveMe function 271–272
moving through DOM 140–144

R

S

Get even more for your money.

Have it your way.